EMBATTLED COURAGE

Nowhere do events
correspond less to men's expectations
than in war.

—Livy, *History of Rome,* XXX.20

EMBATTLED
COURAGE

The Experience of Combat in the American Civil War

973.7
L 744e

Gerald F. Linderman

THE FREE PRESS
A Division of Macmillan, Inc.
NEW YORK

Collier Macmillan Publishers
LONDON

Copyright © 1987 by Gerald F. Linderman

The Free Press
A Division of Macmillan, Inc.
866 Third Avenue, New York, N.Y. 10022

Collier Macmillan Canada, Inc.

Printed in the United States of America

printing number

1   2   3   4   5   6   7   8   9   10

Library of Congress Cataloging-in-Publication Data

Linderman, Gerald F.
  Embattled courage.

  Bibliography: p.
  Includes index.
  1. United States—History—Civil War, 1861–1865—
Moral and ethical aspects.   2. Courage.   3. Combat—
Psychological aspects.   4. United States—History—Civil
War, 1861–1865—Social aspects.   I. Title.
E468.9.L56   1987   973.7   86-33515
ISBN 0-02-919760-0

Photos courtesy of the Library of Congress.

For Barbara

Contents

ACKNOWLEDGMENTS   *ix*

Introduction   *1*

PART ONE   COURAGE'S WAR

1. *Courage at the Core*   7
2. *Courage from Battlefield to Hospital*   17
3. *Courage as the Cement of Armies*   34
4. *The Uses of Courage*   61
5. *Courage and Civilian Society*   80

PART TWO   A PERILOUS EDUCATION

6. *Unexpected Adversaries*   113
7. *Sword and Shovel*   134
8. *Unraveling Convictions*   156
9. *The New Severity*   169
10. *A Warfare of Terror*   180
11. *Unraveling Ties*   216
12. *Disillusionment*   240
Epilogue   266

Contents

DRAMATIS PERSONAE   298
NOTES   315
BIBLIOGRAPHY   335
INDEX   351

Acknowledgments

I owe much to many.

Robert Wiebe has generously continued to offer me a rare and inspiriting combination of acute criticism and warm encouragement. Jonathan Marwil met with boundless patience and astute advice my many requests for his assistance. Several friends and colleagues have extended their suggestions and support: John Bowditch, Theresa Canjar, Anne Caravias, Tom Collier, John Eadie, Katharine Ehle, Michael Fellman, Sidney Fine, Tom Leonard, Peter Mazlowski, James Morgan, Bradford Perkins, Bryn Roberts, John Shy, Mills Thornton, James Turner, and Maris Vinovskis.

I am grateful, too, for grants provided by the Horace H. Rackham School of Graduate Studies of the University of Michigan and by the Smithsonian Institution. I am indebted to Forrest Pogue for his support of my work as a Smithsonian Fellow and to James Hutchins for his numberless kindnesses and his faith in the project's ultimate worth. Elizabeth Hall, Pat and Keith Matthes, Lindsay and Aaron Miller, and Helen and Hans Paeffgen made my year in Washington a time of special pleasure.

The staffs of the Graduate Library and the William L. Clements Library at the University of Michigan, the Library of Congress, the Bowdoin College Library, the Southern Historical Collection of the University of North Carolina, and the William R. Perkins Library at Duke University were most helpful, especially in locating sources and granting permission to quote from them.

Joyce Seltzer has been a wise and perceptively provocative editor.

Janet Rose, Jeanette Diuble, Connie Hamlin, and Lorna Altstetter of the University of Michigan's Department of History brought to this work a warm humor just as valuable to me as their help in the manuscript's preparation.

A final, incalculable debt is due my wife Barbara, who creates a peace within which it becomes possible to think about war.

Introduction

Every war begins as one war and becomes two, that watched by civilians and that fought by soldiers. Separation may begin soon after a society declares itself at war. Although twentieth-century conflicts have increasingly visited suffering on civilians, the experience of young men who go off to fight has always differed from that of those who stay at home. Combat changes soldiers more profoundly than participation on the home front alters even the most ardent civilian. Conceptions initially embraced by society at large—national war aims, attitudes toward the enemy, views regarding the character of the fighting—retain vitality for civilians long after the experience of the soldier has rendered them remote or even false. The divergence of outlooks leads inevitably to tension.

As the struggle advances, political leaders may become aware of the need to keep the two wars proximate, ordinarily by realigning civilian comprehension to encompass more of the realities of the soldiers' war. If, after differences can no longer be denied, they are permitted to grow, soldier morale and, depending on the course of battle, even the cohesiveness of the nation's military forces may be jeopardized. In the postwar period, the problem becomes less urgent but no less significant. As soldiers return and the military and civilian spheres recombine, two wars must again become one in the public's understanding. At stake are the social integration or isolation of the veteran and the society's receptivity or resistance to new wars, for both determinations will depend heavily on which war comes to prevail in the historical memory of a people.

The young men of the 1860s carried with them into military life a strong set of values that continued to receive reinforcement from home. In a day of simpler assumptions, when one's actions were thought to be the direct extension of one's values, they attempted to apply their values in combat, in camp, and in hospital. But the Civil War regularly betrayed the confidence with which Union and Confederate soldiers sought to fight it; much that they encountered was at odds with their expectations. As they wrestled with the unforeseen, they were changed. The experience of combat frustrated their attempts to fight the war as an expression of their values and generated in them a harsh disillusionment.

From that experience two composites of the Civil War soldier emerge, the first roughly characteristic of the war's early phases, 1861–62, and the second of its final years, 1864–65. The problem of such generalized portraits is that in a canvas so crowded no individual seems to fit. But here the gravity of change—the dissolution of the first composite and the emergence of the second—is far more important than the fact that single soldiers seldom matched in every particular the portrait presented.

The focus of this book falls on the volunteers of 1861–62, those who fought the great battles of the East and of Sherman's campaign, who arrived early and tried to fight the war to its end. They were the sons of farmers and landholding gentry; the sons of small-town shopkeepers and mechanics; the sons of city artisans and of commercial and intellectual elites. Those young men were white; were the possessors of basic schooling; were imbued with an American-Victorian morality; and, if not men of means, were confident of their ability to gain that status. Their families dominated social, political, and economic life.

The soldiers studied here thus do not represent all of the war's participants. This book does not examine the Union Army's important ethnic components, nor does it treat the experience of the 180,000 black soldiers who fought in the Civil War. Apart from Mosby's forces in northern Virginia, it omits consideration of border state irregulars, and it views those who became regular soldiers in 1864–65, few of whom left accounts, through the eyes of others who generally thought them bounty-jumpers, cowards, and the refuse of the cities. Finally, only infrequent distinctions are made between Confederate and Union soldiers, for the evidence confirms David Donald's judgment that during the Civil War "Northerners and Southerners showed themselves to be fundamentally similar, fundamentally part of the same . . . people."[1] In 1861 everyone assumed that the application of moral values to the struggle would determine both the forms and the results of the war. By 1865 those soldiers who survived had learned otherwise.

This story has elements in common with some of the wars of our century: the gap between the expectation and the actuality of war; the threat that gap posed for soldier–civilian solidarity in wartime; and the efforts of a postwar society to refashion the soldier experience to fit civilian comprehension of the war. There are as well elements of particularity: While the war was too long and too harsh a war not to have altered soldier values, for example, it was not quite long enough or harsh enough to overthrow those values within civilian society. Consequently, the price of adaptation exacted of soldiers by a war different from the one they had marched off to fight was severe. They were frustrated by what they had expected to do and could not do and horrified by what they were sure they would never do and then began to do. They grew to respect and even admire the enemy, but they went on killing him—and took satisfaction from it. They loved and longed for their families but grew to resent and to distrust and to want to punish many at home. They became more and more reliant on their comrades—and then watched them die. They yearned for the end of the war, never realizing that it would truly end for them only years later, when they surrendered the war they had fought to the war civilian society insisted they had fought.

PART
★ ★
ONE

Courage's
War

1

Courage at the Core

A young private of the Richmond Howitzers, Carlton Mc-Carthy,* recognized immediately how the soldier was expected to bear himself in the Civil War: "In a thousand ways he is tried . . . every quality is put to the test. If he shows the least cowardice he is undone. His courage must never fail. He must be manly and independent."[1]

Numberless other soldiers joined Carlton McCarthy in filling their journals, their letters home, and their memoirs with the moral values they knew to be at issue in the conflict between North and South: manliness, godliness, duty, honor, and even—among the best-educated on both sides—knightliness. At their center stood courage.

Such words often seem irrelevant to contemporary thought. Americans continue to invoke "honor" and "courage" on ceremonial occasions—the Fourth of July, perhaps Memorial Day—but do so with a sense that they are not terms with which we need contend in our daily lives. When they are employed by a government agency, a specialized group, or others who would enlist them in behalf of their limited enterprises, we are often skeptical of their appropriation. The terms retain their old aura of importance, but their meanings seem elusive and their usages

---

Dramatis Personae (pp. 298–314) offers brief biographical descriptions of Carlton McCarthy and other, perhaps equally unfamiliar, participants who are frequently cited in this text.

vaguely discredited. On the eve of the Civil War, however, Americans had hardly begun to confront the industrial transformation that would enlarge experience, multiply the categories of knowledge, and introduce processes requiring behaviors so much more complex that the older, obvious line separating the "right" and the "wrong" would grow indistinct. Prior to the rush of moral relativism that followed in the wake of industrialization and urbanization, conduct remained subject to standards both broad and precise, measures of comportment thought as easily applicable to the pursuits of war as to those of peace.

The constellation of values in 1861, with courage at its center, was not a perfect circle. Not all other values were equidistant from courage. Some stood very close and were almost identical with courage; others were distant and shared with courage only one or two components. But they all served, albeit in varying degrees, to support in the mind of the volunteer soldier the centrality of courage.

Manliness was only slightly removed from courage. Indeed, many soldiers used "courage" and "manhood" interchangeably. A Georgia soldier found in the "grand-glorious" sight of Tennessee regiments intrepidly repulsing Sherman's attack at Kennesaw Mountain "the sublimity of manhood." A Texas private, disappointed at his failure to act courageously in the field at Gettysburg, spoke plaintively of his efforts "to force manhood to the front." Many soldiers called combat the test of manhood. They often spoke of courage as the "manliest" of virtues. In corroboration, the 1861 edition of Noah Webster's *American Dictionary of the English Language* identified as virtues "much valued" by Americans, "chastity in females" and "bravery in men." A failure of courage in war was a failure of manhood. A Union staff officer warned that cowardice robbed the soldier of all his manhood. Another Federal apologized for his pusillanimity at Antietam with the statement that it had been the only battlefield "I could not look at without being unmanned."[2]

In the minds of numerous Civil War soldiers the connection between courage and godliness was almost as intimate as that between courage and manliness. Many thought of their faith as a special source of bravery; religious belief would itself endow one with courage. Such conviction especially permeated the more homogeneous Confederate armies, whose largely Protestant rank-

and-file noted that those of their commanders whose spirituality was most ardent were those who possessed, in the words of a Southern artilleryman, "the most intense spirit of fight."[3] Robert E. Lee, Stonewall Jackson, and J. E. B. Stuart, with their fervor for combat and their equanimity under fire, seemed to demonstrate that God bestowed courage directly on those of great faith.

Others' courage might be enhanced obliquely via a related conviction that God protected those who believed in Him. Many a soldier was certain, in the words of a South Carolinian, that God's "unseen hand" had carried him safely through a furious battle. A Louisiana sergeant, Edwin Fay, the target of Federal balls that narrowly missed, did not "believe a bullet can go through a prayer," for faith is a "much better shield than . . . steel armor." The common understanding was that the more complete the soldier's faith, the greater would be God's care. Perfect faith seemed to offer the possibility of perfect safety. If only my comrades and I possessed Stonewall Jackson's faith, a Confederate reasoned, we would find it unnecessary to give thought to our personal safety.[4]

Such conviction of God's direct interposition was itself an inducement to courage, for soldiers agreed that a prime enemy of courage in battle was the apprehension rooted in fear for one's safety. Accordingly, it was common to find in both armies on the eve of battle numbers of men who sought to shore up their courage by attempting to reinforce their religious faith. George Armstrong Custer was one who felt that by professing his belief he consigned himself to God's keeping. His anxiety, he wrote his wife, Libbie, was thereby dispelled. Because his fate thenceforth rested "in the hands of the Almighty," he was made brave.[5] One could not always tell, of course, if one's faith were sufficient to ensure survival, but with the outcome resting with God, soldiers felt relieved of a burden that would otherwise inhibit heroic action. "Leave all to Him" was a formula on which many drew for battle courage.

Those of less substantial faith often promised greater attentiveness to religious prescriptions in return for divine protection. Bargaining with God, soldiers approaching battle threw away their decks of cards and vowed that if they were allowed to live they would never again gamble or utter a profane word or smoke a pipe, that they would control their tempers or carry to the

9

spring all their comrades' canteens or share food with others or go to services or live moral lives or declare publicly for Christ or become ministers.[6]

Godliness bore not only on individual survival but on the outcome of battles. A conviction of wide currency was that God would ensure the victory of the army whose collective faith was sturdiest, a notion requiring no complex extension of logic. As William Poague, an officr in Virginia's Rockbridge Artillery, expressed it, he and most of his men had placed themselves in God's hands: While "the good Lord [shields] our heads in the hour of peril," the Confederates would be wounding and killing Yankees, making inevitable the enemy's defeat on the field. Indeed, soldiers on both sides professed confidence that the benefactions of godliness would manifest themselves on every social level—that the faithful soldier would survive combat; that the army of greatest faith would win the battle at hand; that the cause whose adherents possessed the faith indomitable would prevail in the war. When at the battle of Stone's River Federal troops realized that the Confederates had begun to retreat, a member of the 64th Ohio began to sing the Doxology. "Praise God from whom all blessings flow" was taken up first by his comrades, then by the regiment, and then ran up and down the line.[7]

As courage and godliness were linked, so were cowardice and disbelief. The Catholic chaplain of the 14th Louisiana was convinced that none were more cowardly than those who failed to renew their faith and relieve themselves of mortal sin by taking the sacraments prior to battle. A Protestant soldier of the 47th Illinois was equally certain that the Bible enjoined courage: The soldier's "standard of manhood is high, and he found it in the Book his mother gave him: 'If thou faint in the day of adversity, thy faith is small.'" Such thought found a deft summation in the words of George Cary Eggleston, who, though Indiana born, fought for the Confederacy. Cowardice, he said, "is the one sin which may not be pardoned either in this world or the next." In the mind of the soldier, godliness sustained courage and victory; doubt underwrote cowardice and defeat.[8]

Duty would seem a value more comprehensive than courage, but that inclusiveness denied it the focus and force of courage as a prescription for behavior in war. A precise definition of duty is difficult. Civil War soldiers, particularly those of officer rank, spoke as if they knew their duty, but they seldom felt it necessary to discuss or dissect it. They most often referred to duty to country, but generally the objects and the degrees of obligation remained elusive. Webster's 1861 dictionary identified duty as "that which a person is bound to pay, do or perform," but to whom or to what? Duty to God? To the Northern or Southern cause? To the Union or Confederate government? To one's unit, the regiment? To one's comrades? To one's family at home? There had been in the American experience no encounter with feudalism, and thus there remained at mid-century not even a residue of a hierarchy of duties. The prewar period, moreover, had been a time of expansive individualism, and duty was one of those categories in which individual definitions varied—and prevailed. Though men felt duty's weight, its nature remained amorphous. What emerged, however, was an impetus to persist—to remain at soldiering, to continue to heed combat orders, to persevere in battle. Whatever the individual might conceive to be the object of his duty, the principal way to satisfy it was to act courageously. As the Brahmin Stephen Minot Weld made clear when, wrestling with prebattle suspense, he conceded that "I had all I could do to keep myself up to my duty," actions that met duty's demands also met the claims of courage.[9]

Honor too yielded to the centrality of courage but was of a still different quality. Courage, as we shall see, possessed clear definition, but within the meaning of honor—as within duty's— there were broad areas of intangibility, at least to the mind of the twentieth-century observer. The compilers of Webster's dictionary, failing—or perhaps assuming it unnecessary—to define honor, instead described it. The most important of the fourteen annotations they devoted to it represented honor as "True nobleness of mind; magnanimity; dignified respect for character, springing from probity, principle, or moral rectitude; *a distinguishing trait in the character of good men.*" While courage had to be demonstrated, honor did not. Notions of honor so suffused the opening of the war that the honorable nature of the soldier— especially the Northern and Southern volunteers of 1861–62— was widely assumed. In the works of the South's writer-soldier John Esten Cooke, participation in the war was held to be in itself a mark of honor. An accompanying assumption, held most prominently by those in command positions, was that the forthcoming conflict would in its essence be a contest between gentlemen. Such convictions created for the soldier a task unlike that

11

imposed by the requisites of courage. Assumed to be honorable, he had to act so as to escape any imputation of dishonor. It was not a simple matter; one risked dishonor in many ways—by employing coarse language, by exhibiting disrespect for women, by dropping from the line of march—but by far the gravest lapses—fleeing from battle, for example—were those that revealed cowardice. Thus the single most effective prescription for maintaining others' assumption that one was a man of honor was to act courageously. Seldom could the soldier with a reputation for courage be thought dishonorable, so incompatible did those traits seem. Perfect courage was thus the best guarantor of an honorable reputation.[10]

The linkage between honor and courage manifested itself in Civil War soldiers' frequent references to the "honorable death"—inevitably the courageous death—and the "honorable wound"—inevitably suffered in the course of courageous action.

Wounded at Ball's Bluff, Oliver Wendell Holmes, Jr., contemplated with joyful pride the prospect of dying a "soldier's death."[11] The soldier's desire to uphold his society's values shines forth in such responses, especially when the honorable wound is contrasted with the "million-dollar wound" so prominently referred to during World War II. Clearly, Civil War soldiers gave highest importance to the context in which the wound was sustained, whereas the twentiety-century soldier first measured its severity—serious enough to require evacuation home, not so serious as to kill or disable permanently. The former was prized as a badge of honor and the latter, in a war of vastly different combat experience and broader-based armies less susceptible to middle-class values, as a passport from jeopardy.

Honor more than other values within the soldier's moral constellation possessed aspects that did not attach themselves to courage but were nevertheless critical to the good soldier—the sanctity of one's word of honor, for example. That it should so frequently have been offered with good intent and accepted by others without suspicion struck close to how nineteenth-century Americans thought of themselves. Today it seems remarkable that they so trusted the personal pledges of others—enemies in war—that they would build on that confidence arrangements critical to the war effort. Prisoners of war, for example, were often paroled pending exchange. Ulysses Grant released the Vicksburg garrison on parole. Each was liberated solely on the basis of his assurance that he would not return to soldiering until informed that a captive held by his own side had been released, freeing both to return to duty. In the interim the paroled soldier was expected to proceed on the basis of his word of honor—to go home or, in a few cases where states forbade the return of parolees, to report to one of the detention camps maintained by his own side.

After his division had led the disastrous charge at Gettysburg, George Pickett was angered by orders assigning its remnant to guard Northern prisoners, so "I instructed my Inspector-General to parole the officers and give them safeguard to return [to Northern lines], binding them to render themselves prisoners of war at Richmond if they were not duly recognized [as exchangeable] by their government."[12] There was no mockery in the expectation that a Northern officer released in Northern territory would, if unexchanged, make his way to the enemy's capital and report for incarceration.

Henry Kyd Douglas, a Confederate officer wounded at Gettysburg, was captured and then freed on parole. Very soon, however, he wrote to Washington, D.C., requesting outright release on grounds that a year earlier he had discharged a Union major from parole. (The major's letter of attestation was enclosed.) But here Douglas overtaxed the bonds of trust. Washington, demurring at paroles individually negotiated, refused his request.[13]

Captain Edward Hastings Ripley and his men, part of the Union garrison at Harper's Ferry, surrendered in September 1862 to attackers under the command of Stonewall Jackson. Jackson's men treated the Federals "like gentlemen"—"Not by a word or expression did they give us any indications that we were captives and they the captors"—and took their paroles. Their home state, Vermont, was one of those that did not permit parolees to return home until exchanged, so Ripley's men waited at Camp Douglas in Chicago, separated only by a partition from unparoled Southern prisoners of war and treated identically—that is, abysmally. Conditions were harsh. At least fifteen of Ripley's company died of typhoid. The men gave vent to their wretchedness in fighting and in acts of insubordination and incendiarism, and Ripley complained of the delay in exchange, but apparently no one thought it outrageous that personal pledges should cost soldiers their freedom and expose them to severe and sometimes fatal treatment in the midst of an altogether friendly and sympathetic population. No, they had given their word, and there they remained for six months. Although such instances were rare, they do establish a willingness early in the war to endure much to uphold a conception of personal honor.[14]

When a "foolish" attack spurred by an overzealous color-bearer at Falling Waters, West Virginia, resulted in the capture of 735 Confederates, Wayland Dunaway of the 47th Virginia was one of the Southern officers invited to dinner by their captors, "as friendly as men who had been companions from childhood." At its end, the guests pledged good behavior and were sent without a guard to rejoin the other prisoners. The Confederates were tempted by so easy an opportunity to escape, but "though our bodies were for the moment free, our souls were bound by something stronger than manacles of steel,—our word of honor. We groped our way back."[15]

Intrinsic to a gentlemen's war was the conviction that enemies no less than comrades merited honorable treatment. Accordingly, prisoner interrogations were gentle affairs based on the proposition that a soldier had no right to ask questions whose answers would compromise the integrity of the prisoner or damage his cause. Francis Amasa Walker, a future president of the Massachusetts Institute of Technology, was captured by rebels during Wilderness combat in 1864. His captors were "exceedingly cordial," so much so that he was able to escape. Swimming the Appomattox River, however, he landed among other Confederates, whose colonel asked him whether anyone had escaped with him. Bristling, Walker retorted, "Of course you do not expect me to answer that question." The colonel did not press him.[16]

Even those most impatient with any encumbrance on the waging of war accepted the constraints of honor. When a Southern captain whom he was examining objected, "Why, General, I cannot answer those questions. Did you expect me to?" Philip Sheridan replied, "No, but I thought I would ask them."[17]

Interrogating a member of the 9th Michigan, Confederate General E. Kirby Smith asked how many men there were on the Union side and whether an attack was being prepared, "questions he had no right to ask." The prisoner shot back that the general could reconnoiter for himself! It was apparently beyond the horizons of those men to weigh the value of a piece of military intelligence against the claims of honor or to contemplate coercion to extract it. After Francis A. Walker's retort, General Jacob

Hoke told the prisoner that he *did* expect an answer to that question regarding other escapees. When Walker again refused, Hoke muttered ominously that General Beauregard would attend to the matter. "He will get the same answer," Walker said, and there the affair ended. What is surprising is the solemnity with which Walker regarded the episode as a violation of honor and what he obviously considered a harsh sanction against those who had so compromised themselves—"all chance of hearty comradeship . . . completely disappeared."[18]

Another incident revealed what soldiers were willing to do to uphold the word of honor. Shortly before Antietam, a young Federal staff officer rode up to one of the colonels in General Jacob D. Cox's brigade, insisted that there were no enemy ahead, and urged him to speed his advance: "Why don't they [your troops] go in faster? There's nothing there." Stung by the reproach, the colonel pushed ahead vigorously and, just as he discovered the faultiness of the young man's estimate, was captured by Confederate cavalry. Later, Cox met the colonel walking from the Confederate line to the Union rear. "But where are *you* going?" the colonel asked his general. Into the gap ahead, Cox replied. At that answer the colonel gave a start—Cox thought it "involuntary"—and blurted out, "My God! Be careful!" Immediately, however, he checked himself—"But I am paroled"—and turned away. Cox, no fool, brought up a brigade before advancing.[19] Here not even the soldier's desire for battlefield victory or the desire to protect comrades enjoyed decisive priority over the demands of honor.

Knightliness might be described less as a distinct value than as an extension and an exaggeration of honor. Its influence was not broad. The men in the ranks paid it little heed, and serious interest confined itself to two narrow social strata: the Southern upper class, especially Virginia gentlemen, and New England Brahmins. Here its impact was intense, and each group wielded in its section of the country an influence far beyond its numbers.

Those who aspired to knightliness imposed on warfare a set of romantic images derived from the writings of Sir Walter Scott, especially his Waverly novels. George Cary Eggleston found that the libraries of Southern planters, although "sadly deficient in the literature of the present," contained Scott's novels "in force, just as they came, one after another, from the press of the Edinburgh publishers." John Esten Cooke had had Scott—"his ultimate literary ancestor"—read to him as a child. Five hundred miles to the north the boy Oliver Wendell Holmes, Jr., had enthusiastically lost himself in the Waverly adventures. Mark Twain would later charge, not entirely in jest, that Scott should be held responsible for the Civil War.[20]

To those imbued with knightliness, warfare seemed a joust and the soldier a knightly warrior or holy crusader, an exemplar of brave and noble manhood. Their influence at the outset of the war tended primarily to intensify certain aspects of courage's war. Knightliness elaborated and sharpened the appeal of the honorable death; as its principal incarnation, J. E. B. Stuart, put it, "All I ask of fate is that I may be killed leading a cavalry charge."[21] Fascination with the duel accentuated the attractiveness of individualized combat. The idealization of the mounted warrior wrapped the cavalry, especially the Confederate horse, within an aura of romance. The chivalric ideal—*sans peur et sans reproche*—both enhanced the soldier-knight's determination to do his duty without regard for consequences and harshly increased the onus attached to his feelings of fear. The accent on gallantry and courtesy strengthened ties between enemies. Had the impulse to knightliness been able to sustain itself, the Civil War would have been a most polite war.

Manliness, godliness, duty, honor, and knightliness constituted in varying degrees the values that Union and Confederate volunteers were determined to express through their actions on the battlefield. But each, as an impulse to war, remained subordinate to courage. Young Americans would most often cite "duty" as having prompted them to enlist and "honor" as having held them to soldiering through their terms of enlistment, but the pursuit of courage—and its obverse, the flight from cowardice—proved the ultimate sanction. Courage served as the goad and guide of men in battle.

2

Courage from
Battlefield to Hospital

Courage had for Civil War soldiers a narrow, rigid, and powerful meaning: heroic action undertaken without fear. To those aware of twentieth-century war's powers of destruction and intimidation, that standard is likely to appear both hollow and hopelessly unattainable, but over the past century definitions of courage have evolved in delayed rhythm with changes in the nature of combat, and ours are no longer those of the 1860s. Americans would enter World War I holding to the Civil War conception of courage, but it could not maintain itself against an immensely more powerful weaponry. A courage earlier thought decisive in war as an extension of the will of the individual yielded to the power of the machine gun and a long-range artillery capable of obliterating men and, seemingly, even the landscapes over which they fought. The power of the soldier to produce effects that he willed dwindled, and through four years of impasse on the Western Front British, French, and German trench soldiers were likely to feel themselves so subordinated to the destructive processes of war that they came to think of themselves less as actors in war than as victims of war. Men were compelled to concede the limits of individual will and the exhaustibility of courage.

Charles Moran, later Winston Churchill's physician but during three years of the Great War a medical officer in Flanders, still held courage to be "the master quality," but on the basis of his observations of trench warfare he began to liken it to a bank account. Each soldier had only so much courage-capital and expended it bit by bit, not in what he did but in attempting to meet what was done to him. When a man's courage had been used up—as inevitably it would be—he was finished as a soldier. Again in World War II, courage moved farther from the Civil War notion of assertive action. For Dwight Eisenhower, perseverance became courage; heroism, he declared, was "the uncomplaining acceptance of unendurable conditions." Here Eisenhower marked a transition from active to passive conceptions of courage. In a war that John Steinbeck saw as "weapon against weapon rather than man against man" and that James Jones believed to be industries versus industries, with the infantryman of no more import than a mosquito, it was less often assumed that the soldier could, through the power of will, surmount situations presented by war; he could at best endure them.[1]

Subsequent wars have accelerated the separation of courage and will. To a Marine officer in Korea, expressions of traditional courage were symptomatic of the wreckage of the soldier—the loss of one's mind and of one's instinct for self-preservation. In Michael Herr's depiction of Vietnam combat, courage was no more than undifferentiated energy cut loose by the intensity of the moment, "mind loss that sent the actor on an incredible run," presumably a reaction primarily reflexive and physiological. Tim O'Brien stood Civil War courage on its head: cowardice, he suggested, was *not* fleeing the war in Vietnam.[2]

The experience of twentieth-century war also eroded the Civil War's bond between courage and fearlessness—and its notion of fear as forbidden territory. To feel fear was to be a coward, Civil War volunteers thought. Moran, while granting as a matter of his own observation during 1914–18 that "almost all men felt fear," still spoke of the soldier's "secret battle with fear." Each was "alone in his war with terror." By the 1940s, however, soldiers were willing to acknowledge their fear, both to themselves and to others. In his study of three hundred members of the Spanish Civil War's Abraham Lincoln Brigade, John Dollard found three-quarters of its American combat veterans willing to admit that they had felt fear going into action the first time; after that initial exposure to battle, 36 percent granted that they were always afraid and 55 percent sometimes afraid. More significant was his discovery that eight of ten thought it better to admit their fear and discuss it with their comrades; acknowledgment had thus become the first step in the individual and collective control of fear. "Courage is not fearlessness," Dollard wrote, "it is being able to do the job even when afraid." Thus Steinbeck could write of World War II that it was "the style" "to indicate that you were afraid all the time." And Ernie Pyle, the GI's correspondent, confirmed the parting of courage and fearlessness: "War scares hell out of me. I guess it's because I don't want to die. But I know I'm not a coward." He wrote later, indeed just prior to the Okinawa invasion in which he died, "I have woolies but Marine officers do too, so I don't need to feel ashamed." Twenty years later the Green Beret Donald Duncan spoke in similar vein of his comrades in Vietnam: "We all know we're scared so there is no real reason to mention it, but we do, because if we say it often enough, it loses reality." Finally, Michael Herr again helps to measure, both in expression and in substance, the distance traveled beyond Civil War courage: "I was," he wrote of Vietnam combat, "scared every fucking minute"—and, he added, all the others were too.[3]

Notions of a dauntless, assertive soldier courage have not disappeared from our society. They continue to occupy a niche in popular culture, especially in films, and a more prominent position in the training offered students of service academies and members of elite military units. But the changing circumstances of combat have reduced them from a powerful precept to a fugitive ideal.

No anticipation of such a future troubled those who marched to war in 1861. They were confident that the individual would remain the determinant of war's course, that their personal goals would remain more important and challenging than any collective or organizational requirement. They did not contemplate their inundation by armies of massive numbers or by a war of powerful impersonal processes. They did not feel captive to enormous, aloof forces on which their fates would depend. They did assume that, within God's superintendence, the world's most powerful force was that of the individual will brought to bear on the course of events, including those of war, and that courage was the fulfillment of man's highest nature.

Few Civil War soldiers felt able simply to declare their courage. No man knew how he would behave in battle, Ulysses Grant's aide, Horace Porter,[4] insisted, so courage was never assured until it had been put to trial. Critical to the soldier's Civil War was his willingness to expose himself in a direct test of his mettle against that of the enemy.

The requirement that courage be a fearless courage meant that the soldier's feelings about what he was doing were as important as his actions. Particularly admired—sometimes extravagantly—were those who seemed to possess fearlessness as nature's gift, those so oblivious to fear that it could not exist within the range of their emotional reactions. Such men showed an absolute indifference under fire; they were those ideal officers who were perfectly brave without being aware that they were so. A Union artillery barrage catching Confederates in the open sent them running for cover—all but General Turner Ashby. He was, concluded an observer as moved as the general was unmoved, "totally indifferent to the hellish fire raining all about him." Southern soldiers were convinced that both Stonewall Jackson and J. E. B. Stuart ("he saw everything in battle utterly undisturbed by the danger") lived with no consciousness of the feeling of fear. When in battle, such men appeared to expose themselves recklessly, with no idea that they stood in danger of being killed. Long after others had abandoned uncommon markings as a sure invitation to enemy bullets, Stuart continued to wear in battle his distinctive slouch hat adorned with a long plume. He was widely admired for what others took to be his constitutional insensibility to risk. Similarly, Jackson's "utter disregard of danger" was one of the strongest elements of magnetism drawing Southern rank-and-file to him.[5]

To the relief—and sometimes the alarm—of those many soldiers who felt such *sang froid* was no part of their own natures, there was a wider path to courage. One could—indeed, would have to[6]—test oneself in combat and, applying the powers of will, try to expel fear. Few could hope to achieve the insouciance of a Stonewall Jackson or the fearless courage of an Ashby or a Philip Kearny, but soldiers could at least so diminish their secret fear that they too would become capable of heroic action. Few felt that they would be able to join the company of courage's exemplars, but all knew it essential to prove that they were not cowards—and that was itself a formidable task. The unpressed logic of the situation was perhaps analogous to that of the Puritan wrestling with his conviction of predestination; the individual could never be sure that he was one of the chosen, foreordained by God to heavenly bliss, but he could be certain that if he did not comport himself with piety and purity—that is, as if he *was* among the chosen—he would offer others, and perhaps himself, undeniable proof that he was not. Hence few balked at submitting themselves to the test of battle.

Reduced to tactical terms, courage was preeminently the charge—the boldest actions were assumed to be those of offensive warfare—but there were many other situations to which the tenets of the test were no less applicable, trials of steadfastness as well as advance. In the first years of the war the rank-and-file held themselves to a strict standard, that of fighting "man fashion." They were expected to wait stoically through the tense and difficult period just prior to battle; to stand and receive enemy fire without replying to it (one of Lee's soldiers called this "the most trying duty of the soldier"); and to resist all urges to quicken their pace under fire, to dodge or duck shells, or to seek cover. (Within those assumptions men who at the war's outset had purchased body armor were ridiculed, but the issue became moot when breastplates were discovered to stop nothing except movement.)[7]

Difficult as those tests were for enlisted men, the burden on officers was far heavier. While each of those in the ranks felt the necessity to prove himself to himself, to those comrades around him and, to his family, the officer was compelled to do the same and, in addition, to impress his courage, less by stoic endurance than by positive demonstration, on all those he commanded. A Wisconsin colonel was convinced that "the men who carried the knapsacks never failed to place an officer just where he belonged, as to his intelligence and bravery. Even if [officers] said nothing, yet their instinctive and unconscious action in battle placed upon the officers the unavoidable brand of approval or disapproval."

Not even the highest-ranking officers were exempt. "We knew the fighting generals and we respected them," a New York artilleryman said, "and we knew the cowards and despised them." Of 425 Confederate generals, seventy-seven were killed in the war.[8]

For the officer, the arena was larger, the audience more numerous, the possibilities of courageous demonstration more varied, from the casual to the monumental. In his first battle Robert Burdette, whose Illinois regiment was bracketed by rifle and cannon fire, watched an officer ride down the line, stop to ask a soldier for a match, light his pipe, puff on it as he would relaxing before his hearth, and then ride forward to overtake his skirmishers: "How I admired his wonderful coolness!" A less "natural," more hortatory, but no less admired courage was that of Colonel Emerson Opdycke, who, caught in the rout at Chickamauga, was determined to hold ground vital to General George H. Thomas's stand against the onrushing Confederates. He sat on his horse at the crest of a hill and, though fully exposed to enemy view, continued to point with his sword in the direction his regiments were to fire. Such a pose might today appear appropriate only to his posthumous equestrian statue, but to those who watched, Opdycke was "the very incarnation of soldierly bearing and manly courage."[9]

That passages through the test should sometimes appear effortless or theatrical should not hide its essential characteristics. Its gravity was unquestioned. William Dame was a young, well-educated Southern gentleman whose artillery battery, the Richmond Howitzers, fought under Lee. A teamster—"a dreadful, dirty, snuffy, spectacled old Irishman," certainly no gentleman and not even a soldier—one day insisted on taking the pulses of William and his friends. He then announced that one soldier was excited, another was frightened, that a third "would do all right" in combat, and so on. Some of the judged were pleased, others hated the Irishman for his verdicts, but no one dared either to refuse to submit to the test or to question its results. "Nobody can tell what a dreadful trial this simple thing was!"[10]

Dame and his comrades were apprehensive far in advance of the test of battle, for they knew that mercilessness awaited failure. Seeing in battle a soldier so fearful that he was about to run, Rutherford B. Hayes threatened him with a pistol and vowed that "he would kill him on the spot" if he did not "go in and fight." The man regained control, returned to the battle, and was immediately killed. Hayes was glad to have given the weakling the death of a hero rather than that of a coward. Nor for a moment did he imagine that the dead soldier would have reproved him; Hayes simply assumed his eternal gratitude. Frank Wilkeson, a private in the 11th New York Battery, helped a fellow Union soldier, wounded in the foot, to a field hospital. The doctors, however, discovered powder burns suggesting self-infliction ("The cowardly whelp!") and Wilkeson was "really pleased to see the knife and saw put to work and the craven's leg taken off below the knee." Notwithstanding a "look of horror" that came to the coward's face when he realized that his leg had been amputated, "The utter contempt of the surgeons, their change from careful handling to almost brutality," Wilkeson added, were "bracing to me." The Confederate cavalry commander Wade Hampton reported that he had killed eleven Federals, two with sword and nine with pistol. An afterthought prompted him to add that he had slain two others who had been running and were thus not to be counted. Cowards apparently lost the right even to be numbered among the trophies.[11]

Those who anticipated such reactions from others imposed a meticulous discipline upon themselves. An Illinois private, Robert Strong, suffered attacks of rheumatism and diarrhea so debilitating that the lieutenant gave him a pass. Still he hesitated. "The boys have not had a single fight without my being with them. If I go to the rear and am killed there, I will be ashamed to meet them on the other shore. I am going [back] to the company." A Massachusetts soldier feared at Gettysburg that his lame brother would not arrive in line before battle began: "I was worrying for him every time I heard the skirmishers firing. . . . I can remember well how glad I was to see him when he came limping up," for he would not be called a "skedaddler."[12]

Often the most powerful fear was that one's fear would be revealed—and that meant a prohibition on discussion, frequently even among comrades, of the topic of greatest concern to each soldier. Fear was not an anxiety to be shared but a weakness to be stifled. Soldiers knew their own fear and noticed "pallor on every face," but ordinarily no one spoke of fear. "I was scared," Charles Bardeen recalled fifty years after a mortar barrage. "Prest was scared; I knew he was scared, he knew I was scared; I knew he knew I was scared, and he knew I knew he was scared: yet though either of us if he had been alone would have lost no time in getting to a place of safety, rather than acknowledge to each other we were scared we pretended to deliberate." A private in the 11th Pennsylvania, James T. Miller, drew the contrast between campfire and battle line, between those tales of bravery that could be spoken and those fears that had to be suppressed:

[I]f you could only be with us around our camp fires after a fight and listen to the accounts of the hairbreadth escapes that are told of and hear the loud laughs that greet each one's experience and see the gay reckless careless way in which they are told, you would be very apt to think that we were the happiest set of men you ever saw. But if you should go with us to the battle field and see those that [were] so gay, their faces [now] pale and their nerves trembling, and see anxiety on every countenance almost bordering on fear, you would be very apt to think we were all a set of cowardly poltroons—this picture to be taken just before the fight begins, and the enemy is in sight and the dull ominous silence that generally takes place before the battle begins.

A friend confided to Rice Bull of the 123d New York that he had had a premonition that he would be killed in the next fight. He had told no one else, for he felt ashamed and thought that others would believe such a presentiment was evidence that he was a coward.[13]

The assumption that fear was a special problem only for oneself often brought surprises when words could be found. David Buell of the 8th Alabama, whose manner failed to hide "the deepest anxiety," asked Hilary A. Herbert:

Colonel, does it ever occur to [you] that you may be killed some day in battle?

Yes, very frequently. But why do you ask?

Well, I thought from [the] fact that you never say anything about it, and then from the manner in which you expose yourself . . . recklessly, that you had an idea that you were in no danger of being killed.

O, no . . . I have no idea . . . that I am at all exempt from any of the dangers that confront officers holding such a position as I do. . . . I know that the probabilities are that a colonel of an infantry regiment . . . who does his duty, will in all probability be either killed or seriously wounded. I have . . . simply made up my mind that I must take my chances. . . . That is all there is to it.

Here silence had allowed Buell, "my friend," to mistake Herbert's fatalism for fearlessness.[14] The reticence was unfortunate, for Civil War soldiers were thus unable to draw on that reassuring conviction of mid-twentieth-century soldiers that battle fear was "normal." Instead, the terrors of combat seemed to grow larger because so often they were suffered wordlessly.

Soldiers did not often challenge those harsh reactions to evidence of fear in battle, because they considered the results of the test decisive and unalterable. They thought of the test as if it were a litmus revealing their single essence, either courage or cowardice. Leander Stillwell of the 61st Illinois was certain that war brought out "all the latent force of character a man possessed." John Esten Cooke observed that peril aroused fierce pride and courage in the brave but unnerved the coward. Thus the test did more than reveal the soldier's basic nature; it intensified it. Joshua Lawrence Chamberlain, the hero of Gettysburg's Little Round Top and a man as reflective as he was brave, believed that the test of war made the good better and the bad worse. All soldiers spoke as if its results were final—though in practice negative results brought damnation ("Was I to run and prove myself a coward?") much more readily than positive results brought certainly to oneself or others that one was a soldier of courage. A lieutenant colonel, so badly frightened that he "soiled his breeches," "never got over that scare" and during the next fight left for home. "Cases of recovery from the disease of fear . . . are rare," Horace Porter concluded.[15]

Regulations ordinarily permitted officers of both armies simply to resign their commissions and return to civilian life, but all understood that to do so on the eve of, or during, a campaign invited the imputation of cowardice. Confederate General Frank Paxton made clear to his wife on September 22, 1861, what was at stake:

> To return home, all I have to do is to resign my office, a privilege which a man in the ranks does not enjoy. Then your wish and mine is easily fulfilled, but in thus accomplishing it I would go to you dishonored by an exhibition of the want of those qualities

which alike grace the citizen and the soldier. An imputation of such deficiency of manly virtues I should in times past have resented as an insult. Would you have me merit it now?[16]

It was theoretically possible, though in practice unusual, to regard positive outcomes with the same decisiveness. James A. Connolly, an Illinois soldier serving in the Army of the Cumberland, was put up for promotion to brevet lieutenant colonel. He had earned it, he was certain, for he had entered combat "with fear and trembling" and had conquered both. On the other side, John O. Casler of the Stonewall Brigade showed a similar confidence in retrospect: "I do not consider myself a hero [but] neither do I consider myself a coward, for I have been in positions that tested me thoroughly, and such as a coward could not stand." Great numbers, however, failed to find confirmation of their courage and continued to look to the next test of battle with no less apprehension than they had to the last. Tension persisted. If the soldier's courage once fails, Carlton McCarthy warned, "he will be told he's a baby, [will be] ridiculed, teased, and despised."[17]

As if this test of one's fundamental nature were not sufficiently severe, nineteenth-century Americans added to its gravity. Civil War armies were youthful armies. Soldiers under eighteen numbered more than 10,000 in the Union Army and made up perhaps 5 percent of the strength of Southern forces. Dunaway watched a twelve-year-old Confederate cannoneer playfully roll over backward each time he pulled the lanyard. In both armies, eighteen-year-olds constituted the largest single age group during the first year of war. So for some the test that divided courage from cowardice came also to separate manhood from boyhood. One who passed welcomed the assurance that he was no longer a "spoiled" and "finicky" boy; he had been made a man. Stephen Crane would later celebrate the transition in *The Red Badge of Courage*. Rallied from a retreat, Henry Fleming and his boyish comrades, frightened, anxious, and only tentatively in control of themselves, settled down sufficiently to fire a volley at the pursuing rebels. When the smoke lifted and no enemy remained in sight, the Union soldiers leaped into "an ungainly dance of joy." A few moments earlier, they had felt divided and impotent, but pride and trust had arrived, Crane tells us—"And they were men."[18]

A corollary of the test of male maturity was for some soldiers the assumption that they were also testing themselves against womanly influences in their lives or womanly characteristics in themselves. Rutherford Hayes, whose relationship with his mother and sister had been unusually dense and constricting, found liberation in the "man's world" of army life, which despite its dangers was to him a delightful existence devoid of bothersome women and babies. There were also hints that passing the test, and thus confirming the dominance of one's masculinity, bestowed permission to express occasionally one's softer, feminine side. Joshua Chamberlain listed among "the highest qualities of manhood" called forth by war the "tenderness of caring for the wounded and stricken—exhaustless and unceasing as that of gentlest womanhood which allies us to the highest personality." Those who had passed combat's test could afterward help the wounded on both sides "with the kindness and tenderness of a woman," could relieve in softness the hard and driving spirit of combat. Wounded in battle, Chamberlain accepted as high tribute the words of one of his regimental commanders, "General, you have the soul of the lion and the heart of the woman." The sequence of compliments was, however, critical. To express oneself in womanly ways before meeting the test, before proving onself the lion, was to reveal womanish weakness.[19]

The demands of courage did not disappear with the soldier's withdrawal from battle. Not even a wound provided the immediate exemption one might anticipate. The soldier was expected to depart from the field courageously—that is, with no exhibition of pain—a remarkable expectation based on the "sublime self-abnegation of the true soldier,"[20] the assumption that the wounded *could* retain control of themselves if imbued with the right values.

Sparse indeed are soldier accounts that do not express admiration for some heroic departure from the battlefield. Robert Stiles, an artilleryman in Lee's army, told of a Louisiana captain who, while cheering on his gunners, was struck by a shell that carried off his "bridle arm" at the shoulder. The captain caught the reins in his right hand; swung his horse in order to hide his wound from his men; called out, "Keep it up, boys, I'll be back in a moment"; started down the hill; and fell dead. Chamberlain, wounded at Petersburg, concealed his hurt, steadying himself with the point of his sword until the charge passed and he felt that he could withdraw honorably. George Eggleston's brother, his arm torn away, held up the bleeding stump and called out, "Never mind, boys; I'll come back soon and try 'em with this other one." A cavalry lieutenant asked his captain for permission to leave the column. "What for, Mr. Hoyer?" "Because I am mortally wounded, sir."[21]

Those who reached the military hospital found that though it might offer respite to the body, it seldom permitted any relaxation of the will. Thirty years later Oliver Wendell Holmes, Jr., would tell a Harvard audience that "the book for the army is a war-song, not a hospital-sketch," and in obvious ways hospital and battlefield presented contrasting experiences of war, but there was no dichotomy in expectations of soldier comportment. The battlefield's values extended to the hospital and in ways intensified there. The body's debility and the removal of comrades' support contributed to the necessity of what William Howell Reed, a Sanitary Commission medical worker, called "the harder heroism of the hospital." He and his fellow workers—Sanitary Commission and Christian Commission and nurse volunteers—dedicated themselves to the alleviation of the soldiers' suffering. No one could mistake the selflessness of many of them, for to enter army hospitals was always to risk one's own life against disease and against injurious medical treatment. Louisa May Alcott had worked only a month as a volunteer nurse at Georgetown's Union Hotel Hospital when she contracted typhoid fever. The preferred treatment—massive doses of calomel—resulted in a mercury poisoning that caused the loss of teeth and hair and the slow degeneration of the nervous system. She lived until 1888 but was never again entirely well. Her nursing supervisor, the New England feminist reformer Hannah Ropes, succumbed to typhoid pneumonia after eight months. Walt Whitman visited Washington area hospitals from late 1861 until June 1862, when his physical collapse brought doctors' warnings that he must not return.[22]

Dedicated as they might be, however, such people took up roles not designed simply to make the wounded more comfortable. The problem confronting them was their inability to aid recovery in any medically significant way. Few of the nurses had received training, and in any case the state of medical science had little to offer. Still ignorant of the relationship between germs and infection, doctors amputated wounded limbs and then administered stimulants in misguided efforts to forestall sepsis. Nurses could wash and feed the wounded, could "clean" wounds, bind them with linen and, as theory held beneficial, keep them moistened with water. In the end, however, medical workers had little choice but to rely on the teaching of Florence Nightingale: Nature was the healer, and the task of the nurse, nature's partner, was to encourage in the wounded soldier a receptivity to nature's actions, a task more moral than medical. Indeed, here some nurses felt themselves better qualified than doctors, who were present "because their work proceeded either from obedience to military duty or a contract for pay." They were thus inferior as healers to the nurse volunteers, who were there out of selfless concern for their patients. "Apothecary and medicine chest might be dispensed with," Hannah Ropes said, "if an equal amount of genuine sympathy could be brought home to our stricken men."[23]

In practice, however, nurses could do little (and doctors little more). Though nineteenth-century Americans were well acquainted with chronic illness and death, especially infant mortality, in ways that must have generated some protective emotional callus, virtual impotence amid so much pain surely distressed medical aides. Their reaction was to encourage the soldiers to live—and especially to die—in harmony with soldierly values, to accept pain and death within the framework of those values. The presence of women, the hospital agent Julia Wheelock Freeman said, brought forth "the better angel" of the soldier's nature. "A kind, cheerful look, a smile of recognition, one word of encouragement, enables him to bear his sufferings more bravely."[24] So vital did that seem to nurses that their desire to encourage the courageous death frequently became the determination to compel it.

The nurses' working proposition was the supremacy of the individual will as an extension of courage: Suffering was a refining and properly subduing influence to be borne cheerfully and quietly. No matter how severe the wound, the soldier possessed the spiritual power to triumph over pain. Tending wounded soldiers in May 1864, Reed wrote of a Union soldier shot through both lungs:

> In one corner, upon a stretcher, lay a soldier, whose open, manly face, high forehead, and clear, intelligent eye, bespoke an excel-

lent character. . . . I recall his cheerful courage, his pleasant companionship, his bright smile, which seemed to me to light up that
room of suffering and death with a radiance from the other world.

Reed also cited with approval an episode in which a young con-
script lay dying of lockjaw; while his body twitched with pain,
he had resigned himself to God's will and thus his face bore an
expression of serenity. Such cases were the assurance that one
could remain in control if one's values were the proper ones.[25]

Pain expressed, however, was weakness revealed. "Our
American man," Whitman wrote, ". . . holds himself cool and
unquestioned, master above all pains and bloody mutilations."
Thus wounds offered opportunities to demonstrate a courage
transcending even that of the battlefield. Mary Livermore, a
Sanitary Commission organizer and frequent traveler to battle
sites and hospitals, thought that "it may be easy to face death on
the battle-field, when the pulses are maddened by the superhu-
man desire for victory. . . . But to lie suffering in a hospital bed
for months . . . requires more courage." Hospital courage meant
staying calm and not complaining, even to the point of death.
"He made no display or talk; he met his fate like a man." The
coward, on the other hand, abject and groveling, gave voice to
his pain. Soldiers often contrasted their wounded comrades' "stoical bravery" ("A Union soldier, if so severely wounded that he
could by no possibility assume a cheerful countenance, would
shut his teeth close together and say nothing") with the faint-
heartedness of the enemy ("a rebel, if he could boast of only a
flesh wound, would whine and cry like a sick child").[26]

In their efforts to bolster the impulse to courage, hospital
workers were certain that they were successful. Whitman
recorded the testimony of a doctor who in six months among the
wounded had seen none who had died "with a single tremor of
unmanly fear," and the poet's own experience bore out the claim:
Not one case of a soldier's dying "with cowardly qualms of terror." He thought that record was the "last-needed proof" of
American democracy. Mary Livermore did encounter a dying
soldier who told her, "I have lived an awful life, and I'm afraid
to die. I shall go to hell." "Stop screaming," she commanded.
"Be quiet. . . . If you *must* die, die like a man, and not like a
coward." God, she assured him, was willing to pardon him. Later
a Methodist minister arrived to urge trust in Christ and to sing

hymns. Finally, the soldier said, "It's all right with me, chaplain! I will trust in Christ! God will forgive me! I can die, now!" Mary Livermore watched as his face grew rapturous. "I looked at the dying man beside me, and saw, underneath the deepening pallor of death, an almost radiant gleam." It was, she reported, the only case of fear of death that she encountered.[27]

Often hospital workers thought of themselves as observers serving in behalf of soldiers' families. Those at home would want to know about their son's or husband's comportment at the end. Especially were they anxious to learn his last words, that they might reveal an ultimate success in pursuit of courage or godliness. Thus the state of one's courage remained until the end—and especially at the end—a matter of the most intense concern, both to the soldier and to those who surrounded him.

The harsh dichotomy between courage and cowardice was sometimes diminished by removing cowardice from the realm of individual will. Cowardice might be mitigated, for example, when seen as a form of insanity. Sergeant Fay wrote his wife that Lewis Peters, a fellow Louisiana townsman who had shot off his hand "to get to go back home," was "not thought by most persons to be in his right mind." There was some softening, too, in occasional metaphorical references to cowardice as an illness. A South Carolina volunteer called it "chicken heart disease." Ira Dodd, a Union enlisted man describing regimental officers whose health "failed suddenly" and who quickly resigned, generously referred to their affliction as "cannon fever." Reed described a wounded solder whose loud moans issued from "a wild delirium." Clearly he was not himself. Sometimes even environmental influences might be considered. Nurse Jane Woolsey suggested that while the wounded under her care were ordinarily "marvels of good and even gay humor," those who were sullen might be so because they were city "roughs." But such flexibility was both rare and superficial.[28]

A more accurate gauge of the weight with which courage's war bore down on soldiers was to be found in their discussions of wounds as desirable, even valued, acquisitions. Rutherford Hayes "fiercely wished" a wound—and was rewarded with five. The colonel of the 9th New York complained to a wounded fellow officer: "You are a lucky man, Colonel. I'd give a thousand dollars if I had your wound. I am afraid my friends in New York will think me a coward because I never can get hit." When his wife's brother was struck by a bullet, Benjamin Harrison wrote to her: "I almost envy John his honorable wound." William Dame insisted that the wounded making their way to a field hospital were "as cheerful a lot of fellows . . . as you can imagine. Wounded men coming from under fire are, as a rule, cheerful, often jolly. Being able to get, honorably, from under fire, with the mark of manly service to show, is enough to make a fellow cheerful, even with a hole through him." If there was here some ambivalence between the wound as emblem of courage and as a safe-conduct from combat, none was retained in civilian translation. Searching for his wounded son on the field at Antietam, Oliver Wendell Holmes, Sr., observed of the survivors that the "wounds they bore would be the medals they would show their children and grandchildren by and by. Who would not rather wear his decorations beneath his uniform than on it?" One of Louisa May Alcott's patients, shot through the cheek, requested a mirror; his image worried him. "I vow to gosh, that's too bad! I warn't a bad looking chap before, and now I'm done for; won't there be a thunderin' scar? and what on earth will Josephine Skinner say?" To Alcott the answer came easily: His fiancée would surely admire his "honorable scar," "lasting proof that he had faced the enemy, for all women thought a wound the best decoration a brave soldier could wear."[29]

Reinforced by such conceptions, the impulse to courage was indeed potent. "Death Before Dishonor" might ring today in many quarters as no more than a hopelessly hackneyed line from hoary stage melodrama, but for Civil War soldiers it had both vivacity and pertinence. When Weld learned that officer "X" would be dismissed from the army for asking a hospital attendant for something that would make him sick, he decided that X "had a great deal better have been killed." A Confederate chaplain, Charles Todd Quintard, said in praise of General Benjamin Cheatham that he "understood thoroughly that it was better that a leader should lose his life than his honor." As George Stevens of the 77th New York watched the ritual dismissal of a New Jersey officer caught in cowardice, he thought, "how much better it would have been to have fallen nobly on that field of battle, honored and lamented, than to live to be degraded and despised." A Wisconsin private wrote home that he "would rather have been *under ground,* than to have been branded as a coward before the whole Reg't." An Indiana small-town soldier, Theodore F. Upson, told of his colonel's confrontation with one of the regiment's skulkers. "Get up . . . Cherry. Go to your Company and show yourself a man for once. You ought to be ashamed of yourself." "I will go, Colonel, since you insist, but I am sure if I go up there I shall be killed." "You had better be killed than have the reputation of a coward." Cherry went up on the line and was killed instantly by a shot from a Confederate battery.[30]

3

Courage as the Cement of Armies

As Robert E. Lee began his first invasion of the North in the early autumn of 1862, one of the most renowned regiments marching in his Army of Northern Virginia was the 1st Virginia of James Longstreet's corps. In its ranks was an ordinarily buoyant, gregarious, and sweet-tempered private, the son of immigrant parents who had met during the crossing from Ireland, married, and raised in Richmond a large family that in time became one of the city's wealthiest and most popular. On the afternoon of September 14, however, John E. Dooley found himself in a situation so menacing that all equanimity disappeared.

The "Lost Order of Antietam" had revealed to the Northern commander, George McClellan, how widely separated were the units of Lee's army, and Union divisions were pressing northwestward through Maryland against the Confederate rear at South Mountain. Dooley's regiment was one of those Lee ordered to return to Turner's Gap by forced march to join D. H. Hill's division in stemming the Yankee advance. That help arrived too late. Hill's men had already been enveloped and routed by stronger Union forces, so that as the 1st Virginia pressed up the mountain, it passed Confederate stragglers and limping wounded. "The appearances of things are to say the least very discouraging," Dooley wrote. Soon Northern batteries began to

34

sweep the road over which the Virginians marched. The casualties, the confusion, the absence of firm command frightened John Dooley. The force of Union round shot seemed to multiply as it splintered rocks and sent their fragments hurtling at the Confederates; the noise of the bombardment magnified as it resounded from ridge to ridge.

At the edge of a field on the brow of the mountain, the regiment established a line, only to be attacked by swarming Federals. "There was not a fair fight here," and Dooley joined his friends in withdrawing from one position to another. Thirty minutes later, at a last line, "lying on our faces while shell and shot and bullet screamed and whistled over our heads," he "considered it a great want of prudence . . . to remain." As he was about to flee, a captain of the 11th Virginia came up and clapped him on the back: "Hurrah for you! You are one of the 1st [Virginia]. I know you'll stand by us to the last!" He said nothing more. He delivered no order, spoke no threatening word, but what he said fixed Dooley to the spot. "What could I do under such circumstances? Was I to run and prove myself a coward? No Sir! So I just laid [sic] down with the others who were making a last *stand*, lying [down]."

John Dooley was not required to pay the price of his resolve. The Federals soon broke off the attack, and under cover of night the Confederates slipped away and joined the forces Lee was hurriedly concentrating at Sharpsburg. Dooley's company, however, was no more than a slender accession: Only he and the captain remained to prepare for the battle at Antietam Creek, where once again the power of the ideal of courage held him in combat.[1]

With soldiers like John Dooley so painfully sensitive to their actions in battle as the fulfillment or failure of the most basic values, courage moved beyond individual concern to take on critical social and military importance. It became integral to the way soldiers—and armies—fought.

By far the most important function of courage was to sustain the minimal discipline required to organize armies, to bring them together on the battlefield, and to motivate their soldiers to fight one another. Such a role may seem anomalous to twentieth-century Americans inured to discipline established by extensive military training and enforced by a strong system of military justice and by the public's willingness to respect and even to extend into civilian life the penalties imposed by that system. But in the Civil War indiscipline was chronic,[2] and without the power of the ideal of courage both to impel and compel men to combat, neither the Union nor the Confederate government could have mounted so comprehensive an effort. In courage was the armies' cohesiveness.

The extraordinary lack of formal discipline within Civil War armies sprang from the strength, vitality, and persistence of soldiers' local sources of identity and support. As Ulysses Grant would later point out, the United States before the war was a country divided into "small communities" and "localized idioms."[3] The farmboys and small-town youth who filled the ranks did not at first experience the war as a rupture with community life rendering them susceptible to new idioms and new rules. It was to be an adventurous outing, perhaps slightly dangerous, but it would remain in its essentials an extention of home life. Soldiers might welcome the temporary suspension of small-town superintendence, but they would not hesitate to invoke small-town values to resist any new set of restrictions.

Small-town individualism and egalitarianism contributed nothing to military discipline. The first expressed itself as opposition to any development threatening to submerge the individual in the collectivity. Volunteers on both sides fiercely resisted subordination to a military hierarchy. The Southern soldier, Carlton McCarthy insisted, was "an individual who could not become the indefinite portion of a mass, but fought for himself, on his own account." The Confederate rank-and-file, Herbert observed, "failed utterly to understand . . . why, as soldiers enlisted in [the cause of constitutional liberty], they were not each and all entitled to be treated as free men." Northern perceptions were identical. "It is not necessary for one to lay down his manhood when he takes up the dress and arms of war," an Indiana soldier maintained. "After everything was done that could be done to make a model soldier of an American volunteer," a Federal from Wisconsin said, "there was still left a reserve of individuality."[4]

Such insistence was a source of despair for leaders on both sides. Sherman was appalled that individualism should threaten to dominate combat. He complained after First Bull Run that "each private thinks for himself," an observation that for a time reduced him to black pessimism. "I doubt if our democratic form of government admits of that organization and discipline without which an army is a mob." As slavery had weakened the South, democracy had weakened the North—and no one, he added, could say which was the greater evil.[5]

The egalitarian spirit expressed itself in resistance to distinctions between persons, even in armies conceived from the outset as loose groupings of individuals. Holmes might believe that "the lines of nature . . . establish orders and degrees among the souls of men," but that was a snobbish Brahmin judgment that few tolerated. Northern citizen-soldiers, as Colonel Grenville M. Dodge of the 4th Iowa discovered, simply refused to be "bossed." Nor did any sense of natural distinctions induce the Confederate soldier to relinquish what McCarthy called "the right of private judgment," which extended even to the soldier's prerogative to decide when his unit could not accomplish its mission in combat and when, accordingly, he might surrender.[6]

The target of those determined to retain "the right of private judgment" was the officer. Frank Wilkeson put confidently and bluntly the sentiment of the ranks: Enlisted men were the equals of their officers—"and not a few . . . the superiors"—in courage, intelligence, and military ability. The result was a strong bent to resist the orders of any officer whose superior qualifications were not immediately apparent to the privates.[7]

A Federal general of volunteers, John A. Logan of Illinois, explained that the men had known at home "no discipline or superior authority" and were thus "absolutely ignorant of . . . the proper deference due superior officers." If he thought, however, that informing them of the deference due would dissolve their antagonism to orders, he was grievously mistaken. Men inclined to resist officers in general knew that their own officers were particularly vulnerable. Most companies were made up of residents of the same county. Some were even more intimately connected, with a nucleus drawn from a single church or business enterprise. While social distinctions were by no means absent from home communities, no relationships there (among whites) remotely approached that, for example, between a prewar Regular Army colonel and a career private. Thus volunteers could not but continue to think casually of their company and regimental officers; they had little "awe and reverence" for those who were boyhood companions and friends or neighbors of long standing.[8]

One might expect the problem to be less serious in the Confederate Army. Would not a society one of whose pillars was slavery have inculcated a strong sense of status and a keen ability to recognize superiors and inferiors? It seems not. Richard Taylor, whose standing as the son of President Zachary Taylor and the brother-in-law of Confederate President Jefferson Davis would appear to have commanded the utmost deference, complained that among his Texas soldiers "distinctions of rank were unknown. Officers and men addressed each other as Tom, Dick, or Harry, and had no more conception of military gradations than of the celestial hierarchy of the poets." Mark Twain and fourteen friends from Hannibal who organized themselves in the Marion Rangers refused orders to cook—that was "a degradation"—to go on picket duty, or even to attack a house occupied by the enemy. The sturdiest prop supporting their resistance was their inability to think of Brigadier General Thomas Harris as other than "the sole and modest-salaried operator in our telegraph office" at home in Hannibal.[9]

A relatively small number of Southern gentlemen held to a well-developed sense of hierarchical relationships and a desire to compel the observance of social gradations; a significant proportion of them, however, chose to enlist in the ranks. As one of them noted, "the higher the social position, the greater the wealth, the more patriotic it would be to serve in the humble position of a private." Extending beyond the desire to demonstrate selflessness in the cause was the determination to prove that their abilities were independent of social status and, most important, that their worth did not rest on rank—exactly what other privates were intent on establishing. Gentlemen, moreover, often gravitated into local units whose ranks were filled with those of similar standing—the Richmond Howitzers, the Rockbridge Artillery, the Washington Artillery of New Orleans. In such blueblood units the same issue—equality—came to the fore, this time as intraclass equality. Southern gentlemen might uphold the necessity of a societywide sense of social subordination—Eggleston spoke of the "fixed" social status of every person—but they spent much of their time as soldiers resisting their own subordination at the hands of their officers. "It took years," Mc-Carthy observed, "to teach the educated privates . . . that it was their duty to give unquestioning obedience to officers because they were such, who were awhile ago their playmates and associates in business."[10]

The view then was the same from both social ends of the Confederate Army. John Dooley knew from long observation "the meager discipline in the Southern armies, their spirit of insubordination and levelling of distinctions." Robert E. Lee lamented after Gettysburg: "Our people are so little liable to control that it is difficult to get them to follow any course not in accordance with their inclination." As the historian Ella Lonn so well put it, "All Southern soldiers had a strong consciousness of themselves as free moral agents; they were wholly unaccustomed to acting on any other than their own motion. They were unused to control of any sort and were not disposed to obey any one except for good and sufficient reason, fully stated."[11]

The mobilization of armies was not, as it would become in the twentieth century, a matter of persuading or compelling young men to accept a status of powerlessness. Both governments would have preferred organization from the top down—with Washington and Richmond issuing administrative *ukases* that would call forth rapid and respectful obedience from every town within their territories—but at the outset neither deluded itself into thinking such centralized control possible. Sherman complained that the national government did not yet have "the right, and also the physical power, to penetrate to every part of our national domain" and "people even of small and unimportant localities, North as well as South, had reasoned themselves into the belief that their opinions were superior to the aggregated interest of the whole nation."[12]

At best, Abraham Lincoln could solicit the cooperation of governors and promise federal monies to help equip regiments that state leaders might agree to raise. Governors in turn engaged local notables, who in exchange for officers' commissions would draw on their community reputations to enlist townsmen. Sometimes governors had the power to appoint; sometimes they could advance their nominees only by recommending to the men those they hoped the men would approve; sometimes it was understood that rank would be distributed according to the number of men a recruiter was able to gather about himself. Often local figures on their own initiative would organize a nucleus, offer the unit to the governor, and request his confirmation of their rank. Ordinarily a man's ability to recruit signified local prestige or position sufficient to win the men's initial acquiescence in his elevation to command. (James A. Garfield formed the 42d Ohio around a core of his students at the Western Reserve Eclectic Institute of Hiram.) But even in those states whose governors held full authority to appoint regimental officers, the politics of the situation required great caution and often abnegation. The system almost always contained ways for the men to ratify or reject particular officer appointments. The most common was the election of officers, and that aggravated further the problem of discipline.[13]

Officer elections projected directly into the army the allegiances of the locale. At the war's outset Sherman, away from Ohio so long that the men of his home community would not elect him "to my appropriate place," had to find another avenue to a commission. In Eggleston's Virginia unit, even corporals were elected; through the first eight months of the war Eggleston knew of no noncommissioned officer appointed or demoted by his captain without a company vote. The principle that rank was acquired from the men was bad enough, but even more troublesome was the civilian assumption that powers derived from an electorate could be withdrawn by that electorate. Eggleston reported that officers chosen by the rank-and-file were often later subjected "to enforced resignation upon petition of the men." Officers thought too severe were simply not reelected.[14]

Commanders thus found it necessary to go far to accommodate these "free moral agents." For a time a company captain of the 21st Georgia directed his men with words that seemed suggestions rather than orders: "Gentlemen of the Banks County Guards! Will you please halt?" As late at November 1863, General E. F. Paxton assumed command of the Stonewall Brigade in tones so respectful as to seem supplicatory: "The Brigadier commanding, assuming the position, embraces the opportunity to express his appreciation of the honor received in being assigned to [this] brigade. . . . He hopes to merit your good opinion by his efforts to provide for your comforts and promote your efficiency, and by his participation with you in all the dangers and all the hardships of the service. He expects that such example as he may set, of attention to duty and obedience to orders, will be followed by the officers and men of his command."[15]

The chastening experience of John Beatty, lieutenant colonel of the 3d Ohio, demonstrated a common interplay of forces. When he discovered that his men were not staying in camp, he attempted to enforce discipline. But his approval of court-martial judgments "brought down upon me not only the hatred and curses of the soldiers tried and punished but in some instances the ill will of their fathers, who for years were my neighbors and friends." Rigor, moreover, not only cost him all popularity but aggravated insubordination. Some men drifted away for days, and those who remained refused to drill. When Beatty executed a general's order by buckling to a tree a drunk and rebellious soldier, the whole regiment rose in protest: "The bitter hatred that the men entertained for me had now culminated." Still, Beatty was able to face them down; confronted with his vow that he would die before permitting them to free the miscreant, they dispersed. Later, he negotiated with the regiment's timorous and incompetent colonel an understanding that that officer would resign in exchange for Beatty's promise not to bring charges against him. The colonel, however, soon reneged and again roused the men against Beatty by promising furloughs. The soldiers cheered the colonel, decried the conspiracy to displace him, and gathered 225 signatures on a petition demanding that *Beatty* resign. Beatty again persevered—the colonel was at last persuaded to depart—but not many officers were willing to risk as much as he had against the powerfully coercive influences of camp and home.[16]

Sheridan expressed the belief that he should trust his reputation to the common soldier. He might have added that very often officers had no choice but to do so.[17]

With home town values furnishing such abundant fuel, the inability of the armies to seal off soldiers from nonmilitary influences made it likely that sparks of indiscipline here and there would erupt into flame.

The Civil War was a most unmartial war. Civilians swarmed everywhere and seemed to do everything. Training remained ludicrous as long as it was undertaken close to home. Volunteers' families would arrive, pitch tents, and sometimes build brush houses, and they were not there solely to watch the proceedings from a respectful distance. "Crowds of men, women, and children visited our camp daily," a Rhode Islander wrote, and "each day seemed a holiday."[18]

A pristine military atmosphere was no more likely in combat areas. There too, civilian influences abounded. Many officers brought servants from home or hired them en route. In an extraordinary instance the colonel of New Orleans's Washington Artillery went to war with a German serving as his major-domo, the German's wife as his *vivandière* (canteen-keeper) and the French chef of Victor's Restaurant (accompanied by a pet fox) as his personal cook. Army wagonmasters and teamsters were civilians, as were the commissary clerks. The military establishments did not feed their officers but paid them allowances for food, which they secured by entering the civilian economy. Sutlers arrived to purvey varieties of nonspartan foods and notions to both officers and men. Wealthier families frequently visited their soldier sons. Wives of high-ranking officers were sometimes able to remain with them throughout the winters. In November 1861 a member of Stonewall Jackson's staff in camp near Winchester, Virginia, noted "a very general congregation of officers' wives at the farmhouses in the neighborhood," which soon expanded "until women and children are as common in the camp as black-berries in August."[19]

Army units themselves were a considerable part of the traffic in and out of combat zones: Large detachments were sent home to recruit; Union regiments were ordered home to vote; and contingents were dispatched to guard against city disturbances. Combat often took place in the midst of civilian populations, people whom soldiers found so like themselves that they felt none of the apprehension of being in a strange land and none of the isolation that would heighten their sense of dependence on the army. Northern privates might write home of their shock at the discovery that some Southern women used snuff, but within their initial assumption that the line between combatants and noncombatants would remain inviolate and that their lives were protected against civilian acts of belligerence, they felt quite comfortable in the homes of Southerners.

Thus the Civil War soldier, moving from peace to war but seldom severed from civilian influences, suffered little serious sense of discontinuity. He at first surveyed the war as he had his locale, and he found little cause to doubt that he remained master of his own destiny. In ways that twentieth-century war would no longer admit, the Civil War was thought an extension of, not a hiatus in, peacetime life. As Joshua Chamberlain would later observe, soldiers continued to think in ways "related to a condition of domestic peace, and did not contemplate a war at the center of life."[20]

Adding immeasurably to indiscipline was the failure of the armies—at the outset, both armies; beyond the second year, the Confederate Army in greater measure—to provide logistical support sufficient to sustain soldiers in the field without recourse to activity prejudicial to discipline. Soldiers have always violated regulations in order to enhance personal comfort or pleasure. When, however, the objective was the soldier's survival or, at a minimum, the maintenance of his health, the requisite "indiscipline" was of a special order. Because at the outset of the Civil War neither army could provide basic sources of nourishment, shelter, and warmth, soldiers' determination to survive by foraging fostered a structural indiscipline whose forms and results would profoundly influence the later stages of the war.

In order that the Civil War might be fought, the Union and Confederate high commands felt it essential to establish discipline in concentric spheres: Soldiers had to be held within military jurisdiction, held to camp discipline, and, at the center, held in battle. Efforts within the first sphere were largely unavailing; throughout the war desertion remained a terrible problem. Nonbattle discipline, too, continued to appall military leaders North and South. Ironically, discipline was best where it was most required—in battle—and here courage was the key. In certain conditions the soldier could forsake his unit without seriously impugning his courage. He could almost always disobey, straggle, wander, or commit varieties of mischief without calling his courage into question. Only in battle was he willing to concede a connection between courage and discipline. As Carlton McCarthy put it, the soldier was "ever ready to fight, but never ready to submit to the routine duty and discipline of the camp or the march."[21]

That acknowledgment did not mean, however, that officers had only to issue orders in or around battle. In their attempts to command, they discovered that they secured obedience only as their men judged them worthy to command and as they could persuade their men that the order at hand touched an issue of courage.

Occasionally, it is true, soldiers were so impressed by an officer's courage that their trust embraced all his orders. Stonewall Jackson was the foremost example. A Confederate officer spoke of his own "desire to emulate the action of the best men on the field";[22] by his fearlessness, Jackson persuaded more of his soldiers than did any other in direct command of field forces that he was the best man on the field. But such a consensus was rare. Seldom was the commitment of the rank-and-file so profound that it disposed of the need to examine orders, often separately and always critically.

Most common soldiers simply refused to equate worth with rank. Men measured the individual, Abner Small of the 16th Maine said, and not the grade of his commission. Seldom was there charity in their original assessments; many shared the view of the Michigan sergeant who decided that officers frequently lacked "the excellence of character" that would entitle them to their positions by "naturally" drawing the men's respect. Convinced that differences in character constituted the only important distinction between men, privates subjected each officer to their examination. Each had to prove by the quality of his leadership his right to rank, a tenet that the most perceptive officers comprehended and accepted. Henry Abbott of the 20th Massachusetts seldom claimed a power based on his rank rather than his example; officers, he knew, must be worthy of their men.[23]

Most officers, lacking the heroic presence of a Jackson or a Stuart and thus unable simply to issue orders, had no alternative but to prove themselves exemplars of courage. A device widely employed in the war's first years was conspicuous exposure to enemy fire. Such generals as George Armstrong Custer, D. H. Hill, and Alfred Torbert rode along the line ignoring enemy bullets and shells. John Pelham, "Pelham the Gallant" of the Confederate artillery, directed his men to lie down while he remained on his horse, "intent solely upon the movements and designs of the enemy, wholly careless of the 'fire of hell' hurled against him." John Beatty brought to an end his tribulations with the 3d Ohio when at Perryville he ordered his men to the ground while he remained standing under "shot, shell, and canister . . . thick as hail," a gesture that at last won over the regiment. "[N]ow they are, without exception, my fast friends."[24]

It was as if officers were required to bank courage, with their deposits compelling equal contributions by the men and the joint balances then becoming available to officers to draw down when they thought them required. Wounded in a charge against Northern cannon emplaced on a hilltop, a Mississippi lieutenant colonel refused to be evacuated: "Tell the Twenty-first they can't get their colonel till they take those guns!" The second and third charges failed, but not until he fainted could the men carry him off.[25]

Some officers whose civilian identities automatically triggered rank-and-file animosity could use demonstrations of courage to override initial unpopularity. A newly commissioned brigadier general, Carl Schurz, found that among John C. Frémont's men of the Western Department he was distrusted as a "politician." "But by a display of courage in battle, he succeeded in dispelling many of their objections." When Prince Charles Polignac, a French aristocrat and brigadier in the Confederate service, was assigned by General Richard Taylor to a Texas brigade, the men bridled at having a "foreigner" as their commanding officer. They wanted no "damn frog-eating Frenchman" whose name they could not pronounce and whose orders were "Greek" to them. Taylor nipped the mutiny by promising to remove Polignac if dissatisfaction remained after their first action. Polignac then distinguished himself in an engagement against Union gunboats sent up the Washita River. "By his coolness under fire, [he] gained the confidence of his men. . . . They got on famously, and he made capital soldiers out of them." Courage was the sovereign value.[26]

Once exposure to battle had established a tentative reputation for bravery and had begun to build credits, the officer had available to him several ways of drawing out the men's courage. He might do so with gestures of reassurance. Enlisted men often described as "contagious" their commander's calmness under fire. Fearing that his men would waver under the climactic Southern artillery barrage at Gettysburg, Schurz serenely walked up and down smoking a cigar.[27]

Of one of his attempts to relieve Vicksburg, Richard Taylor wrote:

With the exception of Green's command, the troops on the right of the Teche [River] were raw, and had never been in action. As shot and shell tore over the breastwork behind which they were lying, much consternation was exhibited, and it was manifest that an assault, however feeble, would break a part of the line. It was absolutely necessary to give the men some *morale;* and, mounting the breastwork, I made a cigarette, struck fire with my *briquet,* and walked up and down, smoking. Near the line was a low tree with spreading branches, which a young officer, Bradford by name, proposed to climb, so as to have a better view. I gave him my field glass, and this plucky youngster sat in his tree as quietly as in a chimney corner, though the branches were cut away [by enemy bullets]. These examples, especially that of Captain Bradford, gave confidence to the men, who began to expose themselves.[28]

An officer might use courage to shame his men to a corresponding courage. The Virginia soldier William W. Blackford thought that Stuart's presence itself possessed the power to rebuke those not acting courageously. Where Stuart was, men "were ashamed to be anything but brave." But others were required to offer gestures of courage. In the wake of the Union defeat at Chickamauga, the commander of a portion of Burnside's cavalry screening Knoxville resolved to halt the movement of his men, who were being "driven back by the hot fire" of Southerners. He "would walk deliberately up to the rail pile and stand erect and exposed till his men rallied to him. For hours he did this," until in mid-afternoon he was fatally wounded.[29]

Discovering that a skirmisher had violated his orders by lying down, D. H. Hill forced the man to stand with him under fire and to load his rifle for Hill to fire—after taking a long, long aim.[30]

No one came closer to epitomizing these conceptions than Philip Sheridan at Cedar Creek. When Jubal Early flanked the Union left and attacked with such ferocity that Confederates penetrated to the rear of Sheridan's army, Federal units were sent flying in retreat. At Winchester, Sheridan learned of the disaster and set out to ride 14 miles down the Valley Pike, everywhere rallying men whose defeat he would not accept. Swinging his hat, pointing southward, he shouted, "Turn back, men! Turn back! . . . You'll have your own camps back before night!" "The effect," Bruce Catton wrote, "was electric." The men, shouting

"Sheridan! Sheridan," rallied, returned to the firing line still held by Sixth Corps, and that afternoon launched a counterattack that ruined Early's army. In the words of a brigade historian: "Such a scene as [Sheridan's] presence produced and emotions as it awoke cannot be realized once in a century." Sheridan's biographer too thought it an epiphany: "Rarely in military history has the presence of one man affected so positively the outcome of battle."[31]

Here was an exhibition of courage so individualistic, so highly visible, and so powerful that it seemed to attain its results not by osmotic effects of reassurance or shaming but by the direct transfusion of courage from a commander to his men.

If officers made no attempt to demonstrate courage, or if the men found the results of their efforts ambiguous, those in the ranks often decided to "try out" their officers. They could not force an officer to thrust himself forward in battle, but they thought they could learn elsewhere what they needed to know. Sometimes that godliness so proximate to courage provided the signal sought. When the 65th Ohio's new commanding officer arrived and everyone wondered what kind of man he was, a private idled near headquarters one night and then reported, "Boys, Harker's all right. I peeked in his tent, and saw him reading his Bible." More often, the men probed the way an officer invoked discipline. Several privates might ostentatiously violate a camp rule, and all would watch the officer's reaction. If the punishment was deemed just, he won a measure of respect—if just and clever, even more. But if it was too severe for the infraction, the officer would discover that he had invited a problem far more serious than the one he had settled. He who punished harshly was counted a martinet, and to many that signaled qualities antithetical to courage.[32]

John Casler wrote of a pretentious and demanding regimental adjutant, "a fop in kid gloves" who "wanted to be very strict." "Some of the boys prophesied that he was a coward. Sure enough, when the battle commenced he showed the 'white feather' and disappeared." Several days later the adjutant returned to camp; the colonel asked him how the battle had gone at Winchester—80 miles to the rear—and dismissed him from the regiment. Here was another demonstration that discipline could not be invoked in ways divorced from courage. (A sanguine Texas general once proposed to solve the problem of discipline simply by extending the requirements of courage from combat to the enforcement of regulations. He insisted that it was as much the duty of company officers to lose their lives in support of discipline as to die on the battlefield. But that was not a position to which any noticeable number of officers rallied.)[33]

Nor were the men impressed by attempts to win them over merely with gestures seeming to renounce officer formality or officer prerogatives. Soldiers lauded Stonewall Jackson's willingness to join them in the mud and to put his own hands to the rebuilding of a critical bridge. The same conduct by an unproven officer would have been resented. On the march Benjamin Harrison sometimes carried on his saddle the guns and packs of exhausted soldiers or even gave over his horse to sick soldiers; in camp he made coffee and carried it to those freezing on picket. But kindness and consideration in a man of Harrison's proven courage would become in another officer weakness and a shallow appeal for sympathy.[34]

The effort of hard-pressed officers to establish their courage as the essential link between command and compliance was shaped by the patterns of indiscipline confronting them. Some indiscipline was self-indulgent. As in all wars, soldiers disobeyed standing orders so as to improve their own lot, with motives ranging from a moment's frivolous pleasure to the preservation of bodily health. Some acts of indiscipline, however, were understood to convey meanings as socially significant as they were personally gratifying. They were designed to puncture officer vanity and to punish officer aloofness; to defend against officer infringements of the enlisted man's dignity; and to resist excessive punishments decreed by officers.

The men devoted much effort to the deflation of the officer whose character in their judgment did not merit the command conferred by his rank. Since so many officers fitted that description, soldiers' reminders of their fundamental equality targeted both officers as a class and individual offenders. In winter quarters Casler's Virginia regiment organized a theater featuring a blackface minstrel troupe whose performances burlesqued officers, including doctors, quartermasters and commissaries. Another winter pastime was the snowball battle between regiments; officers who expected only to watch were pelted or "captured," pulled from their horses, and their faces washed with snow. (Longstreet seemed at first unperturbed by a snowball salute but soon threatened to cancel furloughs for the winter if it did not halt.) As the need arose, individuals were subjected to tactics ingeniously calibrated from the gentle to the devastatingly cruel. Enos Vail of the 20th New York thought the regimental surgeon, a major, "decidedly gruff." He and his friends seized the doctor and repeatedly bounced him into the air from a tent fly, "a great blow to his vanity." General William S. Rosecrans received a less presumptuous but more clever rebuke. When he decided to perfect camp discipline by walking among the tents at night and upbraiding those who had not extinguished lights or who continued to sing and talk, the men decided to retaliate. The next time he came by, flailing at the canvas with the flat of his sword, they pretended to mistake him for the regimental wagonmaster playing a joke on them. From within their tents they shouted back, abusing the general with "all sorts of rough camp chaff" and revealing only innocent astonishment after they had forced Rosecrans to identify himself.[35]

Company I of the 9th New York held in contempt the bravery of its newly arrived commander, Captain Barnard. "A variety of insults were heaped upon him openly, the moment he entered our quarters, and . . . when he came out to take command, the Company refused to a man to obey his orders. And this, too, after he had made a speech to the effect that the insulting remarks . . . must be stopped, and that he would shoot another man under the same circumstances, etc.; but all in vain." During the day Barnard was hanged in effigy and caricatured on his own tent-flap; at dress parade, mention of his name drew "three groans." That night the company area was "a perfect bedlam, so that the poor man dared not step out of his tent. This was the last of Captain Barnard. In the morning, the Major sent in a request that the Company cease their demonstrations, as Captain Barnard had already sent in his resignation."[36]

Mockery sometimes became a high art. When in Wilbur Hinman's Ohio regiment its temporary commanding officer, Colonel William H. Young, grew angry that those in the ranks were anticipating a drill order, he shouted at them, "*Will* you wait?" "The boys picked up this expression, and to the day of our discharge kept it in active service." Whenever the colonel came into sight, a dozen would cry out, "*Will* you wait?" "It always an-

noyed him, and that is probably the reason the boys kept it up."
"Nothing was more keenly relished than a joke on an officer."
When half-rations made long night marches unusually onerous,
a member of Hinman's company would yell out a riddle touching
on the "tender spot" of an officer. Another would shout an answer laying bare that vulnerability, and all would enjoy the officer's loss of temper and futile search for culprits.[37]

When annoyance with pretentious style was combined with
skepticism regarding an officer's courage, the sardonic element
intensified. In September 1862 Hinman's company, advancing
"madly" in battle line through woods and thickets, heard a dozen
shots in the distance. Captain Orlow Smith "was sure the battle
had come at last" and shouted "frantically," "There it comes now!
Steady, Company G!" But there was nothing coming. Thereafter
any stray shot would bring a cry, "There it comes now! *Steady-
y-y* Company G!"—"and then everybody would laugh—except
Captain Smith." A variant was the alacrity with which the men
cheered a despised officer—in tones mocking and derisive. Those
were forms of indiscipline effective in retaliation and, one would
guess, in inhibiting an officer's readiness to repeat the offending
behavior.[38]

Insistence on equal treatment underlay much indiscipline.
Leaving the Shenandoah Valley on its way to Fredericksburg, a
company of the 21st Georgia passed a farm offering apple brandy
for sale. The captain detailed men to carry over the canteens,
but at the stillhouse they encountered a cavalry guard who announced that Jubal Early had forbidden purchases. Had the general had any cider? Yes, a canteen filled and a keg tied on his
ambulance wagon. "Then we will buy what we want"—and,
with the captain in at least temporary alliance, they did. Such
insistence could turn harsh. Union soldiers assigned to picket duty
on Christmas Day during Sherman's march through Georgia fired
repeatedly, creating false alarms that brought the reserve running up each time, until the pickets were bought off with punch.
Still unmollified, the guards seized local civilians, looped rifle
slings around their necks, and threatened to hang them unless
furnished with a Christmas dinner and whisky.[39]

When soldiers were convinced that officers had offended their
personal dignity, the resultant indiscipline ranged from simple
disregard of a command to explosive reaction. A colonel's order
requiring soldiers to obtain passes before leaving the regiment

was, the fifer Bardeen reported, one of the rules he and his comrades never "regarded" and would "love" to see enforced.
LeGrand James Wilson's Mississippians considered "repugnant"
the idea of carrying passes to town and swore to march home if
the regulation were not lifted. When a Massachusetts officer
whistled for Drummer Phillips, age fourteen, the boy replied
that he was not a dog and would not answer a dog's summons.
For that impertinence the officer ordered him tied to a tree, but
an appeal to the colonel brought deliverance to him and a rep-
rimand to the lieutenant. General John White Geary, a Union
division commander, caught a soldier he thought a skulker and
threatened him with the flat of his sword. When the private replied, "Put up your sword or I'll shoot you," Geary apparently
concluded that such assertiveness was incompatible with cowardice and apologized.[40]

Military courtesy was always a matter of special sensitivity,
and privates often expressed their judgment of an officer by with-
holding their salutes. Still, as if to ensure that officers should not
be able to count on any consistency of soldier reaction, enlisted
men sometimes took umbrage that military courtesy was not rendered *to them*. A color corporal, John Ovendorf, met on the company street a new second lieutenant and saluted him, but "the
officer failed to return the compliment." Ovendorf muttered, "I
will never salute you again." Overhearing, the lieutenant called
him "a vile name." To that the corporal responded with a blow
so powerful it appeared to kill the officer. But "nothing was ever
done about the matter." The men thought Ovendorf in the right:
Had he been placed on trial, "he would have been acquitted and
the officer punished."[41]

An officer determined to impose punishments the men
thought unreasonable could incite sharp counteraction. Charles
Sidney Winder, whose imagination extended no farther than the
letter of the Confederate Army's regulations, resolved to end
straggling among members of the Stonewall Brigade accustomed
to seeking water, taking naps, and staying the night with friends
when the inclination seized them. He ordered a roll call at the
end of each day's march, with absentees to be "bucked"—their
hands tied together and then slipped over their knees and a stick
run through under the knees and over the arms, a position "tiresome and painful"—from sunrise to sunset the next day. Though
other officers tried to dissuade the stubborn Winder from such

harshness, thirty of the men were immediately bucked. "We were all as mad as fury," John Casler recalled, "for it was a punishment that had never been inflicted in our brigade before." That night fifteen of the thirty deserted, and those who remained were no less rebellious. "We marched the next day a short distance, but I would not 'fall in ranks.' I told my captain I did not intend to answer a roll call that evening, and if I was bucked again for straggling it would be the last time; that I would never shoulder my musket for a cause that would treat soldiers in that manner." Before Casler and others developed their mutiny, however, officers had carried the story to Stonewall Jackson. "He sent Winder word that he did not want to hear of any more bucking . . . for straggling. That was the last of it, and the only time it was ever done."[42]

Still, Winder, "very severe, and very tyrannical," was one of those officers whose inflexibility brought their men to the edge of violence—and sometimes propelled them beyond. He was "spotted" by some of the brigade, and "we could hear it remarked . . . near every day that the next fight . . . would be the last for Winder." As it happened, the men were right, though at Cedar Run Winder died by Federal artillery shell rather than Confederate bullet. Such threats were not uncommon. The Southern General Allison Nelson was an "arrogant" West Pointer for whom the men came to feel "an almost uncontrollable hatred," for he had forgotten that he was commanding "*Americans*," "that he was ordering around men who could think as well as himself." In the men's version of the climactic incident, two privates were arranging a coffee-for-chickens trade with a Southern woman when she complained to Nelson that they had cheated her. He immediately ordered the two strung up—their hands tied by the thumbs to an overhead branch so high that they had to stand on their toes. Angry comrades went to Nelson's tent and fired a volley into its side just above their sleeping commander. The men were promptly released to complete their trade.[43]

As Alfred Bellard and friends in the 5th New Jersey were cutting down two privates strung up by a tyrannical captain, that officer appeared and, while expostulating, cut one of the enlisted men with his sword. A near-riot ensued; the colonel and the guard were summoned; threats, challenges and pushes were exchanged. The captain never again tied up a soldier. Indeed, he soon resigned, perhaps because he had felt the force of Bellard's concluding observation: "It was such officers as that who received a stray ball occasionally on the field of battle."[44]

The casualness with which the Louisianian Edwin Fay wrote home of an officer so hated that in combat he would certainly find himself "between two fires" suggests that the idea of officer murder had become common currency. Walt Whitman heard of many officers who no longer dared go into battle or even on picket for fear that they would be killed by their own men. There were claims that many officers died in that way, but confirmation was never offered. Seldom, it appears, was so extreme a step taken. "Many a wearer of shoulder-straps was to be shot by his own men in the first engagement," John Billings of the 10th Massachusetts Battery recalled, but when the battle arrived, "there seemed to be Rebels enough to shoot." The threat alone frequently sufficed. Often the men needed little more than macabre humor with a pinch of menace, as in those cases of objectionable officers treated to mock funeral processions and their own obsequies. ("The men . . . built a coffin of cracker boxes. We made a dummy of straw and old clothes, laid the corpse carefully in. We paraded around the camp, and after a suitable funeral, we buried it with military honors. Our new would-be lieutenant departed the next day, never to return.")[45]

No easier was the lot of the officer who imposed discipline on orders from his superior. That afforded him no shelter from the men's retributions. Neither army's chain of command had developed much tensile strength, and the officer who invoked higher authority simply exposed himself as a puppet deserving even less respect than the martinet. To press AWOL charges at a superior's behest was to court greater anger than would doing so on one's own initiative.

As in the case of military courtesy, men who habitually ignored regulations did not disdain to invoke them to their own benefit. Often the book could be employed against the book, the letter of discipline invoked to thwart the spirit of discipline. Casler's unit was ordered to dig a trench line. After a considerable period of labor, the lieutenant returned to camp, leaving a sergeant in charge, and soon one of the squads—its sector unfinished—decided to join the lieutenant in his leisure. When the lieutenant learned that the proposal had been Casler's, "he ordered me before his august presence and commenced cursing me, and wanted to know why I did not remain and finish it. I replied that we had done as much work as the balance of the corps, and had gotten that much ahead of them, and that I did not consider that we were required to remain there longer than the others, but that if they would have remained I certainly would." Perhaps sensing the ineffectuality of any defense relying on the Confederate Army's devotion to equal-hours employment, Casler then shifted to the attack: "And furthermore you must not curse me, or I will report you to headquarters." The lieutenant ordered Casler to an hour's punishment duty. Casler marched away with the sergeant but soon decided that he would go to the guardhouse before he would pile brush. His resistance was rooted in his sense that the regulations gave him the advantage: "An officer can punish a private, but he dare not curse him." The lieutenant was forced to agree, for he "talked very mildly, and said that he did not want to punish me; that he knew I was a good hand to work, and that he wanted that to be the last time I disobeyed orders. He knew that I would report him, and he wanted to smooth it over. He told me to go to my quarters, and he never cursed me afterwards."[46]

Enlisted men were not slow to discover in literalness new possibilities of humiliating their officers. When a sentry received from the officer of the guard instructions so strict and so detailed that he felt his dignity was infringed, he simply enforced them— to the point of compelling the officer to dismount in the middle of the river. When Benjamin Harrison insisted on a camp guard, a practice Illinois soldiers regarded as tainted by its currency in the Union's more cautious and effete eastern armies, the enlisted men enforced regulations to the letter: Each returning officer was required to go to the gate, to give the countersign, to present his pass, and even to provide a light by which the sentry could read the pass. Harrison canceled camp guard.[47]

So officers were compelled to learn, often painfully, how to command with only infrequent invocation of formal military discipline. The first step was the recognition that courage held primacy among the men as among the officers. Even the detested Nelson drew a cheer from a company that had just lost thirty-four of its sixty-three men at Shiloh when he commended the bravery of its performance. Another tactic, effective if used sparingly, was for an officer to confront an intransigent soldier with an offer to remove his straps and "lick him," thus reversing the threat of violence. But far more potent than the challenge was flexibility, a willingness to gain the spirit of discipline by sacrificing its letter to the men's determination to resist formal control. When a private in Hinman's company shot down a buzzard in violation of Lieutenant Johnston Armstrong's order against the discharge of muskets, the lieutenant delivered himself of "sulphurous expletives, the use of which is strictly forbidden by the Bible." However, at the first halt in the march he formed the company and "made a full apology for his lapse from self-control." The men cheered him for what they deemed a graceful act, and Armstrong had won on two counts. His outburst, whatever the subsequent retraction, would be likely to inhibit other potential offenders, and the response to his apology would make others even less willing to risk the wrath of one so popular. Later, he employed another tactic with equal effect. Discovering four sentries asleep, he hid their guns and shouted, "The rebels are coming!" The men's consternation, clumsiness, and embarrassment were far better insurance against repetition than any formal punishment.[48]

A few officers seemed to know from the outset how to lead their quasi-soldiers. Captain Hilary Herbert, with his Alabama company en route to Richmond in the early days of the war to become a part of the Confederate Army, angered the men with his attempts to keep liquor from them. He placed a guard on one of them, "Morris by name, a big stout double-jointed fellow . . . just recovering from a drunk," but during a change of trains Morris escaped and had to be pried from a barroom. "Captain," he began to argue, "you think I am a fool, but I am not. This company has never been mustered in; you have no more authority over me than I have over you, and I am not going to Virginia with you. I am going to stop right here." "Well, Morris," Herbert answered, "it is all very true that I have no power to compel you to go with me to Richmond, but you have no right to that uniform you wear. It was given to this Company to be used by soldiers in the field. That uniform is going to Virginia with me and the Company. If you do not walk into that car and behave yourself, I will have that uniform stripped from you at once and turn you loose in the streets without it." Morris knew that he had been outsmarted. His courage had been challenged and his dignity imperiled; he "hung his head and took his place in the Company."

Later, in the summer of 1862, Herbert became the regiment's commanding officer, replacing a colonel so unpopular that the unit was disintegrating. Just prior to that officer's resignation, sixty men had deserted in a single night. Herbert assembled the sergeants of the companies most seriously weakened.

> I know very well these men have not gone to the enemy—they did not mean to desert the Confederate cause; they only deserted, as I have learned, because of their belief that they were harshly treated by Colonel Winston, and I know very well, though I do not ask you to affirm or deny it, that these men have joined other regiments in the service, and also that you know this fact and can easily communicate with them. Now, I say to you, that such of these men as shall return to their places within two weeks will be forgiven; no notice will be taken of their desertion. If after that time, however, I lay eyes on one [of] these deserters who shall not have come back . . . he will be court-martialed and shot, if I can bring it about.

All but a few did return. Two who did not—Morris and another—were caught, tried and condemned to be shot, although Jefferson Davis overrode the sentence and pardoned both of them. "Morris afterwards made a good solder" and after the war greeted Herbert with cordiality.[49]

Here was the prescription for the exercise of command: a sympathetic understanding of the men's grievances; a refusal to condemn their actions; a wide flexibility in the reimposition of discipline; a knowledge of the men's likely reactions; and the invocation of military law only as the final sanction. But few knew of such prescriptions and fewer still knew how to apply them. In fact, Herbert had risked much in moving to that final step, for amid such complex patterns of interaction—individual officers and men intent on testing themselves (and suppressing all signs of fear); enlisted men sensitive to the formation within their own groups of collective judgments regarding every man's courage or cowardice;[50] enlisted men testing their officers; officers challenging the men's courage to spur them in combat—the men found exercises of formal military justice extremely repugnant.

In the war's early stages the armies often resorted to public degradations of cowardly or refractory soldiers. If the miscreant were an enlisted man, the ceremony might include the reading of charges, the shaving of the head, the cutting of buttons, the turning of the coat or, if an officer, the snapping of the sword, the ripping of shoulder straps, the smashing of the pistol. Often the enlisted man being drummed out would be compelled to wear a sign specifying his offense—"Coward," "Skulker," "Thief"— and to march in disgrace up and down the ranks of former comrades while the regimental band played "The Rogue's March." Sometimes whippings were included. Sometimes the army undertook to publish in the man's home community the news of his condemnation.[51]

In the beginning, such pageantry impressed on the men the weightiness of the occasion. They were awed and often resolved, as no doubt their commanders intended, to do nothing to bring such obloquy upon themselves. But it was not long before anger and revulsion that the army would treat any one of them that way also appeared. With each soldier constantly—if privately—sensitive to the difficulty of maintaining his own courage, many found intolerable a ceremony proclaiming to the world that one of their number had so spectacularly failed the test. The humiliation seemed unbearably visible, unbearably final. John Beatty thought drumming out "a fearful punishment." "Death and oblivion" would be less severe. Watching the drumming out of two Confederate deserters, Alexander Hunter of the 17th Virginia was no less appalled:

> It seemed worse than a funeral and more solemn, for it meant the burial of manhood and self-respect. After they had been marched up and down twice they were brought back to the center, halted, and, branded in their souls as it were, carrying each his stigma, were permitted to go their way. . . . This unexampled public degradation, [officers and men] reasoned, would kill all self-respect, and in nine cases out of ten ruin a man's future entirely. No gallant conduct or desperate bravery in the field could ever restore the honor that was lost. Dead to all incentive, utterly paralyzed to all exertion, the man would be sent adrift in the world, about as well ticketed to moral destruction as he could well be; for when you break a man's spirit and take all hope away, you do your very worst for him, both in this world and the next. It is all over with him.[52]

Measured by the despair on every face, such ceremonies supplied some of the saddest scenes of army life. Few soldiers wished to watch a second time. Indeed, in Hunter's brigade, the first public degradation "met with so little favor from officers and men that it was universally condemned" and was never repeated.[53]

Resistance intensified as both armies increasingly employed military executions. Here revulsion was even greater. Allen of the 4th Rhode Island found intolerable even the hanging of a Southern civilian who had shot and killed a Union lieutenant drilling black soldiers in front of his house. In August 1863 Robert Carter's Massachusetts regiment was compelled to watch the deaths of five deserters from the 118th Pennsylvania. "It was awful. How impossible it was for us to fathom the agony of their souls, as they marched to their own funerals, saw their own coffins, and their very graves before their eyes. *Oh, it was terrible!*" By miscalculation the ceremony was completed fifteen minutes prior to the time set for execution. "General Griffin now became restless under the awful suspense, and suddenly breaking the dreadful silence, shouted in his shrillest voice to Captain Orne, 'Shoot those men! or after ten minutes it will be murder! Shoot them at once!'" "It was the most dreadful spectacle I ever witnessed," Carter declared, "and I pray that I may never be permitted to see such a sight again."[54]

When soldier executions were even more seriously bungled, as they frequently were, the anguish could become almost palpable. Thomas Galwey and his friends of the 8th Ohio were ordered to attend the execution of two deserters. The firing squad's muskets, loaded the evening before, had somehow been exposed to rain. The first volley slightly wounded one of the condemned. The second volley wounded the same man again and "drove the other into a paroxysm of fear and trembling." The third volley killed the first soldier and only wounded the second. As the second soldier continued to struggle to free himself and the general raged, the spectators stood by, suffering nearly unbearable combinations of pity, disgust, and anger. The provost marshal brought members of the firing party to within a barrel's length of the survivor, but none of the muskets would fire. Finally, he drew his revolver and "discharged all the barrels" into the man's head.[55]

In such spectacles, even the most rigorously performed, the rank-and-file—and many officers—found numerous grounds for opposition. Death, after all, had its own sphere, battle, but the camp should be spared violent death, and thus parade ground executions raised in soldiers a sense of trespass. The agent of death seemed as anomalous as its setting: death "by the muskets of their comrades." The same held true for the climate of death. The men spoke of the "hot-blood killing" of battle and contrasted it with the execution's "cold-blood killing." In combat, Bardeen pointed out, a soldier never knew if or when he would be killed; on the execution ground men were denied the solace of that ignorance. And because the men assumed that only the staking of courage justified exposure to the risks of death, this "cold-blood killing" seemed cowardly to many.[56]

Thus to the rank-and-file public degradations and executions became extreme cases of officer tyranny. Casler and his friends thought it divine judgment that three officers who had sentenced four deserters to be shot should soon afterward be killed in battle. As in response to all other forms of officer despotism, resistance resulted. Sentries aimed poorly when prisoners slated for execution ran to escape. Men selected for firing squads loaded blanks, fired high, or simply failed to pull the trigger. Commanders were driven to draw all guards from outside the condemned men's company or regiment, to designate special loaders, and to lighten the burden on participants by diluting individual responsibility. The Confederate chaplain Quintard wrote of an execution in which twenty-four soldiers were marshaled to shoot one man, and twelve of the muskets were loaded with blanks.[57]

Later in the war there were numerous mock executions, so many that they must have reflected a higher policy in which ceremonies including every ritual except the final volley were designed to arouse that awe ("the solemn presence of death") that deterred without raising the revulsion that intensified indiscipline. When at last the President's pardons were announced, cheers often broke from the ranks of reluctant spectators. Abraham Lincoln knew that "you can't order men shot by dozens or twenties. People won't stand it." He knew that executions remained loathsome to his soldiers. Military justice could serve only a limited role in enhancing combat performance, and one is brought back to the demands of courage on the individual soldier.[58]

When Sergeant Fay dismounted to remove a fence rail and his horse charged without him, he was unconcerned that the Confederate Army might punish him for missing the fight. He did, however, solemnly resolve that next time he would *lead* the charge. When Eggleston reflected on why he felt impelled to fight Yankees, he gave no thought to formal sanctions; no, the fear of personal dishonor was such a stimulus, the source of greater terror than death, that officers issuing orders were, he insisted, unnecessary to the waging of the war. In the end it was the pursuit of courage and the flight from cowardice that upheld the discipline essential to the cohesiveness of Civil War armies.[59]

4

The Uses of Courage

The conditions of combat alter more rapidly than men can adjust their conceptions of combat. In the Civil War soldiers at first were not much troubled by the discrepancy between their persistent idea of combat as an individualized endeavor and the reality of increasingly depersonalized mass warfare, because their notions of courage helped to conceal the gap.

The primacy of courage promised the soldier that no matter how immense the war, how distant and fumbling the directing generals, or how powerful the enemy forces seeking his destruction, his fate would continue to rest on his inner qualities. Courage also offered ways to cheer those who suffered ruinous defeats in battle, to defend the soldier against the grisliness of the battlefield, and to conceal the destructiveness of the conflict by fostering good-will toward the enemy.

Underpinning discipline in battle remained courage's most important role, but its other functions—as the assurance of success; as a substitute for victory; as an insulation against battlefield trauma; and as a tie between enemies—were hardly less vital to the waging of the war.

Courage was the individual's assurance of a favorable outcome in combat. Put as simply as it appears to have been understood in 1861, the brave would live and the cowardly would die. Stiles of the Richmond Howitzers offered the sort of episode commonly recounted. Preparing to leave the Fredericksburg lines, members of his battery were lifting an ammunition chest from its hole to its carriage when a Northern battery across the river fired a long-range shot that the Confederates could see arching toward them. One Southerner sought shelter by leaping into the hole. Seconds later, the shell's explosion sent the carriage hurtling after him; it crushed the head of "the only man who had not stood his ground." Stiles was only one of the war's many moralists to invoke Napoleon's words: "Behold the just fate of the coward." What here remained implicit—that the courageous would be spared—was made precise by Edwin Fay: "I have always believed the most daring came off with fewest wounds."[1]

There was comfort even for the soldier of courage who might prove himself the exception by being shot down: Those at home would join celebration to their mourning of his death. If the good did die, they died good deaths. The conviction early in the war, again reduced to the most direct terms of popular belief, was that the hero's death was a happy death. As an infantryman in Lee's army, Hunter watched from the heights above Fredericksburg the charge of the Union's Irish Brigade. He and those about him were "filled with wonder and a pitying admiration for men who could rush with such unflinching valor, such mad recklessness into the jaws of destruction." Though that evening the Irish Brigade could count standing only 250 of the 1,400 who had charged, Hunter said of the fallen that because their behavior had been "superb," "none of the bitterness of death was theirs." "A brave man dies but once, a coward dies a thousand times."[2]

Courage also served as victory's surrogate in the face of battlefield defeat. The soldier's goal was twofold. He strove to defeat the enemy but also to attain the highest standard of courage; thus the military outcome of a particular engagement, while mirroring the effectiveness of his side's participation, need not reflect the *quality* of his side's performance. By applying that calculus, armies beaten in such battles as Fredericksburg, Chancellorsville, and Gettysburg could ignore the outcome as measured by traditional indices—the comparative numbers of dead and wounded, the army forced from the field—and stress instead the triumph of comportment to the exclusion of results.

The battle of Ball's Bluff in mid-October 1861 was a reconnaissance in force gone terribly wrong. Two Massachusetts regiments, the 15th and the 20th, crossed the Potomac near Leesburg and blundered into a superior Confederate force that pushed them back against the river; 200 Federals were killed or wounded, 700 were captured in the debacle. Two months later, on Christmas afternoon, the 20th Massachusetts formally accepted a beautiful silk memorial ensign, a state flag bearing on one side the words "Ball's Bluff," the Massachusetts pine tree and the inscription "Stand in the Evil Day" and on the other side the state motto and an arm whose hand grasped a sword. The flag was the gift of the sisters of Lieutenant Putnam (killed at Ball's Bluff) and Lieutenant Lowell (wounded at Ball's Bluff, later killed in battle in 1862). The presenter was John Palfrey, the father of the regiment's lieutenant colonel (to be discharged as disabled, 1863), who read a letter from Charles Eliot Norton, editor of the Loyal Publication Society. It promised the soldiers that Massachusetts "will never forget your hard, faithful, glorious though defeated services on that day." Norton at least acknowledged the outcome; many did not, and from their panegyrics a reader might conclude that lost battles had been won.[3]

Northerners' accounts of the Fredericksburg defeat carried the same message, if anything intensified. They acclaimed the courage of Union soldiers exactly as if that bravery had carried the day. A colonel of the 77th New York wrote: "None were ever more brave or more desirous to test their valor. The heroic deeds of those who did advance against the enemy will ever redound to the glory of our arms." Walt Whitman reported that "never did mortal man in an aggregate fight better than our troops at Fredericksburg. In the highest sense, it was no failure." Though the attackers could see before them strong Southern batteries and rifle pits, "Yet all the brigade went forward unflinchingly. . . . [S]till the men advance with unsurpassed gallantry—and would have gone again further, if ordered." Currier & Ives pointed the same moral in their print of the battle: "This battle shows with what undaunted courage the Lion-Hearted Army of the Potomac always meets its foes."[4]

Even those who acknowledged defeat often found palliation in courage. Chamberlain of the 20th Maine spent the night following the battle in "a ghastly bivouac among the dead," building breastworks of bodies stripped of clothing. Still, their valor had been "splendid" if unavailing and their ghosts were "glorious." Colonel George B. Sanford of the Regular Army's 2d Dragoons was remorseless in his description of the battle: "[T]he most desperate piece of fighting in the war, as from the first men realized the utter futility of the attempt. It was simply to go up and be killed without even the hope that finally the position would be taken." Nevertheless, courage offered some redemption: "It was a horrible battle, relieved only by the wonderful gallantry of the men and officers." Such distinctions between battlefield conduct and battlefield verdict carried Unionists through the long months between mid-1861 and mid-1863 as Federal forces suffered heavy defeats at the hands of Confederate armies in the East.[5]

This conception of courage as commensurate with military success also found expression on the tactical level. During the first Peninsula campaign a Confederate battery followed the manual perfectly in setting up its cannon under heavy Northern fire, "every piece, limber, caisson and man in the exact mathematical position in which each belonged, and every man [in] the very attitude required by the drill-book." Robert Stiles thought it "a beautiful movement." He was proud of his comrades' "staunch soldierly stand" and agreed that they deserved the cheers directed to them by nearby Confederate infantry, for they had shown themselves "equal to the most trying duty of the soldier . . . standing and receiving fire without replying to it." Their courage stood resplendent, with no consideration of the military purpose to be served. Stiles had not a word to say about the tactical success or failure of the maneuver.[6]

Courage also helped to insulate the soldier against the trauma of combat. Its code ordained that the soldier react to the sights of the battlefield with *sang froid*, the ability to remain unmoved by the horrors of war. Consider the manner in which John Esten Cooke chose to establish the bravery of John Pelham, the Confederate artillerist: "He saw guns shattered . . . or men torn to pieces, without exhibiting any signs of emotion . . . the ghastliest spectacle of blood and death left his soul unmoved—his stern will unbent." Similarly, when a Northern volley struck at head level a line of Mississippians and they lay eyes open, faces bleached by "a sickly summer rain" and foreheads "stained with ooze and trickle of blood," Stonewall Jackson passed by, looked long, but did not shudder. "Not a muscle quivered," Stiles admiringly reported. "He was the ideal of concentration—imperturbable, resistless."[7] To tremble might signal horror, and to feel horror was to yield to despicable effeminacy.

As courage served to detach the soldier from sights that might otherwise unnerve him, godliness further removed him from the edge of pain. A Virginia gunner who had declared for Jesus after two of his comrades died at Chancellorsville remained safe through the first two days of Gettysburg. On the last day of battle, "all thought the struggle over," and the soldier sent home word that he was unhurt. Suddenly, however, "a terrific fire burst thundering, flashing, crashing" on the unit's guns and he was hit. A friend saw what happened: "There lay our noble comrade, each . . . limb thrice broken, the body gashed with wounds, the top of the skull blown off and the brain actually fallen out upon the ground in two bloody, palpitating lobes." But the friend voiced no shock, for in his eyes God's "chariot and horses of fire had caught [the dead man] up into Heaven." Similarly, Burdette of the 47th Illinois lost comrades but not equanimity: "Oh, I never stand beside an open grave that I do not see the Son of God standing on the other side in the resplendent beauty and glory of the perfect Life."[8]

Courage was also the primary bond between enemies.

Civil War soldiers valued courage in and of itself. Accordingly, it was unlikely to attach itself to anyone unworthy. Given particularly the kinship of courage and godliness, courage could hardly be exercised by evil men or incorporated in an evil cause. If courage was a universal virtue of constant quality—and all soldiers thought it was—it became difficult to deny that demonstrations of courage were proofs of an ennobling purpose.[9] Should the foe then prove courageous, a basis for mutual respect and sympathy would be created. Another fundamental assumption—that one's achievements in war were enhanced by the worth of the enemy—reinforced this effect of courage. The worthier the antagonist, the worthier must be the force that is able to overcome him.

At the outbreak of the war ferocity characterized each side's image of the other. Southerners denied that those who confronted them were American soldiers. No, the Union Army was an assemblage of immigrants, of European marauders, a "hireling host," "the refuse of the earth." By their nature such people would invade and ravage other people's land. From the Northern side, the enemy appeared less distant but just as deplorable: Southerns were traitors. Writing to his brother Henry on the eve of his entry into the Union Army, Charles Francis Adams, Jr., decided that he "could fight with a will and in earnest" against the rebels. "They are traitors, they war for a lie, they are the enemies of morals, of government, and of man. In them, we fight against a great wrong." Occasionally, such images persisted to color actual observations of the enemy. A Vermonter watched Confederate troops of Jackson's command cross a pontoon bridge following their capture of Harper's Ferry in the early autumn of 1862: "They were silent as ghosts; ruthless and rushing in their speed; ragged, earth colored, dishevelled and devilish, as tho' they were keen on the scent of the hot blood that was already streaming up from the opening struggle at Antietam, and thirsting for it." But such views, so abstract and impersonal, seldom survived close contact with the enemy. A Union solider later realized that "the two armies became familiar with each other on the skirmish line; and familiarity bred *respect.*"[10]

Courage dissolved antipathy. At first, individual soliders might simply discover themselves silently admiring certain actions on the other side. Respect arrived with incidents small or large. To John DeForest it came as he watched a Texas major who very casually exposed himself during combat: "[M]any men in the line of battle added their bullets to the deadly flight which sought his life, while all our brigade watched him with breathless interest. Directly in front of me the horse reared; the rider dismounted and seemed to examine him; then, remounting, cantered a few yards; then leaned backwards and slid to the ground. Away went the horse, wildly, leaving his gallant master dead." To Pickett it came with that doomed charge of Meagher's Irish Brigade at Fredericksburg; he wrote his wife: "Your soldier's heart almost stood still as he watched those sons of Erin fearlessly rush to their death. The brilliant assault . . . was beyond description." Appropriately, it came to a Union color sergeant in the attack of Pickett's men at Gettysburg. No charge was "more daring," and Federal observers felt an "unbounded sympathy" for those who made it. Shortly, each side began to *express* its admiration of such feats. Indeed, Pickett said that at Fredericksburg "we forgot they were fighting us, and cheer after cheer at their fearlessness went up all along our lines."[11]

Such incidents, multiplied, led to a generalized respect for those fighting on the other side. Some soldiers reminded their comrades that the enemy's cause was evil and that honoring his valor seemed to honor his cause. A few remained impervious to the enemy's courage. The Confederate General Daniel Harvey Hill continued to hate Yankees with an unabating intensity. But most found that they felt less and less resentment against those they faced in battle. Eggleston later recalled that the war had taught him "the courage and manliness" of Northerners. Holmes spoke of the "brotherhood for the enemy"; those "doing their best to kill one another felt less of personal hostility, I am very certain, than some who were not imperilled by their mutural endeavors." Other soldiers noted, sometimes with surprise, their freedom from malice. Mark Twain, a Confederate volunteer whose enthusiasm and military career both expired quickly, later used that discovery to condemn war as "the killing of strangers against whom you feel no personal animosity; strangers whom, in other circumstances, you would help if you found them in trouble, and who would help you if you needed it."[12]

Bruce Catton called the Civil War a war between men "who, when left alone, got along together beautifully." Given the flimsiness of discipline, the rank-and-file were frequently left alone. One result was the local, informal enlisted men's truce, the private cease-fire "to gas a little." It was most easily arranged when the armies occupied opposite banks of a river. Privates swam out to an island to talk and trade, for Federals craved tobacco, Confederates were always short of coffee, and no one was averse to swapping newspapers. Such parleys further reduced animosity. Opening jibes ("I say, Johnney Reb, why don't you wear better clothes?" "We uns don't wear our best clothes when we go to kill hogs.") soon yielded to cordial explorations of sentiment on the other side. The answer to the question, "Ain't you tired of this thing?" was likely to be yes. Responses to "Why have you come down here to take away our niggers?" were likely to reveal to Confederates Northern attitudes about blacks much closer to their own than they had expected. Afterward, soldiers gave notice ("Are you dressed yet?" "Look out, Yanks, we're going to shoot.") before resuming hostilities. Officers tried to prevent local truces and to terminate those under way, but here again circumspection was called for. When a Confederate officer compelled the resumption of battle and irate Northern soldiers on the other side of the Chattahoochee, concentrating their fire, shot *him*, the Southern rank-and-file agreed that he got what he deserved.[13]

Soldiers found it reasonable that at certain times and in more or less formal settings army should fight army, but in their judgment that did not require that men fight men continuously or that even in battle men should fight without restraint. Alfred Bellard remembered a wounded but sharp-tongued Confederate of the 8th Alabama whose words so lacerated a Federal that he tried to club the prisoner, only to be stopped by an officer. That episode was, however, "the only exhibition of brutal passion that came under my notice." At Fort Pillow and at the Battle of the Crater, Southerners would later commit against black soldiers what some Northern soldiers would become convinced were atrocities, and soldiers on both sides, especially in border state areas, would treat with excessive harshness irregulars loyal to the other side, but comparable episodes involving white Union and Confederate front-line troops were rare. Fifer Bardeen's assertion that combat soldiers, when not in action, felt themselves to be "men and brothers" no doubt exaggerated their intimacy, but the recognition of courage in one another did moderate hostility. As Casler put it, "Each knew he met foemen worthy of his steel, for they had been tested on the field of battle."[14]

The rapport evident in informal truces extended to instances of what might be called delicacy in combat. Once soldiers granted the opponent's courage, it seemed necessary to proffer to him general notions of openness and equity, and "giving the other fellow a fair chance," as it was put, sometimes meant renouncing a combat advantage. When General John Bell Hood realized that the enemy troops he was about to attack were unaware of Southerners' presence, he ordered, "Major, send a shell first over their heads and let them get in their holes before you open with all your guns." When a Northern sentry challenged a Southern soldier approaching his post and the latter answered, "A friend," the Confederate decided that to kill the sentry in an action based on a lie and a deceit was not permissible. After the war, a Michigan officer apologized to the Confederate cavalry leader Wade Hampton because at Gettysburg he had tried to saber the South Carolinian from behind.[15]

Indeed, in the early years courage as a bond between enemies possessed power enough to weaken war's primary assumption, that the first purpose was to kill the enemy. With growing awareness of the enemy's courage, one's reactions might progress from regret that a brave opponent had been killed, to hope that another would not be, to demonstrations of pleasure and congratulation that he had not been. Frank Wilkeson traced such a pattern.

> I saw an officer on a milk-white horse ride forth from the woods in the rear of the Confederate work. Confident that he would be torn to bits by shells, I dropped my pipe, and glued my glass on him and waited for the tragedy. He trotted briskly over the plain where shell[s] were thickly bursting, and into the fort. I saw him hand a paper to the officer in command of the work. He sat calmly on his horse, and talked and gesticulated as quietly as though he were on dress parade. My heart went out to that man. I hoped he would not be killed. I wished I had the aiming of the guns. He lifted his hand in salute to the visor of his cap. He turned his white horse and rode slowly across the open ground, where shot and shell were thickly coursing. Dust rose above him. Tiny clouds of smoke almost hid him from view. Shot struck the ground and skipped past him, but he did not urge his horse out of a walk. He rode as though lost in meditation and deaf to the uproar that raged around him. He rode into the woods, disappeared in the timber, and was safe. With a "Thank God that brave man was not killed," I rejoined my gun.[16]

Not everyone kept such sentiments to themselves. Rice Bull of the 123d New York described a "gallant deed," a Union courier running a half-mile under fire, waving his hat and shouting at the enemy. When he at last made it to safety, opposing Southerners set off a great appreciative yell. Indeed, occasional incidents reveal the ability of courage even to *suspend* the soldier's sense of killing as the first necessity. Robert Strong and others of his unit pushed back Confederate skirmishers in a woods, but one Southerner would not withdraw with the others. He stayed to fire and then left with "some pretty bad words" and a derisive slap at his backside. One of the Federals was angry and shouted, "Kill him, the Rebel son of a bitch!" but others said, "No, don't"; it would be a pity to kill so brave a man. Ultimately they cheered the Confederate.[17]

An artillery duel opened the battle of Perryville, with the Federal battery commanded by Colonel Charles Carroll Parsons, a West Point graduate, and the Confederate battery by Captain William W. Carnes, an Annapolis graduate. Carnes managed his guns skilfully, his shots killing or wounding nearly all of the opposing officers, men and horses, but Parsons, "with great bravery and coolness," continued to fight with his last cannon even as the Confederate infantry began to advance. An infantry colonel ordered fire directed at Parsons, who, in anticipation, drew his sword and stood at parade rest. So impressed was the colonel by this "display of calm courage," that he ordered rifles lowered: "No! You shall not shoot down such a brave man!" Parsons was allowed to walk from the field.[18]

Occasionally reputation alone served as protection. When at Antietam Confederate cannoneers saw mounted officers surveying their lines and proposed sending shots at them, a gunner objected: "No, that's the Chief of Artillery [General Henry J. Hunt]. He's a brave man, and I won't fire at him. Wait until the battery comes, and we'll fire at that." A Pennsylvania colonel claimed to have struck aside the weapon of a skirmisher aiming at the Confederate cavalier Turner Ashby, who did not realize that he was in danger. "Ashby is too brave to die in that way."[19]

Nothing said here should suggest that Civil War combat ordinarily was anything but fierce and furious. In a war in which generals resolved to parade themselves under fire and officers exposed themselves to fire in order to establish the right of command, in a war in which soldiers stiffened themselves not to seek cover from enemy shells and anticipated the charge as the essential combat experience, men had patently invested so much of themselves in fighting that it was sure to be vehement, whatever the frequency of their truce-time assurances to one another that common soldiers could easily end the war if only left alone by generals and politicians. When Ira Dodd of the 26th New Jersey observed that there "was never a war fought . . . with less bitterness between those who met each other on bloody fields," he bracketed his thought with another, that no war was fought more sternly. To Edwin Forbes, "It seemed scarcely possible that within so short a distance were men [bantering and singing and 'free from actual malice'] who at a moment's notice might engage in deadly conflict"—but it happened daily. Of the functions of courage, only this one, courage as a bond between enemies, had any propensity to mitigate violence; all others heightened the intensity of the conflict. These were, after all, men determined to prove to themselves and others that they possessed qualities vital to their self-conception. This was not a war against foreign foes, in which ferocity could feed on cultural misperceptions. Here each side understood the other comprehensively if not completely, and participants on both sides were determined to demonstrate precisely the same thing, at the cost of their own lives and those of the other side.[20]

In an admission rarely found in postwar military memoirs, Ulysses Grant conceded that in a conflict whose initial assumptions equated abstention from combat with cowardice and bound discipline to courage, he had in his 1861 Missouri campaign committed 20,000 men to battle at Belmont with no orders and with no prior intent to do so. "I did not see how I could maintain discipline, or retain the confidence of my command, if we should return to Cairo without an effort to do something."[21] Clearly, the soldiers' impatient determination triggered engagements more frequent and fiercer than they might otherwise have been.

If courage's war intensified combat, so did it tend to contain violence within the limits of formal battle. Violence diminished so rapidly beyond battle that, set against twentieth-century war, the peripheries of warfare were almost bloodless. A Pennsylvania infantryman wounded in battle, captured, and held in the Andersonville prison camp for fourteen terrible months could still speak in undiminished praise of combat soldiers on both sides, those men "who daily tested each other's fidelity, bravery, and courage." In such a phrase lay both the intensification and the delimitation of combat. Wherever soldiers perceived that their courage was being tested, the fighting was stiff and bloody; where they found the setting inappropriate to contesting courage, contacts between combatants were likely to remain tranquil. In short, the appropriateness of any aspect of war to that daily testing was the criterion by which soldiers tried to regulate their own participation in combat. By extension, they would resist bellicosity on peripheries where they thought courage was not in question. When a vindictive senior colonel ordered his troops to loot and burn Darien, Georgia, Robert Gould Shaw restrained his own regiment and denounced the enterprise, in part because there was "not a deed performed from beginning to end, which required any pluck or courage."[22]

For officers, occasions of such diminished ferocity raised serious problems of command in several spheres. Generals were infuriated when defeats of the enemy could so seldom be turned into decisive routs. Failure was always attributed to the victors' exhaustion or to unit disorganization, but there was as well a lack of zeal for the pursuit of those forced into retreat. Beatty fired

71

one shot at retiring Confederate cavalry and immediately regretted it—"it would have been criminal to have killed one of these men, for his death could have had no possible effect on the results of the war." From the same set of assumptions both armies developed a distaste for sharpshooting. Dunaway of the 47th Virginia was furious when after the close of the first day's fighting at Gettysburg two "gallant" Confederate officers were killed by rifle shots, "although no Yankee was in sight." Sharpshooters hidden in a wooden building were responsible for that "murderous villainy."[23]

Most Civil War soldiers liked picket duty. Bardeen called it "the soldier's romance." At its best, it offered individual responsibility, rare privacy, and, even at its worst, a "more social relation" with officers. But soldiers rejected picket as a proper sphere of combat. "[T]he men on both sides," Galwey noted, were "accustomed to see one another on picket and . . . unwilling to harass or to be harassed unless an advance, retreat, or some decided movement is attempted by the opposite side." Indeed, pickets would often warn one another if an advance were impending. Occasionally the capture of an opposing sentry might be considered an achievement, but firing while on picket was "mere wantonness," and killing while on picket was "assassination"—so Bardeen's regiment taught him. Michigan's Alpheus S. Williams was always unhappy when picket fire broke out and always glad when it ceased, for it could have no effect on the war's outcome and was "a miserable and useless kind of murder." "Wanton cruelty," Hinman called it.[24]

Southerners fully reciprocated those sentiments. When Herbert discovered that his 1862–63 winter quarters lay within range of a two-gun Federal battery only three-quarters of a mile distant and that there were pickets just across the river, he was not alarmed: "We were now real soldiers on both sides and well knew that mere picket shooting helped neither side and was only murder." The Union pickets saluted Herbert, and he acknowledged their courtesy.[25] Real soldiers did not kill one another when neither side had staked its courage.

Here again, courage was influential in setting the categories and modes of combat. Numberless Civil War soldiers accepted its centrality and attempted to fight the war as an extension of courage and the values clustering about it. They would have preferred a war in which privates continued to tell one another that it was unmanly to dodge or duck a shot, in which officers persisted in exposing themselves to enemy fire as an example to their men, in which all continued to damn spade and shovel as the instruments of despised defense.[26] Had the will of the combatants prevailed, that was the kind of war men would have continued to fight.

Above all, the combatants wanted this to be a war in which men retained control. The determination of soldiers to maintain mastery, over events and over themselves, can be measured in the way participants treated the problem of emotion in combat.

Many Civil War soldiers experienced in combat a swelling exhilaration, an elevation of feeling that fitted J. Glenn Gray's description of one of the "enduring appeals of battle": the "delight in destruction." In *The Warriors*, his remarkable book of reflections on the combat experience of World War II, Gray wrote: "Anyone who has watched men on the battlefield . . . finds hard to escape the conclusion that there is a delight in destruction. . . . Men who have lived in the zone of combat long enough to be veterans are sometimes possessed by a fury that makes them capable of anything. Blinded by the rage to destroy and supremely careless of consequences, they storm against the enemy."[27]

Eighty years earlier the delight in destruction was no less discernible, but it was called by other names. Vail said of the first day's fighting at Gettysburg that "our fighting blood was up and we were insensible to danger." Nisbet spoke of "the 'gaudium certaminis' [delight or joy in battle] which battle ever brings to the heart of the true soldier." Stillwell maintained that "a soldier on the fighting line is possessed by the demon of destruction. He wants to kill." The Confederate cavalryman Thomas Rosser referred to "fury's mad delirium." Rice Bull noticed that the nervousness and trembling felt just prior to the fight became rage and fearlessness in battle. When the momentum of the charge up Missionary Ridge carried it beyond the orders of Union commanders, and company officers who at first tried to stem the rush soon joined the surge, "Everyman," said Hinman, "was in a paroxysm of jubilant enthusiasm." Rufus Dawes described in similar manner an action at Antietam in which his Wisconsin regiment lost in killed and wounded 152 of its 314 men:

> Another line of our men came up through the corn. We all joined together, jumped over the fence, and again pushed out into the open field. There is a rattling fusilade [*sic*] and loud cheers. "Forward" is the word. The men are loading and firing with demoniacal fury and shouting and laughing hysterically, and the whole field before us is covered with rebels fleeing for life, into the woods.

Perhaps it was with such experience in mind that Robert E. Lee said in the wake of his victory at Fredericksburg, "It is well that war is so horrible, else we should grow too fond of it."[28]

The delight in destruction was thus no less a presence in Civil War combat than in World War II, but it was perceived differently. A World War II soldier, Guy Sajer, describing his experience as a member of the Gross Deutschland Division fighting the "Ivans" of the Red Army on the Eastern Front, noted that "the almost drunken exhilaration which follows fears induces the most innocent youths on whatever side to commit inconceivable atrocities. Suddenly . . . everything that moved through the din and the smoke became hateful, and overwhelmed us with a desire for destruction." Civil War soldiers tried to guard against that sense of being overwhelmed; they were wary of any loss of self. If they were overcome—as happened at times, for they could not always resist such powerful emotion—they continued to insist that such experiences were exceptional and extrinsic. "The satisfaction in destroying," J. Glenn Gray wrote, "seems to me peculiarly human, or, more exactly put, devilish in ways animals can never be." That it was "devilish" those of the 1860s would have agreed; that it was human they were at great pains to deny.[29]

Some soldiers, it was true, cultivated the delight in destruction. Stonewall Jackson described to others the state of "delightful excitement" he attained in combat. Custer called the cavalry charge "the fiercest pleasure in life." The Union General Philip Kearny, killed at Chantilly, Virginia, on September 1, 1862, was reported to have told Custer, "I love war. It brings me indescribable pleasure, like that of having a woman." His guiding aphorism

> Let us fight for fun of fighting,
> Without thought of ever righting
> Human Wrong

pointed in the direction of the delight in destruction. Sherman found in battle "something to make him forget himself, completely, utterly," as if he were again lost in rapture he had discovered elsewhere—incongruously—only in painting pictures.[30]

One would think that every front-line soldier would welcome such experience. In the "fury" of which Gray spoke, all sense of personal danger seemed to disappear, and that, as the source of fear and thus of cowardly behavior, was what all strove to throw off. But great numbers of Civil War combatants, it appears, lost sight of that possibility in continuing to think of such feelings as unnatural, or at least as standing utterly apart from their real selves and in no sense a higher realization of self. To the contrary, those who experienced Gray's delight in destruction described it in terms of loss, a loss of control, of consciousness, of health, or of mind. When Joshua Chamberlain, after the war, listed those "highest qualities of manhood" that combat had "called forth," the first was courage, and the one cited next was "self-command." To feel oneself subject to "an almost uncontrollable impulse," to acknowledge alien intrusion—possession by Stillwell's "demon of destruction" or Dawes's "demoniacal fury"—was an occasion not for celebration but for the gravest concern, because to relinquish control was to surrender self-direction and thus one's individuality.[31]

When experienced in less menacing ways, combat exhilaration was often described as an uncommon state—as a drunkenness, for example. Storming the Fredericksburg heights at the time of Chancellorsville, Dodd forgot the fatigue, the thirst, the wounds, the enemy's fire, the dead and suffering comrades, forgot all but the charge: "Is there any intoxication like the joy of victory?" Those who assaulted Missionary Ridge were described as "completely and frantically drunk with excitement." It was likened to a dream state. Poague recalled that in his first battle, actually a Shenandoah Valley skirmish, a "curious mental exaltation seized us; an inward questioning as to whether it was all a dream." At times both dream and intoxication entered the description. When Ripley charged Confederate guns in Peninsula fighting during the fall of 1864, "it was a dream, so great was the intoxication of the excitement." Some felt it as a state of physical abnormality: seized by "the fever of the rush"; "gone wild with battle fever"; "wild with uncontrollable delirium"; "delirious with . . . wild excitement." It became even a species of dementia, a temporary insanity: the charge raising "one mad desire" to trample down everything. J. Glenn Gray chose to call such feelings "the delight in destruction," a term not perhaps carrying approbation but certainly conveying appeal; Civil War soldiers chose instead to describe those feelings in ways making clear that, as violations of the nineteenth-century ideal of the discerning mind and the controlling will, they were not cherished.[32]

Significantly, Civil War soldiers were convinced that excitation threatened the courage they sought to exemplify in combat. Although Garfield ordinarily admired General William S. Rosecrans, one side of the commander of the Army of the Cumberland alarmed him: In battle Rosecrans was sometimes swept away by excitement, losing all control of himself and others. Cox acknowledged that General Robert H. Milroy was brave, "but his bravery was of the excitable kind that made him unbalanced and nearly wild on the battle-field." For several years Philip Sheridan was held back by a reputation for battle "wrath and fury" that might stimulate the troops but clearly made him unfit for high, independent command. Horace Porter summarized the suspicions of the day: A courage born of passion or excitement might fail when it was most needed. Fierce fires soon burn out. Significantly, as godliness could serve as a protection against fear and injury, it could also guard against this frenzied courage. Poague recalled:

> I was at no time frightened, nor was I excited after we reached the battle line. I was conscious of being in danger, but right there I felt was the place where I ought to be. The thought repeatedly came to me that I was in the hands of a kind heavenly Father, and that His merciful care and protection were over me. With all this was a most novel sensation, hard to describe, a sort of warm, pleasing glow enveloping the chest and head with an effect something like entrancing music in a dream. My observing, thinking and reasoning faculties were normal.[33]

The ideal courage was a cool courage. A fellow officer of the 20th Massachusetts wrote of Lieutenant Henry Ropes's death at Gettysburg: "His conduct in this action, as in all previous ones, was perfectly brave, but not with the bravery of excitement that nerves common men." He was "absolutely cool and collected, apparently unconscious of the existence of such a feeling as personal danger. . . . It is impossible for me to conceive of a man more perfectly master of himself." Burdette admired Colonel

McClure as "the father of the regiment," the "Old Man" and a "fighting colonel," but he singled out a particular point of praise: "Under fire, his calmness was contagious. His courage rose above excitement."[34]

Accompanying the respect accorded to calm self-control was an intense suspicion of any immersion in collective emotion. Courage was to be not only cool but individualized. As almost every Civil War memoir makes clear, soldiers admired most those whose actions set them apart from others. In the course of a confused Peninsula collision in 1862, Philip Kearny, whose men had earlier serenaded him and chanted "Ker-nee! Ker-nee!" realized that his command was fighting ineffectively because soldiers were ignorant of the precise location of the enemy. "You don't know! Then, find out! Here, I'll show you!" His remedy was to ride across the field in order to draw to himself fire that would reveal the Confederate position. "There! There's the target! Now go in and kick those rebels out!"[35]

At the battle of Stone's River, fright sent John Beatty's Union brigade fleeing past him toward the rear. For a moment it appeared that he might be able to rally them by calling them to the colors he waved over them, but then his horse was shot and the retreat threatened to become a rout. Later in the battle, angered by his men's unwillingness to advance, Beatty rode forward alone to mark the line to which, his gesture said, his skirmishers were to return. Though "a hundred muskets" opened on him, he completed his solitary tour. At Five Forks a wounded and bloody Chamberlain by himself reversed a Federal retreat—and was cheered by the troops of both armies.[36]

In the first Peninsula campaign, Berdan's sharpshooters found themselves exchanging fire with concealed Southerners who had killed New York Private John S. M. Ide.

> On learning of the fall of this man Col [William Y. W.] Ripley, notwithstanding the dangerous approach to the fatal spot, and that his field-duties did not oblige him to thus expose himself, boldly walked down the lane which was at the time completely under the rebel fire. With a quick step, but erect, this good officer advanced, the admiration of hundreds of eye witnesses, while bullets plowed and dusted the ground around him. On reaching the body of the prostrate rifleman he inquired into the manner Ide had been shooting, then picking up the fallen man's rifle, screwed

up the telescope one notch, believing that Ide had been shooting under. "I'll try him a shot at one notch higher anyway," he said; then taking position, the man in the tree top was discovered, a quick aim and interchange of shots followed. Ripley escaped harmless as the ball spattered in the log building behind him. But the grey-backed fellow—well, there were no more shots from that tree top. Whether killed or scared to death, it was a sure case of a "gone Johnny."[37]

The most celebrated episodes, those that would be celebrated at veterans' reunions for fifty years, exemplified "what one man could do to change the whole face of a battle"—often Rosecrans at Stone's River, preeminently Sheridan at Cedar Creek.[38]

Ambrose Bierce, whose writings on the Civil War were caustic yet tinged with the nostalgia of a lingering emotional allegiance to a set of values his intellect had discarded, was able to push precisely to the threshold of parody the elements of this conception of courage. In his story "A Son of the Gods," a Civil War army (side unspecified) halted to consider whether the enemy awaited it beyond the crest of a hill. As its commanders pondered, a young officer on a white horse offered to ride out alone on scout. Ten thousand watched him. "How glorious! Gods! what would we not give to be in his place—with his soul!" He was "this military Christ" whose act spared the lives of those who would otherwise have been sent out in lines of skirmishers. He twice drew enemy fire, of course revealing the enemy's positions, and those behind, energized by his courage, charged without orders—only to find the hero dead. The author both mocked and joined the men's mourning: "Would one exception have marred too much the pitiless perfection of the divine, eternal plan?"[39] That Ambrose Bierce seized so perceptively the war's central values—an individualized, self-possessed, exemplary, and ultimately heroic courage—and could not overthrow all loyalty to them may reflect the fact that he served in the Union Army during the war's first years. That the situation he created to illustrate those values threatened to topple into bathos and burlesque may reflect the fact that he served as well in the war's final years.

In the next century Theodore Roosevelt would say, "All men who feel any power of joy in battle know what it is like when the wolf rises in the heart."[40] Those who set out to fight the Civil War carried with them a framework of values leaving no place for the wolf. They may have felt Gray's delight in destruction, but they neither welcomed it nor granted it a place within their moral construct. Such episodes, they wished to conclude, were but temporary lapses from the soldier's true self. Northerners and Southerners alike knew the kind of war they wished to fight, one in which cool, logical thought and individual will would shape the war within courage's constellation of values.

5

Courage and Civilian Society

Within its formidable framework of individualistic, internalized moral values, courage became the filter through which soldiers sought to comprehend the war—and ultimately to endure its bloodshed. Rarely did they derive any of the war's meaning from notions of large-scale forces at play, of clashing economic systems, or of antagonistic cultures. That sense of enormous impersonal and ideological forces on which one's fate depended, which would imbue soldiers of the twentieth century's world wars, was scarcely to be found in the first stages of the Civil War. For its soldiers, the war reduced itself to other men, comrades and adversaries, whose actions were informed by familiar moral values, to courage pitted against courage.

Not surprisingly, Americans at large also came to see the war in the simple images of courage. For them, as for their soldiers, even "The Cause" reduced itself to a manifestation of courage.

Prior to the war a single action undertaken by each side had struck those on the other side with a force so overwhelming that it seemed to suppress all reservations regarding war, to remove all complications, melt all moral ambiguities, confirm all suspicions, and harden all sympathies. The South's terrible willingness to open fire on Fort Sumter and Abraham Lincoln's outrageous call for troops to be turned against the people of the South were actions so dramatic as to erase from the consciousness on either side any cognizance of antecedent moves and responses leading to them, and particularly of one's own side's contributions to the sequence. Nothing remained save that monstrous action of the other side. Northerners felt they were the targets of decisive Southern action; Southerners were convinced that they had been made the prey of the North's initiative. Peace sentiment in the North wilted; Union sentiment in the South sank beneath the level of public discourse. The South meant to destroy the Union; the North meant to invade the South.

Thus citizens of each section spoke of the other's action not as the undesired but comprehensible climax of a lengthy sequence of events but as a beginning, "the mighty reveille."[1]

Southerners welcomed the new clarity of vision. William Poague, as he prepared to enlist in the Rockbridge Artillery, had no difficulty locating the culprits: "The North was the aggressor. The South resisted her invaders," for invasion was implicit in Lincoln's call for volunteers. Poague dismissed the Fort Sumter episode as a case of South Carolinians manipulated by Northerners into firing the first shot. Robert Stiles, whose Georgia-born father had raised his family in New York and Connecticut and had sent Robert to Yale, went South just after Sumter to join the Richmond Howitzers. He was motivated by no desire to preserve slavery or to exercise the right of secession but simply "to defend his own hearth-stone," a phrase capturing Southern soldiers' central conception of the war. Alexander Hunter employed the same term: He and his friends fought "for their hearthstones," defending their homes "against the hirelings of Lincoln," whose call had transformed the issue into one of "home, kindred and country." When Hunter was captured during the Peninsula campaign, a Federal general's aide, a "spruce young fellow in a natty uniform," asked him, "What are you Rebels fighting for, anyway?" "The question struck me there and then as supremely ludicrous. Here were we Virginians standing on our own soil, fighting on our native heath against an invading army, defending what every man holds dear—his home and fireside. As well ask a game-cock why he crows and bares his spurs on his own dunghill." Hunter's sarcastic reply, "We are fighting to protect our mint-beds," mocked a question worthy only of ridicule. Its answer, he was sure, was apparent to all.[2]

The issue was less exigent but no less vivid on the Northern side. "The Union" was after all an abstract conception with few practical manifestations in the daily lives of Northern farmers and small-town dwellers. But one can recognize that for Sumter to mobilize Northerners as it did—it incited, Cox wrote, "a popular torrent which no leaders could resist"—Union must have acquired compelling substance. Eric Foner has suggested a way in which the abstruse may have found passage into the tangible: The South's challenge to the government of the United States was deemed a challenge to republican government, and since Americans believed republican government the source of freedom, that government's destruction would be the destruction of their personal liberty. Undecided on the issue of abolition, John Brobst of Gilmanton, Wisconsin, pronounced secession intolerable and joined the 25th Wisconsin. "Home is sweet and friends are dear, but what would they all be to let the country go to ruin, and be a slave. . . . If I live to get back, I shall be proud of the freedom I *shall* have, and know that I helped *to gain* that freedom." Though it is not easy to comprehend how any of secession's practical effects could penetrate the daily life of small-town northwestern Wisconsin, Brobst felt deeply that secession had deprived him of his freedom and that he had to fight to reclaim it. Whatever the process, preservation of Union had acquired personal meaning powerful enough to separate decisively those who believed in Union from those they thought threatened Union.[3]

The same obliteration of nuance and abandonment of earlier priorities appeared in the North. Before April 12, 1861, many Abolitionists, including Wendell Phillips, had held to a policy designed to separate the North from slavery's contamination. Samuel Gridley Howe regarded political union as no more than a fetish. But with Sumter any call to let the Southern states go in peace became intolerable to almost all Abolitionists; they quickly swung round to favor Northern military action. As Walt Whitman chanted: "Not the Negro, not the Negro. The Negro was not the chief thing. The chief thing was to stick together."[4]

On both sides the resulting syllogism was simple. The way to reestablish Union or to preserve freedom by repelling invasion— or, for many, many fewer, to destroy or to defend slavery—was to defeat the enemy, and the prime requisite of military victory was courage. Again, Walt Whitman gave words to the perception of many. Sergeant Calvin Harlowe of the 29th Massachusetts was a member of the garrison of Fort Stedman when it was attacked by Confederates. When the attackers demanded surrender, Harlowe urged his comrades to fight on, and he shot a Southern captain before he was killed. "When I think of such things," Whitman said, "all the vast and complicated events of the war, on which history dwells and makes its volumes, fall aside; and for the moment at any rate I see nothing but young Calvin Harlowe's figure in the night, disdaining to surrender." Civilians, no less than soldiers, viewed the war through the filter of courage.[5]

The influence of home was profound. Soldiers' families enforced and reinforced the centrality of courage. The town ladies' aid society ordinarily presented to the unit leaving for war a set of colors, usually regimental and national standards, emblems that it was assumed would heighten their courage, as the Bibles distributed at the same time would strengthen their godliness.

The most poignant measure of such efforts was there in the last messages left by wounded soldiers who thought themselves dying. Rufus Dawes, commander of the 6th Wisconsin at Gettysburg, described a young corporal shot through the breast who "came staggering up to me before he fell and opening his shirt to show the wound, said 'Colonel, won't you write to my folks that I died a soldier.'" So often the intent was the same, with only the words varying. "Doctor, see that my record is right at home. Tell them I died at my post doing my duty." "Tell mother I died doing my duty." "Tell my mother I did not die a coward." When Oliver Wendell Holmes, Jr., suffered his first wound at Ball's Bluff, his foremost concern was that friends and family should know that he had done his duty. Clearly, townspeople had conveyed their expectation that their soldiers would act courageously.[6]

Courage, the vital value, stood as one of several in its constellation. All, however, were inseparable in the American mind. Those at home assumed that one could not be virtuous in courage and unvirtuous in other aspects of life. A brave or even an efficient wastrel would have struck Americans of the 1860s as an absurdity. There was as yet little separation of the spheres of life, little notion, for example, of professionalism in soldiering—that is, the possibility of high competence in one sphere, in soldiering as a craft, rendering inconsequential the basic nature of the person and his behavior in other spheres. James A. Garfield possessed no military knowledge—nor any doubt of his fitness for military command. "Pluck" he thought infinitely more important than "military science." The regulars, of course, sputtered at the idea. George Gordon Meade said that the officers "have no control or command over the men, and if they had, they [would] not know what to do with them." The men in turn argued that strict discipline did *not* produce combat effectiveness. Only in principle was the unit of such discipline "the perfect military machine." In combat it was weakened by the men's hatred of unjust treatment, "by a lack of confidence in and personal respect for their leaders." In the best regiments, John Billings said, "manliness and self-respect were never crushed out by tyrants in miniature." Richard Taylor replied that courage must be "disciplined, subordinated valor" willing "to be welded and directed to a common end"; otherwise, courage was merely the kind of indiscipline that pushed charges too far, for example. To those of an incipient professionalism, it seemed a debate without limit or resolution, but other Americans simply accepted as self-evident the proposition that the man who possessed courage possessed as well military competence and every other important virtue. Theirs was not precisely Plato's belief—that courage is one of the four parts of virtue and that without justice, wisdom, or moderation one is not truly courageous—but rather that the courageous man would not be unjust, unwise, or immoderate.[7]

If courage was evidence of a virtuous nature, obviously unvirtuous behavior seemed to make courage unlikely. Colonel Scammon of the 23d Ohio for that reason tried to outlaw gambling among the men: "It makes men *bad* and bad men cannot be good soldiers." Henry Abbott, whom many in the Union Army regarded as an exemplary officer, attempted to suppress card-playing *and* profanity *and* drinking. He came down on intemperance with a severity exceeded only by that accorded to cowardice.[8]

Civilians valued highly all manifestations of goodness, religious faith, and purity in personal habits and denounced their opposites. When soldiers recuperating from their wounds stole away and got drunk, Nurse Hannah Ropes was unforgiving. To her, a binge was not to be condoned as a reaction against the experiences of battlefield and hospital but was the unmistakable sign of a character defect. "Alas for the poverty of true manliness, the great overmastery of human weaknesses! How often, with the puling infirmity of absolute imbecility, do these men excuse themselves [by saying] 'I have such a habit' . . . as though the price of the greatest gift heaven ever proferred . . . human manhood . . . must be paid for less than the old patriarch's mess of pottage!" When she caught one of the culprits, she made him repeat the Commandments.[9]

The offender's willingness to yield to Hannah Ropes's chastisement may have reflected a conviction that beneath its pompous righteousness her denunciation made a vital point. Soldiers accepted civilian insistence that impurity was wrong on grounds that held the moral and the practical inseparable. Impurity was a source of weakness and thus of failure, and he who failed as a man was certain to fail as a warrior. The soldier's concern for purity was no prim affectation.

John Dooley thought it important that the Union wounded cursed, while his wounded Confederate comrades did not. A Mississippi officer took care to write even the word "devil" as "d——l." Fifer Bardeen recorded with satisfaction that his was a "clean-mouthed" regiment whose members "checked" vulgar stories. While on a march, he picked up two castaway items, a bawdy book and a letter. He read a paragraph of the book—fifty years later it remained "branded" on his memory—and enough of the letter to learn that it was a wife's confession to her soldier husband that, pressed for rent money she did not have, she had "finally succumbed" to the landlord. "Think of throwing away a letter like that without even tearing off the address." The fifer burned both items. Drink or blasphemy or exposure to immorality weakened the man, which weakened the soldier.[10]

Such matters were of solemn concern to families sending sons to war, for those at home invariably assumed that camp life was corrupting and that moral degeneration would befall the soldier too weak to resist its dissipations. Here was a hazard that seemed to some more dangerous than combat itself. Advising a brother-in-law about to enter the Union Army, Benjamin Harrison implored him to "avoid with more care the *vices* of the camp than you would the enemy's *bullets* . . . they are more deadly. Private James Newton wrote home to DePere, Wisconsin, in mid-1863:

Oh! My Mother pray for me, that God will keep me from the many temptations to which I am exposed. I presume you have often heard of the vices of the camp, but you did not realize it. No person can ever realize it until they have been placed in some such a position as I am now, and then they will begin to realize what is meant by the vices of the camp; then they will see all kinds of iniquity openly practiced without being reproved by any one.

When a box from home arrived containing a bottle of whisky or brandy labeled by a parent "To be used in case of sickness or wounds," few recipients smiled.[11]

Those concerns manifested themselves in the ways families instructed young men departing for war "gay as larks, merry as crickets, playful as kittens." Parents admonished their sons first to be brave and then to be careful. "My son, do your duty, die if it must be, but never prove yourself a coward." "Harry, don't be shot in the back!" Those who showed more apprehension about their soldier's survival than his conduct in combat did so apologetically. General Ripley's sister thought the war "terrible"—"It makes me sick to think of it."—but immediately entreated him not to be "vexed" with her because she felt that way, because "I have not more patriotism." She momentarily stiffened—"I would not have you act the coward"—and again gave way to her fears—"but don't be rash and throw yourself into the very face of death unnecessarily." Finally, she returned to apology: "There is not much of the spirit of '76 in me."[12]

Injunctions to preserve purity were only slightly less powerful. When the young men of a Protestant parish joined the Chicago Mercantile Battery *en bloc*, they were told "to guard well their health and morals" and "to return to us, if they came at all, as good and pure as they were leaving us." At the Washington Artillery's mustering-in service at Christ Church, New Orleans, the rector "enjoined all to remember that they were educated to be gentlemen, and it behooved them to bring back their characters as soldiers and gentlemen unblemished with their arms." Ripley's mother felt none of her daughter's reservations: "Return to me, my son, when this war is over, unstained by corrupt principles and practices and bad habits I earnestly entreat you." On his departure for the Confederate Army, Carlton McCarthy received numerous charges from his father: attend preachings; read your Testament; eschew drink and profanity; continue to pray; seek out those of good character; trust in the Lord in battle. "I would rather hear of your death than of the shipwreck of your

The stance and expression of an Ohio soldier convey the youthfulness, hopefulness, and determination that marked those who marched to war in 1861. In both Union and Confederate armies, eighteen-year-olds constituted the largest single age-group during the first year of the war.

Young, confident Confederate soldiers pose in a sportive mood prior to the First Battle of Bull Run. The dagger flourished at the left, the soldiers' pipe-clay cross-belts, and the cock plumes of the officer's shako at the right rear mark a time before campaigning compelled a "simmering down" of gear—and of assumptions about combat.

Above left: The attack at Gettysburg by 15,000 Confederate soldiers, led by the division of Major General George E. Pickett, became the most renowned charge of the war. Even while shattering the assault, Union soldiers admired its daring, while on the other side many of the attackers were perplexed that their courage could not conquer. *Above right:* The exemplar of knightly courage, Confederate Major General James E. B. ("Jeb") Stuart told friends, "All I ask of fate is that I may be killed leading a cavalry charge."

Above left: Robert Gould Shaw, colonel of the first regiment of Northern black soldiers, the 54th Massachusetts, was killed leading his men in an audacious attack on the fortifications of Battery Wagner in Charleston harbor on July 18, 1863. *Above right:* A paladin of courage, Joshua Lawrence Chamberlain was one of the war's hardest fighters. He was awarded the Congressional Medal of Honor for the bayonet charge into which he propelled the 20th Maine at Gettysburg, thus preserving the Union's critical position on Little Round Top.

The Currier and Ives lithograph depicting an ordered Battle of Fredericksburg, December 13, 1862, is one of many representations of the dauntless, assertive courage that dominated soldiers' thoughts and mobilized them in battle through 1861 and 1862.

The son of President Zachary Taylor and the brother-in-law of Confederate President Jefferson Davis, Richard Taylor became commander of the main Confederate force in Louisiana. Dismayed by the indiscipline of his soldiers, he complained that they had no more conception of the significance of military rank "than of the celestial hierarchy of the poets."

A group of nurses and officers of the Sanitary Commission gathered at Fredericksburg, Virginia, in May 1864 while assigned to aid Union wounded evacuated from the battles of the Wilderness. Medical workers encouraged their soldier-patients to demonstrate in the hospital a courage no less exalted than that of the battlefield.

In carrying messages between families and their soldiers, inspecting hospitals, and visiting battlefields, Mary A. Livermore, the co-organizer of the Sanitary Commission's Chicago branch, found numerous opportunities to remind soldiers of the standards of courage and personal purity to which those at home attempted to hold them.

A Union field hospital at Savage Station, Virginia, June 30, 1862. So appalling were such places that they came to haunt the minds of Civil War soldiers. A Confederate artilleryman wrote that "the screams and groans of the poor fellows undergoing amputation are sometimes dreadful,—and then the sight of arms and legs . . . as they are thrown into great piles, is something one that has seen the results of battle can never forget."

Oliver Wendell Holmes, Jr., in an 1867 portrait. Battle experience transformed his idealistic zeal into profound disillusionment. Exhausted, distraught, and convinced that such terms as "gallantry" and "duty" were no longer pertinent to combat, he resigned his commission in the 20th Massachusetts in 1864.

faith and good conscience." A Chicago mother inquired of her son sent on duty down the Mississippi: "[D]oes he drink, swear, or smoke? Tell him his mother would rather he would be sent home dead, than that he should return alive and dissipated."[13]

If the soldier were sent home dead—or, more likely, buried where he fell—those at home hoped desperately for last words that would confirm that their soldier had preserved his decency. The dying were most concerned to fix their courage, but families were equally anxious for reassurance of the soldier's purity. They cherished worthy last words as a special remembrance, as a moral summation of the life about to be lost and as a declaration of religious faith. Such avowals were a matter of urgency. On Virginia battlefields the medical attendant William Howell Reed used his brandy flask to restore the wounded sufficiently to secure their names and last messages. When no last words were obtainable, those at home were often distraught: "If I could know what his thoughts were as he went away from earth!" When they were forthcoming, the bereaved were relieved and consoled. The parents of a dead Union soldier wrote to Nurse Jane Woolsey: "You wrote you thought he was praising God. It was the greatest comfort to us of anything."[14]

Few at home foresaw that their soldiers' departure from the town's depot, ears filled with homilies, might carry them to such dark destinations, and thus the community quickly turned to persuading others to enlist. Ira Dodd noticed that after the heady enthusiasm of the first departure the impulse became "solemn and compelling," an impulse whose spirit inquired of others, "Why do you not go to the war?" It drew some of its substance from community competitiveness, town contesting neighboring town in furnishing the war with its soldiers. Frequently, however, the atmosphere moved beyond benign local pride and became imperious. Townspeople might hoot at militia officers who had decided not to go to war; the town's newspaper might run their sketches side-by-side with the white feather of cowardice.[15]

Those who most imperatively urged enlistment were women. They no less than soldiers expected courageous behavior and anathematized cowardice. Their special weapon might with justice be called sexual intimidation. A Richmond clerk reported in May 1861 that the "ladies are postponing all engagements until their lovers have fought the Yankees." Henry Morton Stanley, not yet an explorer but a counter clerk in an Arkansas store, decided that he would stand apart from the war. He was Welsh and scarcely two years in this country; it was not his war. Then he received, he thought from a young woman of whom he was fond, the gift of a petticoat. As intended, that sent the embarrassed recipient scurrying to enlist in the Dixie Greys. When Confederate officials organized draft-eligible men to mine "saltpetre," the potassium nitrate essential to munitions manufacture, "the ladies shamed [the diggers] and called them the 'saltpetre boys,' and told them to go and get a musket and go into the army, that [the women] would dig the saltpetre." Hunter said that in Fauquier County, Virginia: "The first question [ladies] asked . . . was: 'Is he a good soldier?' In their opinion that was the highest praise a man could have, and they hated a coward as they would some vile, unclean thing." Asked if her husband was a soldier, a Southern woman replied, "He would not be my husband if he were not in the army!"[16]

Female advocacy of the prescripts of manhood was not always so straightforward, as the situation of Richard Harding Davis's parents attested. Rebecca Davis considered herself a pacifist. She disparaged as romantic notions all representations of gallant heroes dying for "The Cause," and she contrasted them with the real army as she viewed it, a collection of county jail inmates, draftees, and impoverished immigrants. During a visit to Boston in 1861, she tried to puncture the inflated war talk of New England's sages and to counterpose "the actual face of war" as she had seen it near her Wheeling home: "the political jobbery . . . the malignant personal hatreds . . . burning homes and outraged women . . . brutish men." For the conflict itself she felt an "inexpressible loathing"; she insisted that wrong and tyranny existed on both sides. Yet when Lemuel Clarke Davis, her twenty-seven-year-old husband and a Philadelphia journalist, was drafted and chose to avoid service by paying the $300 commutation fee, she twitted him for "nursing his rheumatism into one foot very assiduously ever since Saturday. Of course I don't guess for what." For a woman to object to the war was one matter, to countenance the abstention of her husband quite another.[17]

Women promised rewards to the willing, ordinarily less mixed than those offered in this Southern poem:

> And now, young man, a word to you:
> If you would win the fair

> Go to the field where Honor calls
>   And win your lady there;
> Remember that our brightest smiles
>   Are for the true and brave,
> And that our tears are all for those
>   Who fill a soldier's grave,[18]

which seems to be the promise of a heart to be won only at the price of a life.

After the war, novelists would resort to a formula in which the heroine withheld love from the young man as a civilian but bestowed it on him as a soldier. In Joseph Kirkland's *The Captain of Company K*, William Fargeon, though obviously successful as a Chicago merchant, philanthropist, Sunday School superintendent, and patriotic orator, loved in vain Miss Sara Penrose. "But who could imagine you as a soldier?" she asked. Will had to concede: "There's not a soldierly hair in my head." He was nevertheless elected captain of his company. While busy with arrangements for its departure, he ignored a summons from Sara, and at that point she began to respect her formerly attentive suitor. When he returned from battle, eyes sad and lips stern, women in the street seized his hand. Sara exclaimed, "But, oh, how changed you are!" His face had been strengthened by battle, by a wound requiring amputation of a lower leg, and by the contemplation of death. He proceeded to retrieve his fortune, become a surgeon, and win Sara in marriage. Though the formula today appears fraudulent and hopelessly sentimental, it caught an interplay of values familiar to Americans of the Civil War years—as the real-life courtship of Henry Higginson shows. Ida Agassiz had rejected his earlier proposal, but Higginson went to war, "Reckless, possibly, of his life, came back wounded, moved her compassion, and gained his wish": She agreed to marry him.[19]

Whether the incitements to military service were pointed prods or simply vague atmospherics seeming to invoke "duty," the results could be harsh. As a student at Yale's Sheffield Scientific School, Clarence King responded with some passion to what he considered the South's outrages against freedom, but, perhaps in reflection of the influence of his Moravian pacifist grandmother, he feared that "the act [of killing] would crucify in me many of my noblest impulses." Such divided thought was "tearing my soul in two" and stoking worries in King that he lacked the courage to lead men. How could a civilian possess qualities so widely assumed to be the property of combatants? King threw himself into intense athletic competition and challenged any who shared his doubts: "Don't think that because I show you my tender side . . . my weak side . . . that I have no fire, no firmness, no mental power. Don't think I never lead men, for in my way I do." As he and his friend Dan Dewey trained near the Canadian border for a regatta, suspicious United States marshals detained them and required them to swear to affidavits attesting to their draft-exempt status as students. That goaded Dewey into enlisting. One can only guess at the distress that his death in a Louisiana battle in April 1863 must have caused Clarence King.[20]

Age did not always provide immunity against such pressures. Although almost forty and exempt by virtue of a leg 2 inches shorter than the other, Frederick Law Olmsted felt a passion to participate and in pursuit of a war "mission" took up work as executive secretary of the Sanitary Commission. As he later explained his sacrifice of ease, income, and health, "It is a day for heroes, and we must be heroes along with the rest." Theodore Roosevelt, Sr., who hired a substitute, drafted a bill authorizing the appointment of Allotment Commissioners, men who would persuade soldiers to permit part of their pay to be sent directly to their families, saving that portion from gamblers and sutlers. He lobbied the bill through the Congress, accepted Lincoln's appointment as one of the commissioners, and worked assiduously in the camps. His efforts, however, did not assuage his son, who at age four had already imbibed the warrior ethic. Theodore Junior was outspoken in his disapproval of his father's path and in his admiration of two uncles who were fighting for the Confederacy.[21]

Martial home influences seldom confined themselves to those within the locale; soldiers away at war remained within their orbit, and townspeople continued to exert pressure to keep their men in the fight. So odious was the thought of desertion in 1861–62 that the home folks made even official furloughs the occasion of patriotic instruction. In July 1862, when Francis Amasa Walker of the 7th Massachusetts returned home unannounced from the Peninsula campaign and "its miasmatic exhalations, its stench of dead horses, and its still more disagreeable memories," his mother only asked, "You haven't left the army, have you?"

Southern soldiers whose homes were in or near battle zones found that their unofficial visits drew the same well-tempered welcome. Casler described a reaction to what he had hoped would be a respite from war:

> My dear old mother . . . spent many an hour on her bended knees praying [not only] for her dear and only boy, but [for] others as well, for she had relatives who wore the blue. She could often hear the raging of the battles, as several were fought near my home. But as dearly as she loved me she would not let me stay at home long when I happened to get there, but advised me to return to my command and be a faithful soldier. She would rather hear of my death on the field of battle, although it would nearly break her heart, than to hear of my being branded as a deserter.[22]

Women in both North and South set themselves staunchly against desertion. A letter addressed to the soldiers of the Confederacy by "The Women of the South" and published in many newspapers in 1862 spoke fiercely: "Never turn your backs on the flag, nor desert the ranks of honor or the post of danger. Men guilty of such infamy would sell your blood and our honor. [T]he black title of tory and deserter will cling to them, disgracing their children's children." (Governor Zebulon Vance on North Carolina later extended that sentence: Deserters would be ostracized "even to the third and fourth generations.") Another appeal from "The Women of the South" appeared during the summer of 1863: "It is impossible for us to respect a coward and every true woman who has husband, father, brother, or lover . . . had rather see him prostrate before her with death's signet on his noble brow that has never been branded by cowardice or dishonor, than have him forfeit his good name and disgrace his manhood by refusing to do his duty to his country."[23]

Soldiers could seldom ignore such sentiments. A Louisiana captain who wished to resign his commission first took soundings at home and received this reply: "[A]ll the women about Minden say you should not desert your [company] in the hour of extremity and they are all down on you." Captain Wimberley did not let such feelings deter him, but neither could he take them lightly; he went home armed with a "certificate" signed by most members of the company attesting that "they were willing for him to go if he wanted."[24]

Though propelled by desires as strong as Wimberley's, Sergeant Edwin Fay of the same company struggled with home influences too strong to overcome. His military ambition "satiated," he was anxious to depart "this horrid war," to go home, to send a substitute, and to resume schoolteaching, but he worried about the taunts of Minden's women. He cautioned his wife to tell no one that he was campaigning to be discharged, but in the end it was Sarah Fay who blocked his return. She needed only to tell him that she wanted him to come, but, though often ill and sometimes feeling that she could no longer bear his absence, she would not give her blessing to his plans. Indeed, she objected even to his efforts to transfer to the other side of the Mississippi, closer to home. Fay was by turns acquiescent—"I will endeavor to never give you cause to blush or reason . . . for my child [to be taunted]"; hurt—"I don't mean to stay long with you [on furlough], for I saw how unwelcome I was to some of the Family when last home"; and bitter—one of his acquaintances, "a proud man [who] could not bear the jeers of others and volunteered," sickened and died, "another victim of the inexorable tyranny of public opinion." Conceding that Sarah was more patriotic than he, he had to remind her that words were cheap: "Ah me, if patriots at home only knew what it was to be a soldier they would cease talking about patriotism." Each of his schemes to leave the war broke against Sarah's opposition.[25]

Not even battle injury was always sufficient to cancel women's compulsion to see their soldier stay on duty. A New York mother wrote Nurse Woolsey:

> I am glad to hear from you that my boy is better. Do you think he is likely to be soon strong enough to rejoin his regiment, or would it be better for him, as he is so young, to return home? I am anxious to know, too, what character he bears as a soldier. I cannot think he is strong enough for the hardships of camp life, but as I have his own honor at heart more than my desire to see him again, I hesitate to apply for his discharge.

Sentiments of such stalwartness were remarkably persistent in some quarters. Making their way home after Appomattox, survivors of a Confederate unit asked a woman for food. Considering carefully, she questioned them, "You are not deserters?" "No," they were obliged to answer, "we have our paroles."[26]

In other ways, too, those at home strove to make soldiers aware of their duty. Robert Gould Shaw discovered that, set against parental desires, his own mandate hardly extended to the choice of assignments within the Union Army. In February 1863 Governor John A. Andrew of Massachusetts offered him the colonelcy of the first regiment of Northern blacks. When he refused the appointment, his mother complained of "the bitterest disappointment I have ever experienced" and wondered whether her son had inherited from his father "a habit . . . of self-distrust in his own capabilities." When Shaw reversed himself and accepted the commission, his mother wrote him, "God rewards a hundred-fold every good aspiration of his children, and this is my reward for asking [for] my children not earthly honors, but souls to see the right and courage to follow it. Now I feel ready to die, for I see you willing to give your support to the cause of truth that is lying crushed and bleeding." It was no surprise that prior to his acceptance Shaw should have felt "ashamed of myself, as if I were cowardly."[27]

The vehicles of home influence were many: letters, army chaplains, visiting relatives, hometown newspaper correspondents, relief workers, hospital volunteers—even strangers. As Casler's unit passed through Loachapoka, Louisiana, a young woman threw a bouquet to Confederate soldiers aboard a troop train. Among the flowers was a slip of paper on which she had written: "A soldier is the lad I adore. Nannie J. Reevs." Northern women preparing large medical aid shipments inserted their own notes of encouragement: "We send these supplies to the noble boys that beat back Bragg's army! We are proud of them!" "Dear wounded soldiers! We shall never forget your gallant conduct at Murfreesboro and Stone['s] River!" Soldiers could not help being acutely aware of the civilian community's claim to exercise oversight of their lives. Home was far away, Ira Dodd said, but he and his comrades were not unwatched. "We fought with the feeling that we were under the straining eyes of those who loved us and had sent us forth." Soldiers seemed often to ask, "What will the folks at home say about us?" and to speak freely of the importance of their surveillance.[28]

During the war's early years most soldiers regarded such watchfulness less as a burden than as a support for their own intentions, protective and ameliorative rather than intrusive or oppressive. Dodd said of the home folks' approval that he and his comrades "valued [it] more than life." They often deferred to home voices and welcomed them as the bearers of benefits.

Many soldiers, for example, thought that home influences helped to counter the demoralization of camp life; letters were "a means of grace." A Union soldier wrote from Fortress Monroe, Virginia, on February 3, 1862:

> One of our men was drunk, and fought and swore so shockingly, day before yesterday, that we had to send him to the guard-house. To-night he is taking a good repenting cry between the blankets. Do you know why? He got a letter this afternoon from his mother, and I have no doubt that she spoke of the Sabbath-school, the church, and the prayer he used to say when a little fellow at home, when his mother tucked him in bed. He instantly made for the blankets; and though he thinks none of us know it, we all know the poor fellow is there sobbing his heart out.

The writer complained that soldiers did not get "letters enough." "You can have no idea what a blessing letters from home are to the men in camp. They make us better men, better soldiers." In reality, the volumes of letters sent and received were remarkable. On the Union side, 45,000 were sent daily via Washington to members of the Eastern armies and an equal number went off from soldiers to those at home. Ninety thousand more passed daily via Louisville for and from soldiers in the Western armies.[29]

A Federal soldier writing from Memphis in December 1862 accorded letters a singular ability to alter the mood and behavior of the men:

> Sometimes our expeditions and reconnoissances take us away from camps for a month at a time, so that we neither receive nor send any letters until our return. The men always become rough and somewhat demoralized on these occasions. They become profane and boisterous, some of them obscene and quarrelsome, and there will be bad blood among them, with the prospect of several fights.
> . . . By and by we get back to camp, and a big mail awaits us. All the men will have letters and papers from mothers, wives, sisters, and friends; and there is a change immediately. A great quietness falls on the men; they become subdued and gentle in manner; there is a cessation of vulgarity and profanity, and an indescribable softening and tenderness is *felt*, rather than perceived, among them. Those who were ready to shoot one another a few hours before are seen talking with one another, and walking together, sometimes with their arms around one another. It is the letters from home that have changed the atmosphere of the camp.[30]

Soldiers assumed that the love of women at home sustained their efforts to lead morally blameless lives. Custer wrote his wife Libbie: "I can tell my little one something that will please her: I have sworn far less during the late battles than ever before on similar occasions—all owing to the influence of my beloved darling." Later he reported with pleasure that he had "not uttered a single oath, nor blasphemed, even in thought" since he had last seen her, although it would be several years before her influence brought him to forswear playing cards for money stakes. "Loving so fine a being truly and devotedly as I do, it seems impossible that I ever should or could be very wicked."[31]

Everyone expected that such influences would advance courage in battle as well as purity in camp. A woman's love was a stimulus that, often by admonition, sometimes by inspiration, would propel the soldier's combat performance, as he might have put it, above self. Dodd touched a thought—"[Dear Girl,] She shall never have reason to be ashamed of me"—that echoes in almost every correspondence. Garfield wrote to his wife: "Whatever betide, I hope you will never have cause to blush on my account." Benjamin Harrison wrote to his: "If God gives me strength I mean to bear myself *bravely*—come what will, so that you may have no cause to blush for me, though you should be forced to mourn." "Dear domestic ties," Harrison declared, "were only the stronger incentive to quit myself well in the fight." As he watched women dress the wounds of soldiers hit in the battle of Franklin, Captain Thomas J. Key of an Arkansas artillery battery mused: "Oh, woman, what would inspire men to breast the storms of bullets and face death fearlessly except thy happiness and thy influence!" As Abraham Lincoln shook hands with Libbie Custer at a White House reception, his words implied that because of his recent marriage Custer would not again go "into a charge with a whoop and a shout." But Libbie Custer would have none of that; she told her husband that she hoped he would continue to attack with his usual élan. He did, and Libbie regularly celebrated the results: "I feel that the angels in Heaven sang glad songs over your victory." He responded with his own grandiloquence: The only reward he asked for his gallantry was that she should hear of it and "be proud of her Boy."[32]

Occasionally women devised ways to incorporate such sentiments in larger community settings. In mid-1863 Mary Livermore and a friend proposed that Chicago hold a great Northwestern Sanitary Fair to raise funds for hospital relief. They began its organization at a women's convention on September 1; solicited advice and contributions from New York, Boston, Philadelphia, and Pittsburgh; and asked men's organizations to donate manufactured items that could be sold. The city's businesses suspended much of their activity during the days of the fair in October. Six thousand visitors a day watched pageants, looked at patriotic tableaux and the American flags "everywhere displayed," attended lectures, and inspected collections of Northern battle flags and captured Southern banners, weapons, and slave shackles. The climactic event, Soldiers' Day, offered "a grand dinner" for eight hundred Union soldiers convalescing or awaiting exchange in the Chicago area.

At twelve o'clock precisely, all being in readiness, the doors were opened, and the guests of the day marched into the hall. It was a bronzed, scarred, emaciated, halt, blind, deaf, crippled, skeleton corps, some without arms, some swinging painfully on crutches, some leaning feebly on those stronger than themselves, all bearing evidence in their persons that they had suffered for their country. "Brave Boys are They!" crashed the band. The ladies waved flags and handkerchiefs, and, according to the programme they had marked out for themselves, essayed a cheer. But it was drowned in audible sobs, as they gazed on the poor boys who were their guests. They were slowly seated at table, and then with eyes humid with tears, and voice tremulous with emotion, Anna Dickinson, a fair young girl orator at that time, welcomed them in eloquent words. . . .

Grace was then said by the chaplain of Camp Douglas, and the waiters darted off for soup, fish, turkey, game, vegetables, pies, puddings, ices, tea, coffee,—anything that was called for. The poor fellows were served as brothers and sons would have been at home. Their food was carved for them, and their not over vigorous appetites were coaxed and catered to as though feasting were the supremest joy of life. Dinner was soon over, and then came the after-dinner talk. Speeches were made by chaplains and officers who happened to be present.

"Three cheers for Abraham Lincoln! a diamond in the rough!" proposed a manly voice; and so mighty a cheer thundered through the hall, that our guests seemed no longer invalids. Then "Three cheers for the ladies of the Northwestern Fair!" shook the hall again. The ladies, in their enthusiasm, responded by "Three cheers for the soldiers!" given with an accompaniment by the band and with the waving of flags and handkerchiefs.

One of the chaplains proposed that the soldiers should give the ladies a specimen of their battle cry, as they charged, double quick, on the enemy—and, unconsciously to themselves, the men took the attitude, and their faces assumed the determination of the charge as they uttered so prolonged, unearthly, and terrific a yell as beggars its description. We can imagine its power on the battle-field.

The excitement was now at a white heat, and there was no vent for it but in music. The band played "The Red, White and Blue"— the boys joining in rousingly with their bass and tenor; the ladies adding soprano and contralto, and for the next hour all sang together, until the entire *repertoire* of patriotic and soldier songs was exhausted. "Let us not forget our dead!" said Chaplain Day. "They who went out with us to the conflict, but whose slumbers on the battle-field shall not be broken until the reveille of the resurrection morn shall awaken them. Let us remember that—

> "'He who for country dies, dies not;
> But liveth evermore!'"

All stood in solemn silence, with uncovered heads, while the band wailed a dirge for those to whom God had granted a discharge from the conflict, and promoted to the ranks of the crowned immortals. A doxology was the only fitting close to the hour, and a thousand or more of voices joined in singing "Praise God, from whom all blessings flow!" Then with swelling hearts and quivering voices, with tremulous clasping of the hands, and broken words of thanksgiving, the boys slowly returned to the hospitals.

"We are not worth all this. We have not earned this kindness," they said. "But on our next battle-field, the memory of this day shall make us braver and stronger."[33]

No war better exemplified John Keegan's observation that battle is essentially a moral conflict. Those of the Civil War understood it to be so in the most profound and comprehensive sense of the term: The conflict was one in which the moral nature of individuals contested against the moral nature of other individuals. Courage's agents did not doubt that one generated power and force to the degree that one approached purity of virtue. When Thomas Nelson Page's biographer noted that for the Southern writer the war "was as religious and moral as it was civil," he might have been speaking of all Americans.[34]

The influence of the family and community on the soldier in the field was intensified by the almost universal resort to a language of heroism. Undermined, denounced, and partially abandoned as a result of the combat experience of World War I, this vocabulary flourished in the Civil War. It remained throughout the war the foundation of public discourse, the language of speechmaking, Sunday sermons, newspaper reportage, and even soldiers' letters.

As Mary Livermore's description of the Northwestern Sanitary Fair illustrated, it was an idiom of elevated sentimentality, one less heedful of recounting what was observed than of confirming that proper values motivated what was observed. "Brave" soldiers stood "firm as a rock," "receiving fire" "nobly" and then returned fire "with spirit." Their commanding officer was "bold as a lion," a "noble fellow" who "fell" and was "committed to his last resting place," a grave "watered by the tears" of his comrades. Those of his men who survived the fight could be assured, however, that their sufferings would be "made sacred" and their perils "made proud," and so on.[35]

Surprisingly, soldiers writing from battle zones sometimes employed a comparable order of euphemism. Stephen Weld wrote to his father on April 29, 1863:

> At the lower crossing [of the Rappahannock], I witnessed *one of the prettiest sights of the war.* It was our men driving the rebs from their rifle-pits. Our men . . . opened a heavy fire on the enemy's sharp-shooters . . . and soon all along the line men could be seen running from houses, ditches and rifle-pits. Then our artillery would open up and *make the rascals scatter.* I saw one round shot *knock a rebel head over heels.* Then, too, as the rebs ran . . . our men would yell and cheer and send *a perfect storm of bullets* after them. Soon our men rushed over in boats . . . and began *popping away.* . . . Then came the *grand skedaddle.* From every imaginable place came a rebel *running for dear life*, with our men cheering at their heels and our artillery *helping to kick them along* . . . a prettier sight I never saw in all my life.[36]

Such language suggested games light-heartedly won or lost and carried civilians and soldiers far from a war of suffering and death. Those subjects, in particular, were meticulously camouflaged. Comrades who were killed had "gone to their long home," had fallen into their "last sleep," or had "gone to mother." Instead of dying, one "dropped off the corruption of a torn and wounded body" or received help from the angels in "loosing him from the clay prison." A Union soldier, soon to risk his life in battle, thought of the "future life, whose invisible veil was about to be lifted from some of us, to reveal the beginning of eternity," and those who were subsequently killed and buried were "left . . . to sleep, where no sound of strife and bloodshed would trouble their rest any more . . . we felt that their sacrifice had gained for them a far greater crown of rejoicing in that beautiful world beyond their humble graves."[37]

Some of the indirection might be explained, as language less than graphic in twentieth-century wars would be, by soldiers' determination not to alarm their families, were it not that soldiers, at least in the war's early phases, were sometimes no more direct in talk among themselves. Just before H. A. Herbert's Alabamians arrived on the field at Second Manassas, Hood's Texas Brigade had broken an assault by the New York Zouaves, "leaving the green sward strewn thickly with dead and wounded lying all about in great baggy, red breeches." Surveying the field exultantly, an Alabamian shouted, "Look, boys, what a bed of roses! Didn't our fellows pluck 'em!"[38]

The language descriptive of courage's war was neither soldier self-delusion nor manipulation employed by high commands or governments; it was, rather, a fair reflection of the structure of values within which soldiers at the outset and civilians throughout the war thought about what was happening. It created in civilian minds less a deception than a disjuncture, with the result that people continued to think and talk of the war in such terms long after they had spent agonizing hours awaiting the casualty lists at the newspaper office, watching military funerals, and trying to comfort themselves or other survivors. Its larger effect was to reinforce all of those conceptions of combat as an exercise in courage rather than as a march to hardship, dismemberment, or death.

A woman friend described to Nurse Woolsey her work at Belle Plain, Virginia, in the wake of the Wilderness battles of May 1864:

We have a Feeding-Station on shore and are putting up another two miles away, on the hill, where ambulance trains halt sometimes for hours, owing to obstructions in the road. The mud is frightful and the rain is coming on again. We are directed to take the return train of ambulances for Fredericksburg.

99

Just as I finished, the train from Fredericksburg arrived. Nothing I have ever seen equals the condition of these men. They had been two or three days in the ambulances; roads dreadful; no food. We have been at work with them from morning till night without ceasing; filling one boat, feeding the men; filling another, feeding them. There is no sort of use in trying to tell you the story. I can scarcely bear to think of it. . . . Yesterday a squad of rebel officers was marched on board a boat lying by ours. I had to pass through their ranks to get supplies from our boat, and shook hand with our boys [male nurses and cooks serving as guards] and saw the [Confederate] officers . . . strong, well-fed, iron looking men, all of them. There's no "give in" in such . . . men as these. Our soldiers from the front say the rebels stand—stand—in solid masses, giving and taking tremendous blows and never being shoved an inch. *It is magnificent!*

No words can express the horrible confusion of this place. The wounded arrive one [ambulance] train a day, but the trains are miles long; blocked by all sorts of accidents, wagon trains, bad roads, broken bridges; two, three days on the way, plunged in quagmires, jolted over corduroy, without food, fainting, starving, filthy; frightfully wounded, arms gone to the shoulder, horrible wounds in face and head. I would rather a thousand times have a friend killed on the field than suffer in this way. It is worse than White House, Harrison's, or Gettysburg by far. Many die on the way. We found thirty-five dead in the ambulances yesterday, and six more died on the stretchers while being put on board the boats. The boats are anything that can be got hold of, cattle scows, anything. Barges of horses are landed by the side of the transports and the horses cross the deck where the helpless men lie. Mules, stretchers, army wagons, prisoners, dead men and officials as good as dead are tumbled and jumbled on the wretched dock, which falls in every little while and keeps the trains waiting for hours. We fed the men at once. We fed all five boats that got off yesterday. There is no Government provision for this, beyond bread; no coffee, no soup, no cups or pails, or vessels of any kind for holding food. The men eat as if starving. These had been three days without food. We are ordered to Fredericksburg to-day . . . as there is more misery there than here.[39]

Her mood was clearly one of pity, disgust, and disillusionment, but she was apparently aware of no anomaly in inserting between descriptions of the wretchedness surrounding her a reference to the magnificence of the battle line, as if the two scenes of war had no connection between them.

The same dissociation appeared in works of literature, where genteel strictures were even more imperative than in personal correspondence. Joseph Hopkins Twichell, a Congregational clergyman and army chaplain who after the war would become Mark Twain's friend and pastor, was nearly overcome by his first experience of battle. At Williamsburg in May 1862 his regiment—the 71st New York—suffered severe casualties. Twichell recorded his reaction to the sight of the dead: "I was like one in a hideous nightmare. It was a sight too piteous for speech. It seemed as if the universe would stop with the horror of it. I could only cry to my own leaded heart, 'It costs too much.'" For this "too piteous" sight he did nonetheless very quickly find words, which he set down "on the march up the Peninsula soon after the battle of Williamsburg":

BURIED ON THE FIELD

They're left behind!
Our steps are turned away:
We forward march, but these forever stay
Halted, till trumpets wake the final day:—
    Good-bye! Good-bye!

They're left behind!
The young and strong and brave:
The sighing pines mourn sweetly o'er their grave;
Mute, moving grief the summer branches wave,
    Good-bye dear friends!

They're left behind!
Four days we staid to keep
A sacred sentry o'er their glorious sleep:—
The drops of heaven above are left to weep;
    Good-bye! Good-bye!

They're left behind!
There let soft sunshine fall
Thro' tremulous leaves; and where sad night birds call,
O moon and stars! kiss through the shadowy pall,—
    Good-bye! Good-bye!

They're left behind!
And fold them to thy breast
In gentle arms, O soil! now doubly blest
By their live valor and death's noble rest:
    Good-bye! Good-bye!

They're left behind!
Comfort!—our heavy souls!
Their battle shout forever onward rolls
Till God's own freedom gathers in the poles!
    Good-bye! Farewell![40]

Religious faith was another buttress of the war's moral framework for both soldiers and civilians. With so many soldiers believing that godliness was a source of combat courage, the influence of religion easily moved beyond the level of the individual and found incorporation in army organization and practice. Indeed, it was pervasive in the Confederate armies, "a deep religious feeling" from commander-in-chief to private.[41] While less conspicuous in the armies of the Union, religion never ceased to receive serious consideration.

Early in the war religious observances were common on both sides. In many units participation was obligatory. The captain of Company E of the 21st Georgia required the men to kneel in prayer each evening after roll call, though the practice must have drawn heavily on the fact that he was their hometown preacher. Members of the 77th and 123d New York and 36th Illinois were under orders to attend divine services, at least while in camp; an observer said of the Illinois unit that "religion is compulsory in this regiment." Campaigning diminished opportunities for formal services, but at the outset a number of commanders seemed to be convinced that military operations should yield to worship. Sabbatarianism was a force in both armies. McClellan's General Order No. 7 of September 6, 1861, read as follows:

> The major-general commanding desires and requests that in future there may be a more perfect respect for the Sabbath on the part of his command.
>
> We are fighting in a holy cause, and should endeavor to deserve the benign favor of the Creator.
>
> Unless in the case of an attack by the enemy, or some other extreme military necessity, it is commended to commanding officers that all work shall be suspended on the Sabbath; that no unnecessary movements shall be made on that day; that the men shall, as far as possible, be permitted to rest from their labors; that they shall attend divine service after the customary Sunday morning inspection, and that officers and men shall alike use their influence to insure the utmost decorum and quiet on that day. The general commanding regards this as no idle form; one day's rest

in seven is necessary to men and animals; more than this, the observance of the holy day of the God of Mercy and of Battles is our sacred duty.

For no less than another year Stonewall Jackson's men remained bound by Robert E. Lee's similar order enforcing rest on Sundays, "unless necessity compels the work."[42]

Such actions expressed piety but also a fear of divine retribution; many were convinced that the army that "profaned the Sabbath" would be chastened and perhaps defeated. James Newton recorded that on April 26, 1863, rain fell on the 14th Wisconsin as it marched from Milliken's Bend, Louisiana, "to punish us I suppose for marching on Sunday." At least as late as Chancellorsville, May 1863, soldiers retained an uneasiness sometimes edging on dread regarding Sunday battle. As Rice Bull put it, "It seemed to me like sacrilege that such a sacred day should be used by men to kill and maim each other."[43]

Such thoughts manifested widespread conviction that on every level the war was being fought as part of God's Plan. In neither section were the clergy neutral—both armies counted a number of "fighting parsons"—and their stance reinforced soldiers' beliefs that theirs was the cause of the godly. The ranks thought godliness a source of protection and of victory as well as of courage. God would ensure the survival of the soldier of perfect faith, the battlefield victory of the army of devotion, the triumph of its cause. Faith promised that the Confederacy would win its independence, that the Union would not be broken.

On the level of the individual, religious conviction gave equanimity to soldiers contemplating the risks of combat. On the eve of battle a Union sergeant felt its calming influence: "I hope for the best and trust in Him who wields the destiny of all." The basis of his trust was likely to be confidence that faith also acted to preserve in battle the lives of the faithful. William Dame and his friends in the Richmond Howitzers did not hesitate to act on that assumption as they broke winter quarters at the opening of the 1864 campaign. They resolved that

. . . during the coming campaign, every evening, about sunset, whenever it was at all possible, we would keep up our custom, and such of us as could get together, *wherever we might be*, should gather for prayer. . . . I may remark, as a notable fact, that this resolution was carried out *almost literally*. Sometimes, a few of

103

the fellows would gather in prayer, while the rest of us fought the guns. Several times . . . we met *under fire*. Once . . . a shell burst right by us, and covered us with dust; and, once . . . a Minie bullet slapped into a hickory sapling . . . not an inch above my head. . . . But, however circumstanced, in battle, on the battle line, in interims of quiet . . . we held that prayer hour every day, at sunset, during the entire campaign. And some of us thought, and *think* that the strange exemption our Battery experienced, our little loss, in the midst of unnumbered perils, and incessant service, during that awful campaign, was, that, in answer to our prayers, "the God of battles covered our heads in the day of battle" and was merciful to us, because we "called upon Him." If any think this a "fond fancy" *we don't*.[44]

Godliness also influenced, on another level, the outcome of an army's battles. The men were aware that on the eve of a fight it was Stonewall Jackson's habit "to wrestle in prayer long into the night" in order to bring himself into harmony with God's Plan. And the men approved, for many were convinced that battles were won because the faith of their commander was powerful. Poague wrote home from the Peninsula on October 26, 1864:

We are all busy preparing for Grant's expected attempt on our lines. . . . By the blessing of Heaven we mean to defeat him in all his efforts. Things in the [Shenandoah] valley don't turn out well for us some how. When I hear of these reverses I can but think of the time past when you used to follow "old Jack" (as he was *affectionately* called by us then) in his glorious races after the enemy as well as his skilful retreats. I cannot help contrasting the characters (*moral*) of the leader of the army of the valley in those days and of its present commander. I fear Gen Early doesn't pray as hard as Stonewall Jackson did to the Lord of Hosts who giveth victory to whom he will.[45]

Others were even more certain that they saw the rewards of godliness—"his direct interposition in our behalf." At Spottsylvania Dame's Confederate companions went to sleep thinking themselves safe within their own lines, but the last three awake felt impelled to look around once more. What they saw were the approaching columns of a Federal surprise attack, and the cannon shot they fired woke the men in time to repulse the Yankees from their sector of the line. "It was," Dame concluded, "the Providence of God to an important result."[46]

The same assurance extended beyond battle to the welfare of one's cause. When their side's fortunes appeared to prosper, Confederate soldiers thought they saw God's intention working itself out. Poague wrote to his mother in October 1864, "If the Lord of Hosts will bless us in future as I believe he has done in the past, our independence is certain." Key was convinced that "if all the army would unite as one man in prayer and faith we would never lose a battle and peace would follow immediately."[47]

Strong as the belief in faith's power to preserve the soldier, army, and cause was, the truly exceptional potency of godliness derived from the ways it permitted people to explain why a soldier died, a battle was lost, or a cause seemed to be failing. As was evident in so many of these soldiers' words, God's Plan was not thought of as a completed script in which His people were, unknowing, simply to speak their lines and act their parts. The thoughts and actions of those here on earth would always to some degree continue to give shape to the results. Negative developments were readily comprehensible when they could be identified as divine reaction against human faithlessness. Consequently soldiers were made skittish even by intimations of others' disbelief.

Under shelling at Chancellorsville, Jake Fogle of the Stonewall Brigade began praying aloud: "Lord, save us this time!" But "a wild, reckless fellow," Sam Nunnelly, only laughed and teased Fogle, "Pray on, Jake"—to the consternation of Casler and other comrades. "Cross and I tried to get Sam to hush."[48]

Russell Conwell, the founder of Temple University, believed that his life had been altered by a wartime incident in which God punished his disbelief. Although his father was a devout Methodist, at Yale he had joined the Free-Thinkers' Club and had subsequently announced to despondent parents, "I am not going to church any more. I don't believe the Bible anyhow." As a captain in the 46th Massachusetts, he permitted a boy named John Ring to accompany him to war. When he forbade him to read his Bible in the tent, John Ring told Conwell, "I love you, Captain, but you are a very wicked man." The regiment was in camp in North Carolina and Conwell was briefly absent, when the Confederates attacked and routed the New Englanders. John Ring went back to retrieve Conwell's ceremonial sword, crossing a burning bridge and sustaining severe injury. His dying request was that Conwell should know he had saved the sword. Told of the boy's death, Conwell was shaken: "[N]o man can describe the horror that came into my soul." Six months later, wounded himself in the battle of Kennesaw Mountain, he sent for a chaplain. Later in the night, an "awful sense of sinking came over me, and I called upon the unknown God for forgiveness . . . a few minutes after my heart was opened . . . the sense of final forgiveness seemed to fill my soul with light." Conwell would later say many times that his subsequent accomplishments in education derived from the obligation he felt to repay the world for the loss of John Ring. Within such a framework, few Americans found it difficult to understand a death so purposeful.[49]

Many soldiers shunned even "strong language" as edging on blasphemy. When an Illinois private employed such words, a friend reprimanded him: "Don't talk so. Some of us will be killed tomorrow in the fight." At Shiloh, Leander Stillwell indulged in "wicked profanity" in the heat of battle and as a result expected "summary punishment on the spot." Sacrilege could even lose battles. Weld was appalled and disgusted that Fighting Joe Hooker had seemed to challenge God at Chancellorsville: "[H]e said that he had a position which God Almighty could not drive him from, and that he had the rebels and God Almighty could not help them. Not much wonder that we were whipped."[50]

Such incidents strengthened faith, but what of disastrous outcomes without any perceptible connection to faithlessness? Key attributed his survival to his faith in God *and* his constant prayers for God's blessing. Favorable results required that he regularly invoke God's protection in prayer; failure to do so would court calamity. Here, then, was a way of explaining failure while leaving intact the assumption of the power of godliness. The soldier had to do his part, the army its part, the people their part. God is on our side, common reasoning went, and God's Plan is one of goodness, so death and defeat signal only that *we* have not yet met the conditions requisite for its execution.[51]

Northern General O. O. Howard contemplated in this sphere the results of his own flaws: "[T]he pride and haughtiness of my heart is more than pen can tell, but I believe God will school me, by failures when I act without Christ, by disappointments and afflictions, [so] as to bring my miserably foolish soul into full subjection to himself." A Southern officer pondering a lost battle—Nashville, a Confederate disaster—reasoned in the same fashion: "[W]hile God was on our side so manifestly that no man could question it, it was still very apparent that our people had not yet passed through all their sufferings."[52]

In parallel fashion, those who pondered the relationship between God's Plan and their apparently failing cause were just as likely to find the fault in themselves. The last letter written by General Frank Paxton before his death in battle lamented, "We are a wicked people and the chastisement which we have suffered has not humbled and improved us as it ought. We have a just cause, but we do not deserve success if those who are here [in the Confederate armies] spend this time in blasphemy and wickedness, and those who are at home devote their energies to avarice and extortion." In short, God's Plan envisioned the triumph of the Confederacy, but God would not effect His Plan until Southern soldiers and civilians were deserving of divine beneficence. Robert E. Lee, too, employed this framework: He suffered military defeats because God ordained it so, but He so ordered not because he opposed the Confederate cause but because Confederates continued to sin. James Garfield not only found God blameless and human beings completely culpable for what in 1862 seemed an irretrievable Union cause, but he discovered God continuing to work out His Plan through the very folly of those mortals: "Gen. McClellan is weakly and wickedly conservative . . . and the President nearly as bad. But out of the very weakness and timidity of our leaders I draw the hope that thus God has willed it—that He is the commander-in-chief of our armies, and there is no [human] will making ends for the war and effectively thwarting the Divine purpose. If McClellan will discipline and mobilize the people into armies, and let them meet the enemy, God will take care of the grand consequences."[53]

The tendency to see God's will in otherwise adverse developments found its most important uses in explaining the deaths of soldiers whom comrades thought spotless in faith and comportment and in comforting those at home whose losses they could not attribute to the individual defects of dead sons or husbands. The popular conception here moved from the notion that death appropriately punished the unworthy, and especially the cowardly, to the belief that death rewarded the worthy. Indeed, for those who died confirmed in their courage and godliness, there was a sweetness in death.

Two days before his first action, William McKinley speculated on his future:

> It may be I will never see the light of another day. Should this be my fate I fall in a good cause and hope to fall in the arms of my blessed redeemer. This record I want left behind, that I not only fell as a soldier for my Country, but also [as] a Soldier of Jesus. I may never be permitted to tread the pleasant soil of Ohio, or see and converse with my friends again. In this emergency . . . my parents, brothers and sisters, and friends [will] have their anxiety removed by the thought that I am in the discharge of my duty, that I am doing nothing but [that which] my revolutionary fathers before me have done, and also let them be consoled with the solacing thought that if we never meet again upon earth, we will meet around God's throne in Heaven.

Paxton, too, was one of those soldiers to whom "death is no enemy, but a messenger expected from God sooner or later, and welcome as the quick path to a holier and happier life." Occasionally, officers might even invoke this conception of death to strengthen courage in combat. Emory Upton told his men prior to a charge: "Some of us have got to die, but remember you are going to heaven."[54]

Those at home tried to shape the events of the war to those beliefs just as assiduously as did soldiers. They too believed that faith and courage mobilized God's protective power. While James B. Sheeran, a Catholic priest, was saying Mass in besieged Charleston in 1864, a 100-pound Parrott shell exploded violently 50 yards away, creating panic among the worshipers. Sheeran was more irritated than apprehensive: "What are you afraid of? Do you think God is not able to protect you from Yankee shells? Is He not able to protect you in church as well as out of it? Keep still, there is not one bit of danger."[55]

Those at home also believed in honoring God by keeping His Sabbath. Libbie Custer was both very concerned that her husband might be required to travel on Sunday and hopeful that she might herself be forgiven for sewing on Sunday. Hannah Ropes's mother wrote to her with characteristic doughtiness after First Bull Run: "Aney Christian Nation that will pitch battle on the Sabbath Must expect to be taught a sence of their duty by hard nocks. I hope our people have learned a lesson they will proffit by."[56]

They too were convinced that God favored their cause. Those at the Northwestern Sanitary Fair sang an "Anthem of Liberty":

> Onward, still onward, flag of our might!
> Onward, victorious, God for the right![57]

They believed in God's Plan—and that their own defects were the sole impediment to its realization. As Nurse Ropes put it: "This is God's war, in spite of uncertain generals, in spite of ill success; in spite of our own unworthiness. . . . Having failed to learn in prosperity, we ought to be glad of the Divine Mercy which gives us another chance in the upheaving of all social comforts and necessities." The days of prayer, thanksgiving, fasting, and humiliation declared in both sections gave the widest social expression to those sentiments. They believed in God's Plan—and took from their faith in it solace in their tribulations. A Northern woman found comfort in the words of her husband, dying of wounds in a Philadelphia hospital: *"It is all right;* if it were not, God would not permit it to be so." When Captain Key received from home news that "bears down my heart like a mighty incubus"—Yankee soldiers, white and black, had been there, cursing, snatching, plundering everything, fighting over the loot, with the children screaming in fright; the medical treatment applied to his four-year-old daughter's "poison in the bone" had caused her teeth to fall out and had ultimately necessitated cutting a portion of her jaw away—his wife *comforted him* by urging him to read Job.[58]

They too believed in the sweet death as the ultimate consolation. A Northern woman said of her husband's death in a hospital that the angels of God had come down to guide his spirit. Mary Livermore comforted a feeble, white-haired Chicago father who had just learned of his son's death in battle: "Your son has only gone a little before you; only a hand's breadth of time between you now." And Nurse Ropes, "flinging all [cheerless] theology to the bats and owls," found herself whispering to dying soldiers: "Who should you fear? The angels are here; God is the Friend who never forgets us, you will never be hungry or tired any more." Louisa May Alcott's vision of death, a vision of peace and repose and home, was similar, though not reached without struggle. On hospital duty in Washington, she offered a wounded soldier help with his meal, but he shook his head, "Thank you, ma'am; I don't think I'll ever eat again, for I'm shot in the stomach. But I'd like a drink of water, if you ain't too busy."

> I rushed away, but the water-pails were gone to be refilled, and it was some time before they reappeared. I did not forget my patient patient, meanwhile, and, with the first mugful, hurried back to him. He seemed asleep; but something in the tired white face caused me to listen at his lips for a breath. None came. I touched his forehead; it was cold; and then I knew that, while he waited, a better nurse than I had given him a cooler draught, and healed him with a touch. I laid the sheet over the quiet sleeper, whom no noise could now disturb; and, half an hour later, the bed was empty. It seemed a poor requital for all he had sacrificed and suffered,—that hospital bed, lonely even in a crowd; for there was no familiar face for him to look his last upon; no friendly voice to say, Good bye; no hand to lead him gently down into the Valley of the Shadow; and he vanished, like a drop in that red sea upon whose shores so many women stand lamenting. For a moment I felt bitterly indignant at this seeming carelessness of the value of life, the sanctity of death; then consoled myself with the thought that, when the great muster roll was called, these nameless men might be promoted above many whose tall monuments record the barren honors they have won.[59]

Obviously there was much in these equations of victory and defeat, of life and death, that would bind soldiers to their families and the home-town folks to those fighting the war. For all, it was a purposeful war, of which God's Plan was but the highest expression. In this vast drama of lives spared or taken, battles won or lost, causes upheld or destroyed, randomness, meaninglessness, chance, and luck were given no role. (Even instances of "lost orders," deemed by some today critical to the outcome of such battles as Antietam, were assigned not to ill fortune but to the will of "a superintending Providence.")[60] More important, the war would not be decided by any superiority of material resources. Northerners and Southerners were certain that victory would tie itself not to more numerous armies or greater numbers of cannon but to divine grace—a linkage that would not be broken as long as the main tenets of this war of courage and godliness, supported in inseparable combinations by home influence, the heroic vocabulary, and religious conviction, remained in place.

★ PART TWO ★

A
Perilous
Education

6

Unexpected
Adversaries

The Civil War could not be fought as its soldiers set out to fight it. As it unfolded, those on both sides discovered that the conflict was much less their creation than they had supposed, that it had gained a life and an impulse of its own. Like soldiers in every war, they encountered much for which they were unprepared, but there was in this war a special poignancy in the breadth of the gap between expectation and actual encounter. Stern experience challenged and sometimes overthrew critical convictions, in the process changing soldiers in ways they found painful to accept and leaving many of them isolated and disillusioned.

In the early months of the war both Union and Confederate soldiers found themselves caught up in a process they called "simmering down." They had all brought from home equipment and supplies inadequately suited for campaigning. Preparing in London for service with the South, Francis Dawson commissioned a maker of surgical instruments to forge a Bowie knife. An Arkansas friend had told him it was the "one indispensable thing," for with it he would be able to seize Yankee muskets and with a single blow sever their barrels. Confederate artillerymen initially flourished sabers and revolvers. Soon they discarded both. Illinois infantrymen arrived with pistols and large knives—"How big we did feel!"—but soon they were gone. Confederate infantry, too, quickly sent home their revolvers and even pitched out an item of government issue, the bayonet. The problem was the absence of transport and the soldier's realization that in matters of weaponry he was to be the army's beast of burden.[1]

That reality arrived early. George Allen of the 4th Rhode Island later recalled that, as he went to war in October 1861, his kit contained

> . . . a full supply of underclothing, woolen blanket, rubber [blanket], three or four pairs of socks, half a dozen nice handkerchiefs, dress coat, fatigue cap, supply of ink, letter paper, and envelopes, portfolio, photograph album, Bible, . . . journal . . . , tobacco, drinking tube, comb and brush, shaving tools, two or three pipes, pins and needles, thread, buttons . . . canteen, . . . patent water filters, [eating utensils], shoe brush and blacking, various kinds of medicine, and flannels for sudden changes of climate or weather, a pair of mittens for the coming winter.

In his haversack were "cold meats, bread and butter, cheese, pie and cake, and other food"—"mostly obtained from home."[2] Such burdens made it inevitable that the route of the first long march would be littered with discarded items. Those who set out carrying 60- and even 80-pound packs were brought down within a few miles. Soon either they or their possessions could go no farther.

Large items were discarded first—overcoats, the quilts so lovingly made by mothers—and then the extra blankets, surplus clothing, knapsacks ("they rubbed the skin off a man's back"), books, gloves, odds and ends. Sometimes before two weeks passed, the soldier had reduced his load to less than 40 pounds, including his rifle (9–11 pounds), cartridge box, a blanket and poncho, a canteen, and a small haversack in which he kept cup and plate; knife, fork, and spoon; soap, towel, comb, and toothbrush; pipe and tobacco plug; rations—hardtack, salt pork, coffee, sugar, salt; and perhaps a change of underclothes. Items not expendable often had to be replaced with more practical designs. Among the infantry, boots yielded to broad-bottomed, flat-heeled brogans and long-tailed coats to short-waisted, single-breasted jackets. Involving the loss of many useful and comforting items evocative of home, this experience was painful. Its only compensation was the opportunity to tease others as the process repeated itself; new regiments always arrived with the same enormous knapsacks, and streamlined veterans chided newcomers as they too moulted for war.[3]

Soldiers usually thought of simmering down as it applied to excessive supplies, but it was a process equally pertinent to baggage of a less material nature. A series of shocks would compel soldiers to abandon or to modify beliefs that in battle proved useless—or dangerous.

The first shock for the Civil War soldier was the extent and deadliness of disease. Those who think Margaret Mitchell intended the measles death of Scarlett O'Hara's husband in *Gone With the Wind* to show he was a milksop would be surprised to learn how many died that way. So rampant was disease in the Civil War that Paul Steiner has called it "natural biological warfare." Union battle deaths—those killed in combat or mortally wounded—numbered 110,000, but twice as many, 224,580, died of disease, and in the Confederate forces the ratio must also have approximated two to one.[4]

Each army suffered two waves of disease. The first consisted of the acute infections of childhood. Here the young men of the cities, who had been exposed at earlier ages to such diseases as measles, mumps, and smallpox and had developed immunity, fared better than country boys, because army life broke the isolation of country regions. Thomas Galwey of a Cleveland Hibernian Guards company proudly observed that "countrymen are not more hardy than city boys." The first wave took a high toll and then diminished as the survivors developed antibodies, but the second—comprising such camp diseases as dysentery, malaria, and diarrhea—struck in force at the outset and continued to increase throughout the war. On the Northern side, 223,535 soldiers had to be discharged for such physical disabilities.[5]

The cases of the 64th and 65th Ohio seem representative. Each entered federal service in the fall of 1861 with nine hundred men, comfortably within the range—845 to 1025—mandated for newly recruited Civil War regiments. By August 1862, however, one hundred from each unit were dead of disease, and three hundred others were gone—absent, sick, or sent home disabled.

Each regiment had been reduced to an effective strength of five hundred before it lost a single soldier killed in action.[6] Here was another and more consequential simmering down.

The commanding officer of Edwin Fay's Louisiana cavalry squadron directed his men not to include the names of sick comrades in letters home. The incidence of disease must have been extraordinary, for only in an extremity would a Confederate officer issue an order he knew would be impossible to enforce.[7]

The frequent transfer of units to areas of unwholesome conditions, or simply of different climate, increased the vulnerability of the men. The 77th New York entered the war in November 1861 with a thousand men; by mid-June 1862 the Virginia Peninsula campaign had left only 250 capable of reporting for duty. Some lay down in their tents and, unable or unwilling to seek assistance, simply waited to die. Stevens recalled that "at times one might sit in the door of his tent and see as many as six or seven funeral parties bearing comrades to their humble resting places. . . . Our army seemed on the point of annihilation from disease." Staff officer Theodore Lyman found a Union Army review in September 1863 disturbing: "It was a somewhat sad sight to look at these veterans, with their travel-stained uniforms and their battered canteens; many of the regiments had no more than 200 men, and their flags so tattered that you could barely read such [Peninsula] names as Fair Oaks, and Williamsburg, where so many of the missing 800 now lie." Lyman had spent the war's first years traveling in Europe; he did not realize how many of the 800 had fallen to infection rather than bullets. In many Civil War books, scenes of men dying of disease are as prominent as scenes of death in combat.[8]

Soldiers of the 1860s were of course accustomed to illness and may have felt death's presence less grievously than we do today. Infant mortality was high; the death of a younger brother or sister was hardly an unusual experience. But if their familiarity with early death was relatively high, still, nothing seems to have prepared soldiers for the extent of army illness. Their public face was that of fatalistic acceptance, of resignation to fever deaths as instances of God's will, but such expressions were frequently stiff with strain. After all, the men were being deprived of friends and commanders were losing fighting soldiers, and those were not heroes' deaths. Courage might protect the soldier in battle, but it offered him little in illness. It might give him a heightened forbearance, but in the grip of largely untreatable fevers the man of courage had but slight latitude for showing qualities superior to those of the coward.

Courage was largely unavailing, and soldiers therefore began to feel despair. Wilder Dwight wrote of the condition of Union troops at Harper's Ferry in November 1861: "There is a hopeless desperation chilling one when engaged in a contest with disease." After Shiloh, when Halleck pursued Beauregard and invested Corinth, the Union Army disintegrated with camp fever. The Federals summoned strength enough to labor for two months, digging classic siege approaches—until Beauregard simply marched away to the south. Garfield was disgusted with the tactical deficiencies of Halleck and other professionals: "If the Republic goes down in blood and ruins, let its obituary be written thus: 'Died of West Point.'" But it was disease that brought Garfield himself down. He too believed in the power of the will to resist sickness, and he had not withheld appropriate instruction from his men. When two who were ill asked permission to return to Ohio, he denied their request and urged that they "wrestle" with their sickness "as with a giant enemy." But the enemy had won; both, with many others, had died, and Garfield was deeply disturbed and "tormented by guilt." "This fighting with disease is infinitely more horrible than battle. This is the price of saving the Union. My God, what a costly sacrifice!"[9]

Disease was one of the shocking realities of the war; camp life was another. It too brought soldiers into rude collision with their expectations.

Soldiers would generally find civilian assumptions about their experiences in the military wrong-headed, but the assumption regarding the nature of army life at first seemed accurate enough. Civilians had held little respect for the prewar regular army; the career soldier was considered dissolute and military life coarse and ruinous to character. Though the volunteers of 1861–62 expected that the encouragement and cultivation of courage would make them better men, they recognized that army life itself would obstruct rather than contribute to their progress—as did the parents who had so carefully shaped and gravely delivered those farewell words of admonition. Still, though forewarned, volunteers found the task more difficult than any had anticipated.

Following the initial waves of illness and homesickness, some actually came to enjoy camp life. Often they were older men and officers, like Rutherford Hayes or Charles Francis Adams, Jr., who found in army activity a release from the complex webs of family relationships and in command responsibilities a pleasing contrast with the dullness of civilian careers. But to the majority of soldiers, camp life came as a series of unpleasant surprises, the most mortifying of which was probably the soldier's discovery that lice had infested his body and clothing. In 1861 the gray-backs, one of Lee's soldiers reported, were hidden from others as a humiliation. A "loathsome" subject, a Federal agreed. Every soldier was infested, he added, even General Ambrose Burnside: "I will guarantee that if every living thing buttoned up under his muddy blue coat had been a soldier, Gen. Burnside would have been pretty nearly a regiment." Soon the searches and killings— a hundred lice per man per day—became public performances, "as acceptable as a daily washing of hands and face," and per-haps even welcome as a brief palliative to what emerged as the principal problem of camp life, a spirit-crushing boredom.[10]

Dooley spoke of the camp life's "monotony and most tedious irksomeness." Beatty complained that he had "hardly enough to do to keep me awake." "Bugles, drums, drills, parades—the old story over and over again." The numbers of corn cakes eaten; pipes smoked; papers respectfully forwarded; "how-do-ye-dos" to colonels and captains and lieutenants and soldiers; the walk-ing, sleeping, yawning—"it is confoundedly dull." Charles Wainwright of the 1st New York Artillery decried "the ennui of weeks and even months with nothing to do" and Dawes noted that a "military life in camp is the most monotonous in the world. It is the same routine over and over every day." Daily schedules in both armies seemed full enough: generally roll-call at six; breakfast at seven; squad or company drill two hours each morn-ing; dinner at noon; battalion drill two hours each afternoon; dress parade at five; supper at six; roll call at nine; taps at 9:30, with guard detail perhaps every two or three days. In addition, both officers and men earnestly planned worthy activities to fill time beyond the hours of training. Soldiers established chapters of Masonic lodges; built chapels; competed in running, wres-tling, boxing, and jumping; organized debating societies, tem-perance meetings, prayer groups, singing classes, reading clubs, spelling schools, theatrical troupes, and grand balls (with some of the men appearing in hoop skirts). Conscientious commanders developed for their junior officers courses of instruction in military regulations, tactics, and strategy. No one gave the problem of monotony more thought than General Joseph Hooker, who as part of his reorganization of the Army of the Potomac following the Fredericksburg disaster instituted regimental snowball battles, with line and field officers participating; regimental and brigade baseball competitions; numerous religious meetings; and spectacular military reviews.[11]

Yet nothing was able to alleviate for long the tedium of camp life. It was the topic that seemed to draw from soldiers their loudest moans. "I am . . . worn out with idleness," Beatty wailed. If I am idle much longer, Jesse W. Reid of the 4th South Carolina wrote, "I will turn to a high land terrapin or an oyster." George Stevens deplored the camp's "inglorious inactivity." But perhaps Vail touched best the depths of soldier malaise in his complaint that mud was causing cancellation of *drills* and beyond picket and guard duty "we had nothing to do."[12]

It was not that camp life was felt to be a suspension of worthwhile activity, a neutral hiatus separating periods of purposive enterprise or a mere delay in entering courage's arena. Rather, the soldier believed that he was being required not only to wait but to rot, and his sense of deterioration was accurate, for the camp remained the locale most hospitable to sickness. (Charles Russell Lowell was surprised that it was so much easier "to make men do their military duty" than to heed regulations designed to enforce a cleanliness that would have reduced sickness.) Stillwell watched the informal division of his regiment into messes of four, eight, or twelve men, with each man doing the cooking in his turn, and deplored the "pernicious" results of careless, unhygienic preparation: six weeks of diarrhea and men dying by the score "like rotten sheep." So it was no surprise that stagnation planted amid such illness and occasional hunger would force from even so stalwart a soldier as Alexander Hunter the lament that "this slow perishing in blank inaction day after day—this long drawn out agony, is more than men can endure." Or, as a North Carolina soldier more gently put it: "If anyone wishes to become used to the crosses and trials of this life, let him enter camp life."[13]

Heroic prewar conceptions of warmaking did not die here, but camp life certainly rubbed some of the shine from them. John Beatty, who was worn out by idleness, described his own disenchantment:

119

> How often, when a boy, did I dream of scenes similar to those through which I have passed. . . . Knightly warriors, great armies on the march and in camp, the skirmish, the tumult and thunder of battle, were then things of the imagination; but now they have become familiar items of daily life. Then a single tap of the drum or note of the bugle awakened thoughts of the old times of chivalry, or regrets that the days of glory had passed away. Now we have martial strains almost every hour, and are reminded only of the various duties of everyday life.[14]

Others drifted to activities that seemed to offer escape from camp life, or at least its temporary obliteration. Civilians often thought soldiers used liquor because it "gives strength and courage," but the rank-and-file derided bottled bravery as "Dutch" (that is, foreigners') courage and resorted to spirits much more commonly as a flight from camp life. Early in the war many units pledged themselves to abstinence, so drinking was for a time restrained as a breach of comradely solidarity. Both armies, moreover, moved officially to restrict the use of liquor. Though available in Union commissaries and sometimes distributed to the men, whisky was not a ration but a medical department supply item to be issued to counteract exposure or exhaustion. John Billings received it three or four times during the war, usually after prostrating marches, and that appears to have been the usual range of frequency in Northern units. In the Confederate Army, official drams came even less often. Union officers could buy commissary liquor whenever they wished, but enlisted men required an officer's authorization—in Vail's New York regiment, an order of the company commander countersigned by the colonel. Often brigade or regimental headquarters inspected incoming parcels to ensure that they contained no alcohol. Standing orders in both armies prohibited the sale of whisky to soldiers by outsiders. Sometimes chaplains attempted to enforce teetotalism; Father Sheeran asked Confederate soldiers for a drink and then galloped off with their bottle.[15]

The results were not impressive. Few clergymen could perform moral patrol duty with more than sporadic effect. Given ordinary levels of indiscipline, the armies' military justice systems could spare little energy to punish drinkers, especially given the multitude of ways enlisted men devised to obtain alcohol. They got it by cultivating civilian suppliers and friendly officers and by contriving innumerable deceptions. When Casler told his captain how he had obtained a permit from the general by claiming that the whisky was intended for the captain's use, the captain "just laughed at the trick." In the opposing army, Hinman was certain that some enlisted men were able to get liquor at all times and in all places.[16]

It soon became evident, moreover, that the weight of soldier opinion had shifted from an initial condemnation of imbibers to the denunciation of those who objected to drinking. Fifer Bardeen's journey into vice was not unusual. At the outset, as a member of the Sons of Temperance, he indignantly poured out on the ground his government-issue gill (one-quarter of a pint) and reported those who had received liquor in parcels from home. But he was bending. In February 1863 he drank an emergency whisky ration for the first time. He began to regret that he had informed; he was, he decided, more ashamed of that than of any other deed. The following Christmas "everybody" was drunk, and on New Year's Day Bardeen was repentant: "I bear witness to [1863's] contaminating effects. Many an evil habit has sprung up in me since Jan 1st, 1863. God grant that the year on which we have now entered be not so." But it was clear both that Bardeen continued to drink and that the force of comradeship had tipped in favor of those who drank; he very much regretted the "absurd scrupulousness" that had brought him more unpopularity than his "more selfish faults."[17]

Like Bardeen, most soldiers neither returned to their prewar sobriety and moderation nor escaped guilt that they were unwilling or unable to do so. They could not easily brush away thoughts that they had yielded to temptation and had thus weakened some vital part of themselves. Still, it seemed to happen to everyone—whether by drink, strong language ("How easy it is for a soldier to swear," Upson mused.), smoking, or playing cards. Dawes described how Union officers began to fill lulls in camp life with drinking, gambling, and horse racing. After Gettysburg, he reported, it became harder and harder not to become "rough, coarse and uncouth." Hayes began to take wine, although by the White House years he would revert to lemonade. Even Benjamin Harrison, the "Christian Soldier," certain that vices were more deadly than enemy bullets, sampled wine, bourbon, and novels, obviously without the lethal results he had feared. They all had assumed that the problem would present itself as free-standing, undisguised temptation to vice; few had foreseen that the sheer unendurability of camp life would make previously forbidden activities irresistibly attractive. One might lose the tug-of-war with the Devil not because of inadequate strength but because of the slipperiness of the ground underfoot.[18]

To be sure, not all vice was of the common sort. Many country boys were encountering city life for the first time. Lieutenant George Howze, a Mississippian later killed at Gettysburg, heard God's voice saying to him, "Take care, young man," and realized his danger. "Temptation was around me in a thousand forms. On every corner of the street the monster stood, clothed in the soft habiliments of a friend." Howze stood firm against "the house of bad repute"—"I thank God . . . I have never entered"—and the billiard saloon, ten-pin alley, and gaming tables: "In none of these things did I indulge. My trust was in God to keep me from [them]." He did succumb to the theater, deciding that it was not "a great sin to go to a moderate extent," for several Shakespearean plays had had "a most glorious effect" on him.[19] For ordinary soldiers the lures of the city that so divided Howze against himself had less to do with their straying than did their aversion to camp life.

The expansion of military experience into areas antithetical to conventional morality had significant emotional and military consequences. That note of moral urgency on which soldiers had left home faded, of course, but it continued to sound in conscience and memory so that the first small breach with those at home opened. Soldiers were compelled to admit to themselves that they were beginning to behave in ways that violated family values.

Some soldiers thought of the hardships and temptations of camp life as a test comparable to that of combat. Theodore Upson of the 100th Indiana wrote to assure his mother that in Sherman's army drinking was the exception rather than the rule; that the enlisted men made fun of drunken officers; that profanity was neither deep nor vicious; that card playing was a matter of amusement and not of gambling. Camp life had tempted and tried them, but she might "search the world over and not find as clean a lot of men as comprise the Army today," for they had been "cleared of . . . dross." Few, however, would find such assurances convincing, and their number could not have included Upson himself, for he had begun to smoke, swear, and drink, and to act toward others in ways he knew he would not have contemplated at home (e.g., accepting excessive change from a Jewish merchant and saying nothing). Whatever his fabrications, he must have felt that he had not passed the test of camp, that he was dim with dross and that actions transgressing family wishes had opened a new distance between himself and home.[20]

The military problem was immediate. Commanders were aware of the deteriorative effects of camp life and worried about diminishing combat capability. When Captain John DeForest observed that his 12th Connecticut, drinking, swearing, and gambling harder than before, were not "so *good* as they were once," he seemed to decry the loss of both virtue and combat effectiveness. General Frank Paxton worried that camp soldiering was making his Confederates worthless and lazy, "a result . . . more disastrous than a dozen battles." Sherman thought that his army, while halted at Atlanta, had begun to disintegrate from idleness. General Grant responded unblinkingly to the logic of the situation. Before hitting upon the approach that led to his capture of Vicksburg, he conducted five "experiments" in an effort to cut avenues through swamps to the city's rear. The men labored amid malarial fevers, measles, smallpox, and Confederate snipers. Though Grant was prepared if one of his experiments should succeed, he had "never felt great confidence" in any of them; still, "I let the work go on, believing that employment was better than idleness for the men." None of the passages could be opened.[21]

Perhaps the men were not as ungrateful as one would suppose. Some of them came to prefer marching to inactivity, and others even welcomed the break-up of winter quarters and the resumption of campaigning. In late March 1862 Berdan's Sharpshooters were happy to receive their marching orders, for they had been chafing and fretting to get away, to do something or to go home. Rice Bull welcomed the 1863 campaign as a change from the monotony of winter drill. To Hinman's Ohioans, "weary of camp life," "the prospect of new adventures [Rosecrans's Tullahoma campaign] was like an elixir." Even in May 1864 regiments and batteries of the Army of the Potomac, joyful "that the season of inactivity was over," cheered its first campaign orders. Others found camp life so oppressive that, an Illinois soldier wrote, they were "willing to go into the jaws of death rather than remain where we are. . . . We are dying faster from the sicknesses of camp than from the casualties of war." His comrades had argued all morning, "often rising into angry and bitter words," each exasperated by the thought that he might be excluded from a dangerous cavalry scouting expedition; those selected "started off in high glee." DeForest called camp life "a healthy [sic!], monotonous stupid life [that] makes one long to go somewhere, even at the risk of being shot." Indeed, some did go the full distance by inviting battle. Not long after Jesse Reid wrote home to South Carolina that "an order to march right to where a battle is going on is one of the most sickening things on earth," he decided, amid severe camp illness, that he was "getting tired of this way of living." "I am anxious to do what fighting I have got to do and be done with it." At winter's end soldiers, unaware perhaps of a most appropriate double meaning, often described themselves as "spoiling for a fight."[22]

Ironically, the fight that soldiers sought quickly presented new elements of disenchantment.

One might assume that Americans of the 1860s were better prepared than their twentieth-century successors to absorb combat's consequences. True, the Mexican War was fifteen years in the past and had exacted fewer than 1,800 battle deaths, but the hunting of wild animals and the dressing of their carcasses; the slaughtering of livestock; the killing, plucking, and gutting of poultry were common in the lives of many young men and must have inured them to the sight of blood. Harold Frederic would later remember of his youth in upper New York that those Thursday visits to Busnell's slaughterhouse, there to watch "with stony hearts" the slaying of several score barnyard animals, were occasions of "our very highest delight."[23] Early railroad and industrial accidents were frequent and often gory. Still, when young soldiers first saw bullets, cannonballs, grapeshot, and canister strike others, their shock was profound.

The first surprise was death's suddenness. "I never shall forget how awfully I felt," Leander Stillwell wrote, "on seeing for the first time a man killed in battle. . . . I stared at his body, perfectly horrified! Only a few seconds ago that man was alive and well, and now he was lying on the ground, done for, forever!" Thomas Wentworth Higginson was looking on as a steamer captain was killed by Confederate bullets: "I shall never forget the strange sensation when I drew his lifeless form into the pilot-house which he had rashly quitted. It was the first dead body I had ever handled and carried in my arms, and the sudden change from full and vigorous life made an impression that no later experience surpassed." The impact was especially vivid for the soldier splattered by a dead man's blood or brains. Disconcerting, too, was the realization that few soldiers died with tidy holes through the chest. Father Sheeran visited the field of Second Manassas: "[T]hose scattered throughout the woods and over the fields presented a shocking spectacle. Some with their brains oozing out; some with the face shot off; others with their bowels protruding; others with shattered limbs." But to him it was Chancellorsville that was "perhaps . . . the most revolting scene I had ever witnessed." "Our line of battle extended over some eight miles and for that distance you see the dead bodies of the enemy lying in every direction, some with their heads shot off, some with their brains oozing out, some pierced through the head with musket balls, some with their noses shot away, some with their mouths smashed, some wounded in the neck, some with broken arms or legs, some shot through the breast and some cut in two with shells."[24]

The magnitude of the destruction administered another shock. No one would ever comprehend the war's 623,026 deaths or 1,094,453 casualties, but soldiers were still stunned by the scale perceptible to them. Riding over the Antietam field following the Confederate withdrawal, Alpheus Williams was dazed by the sight of a Southern regiment cut down in line, 150 bodies in two ranks as neat as if they had been on parade. In another spot he saw bodies "thick as autumn leaves," and he wondered despairingly whether, if the war continued in that fashion, anyone from privates to generals would be left alive. Rice Bull saw at Chancellorsville "a sight that should make a man weep": Southerners caught on an open road by the grapeshot and canister of Northern artillery, terribly mutilated bodies fallen in regimental front. "It was the most horrible sight I looked on during the war." Finally, there was the unexpected variety of death's guises. Soldiers were startled that those wounded in Wilderness combat, not fatally perhaps but seriously enough to immobilize them, should burn to death in brushfires begun by the battle. Union soldiers in North Carolina watched a Confederate soldier cover a retreat by burning a bridge under their fire; later they were appalled to find him, with a leg shot off, "writhing in terrible agony," frying in his incendiary materials, tar and turpentine.[25]

Those killed did not cease to pose problems for the living. Of Shiloh, Henry Stanley wrote, "I can never forget the impression those wide open dead eyes made on me." Following the battle of Williamsburg, Union color sergeant Daniel Crotty of the 3d Michigan realized that the dead had assumed "all possible shapes," one with his face swollen and cast in a "dirty, greenish hue, positively the worst sight of a rebel I ever saw. . . . Horrid sights meet the eye everywhere." From Antietam, Weld wrote home, "The faces of the dead were horrible"; they had been turned black.[26]

Time's passage certainly did not improve either appearance or odor. On July 5, 1863, Bardeen walked over the Gettysburg battlefield: "It is a terrible sight to see on the field the bodies of the freshly slain, but when they lie twenty-four hours, they become unnatural and the sight becomes distressing." At Second Manassas Carl Schurz, the leading German-American advocate of the Union cause, was made so miserable by the dead whose features had puffed up beyond recognition that "he found it difficult to console himself" and in distress wrote Abraham Lincoln a letter so anguished that it edged on insolence: "I do not know, whether you have ever seen a battlefield. I assure you, Mr. President, it is a terrible sight." Father Sheeran recorded at Antietam bodies "black as negroes," bloated and decomposed. He was soon eager to fly back to his monastic cell in New Orleans "to shelter myself . . . from the scenes of bloody strife." Others were repulsed by the related activities of other natural life. Charles Francis Adams reported swine digging up and gnawing skulls: "Such it is to die for one's country!" Robert Gould Shaw saw the bodies of dead Union soldiers mutilated by fiddler crabs. Frank Wilkeson saw black beetles eating corpses. Stephen Weld saw turkey buzzards hovering over the dead: "It was a horrible sight, and made one feel what war was."[27]

If shock at the suddenness, disorderliness, extent, variety, and appearance of death chilled and disheartened the soldier, the problem of the removal of bodies created a disgust equally demoralizing. As Lewis Mumford remarked, meeting death was one thing, disposing of the remains another. Robert Strong called the burial of the dead the "worst of any [disagreeable job] I ever took a hand in," for after three or four days the flesh would no longer hold together as the corpses were lifted. Robert Carter watched Gettysburg dead break apart as they were pushed into trenches, "with not a prayer, eulogy or tear to distinguish them from so many animals." Not surprisingly, many were buried rapidly and carelessly, and as a result their presence persisted. Marching over the Chancellorsville field six weeks after the battle, the 1st Mississippi found the stench still "perfectly awful." The 123d New York came upon the "gruesome sight" of Confederate bodies uncovered by rains. In the Wilderness the 105th Illinois came on limbs protruding from the earth. At Cedar Mountain Dooley of the 1st Virginia "turned half sick from the ghastly spectacle" of bodies only partially buried.[28]

To nineteenth-century Americans the death of an individual was ordinarily understood as an expression of God's will, a piece in His Plan. The deaths at home of elderly family members could be accepted as reasonable and even fitting. The deaths of children, if not so comprehensible, at least took place in a consoling atmosphere of intimacy. But battle deaths were another matter altogether. There was that harshness, sometimes in the manner of dying, frequently in the disposition of the dead. Some combat deaths were grotesque; some remains were entirely neglected.

Some soldiers, it was true, seemed untouched by their encounters with the dead. Writing home, Francis Amasa Walker put the rhetorical question, "Shall I tell you how they [Union soldiers] die?" and then described a wounded Massachusetts boy—knee joints blown out; hands torn off; leg broken; the side of the body punctured—who, Walker wrote without apparent pain or perplexity, died in the cause, "the holy name of freedom, country, law," and fell "under the bright, beautiful banner of freedom." Crotty, at first appalled at the greenish dead of Williamsburg, nevertheless found reassurance in a second look revealing evidence of the superiority of his cause: "The dead of both friend and foe lie side by side, but it is remarked by all that the pleasant smile on the patriot's face contrasts strangely with the horrid stare of the rebel dead." But most were shaken by what they saw. Of that tour of the Gettysburg field, Bardeen wrote, "I should not dare to print or even to tell the horrible sights I saw." Garfield wrote his family of the battle at Middle Creek, Kentucky: "It was a terrible sight to walk over the battle field and see the horrible faces of dead rebels stretched on the hills in all shapes and positions." Years later he would say, as

William Dean Howells recounted, that "at the sight of these dead men whom other men had killed, something went out of him, the habit of his lifetime, that never came back again: the sense of the sacredness of life and the impossibility of destroying it."[29]

Encounters with the wounded, soldiers discovered, could be just as confounding. The dead, after all, were beyond feeling and thus beyond the aid of comrades, but the wounded continued to press their claims on those who remained whole. What the able-bodied could do to help remained, to their frustration, very limited.

The wounded presented still more sights that young men had not thought possible. Dooley saw a fellow Confederate still walking about with a shell-hole in his head, a "large opening . . . in which I might insert my hand." Almost every Civil War memoir contains a passage descriptive of the author's horror on first encountering the pile of arms and legs outside the field hospital tent in which amputations were being performed. And that deterioration appalling in dead bodies could, with its accessories, be even more repulsive in the still living. In the Wilderness Father Sheeran saw many Union soldiers "whose wounds were complete masses of maggots." Robert Strong sickened as he watched a doctor remove maggots from the head of a wounded soldier. Le-Grand Wilson, a Confederate assistant surgeon, required half an hour to cleanse of those grubs the wounds of soldiers struck down at Gettysburg, "certainly the most disagreeable duty I ever performed." He estimated that 90 percent of the wounds he treated were "infected with vermin." Walt Whitman was so unnerved by the sight of so many wormy, mortifying Wilderness wounds that he became ill and had to be evacuated to the North.[30]

A number of circumstances combined to produce such sights. Neither army ever developed a system able to offer the battlefield wounded first aid skilful enough to arrest hemorrhaging and then to transfer them efficiently to medical facilities. As late as mid-1864, when less mobile warfare in the East should have made thorough organization possible, Union wounded were still being evacuated from the Petersburg lines on flatcars—"piled like logs . . . with here and there a half-severed limb dangling from a mutilated body." The wounded were frequently left to their own devices and expected, if ambulatory, to make their own way to help. Comrades could be of only slight assistance. One of the few standing orders more heeded than ignored was the one forbidding soldiers to drop out of the charge in order to aid wounded companions. It was observed because courage was at issue, and to help another might easily be construed as a cowardly attempt to escape combat. To many, the inability to stop and succor or even comfort wounded friends was a source of distress, but that was nothing set beside the agonies of the abandoned wounded.[31]

Those not mobile sometimes waited two or three days for medical attention, and by then many were beyond the need of it. Nearly every wound became infected—no surprise in a day when regimental surgeons commended a porous bag filled with fresh earth as "an excellent absorbent" for suppurating wounds. And when, as happened increasingly as the war proceeded, local cease-fires to bury the dead and treat the wounded proved impossible to arrange, the results were dreadful. Shot through both thighs during Pickett's charge, Dooley remembered the Gettysburg field on the night of July 3, 1863—the groans, the shrieks, the maniacal ravings, the sobs, the sighs, the cries, the oaths, the despair, the death rattles. Not until July 9 would his wounds, by then maggoty, be washed and bandaged. Wilson thought the experience of listening to wounded soldiers "crying piteously" for aid "horrible beyond description" and was convinced that if everyone could see and hear as he had, "war would cease, and there would never be another battle."[32]

Wounds had the power to challenge courage in various ways: by testing the soldier's responses to his own wounds, to the sight of others' wounds, even to the prospect of a wound. The wound almost suffered could permanently strip away one's composure. At Cold Harbor, Weld

> . . . was sitting with a cape of my coat thrown over my shoulder, leaning against the roots of an uprooted pine tree. . . . I finally got tired and threw my legs from one side of the trunk to the other. It was not more than five seconds after I had done this that a shell . . . plunged through the roots of the pine tree, just grazing my shoulder and covering me all over with dirt. It dropped right at my feet. Had I not changed my position, I should have been taken square in the back and crushed to pieces. It made me very nervous about shells. Until then I had not minded them much.

But whatever the power of the near miss to intimidate, it was less than that of the hit. Many a soldier turned out like the one

129

described by Strong, a good soldier who was wounded, recovered his physical strength but was "afterwards . . . afraid of his own shadow." Most feared was the wound that left its victim no alternative but the hospital, a place, whether field hospital or permanent installation, often more terrifyng than the severity of one's wound.[33]

Along with the challenge of combat and the demoralization of camp life, another trial was the experience of the periphery. Soldiers marching into battle found its edges disconcerting. Their own columns retained order, but all around them was evidence of convulsion and disarray—dead, dying, and wounded; scarred trees and buildings; crippled horses; everywhere the refuse of war. Their task was simply to pass as rapidly as possible through the zone, but many found its sights harder to endure than battle itself. "I have always thought," Ripley said, "I should want to pitch in at first, and not wait till I had endured the delightful scenes of 40 or 50 ambulances bringing past their loads." Sherman shrank from the "apparent confusion" and "general apprehension" of the periphery. "I never saw the rear of an army engaged in battle but I feared that some calamity had happened at the front. . . . For comfort and safety [sic], I surely would rather be at the front than the rear line of battle."[34]

Still, the military hospital most haunted the mind of the Civil War soldier. It was easier to die in combat than to go to the hospital—and far more preservative of proper values. No one pretended that such places were other than appalling. William Miller Owen of the Washington Artillery of New Orleans remarked:

> The sorriest sights . . . are in those dreadful field-hospitals, established in barns, under large tents, and in houses. The screams and groans of the poor fellows undergoing amputation are sometimes dreadful,—and then the sight of arms and legs surrounding these places, as they are thrown into great piles, is something one that has seen the results of battle can never forget.* No longer do the rush, roar and boom of shot and shell, and the volleys of musketry bring the fire to the soldier's eye and make his blood tingle

---

*Doctors employed amputation principally as a way to control—indeed, to excise—infection, but frequently the stumps became reinfected. So automatic seemed the resort to amputation that George Allen attributed it to "the grand opportunities for surgical practice" it offered "young army medical students."

through his veins in glorious excitement; but now the saw and the knife prove that all is not glory.[35]

Rice Bull's "first experience in the horrors of war" was a visit to a Union hospital. His "home friend" had contracted typhoid and then gangrene in both feet, and when the surgeon told Bull that only good nursing would enable his comrade to survive, Bull decided to stay with the patient in the hospital's "death-ward." Conditions were frightful. Attendants knew no more than he. "The horrors soon made me decide that I had no further desire for such service." When his friend's toes were amputated and he at last was sent home ("a sad ending of our comradeship"), Bull fled: "Nothing could have induced me to continue in that work."[36]

So dire were hospital conditions that sometimes the best of nurses even in permanent facilities felt almost as Bull did. Hannah Ropes, matron of Washington's Union Hotel Hospital from July 1862 until her death in January 1863, herself suffered from hospital lice and reported that disease from "the itch" to smallpox was rampant throughout the building. A committed Abolitionist, she wrote in mid-December 1862 in fervent support of the cause:

> [T]he cause is that of the human race, and must prevail. Let us work then with a good heart, here and at home. . . . Now is the judgment of this world. Each man and woman is taking his or her measure. As it is taken even so must it stand—it will be recorded. . . . No soul now can stand on neutral ground. Between truth and error there surges and foams a great gulf. . . . Let *us* be *loyal* and *true*.

But she was finding it difficult to work "with a good heart" as the incongruousness of her words set against the realities of her work bore in upon her: "As usual, I have jumped away from the detail of hospital life in writing—facts, perhaps, in the hospital would give a different verdict, so believe for me all the good you can, giving me the benefit of every doubt." Three days later she wrote again: "You have no idea of a hospital, nor has anyone who simply calls in to see me."[37]

Nurses ordinarily continued to wear stalwart public faces and to reassert the values of courage's war. Groans and cries of pain were the adjuncts of every battle, and tearful pleadings that a foot or arm not be taken off those of every field hospital, and they often went unchastised (perhaps because victims' comrades were not generally present to inhibit or to scold), but in permanent hospitals the expectations of proper behavior again tightened. As noted earlier, hospital workers encouraged stoicism. What Reed called "the harder heroism of the hospital" was that, at least in part, because medical workers made it so.

As the war wore on, civilian volunteers' treatment of soldiers seemed to vary with the patients' comportment. Reed, who believed that the best soldiers welcomed disability as an opportunity to demonstrate "the triumph of spiritual power over physical weakness and pain," admitted as much.

> We did have our pets in the hospital, and we could not help it. How different was it to go into one tent and see a poor boy raised in bed, dying of rapid consumption, yet so cheerful, subdued, and quiet in his sufferings, thankful for every word of sympathy, or for any attention to his comfort.[38]

Still, despite all the injunctions directed at the wounded, despite the obvious rewards held out for courageous behavior and the penalties threatening those whose demeanor fell beneath the heroic, so profound was the wretchedness of the patients and the place that the socially approved surface periodically collapsed. A very young soldier dying in the hospital asked a woman to sing for him "Nearer, My God, to Thee" ("Tho' like the wanderer/ The sun gone down,/ Darkness be over me,/ My rest a stone,/ Yet in my dreams I'd be/ Nearer, my God, to Thee"), then "In the Sweet By and By" ("We shall sing on that beautiful shore/ The melodious songs of the blest,/And our spirits shall sorrow no more,/ Not a sigh for the blessing of rest"), and "Home, Sweet Home" ("An exile from home, splendor dazzles in vain,/ Oh, give me my lowly thatched cottage again;/ The birds sing gaily, that come at my call;/ Give me them, with that peace of mind, dearer than all"). Before the last song had ended, the proper atmosphere had become a shambles. Many of the men in the ward buried their faces in their pillows and wept aloud. Mary Livermore, alarmed by such an "excess of emotion"—"This would not do"— hastily called for another song, "Rally Round the Flag, Boys" ("So we're springing to the call from the East and from the West,/ Shouting the battle cry of freedom,/ And we'll hurl the Rebel crew from the land we love the best,/ Shouting the battle cry of freedom").[39]

On another occasion she visited a regimental hospital whose

surgeon was "dead-drunk" and stopped at a bed to offer sympathetic words to a wounded soldier; he wept aloud and then by contagion perhaps a hundred of the two hundred in the wards began to sob convulsively.[40]

Hunter spoke of his own experience of Confederate hospitals: the sick and wounded—many of them illiterate and thus denied the diversion of books and newspapers—"with staring eyes, brooding over their helpless condition, sinking without an effort to rally"; the absence of any familiar faces; the sounds of pain and delirium.

> It was the long nights which came as a terror to every man that lay beneath the roof of the hospital; it was to me as a hideous dream. The vast room with the narrow beds side by side, became like the dim caverns of the Catacombs, where, instead of the dead in their final rest, there were extended wasted figures burning with fever and raving from the agony of splintered bones, tossing restlessly from side to side, with every ill . . . human flesh was heir to. . . . Up and down aisles moved the nurses with muffled footfalls, looking to the eye of the fevered patient like the satellites of the Venetian Doges gliding through the torture chamber.[41]

Those soldiers who remained unwounded had heard what it was like to be hospitalized. A few had seen for themselves. It requires no imagination to work out why memoir references regarding visits to wounded comrades are so slender and sparse. A few generals—McClellan was one, Howard another—occasionally visited hospitals, but ordinarily commanders' reactions were the same as their soldiers'—praying to be spared wounds and, just as fervently, the hospital; distancing themselves as far as possible from this dread aspect of the war. Abner Small of the 16th Maine said of hospitals that there he "grew old at the sight of [the] suffering."[42]

7

Sword and Shovel

Encounters with battle injury and death, with camp, and with hospital appear to have shocked many Civil War soldiers into periods of discouragement and depression. No doubt such collisions temporarily diminished martial élan. (Camp tedium, as an incitement to campaigning, was an exception.) But their effect seems to have been that of a sharp emotional puncture, a painful but slender perforation of the consciousness of the sort experienced by unwitting young men who in all wars discover the naïveté of their expectations. Such shocks do not halt wars, for although a sight might stagger the soldier, its repetition (and others were likely to follow quickly on the first) ordinarily made shallower penetrations until, as Thomas Galwey realized as he looked on the skulls of soldiers killed on the Manassas battlefield, "Horrid sights are, to an old soldier, horrid no longer."[1] The long-term result of cumulative encounters with injury and death was seldom emotional repudiation of the war but rather the realization that the tests of war were more severe, and the personal costs of failure higher, than had been expected. Still, few individuals concluded on the basis of such experience that their own chances of success in war had been decisively impaired or that the rewards of personal triumph were no longer intact.

However, other forces at play in the Civil War signaled something far more potent than combat's cost in lives: that the very *nature* of combat did not fit, and could not be made to fit, within the framework of soldier expectations. Forces of change and novelty made themselves felt less dramatically and drastically, but they slowly chipped away at soldiers' resolve, and their results were over time more profoundly dispiriting. Ultimately, they led many to the realization that they could not fight the war they had set out to fight.

The engine of change was technological modification. An advance in weaponry overthrew the efficacy and then the moral meaning of the tactics soldiers wished to employ, robbing of significance the gestures they had been determined to make. The Civil War's principal weapon remained that of the Mexican War, the single-shot, muzzle-loading musket. Fifteen years earlier its effective range had been roughly 100 yards, and its powers of intimidation had not been great. Ulysses Grant spoke of it derisively: A man might fire one at you all day from a few hundred yards "without your finding it out."[2] In tactical terms, its limitations had enthroned the offensive; charging columns able to survive a single volley from the defending force were likely to be victorious. After discharging their weapons, the defenders had to reload by taking from a box at the belt a cartridge wrapped in tough paper; biting off its end and pouring its powder into a muzzle while holding the musket vertically; freeing the 1-ounce ball from the rest of the paper and inserting it too into the muzzle; using a ramrod to tamp home the ball; bringing the musket to the hip fully cocked and placing a percussion cap on the nipple; and raising the gun to the shoulder.[3] Ordinarily before they were able to complete those motions, the attackers were upon them with all the momentum of the charge.

Civil War muzzle-loaders, however, were no longer smoothbore but rifled—that is, their barrels were grooved in a way imparting to the bullet a spin that extended the weapon's effective range to distances between 300 and 400 yards. Charging columns could be brought under fire much earlier, at a half-mile's distance, and a much higher toll exacted. Even with the persistence of poor firing instruction and wretched firing discipline, rifling strengthened the hand of the defense decisively.

Interestingly, the next stage of technological improvement— the breech-loading repeating rifle—appeared early in the Civil War but never became a decisive factor. The North issued seven-shot Spencer repeating rifles to many of its cavalry units, to Berdan's Sharpshooters, and to a few infantry regiments, but some elements within the Ordnance Bureau were resistant, others simply dilatory, and the numbers provided were never sufficient to bear conclusively on any campaign, despite reports that Confederates thought them frightening (and unfair!). Nonetheless, the introduction of the rifled, single-shot Springfield was in itself sufficient to render established tactics obsolete and thus to threaten values premised on their effectiveness.[4]

The futility of the frontal attack, with each regiment advancing on a two-company front, should have been apparent as early as Antietam (September 17, 1862) in those ranks of dead ranged as neatly as if on parade. Galwey experienced Confederate bullets so thick that "almost every blade of grass is moving. . . . What we see now looks to us like systematic killing."[5] Three months later Federal troops under Burnside attacked Lee's men on the heights above Fredericksburg at a cost of 12,653 casualties against their opponents' 5,309. At Gettysburg it was Lee who on July 3, 1863, sent three of his divisions charging across almost a mile of open ground against the center of the Union line on Cemetery Ridge; of the 15,000 in Pickett's charge, perhaps half returned. At Cold Harbor on June 3, 1864, Ulysses Grant ordered frontal attacks that in less than sixty minutes cost the Army of the Potomac 7,000 killed and wounded against the Confederates' 1,300 casualties. There the principal charges could be sustained only twelve to twenty minutes.

The campaign against Atlanta seemed at first to replicate Grant's advance on Richmond. At New Hope Church and Kennesaw Mountain, Sherman launched major frontal assaults that fared no better than Grant's. At Kennesaw Mountain more than 2,000 of Sherman's men were killed, wounded, or missing, against Confederate losses of 450. Like Grant, Sherman could measure progress only by the retreats that the flanking movements of his superior numbers—not his charges—forced upon his opponents. (When the 1864 campaign began, Sherman's 100,000 had outnumbered those opposite him by 40,000, and Grant's 122,000 had exceeded Lee's numbers by 56,000.) Michael Fitch of the 6th Wisconsin would later pin down precisely the reality of the campaign: "After the rebel army fell back from Dalton [Georgia] and entrenched on a line of hills [at Resaca], it was a mere waste of life to charge them in front as it was afterwards [at Kennesaw]. Nothing was accomplished during the whole of the Atlanta campaign by direct charges on earthworks. Flanking did the work."[6]

Sherman never ceased to yearn for an opportunity to crush his enemies in decisive assault, but he learned, perhaps better than any other Civil War general, what one of his commanders called "the lesson of prudence": Charges on prepared positions had become unbearably costly. Sherman, moreover, appears to have felt less than others a visceral resistance to the prospect of meeting battle on the defensive and to have resisted better than others the impulse to demonstrate courage in the charge; he was thus prepared to apply that lesson.[7]

Ironically, Sherman's first opponent, Joseph E. Johnston, was perhaps the only defensive adept in either army, and it was he who repulsed Sherman's charges while yielding ground before Sherman's otherwise masterly campaign of probing operations and flanking movements. But on July 17, 1864, Jefferson Davis relieved Johnston of his command and installed in his place John Bell Hood, whose devotion to the attack was unsurpassed in either army. Sherman was pleased: "I inferred that the change of commanders meant 'fight.' This was just what he wanted." As Cox put it:

> We of the National Army in Georgia regarded the removal of Johnston as equivalent to a victory for us. Three months of sharp work had convinced us that a change from Johnston's methods to those which Hood was likely to employ was . . . to have our enemy grasp the hot end of the poker . . . we were confident that . . . a succession of attacks would soon destroy the Confederate army.[8]

Sherman was willing to wait for those attacks. At Peachtree Creek Hood lost between 5,000 and 6,000 in killed, wounded, and missing to Sherman's 1,800; at Decatur, as many as 10,000, against Union losses of 3,700; at Ezra Church 5,000 against 600. Describing for Sherman that last combat, soldiers of the 15th Corps assured him that it had been "the easiest thing in the world; that, in fact, it was a common slaughter of the enemy." That change of command, Cox said—and, he should have added, Sherman's willingness to accept a defensive posture—"undoubtedly precipitated the ruin of the Confederate cause." Sherman never broke the connection between courage and the charge. He continued to cite "the courage and spirit" of those Southern attackers who, repulsed again and again, renewed the charge a half-dozen times. But he saw more clearly than others that the charge had become defeat.[9]

137

Civil War soldiers increasingly realized the assault's inefficacy, and not all remained inert in the face of its failure. As the war pressed on, a tendency appeared, provenance unknown, toward tactical variation. Attacks in massed column became less frequent, yielding to open formations supplemented by far greater numbers of skirmishers. Assaults sustained until victory or defeat gave way to advances by rushes, with the men resorting to cover that they had spurned early in the war.

Such departures from the manual's prescribed forms probably began with the combat reactions of the men themselves. To Lyman it appeared that they were saying, We can push this assault no farther, but we won't run—and so they lay down. At Chancellorsville the 12th New Hampshire charged for the first time under heavy musket fire; more than 400 of the regiment's 500 were killed or wounded. "But the terrible experience of the last hour and a half has taught them a lesson that each one is now practicing; for every man has his tree behind which he is fighting." By 1864, as Bardeen noted of the Wilderness campaign, "We could seldom see the enemy, and learned more and more to protect ourselves as we advanced, keeping behind trees and displaying ourselves as little as possible." Beatty pondered whether what he saw at Missionary Ridge on November 25, 1863, heralded the emergence of a new pattern: "I thought I detected in the management [of the battle] what I had never discovered before on the battlefield—a little common sense." Instead of "an extended and unceasing roll, as at Chickamauga and Stone['s] River," there had been a series of probing attacks, "as if seeking the weak place in [the] antagonist's armor," "a succession of heavy blows" that threw off balance and ultimately routed Bragg's Confederates. But Missionary Ridge had been extraordinary on several counts, not the least of which was the unusual success of large-unit coordination. The manual went unrevised, and adaptation was left to those in the field.[10]

Bardeen described, probably with exaggeration, an episode at Spottsylvania in May 1864:

[A] heavy artillery brigade that had come into active service for the first time was ordered to recapture a baggage train. The general actually formed his men in solid front and charged through the woods. . . . [E]very confederate bullet was sure of its man, and the dead lay thick: I helped bury . . . more than a hundred. It even failed with its five thousand men to capture the train, and then our poor little brigade, hardly twelve hundred altogether, was sent in, and advanced rapidly, every man keeping under cover in the thick woods and brought in the train, hardly losing a man.

But such adjustments could never close the gap that technology had opened between enabling will and disabling firepower. Not even the rapid progress made by Union armies in the war's final days could restore the charge to its place as the war's centerpiece. James Newton of the 14th Wisconsin wrote home from Mobile, Alabama, just four days before Lee's surrender at Appomattox:

> Yesterday afternoon a general bombardment took place all round the line, and we were all apprehensive that a charge was going to be made. . . . Since our illfated charge on the fortifications at Vicksburg hardly a man in the Regt can think of charging again without shuddering, and tho' we would go if we were so ordered, it would not be with that spirit and belief in our success, in which every charge should be made.[11]

The range of rifled muskets, paired with the equally unanticipated intensity of fire from so many weapons, denied to the charge the quick decisiveness Americans had expected of it; introduced the likelihood of a long, fierce, and costly war; and forced soldiers to reconsider battle behavior in defense as well as in attack.

Very early in the war, enemy fire began to confound the insistence that the brave never dodged shells or bullets. As they would in so many spheres of warmaking, soldiers here too discovered that they did not control all they had supposed they could. Men might leap over a rolling, nearly spent cannonball, but they soon realized that the projectile's velocity in flight made useless any calculated escape from its path; dodging was thus not only cowardly but futile. Nevertheless, with nothing to commend it, it persisted, largely as a reflexive reaction. Jumping and ducking that first artillery fire, Rice Bull admitted, became "a nervous habit few ever fully overcame." Officers were no more free of it than the men, and an adjustment of the ideal became essential. Early in his service Lyman wrote home: "There is a certain sense of discipline and necessity that bears you up; and the only shell I 'ducked' was the first one," but three months of war changed his story and its tone: "I don't care who knows it,

I did duck when that spherical case came over." Irritated that his men were dodging fire, an Illinois colonel ordered them to stop. Just then a shell narrowly missed him, and he instantly crouched low in his saddle. The men laughed, and he could only reply, "Well, damn it, dodge a little then."[12]

After a general practice had been altered and a standard of behavior breached, soldiers could still be left acutely conscious of their weakness in such matters. As late as the Petersburg campaign, by which time Federal orders instructed soldiers to duck when they saw the distant puff of smoke from a sharpshooter's rifle, Weld still found troubling the sight of his men dodging passing bullets. "Steady, men, that bullet has gone by you by the time you hear it," he explained. "Just then a bullet, which I am convinced was specially meant for me, went whizzing by me and I at once ducked. Every one laughed and I did not blame them, but a more mortified man than I was never lived."[13] It became difficult to know both how to act and why one acted as one did. The realization that so many obviously courageous men dodged bullets was welcome, for it relieved fear of one's own inadequacy. Yet the logical conviction of the uselessness of ducking; the individual's seeming inability to control his reaction; and the residual guilt that he *might* be yielding to personal defeat were disconcerting. Here the experience of war hopelessly smudged an originally pristine index of courage.

The effectiveness of the enemy's fire also reduced officers' willingness to expose themselves to it. The spur to change here was the elementary realization that the price of this demonstration of courage was often being shot down. At Ball's Bluff early in the war, as Confederates fired on Federals from protected positions, officers of the 20th Massachusetts ordered their men to the ground while continuing to walk among them. As intended, privates were impressed and respectful, but at the battle's end only nine of the regiment's twenty-two officers were left alive and unwounded.[14]

Company officers soon decided that such practices were costly beyond any compensatory stiffening of the men's courage. At Antietam, James Nisbet of the 21st Georgia wrote: "Did the officers take shelter? Yes, you bet they did! We had learned to conserve our strength and [had found] that at times 'discretion is the better part of valor.'"[15]

General officers, perhaps feeling that they had fewer opportunities to impress their courage upon their men, were less flexible. On June 14, 1864, in the course of the Atlanta campaign, Sherman spotted at a distance a group of enemy officers—Generals Johnston, William J. Hardee, and Leonidas Polk—in conference and ordered artillery fire brought to bear. Walking away at leisurely pace so as not to appear to his men hasty or even concerned, Polk was struck by a shell and killed. The classic instance had occurred less than six weeks earlier at Spottsylvania. The commander of the Union Army's Sixth Corps, Major General John Sedgwick, noticed a soldier cowering under fire and, striding to him, chided him—"Why, what are you dodging for? They could not hit an elephant at that distance"—only to be shot through the head in that instant.[16]

Consequently, soldiers' applause of their leaders' ostentatious courage veered toward a concern for the officers' safety, at least in cases of officers whose reputations for bravery had been firmly established. Stonewall Jackson became an object of urgent worry. His men wanted him out of danger. "General, let us do the fighting," the commanding officer of the Louisiana Tigers begged him, but Jackson would not relax the standard with which he had entered the war: "Each of us has his duty to perform, without regard to consequences; we must perform it and trust in providence." Others less magisterial could find themselves vulnerable to new combinations of pressure. Father Sheeran joined Mrs. Richard S. Ewell in arguing that there was no justification for the general's practice of "carelessly exposing himself on the battlefield." His death would create despondency, the chaplain contended, and because Ewell was "the soul of the army" would constitute a Confederate disaster far outweighing any power of example in combat. On several occasions Southern columns refused to proceed into battle until assured that Lee would remain safe. "General Lee to the rear! General Lee to the rear!" was the shout. Clearly, the old standard had been turned on itself.[17]

The same circumstances brought change to the conspicuous parading of the general and his staff. At the outset of the war, that was a frequent occurrence, at the end a rarity. On April 2, 1865, General James Harrison Wilson was worried about the progress of his attack against Selma, Alabama: "Regarding it as one of those emergencies which occur but once in a soldier's life and realizing that I had not another man to put in [that is, he had exhausted his reserves], I felt it my duty to show myself on my most conspicuous horse with staff, escort, and red battle-flag in the thickest of the fight." Though his horse was shot down, Wilson was untouched and his victory complete.[18]

Several commanders, to be sure, continued to employ the staff parade with regularity, but its design seemed to shift from the demonstration of coolness under fire to an almost sadistic imposition of a leader's courage on others. Custer grew to relish testing the members of his staff by leading them "where bullets flew thick and fast" and then watching for any betrayal of weakness. Pleased by those whose appearance remained "as calm and collected as if sitting at . . . dinner," he was viciously contemptuous of those who were less strong-willed. The same sour turn appeared in the methods of D. H. Hill, who on occasion apparently attempted by such a display to draw Union artillery fire, wishing simply to "treat" his staff to "a little airing in a fight." Alfred Torbert was another general who insisted on riding along the front line accompanied by his staff and who, perhaps in order that no one should underestimate the importance of the occasion, ordered along additional orderlies, flag-bearers, and cavalry escort. Though in the course of one such exhibition his medical director was killed by Confederate fire, they apparently continued. On the other hand, Lee at Spottsylvania ordered his staff to seek shelter while he alone remained within the Federal field of fire. Enlisted men on both sides were sensitive to the symbols of leadership, and the staff parade's turn toward the perverse did not escape them.[19]

Watching the adaptations of their officers, soldiers quickly became less inhibited in seeking shelter for themselves. The 6th Wisconsin faced its first artillery fire with "heads high" but soon realized "that a discreet and respectful obeisance to a cannon ball is no indication of cowardice." In battle, Carlton McCarthy observed of the Richmond Howitzers, "Experienced men . . . always availed themselves of any shelter within reach. . . . Only recruits and fools neglected the smallest shelter."[20]

The next step, plain to all, was to construct one's own shelter, and here, apart from formal siege operations, the enlisted men took the lead. They began modestly, almost inconspicuously, perhaps sheltering from artillery behind a little mound of earth and then scooping more soil atop it to make it higher. They had at first no special faith in earthworks; indeed, they shared their officers' distaste of them. The watchword at the outset was that only the wretch groveled upon the ground or dug and burrowed, and even General McClellan became a target of spiked criticism "because he had used the shovel at all." But the men had noticed that the officer uninhibited in the presence of the enemy was easily shot down and that from cover they were able to exact a corresponding toll of enemy officers. Soon they discovered the advantages of facing attackers from trenches 30 inches deep and 5 to 6 feet wide, with the excavated dirt piled on the side facing the enemy. Prior to Shiloh, Hinman recalled, "the spade had been considered an ignoble weapon," but the intense fire of that battle had converted the Ohio regiments, and at Corinth those with shovels dug "with alacrity and enthusiasm" and others used bayonets, sticks, or hands "to scratch gravel on every occasion, with great ardor." Thereafter "It was always a wise thing to do, and not in the least inconsistent with the highest development of personal courage." Fredericksburg, Owen noticed, was the first battle Lee's army fought "behind dirt," and Confederates could not have remained unimpressed when "of all the battles this was the most easily won." By 1864, "spades were trumps" in both armies, not only in siege operations but in almost all field movements. Each time Rice Bull's New Yorkers halted within range of the enemy, they dug rifle pits. No urging was needed; it had become "almost second nature, [the] one duty that no one shirked." So it was on the other side: "No sooner would a line be formed when the enemy was near, than every man was busy throwing up a little mound for protection." Sherman noticed shortly after the start of his Atlanta campaign that both sides resorted to immediate entrenching and that even skirmishers were devising defensive works of their own. No orders were given or required for any of this. The men had simply decided to protect themselves.[21]

Not all officers approved of the development. Stiles reported with regret (no matter how high the Union losses) the Army of Northern Virginia's "first real experience" at Spottsylvania and Cold Harbor "of fighting 'in the trenches' and behind 'works.'" He objected to the tendency of digging "to demoralize the men."

> The protection of a little pile of earth being in front of a man and between him and his enemy, his natural tendency is to stay behind it, not only as to part, but as to the whole of his person. I have more than once seen men behind such a line fire their muskets without so much as raising their heads above the curtain of earth

in front of them; fire, indeed, at such an inclination of their gun-barrels upward as to prevent the possibility of hitting an enemy unless that enemy were suspended in the sky or concealed in the tree tops.

So greatly did this desire to fight behind protection increase that I have seen men begin digging every time the column halted, until their commanding officers declared that any man caught intrenching himself without orders should be punished severely.

Hood was even more adamant. Confederate soldiers who sought protection "would imperil that spirit of devil-me-care independence and self-reliance which was one of their secret sources of power, and would, finally, impair the *morale* of [the] Army." In him who fights behind cover, fears multiply—"a brush-heap" becomes "a wall ten feet high and a mile in length"—and he becomes afflicted with a "troubled imagination." On the Union side, Wainwright was also disturbed: Those men entrenching without orders seemed to evince "so much anxiety to make themselves secure; it does not speak well for the morale of the men. I fear they are more willing to be attacked than they are to attack." One can sense in such officers a strained determination to uphold the values with which they began the war.[22]

William Dame insisted that the true power of Confederate defensive positions lay not in mounds of earth 4 feet high and 3 to 5 feet thick, but in "the *men* behind them," "a very thin gray line . . . back of a thin, red line of clay." The military value of "those modest little works" rested in their effect on soldiers' minds: They instilled faith in the defenders while deterring or intimidating Union attackers.[23] Dame's advocacy was important not because it contradicted assertions like Stiles's that digging sapped the digger's martial spirit or because the proposition verged on truism—of course earthworks had no value independent of the soldiers who manned them—but because it made clear his insistence that events remained within soldiers' control, that engineering had no force of its own but counted only to the degree that it reverberated in the soldierly spirit.

Nevertheless, the insistence on the separability of the soldier as digger and the defenses on which he labored almost daily in 1864–65 yielded in the end to the realization that earthworks had become a decisive military influence. As early as Gettysburg it could be seen that the armies were so balanced in the quality of their arms and soldiery, if one were given time to entrench, the other's assault would be almost sure to fail. During the Atlanta campaign Cox concluded that to repel attacks Sherman's army needed only fifteen minutes to dig its rifle pits. As Sherman's failed frontal assaults attested, Johnston's army needed no longer. At Cold Harbor Grant's massed columns, twenty-eight men deep, had shattered against Lee's defenses with a conclusiveness no one could deny. Stiles conceded that in its brevity, slaughter, and disproportion of losses it was "one of the notable battles of history," and he would shortly admit grudgingly: "It is fair to say that, after a while, the better men of the army, at least, learned to use without abusing the vantage ground of earthworks." Wainwright too eventually made his way to the nub of the issue: Those who dig, he admitted, see "that victory has been with the defensive." Hood remained both the exception and splendidly wrong. The prospect of being killed in a futile charge had become infinitely more troubling to the soldier's imagination than any burrowing in the earth. Spades were indeed trump.[24]

Digging was not a practice confined to the war's final years. McClellan had been an early proponent of the shovel, and Stevens reported of the 1862 Peninsula campaign on the Chickahominy:

> The division at once proceeded, as did all the other divisions in the army, to throw up earthworks; making slow advances at certain points by pushing these works further toward the front. . . . Day and night the men worked at the breastworks and bridges. One-third of the army was employed constantly at these works, and the immense lines of entrenchments were marvels of achievements in engineering.

As the reference to the pushing forward of works made clear, however, McClellan's framework remained that of formal siege warfare, and the men remained at that point unenthusiastic about any deviation from open warfare. Conversely, once the swing was under way, not even the last years of the war erased entirely the reluctance to excavate. Digging beyond the presence of the enemy remained anathema. When Hinman's Ohioans were sent to labor for 130 "slowly dragging days" on entrenchments being built to protect Murfreesboro, the "boys did the digging and the officers did the heavy standing around," and the "boys" returned to camp each night "in a thoroughly disgusted frame of mind." The soldier "was willing to endure hard marching and exposure to all the rigors of heat and cold and storm, for that was legitimate soldiering, but he drew the line at grubbing with pick and shovel for forty cents a day" when no Confederate attack was imminent. At the front, however, the evolution toward protected combat proceeded, roughly from enlisted men to officers, from the Western armies to the Eastern, from Federals to Confederates.[25]

Already intricate at Cold Harbor, entrenchments reached their most elaborate forms in the trench warfare of the Petersburg campaign of 1864–65. Soldiers entered that phase of the war looking backward and rejoicing that open warfare had been left behind—"I can stand two months of siege work; no more charging to be required of your humble sergeant-major"—but few continued for long to consider it a change for the better. Stiles spoke in staccato phrases of those who at Cold Harbor endured

> . . . The supreme discomfort and even suffering of "the lines." Thousands of men cramped up in a narrow trench, unable to go out, or to get up, or to stretch or to stand without danger to life and limb; unable to lie down, or to sleep, for lack of room and pressure of peril; night alarms, day attacks, hunger, thirst, supreme weariness, squalor, vermin, filth, disgusting odors everywhere; the weary night succeeded by the yet more weary day; the first glance over the way, at day dawn, bringing the sharpshooter's bullet singing past your ear or smashing through your skull, a man's life often exacted as the price of a cup of water from the spring.

At Petersburg the opposing fortified lines of trenches, protected by ditches, *abattis* (felled trees), and *chevaux-de-frise* (sharpened stakes), were so complex that they began to seem permanent. Here too men occupying them felt unaccustomed levels of physical discomfort. Weld wrote home in July 1864:

> Pleasant life we lead here, I can assure you. Yesterday we had our first rain [in] six weeks. . . . The trenches were half full of mud and water, as [were] all the officers' quarters. I slept last night in a perfect mud-hole, half drenched myself. Today we have a regular dog-day. Hot and sultry, a day that makes one feel dirty and sticky all over.[26]

Beyond the deterioration in conditions surrounding battle, combat now denied soldiers the leisurely recuperation almost invariably available in the first years of the war. As John Esten Cooke observed, the earlier pattern had featured big battles with rests between, "pitched battles once or twice a year, [when we] killed each other all day long . . . and then relapsed into gentlemanly repose and amity." Petersburg, however, was constant, grinding, all-destroying warfare. Soldiers had become accustomed to battles that rendered quick decisions for armies and individuals, ordinarily in a day, or three days at the most, but now combat had become "so incessant and so indecisive," as well as "mad and reckless." From the opening of the Wilderness campaign to the surrender at Appomattox, Michael Fitch noted, it was "a continuous battle." A Rhode Island soldier said that "no one was safe, even for an instant." Darkness no longer brought its accustomed respite; a novelty at Cold Harbor, night attacks became commonplace in the Petersburg trenches. Existence had become a matter of "living night and day within the 'valley of the shadow of death'."[27]

Grant's tenaciousness—his iron resolve to accept, even temporarily, no outcome unfavorable to his army and his awareness that he possessed the resources to persevere even while suffering high losses—had forced the change. No battle was decided faster than Cold Harbor, but no respite followed. Battles were no longer widely separated mountains climbing above the plain of inactivity but numerous hillocks crowded against a background of "continuous and bloody fighting." That deprived death of some of its earlier significance. When a Federal battery opened unexpectedly against the opposing line at Petersburg and a shell mortally wounded a Confederate, his last words were disconsolate: "This is rough on me. If I had been killed in battle I wouldn't have cared, but to be shot in a skirmish it's too bad." Worse, skirmishes had become continuous. The soldier had no time to prepare himself for death, and its setting was no longer one of special drama.[28]

Constant skirmishing combined with earthworks defenses to intensify sharpshooting. Wilkeson spoke for many soldiers in whom the original animus against sharpshooting remained robust; the sharpshooters' new prominence brought from him renewed denunciation in language equating them with lower life forms.

The picket-firing and sharpshooting at North Anna was exceedingly severe and murderous. We were greatly annoyed by it, and as a campaign cannot be decided by killing a few hundred enlisted men—killing them most unfairly and when they were of necessity exposed,—it did seem as though the sharpshooting pests should have been suppressed. Our sharpshooters were as bad as the Confederates, and neither . . . were of any account as far as decisive results were obtained. They could sneak around trees or lurk behind stumps, or cower in wells or in cellars, and from the safety of their lairs murder a few men. Put the sharpshooters in battle-line and they were no better, no more effective, than the infantry of the line, and they were not half as decent. There was an unwritten code of honor among the infantry that forbade the shooting of men while attending to the imperative calls of nature, and these sharpshooting brutes were constantly violating that rule. I hated sharpshooters, both Confederate and Union, in those days, and I was always glad to see them killed.

Wilkeson might have been slightly mollified when he discovered that not all sharpshooters exempted themselves from the demands of homage due courageous behavior. At Cold Harbor, thirsty Union soldiers broke from cover to fill their canteens under the fire of Confederate sharpshooters. As a pair of Federals was racing back, one was hit.

> Instantly he began to dig a little hollow . . . and instantly the Confederate sharpshooters went to work at him. The dust flew up on one side . . . and then on the other. . . . We called to him. He answered that his leg was broken below the knee by a rifle ball. . . . Looking through the embrasure, I . . . with quickening breath, felt that his minutes were numbered. [But] the comrade of the stricken soldier . . . left the rifle-pits on the run; the wounded man rose up and stood on one foot; the runner clasped him in his arms . . . and he was carried into our battery at full speed, and was hurried to the rear and to a hospital. To the honor of the Confederate sharpshooters, be it said, that when they . . . understood what was being done they ceased to shoot.[29]

But a change was under way; old restraints were withering. Expanded distances between combatants seem to have weakened their sense of combat as moral involvement and to have allowed entry to very different considerations. James Wilson noticed during the Vicksburg siege that though pickets at advanced posts never molested their counterparts within talking range, distance sharpshooting had begun to exercise "a strange fascination for men of a sporting turn of mind," and "no one seemed to feel any more compunction in taking a good shot at an unknown enemy than at a deer." At Port Hudson John DeForest, too, recorded a shift in combat's gravity: To relieve the monotony of the siege, some officers took up sharpshooting, and what had once been regarded as base behavior now "seemed like taking life in pure Gayety."[30]

Constraints were impaired from another quarter as well. As some were finding sniper-killing less reprehensible and more gratifying, others were adopting it as an essential component of soldiership. In one of Ambrose Bierce's short-stories, a Sherman scout, sent out to locate the enemy, discovered the Confederate rear guard. Before starting back with the intelligence he paused, tempted to open fire on the Southerners from his cover. "That would probably not affect the duration and result of the war," he reflected, echoing Wilkeson's reasoning—and then abandoning it, "but it is the business of the soldier to kill."[31]

The story was suggestive of a penetration to the level of the common soldier of that war of attrition being waged in Wilderness thickets and Petersburg trenches by Ulysses Grant. Beatty and Wilkeson might have continued to argue that one does not take lives when such deaths are inconsequential to the war's outcome (and Bierce's protagonist at least cited the point), but Grant's war insisted that no loss of soldier life was without significant effect on the results of the war. He may also have understood that continuous fighting would more firmly establish the habit of killing and would make distinctions more difficult, or at least raise the level of resistance to exceptions. If it were to be established that the soldier's function was to kill rather than to differentiate important and unimportant killings, and if he, like the Bierce character, were to accept that it was his "business"—rather than his "duty"—so to kill, the measure of success would be much simpler than those complex calculations of feeling and deportment required by courage's war. Being good at one's business is after all subject to quantitative measurement—in war, the numbers killed.

Reporting on the North African campaign of World War II, the correspondent Ernie Pyle noted a turn in the attitudes of combat soldiers with whom he had not spoken for some time:

> The most vivid change was the casual and workshop manner in which they talked about killing. They had made the psychological

transition from their normal belief that taking human life was sinful, over to a new professional outlook where killing was a craft. No longer was there anything morally wrong about killing. In fact, it was an admirable thing. I think I was so impressed by that new attitude because it hadn't been necessary for me to make the change along with them. As a noncombatant, my own life was in danger only by occasional chance or circumstance. Consequently I didn't need to think of killing in personal terms, and killing to me was still murder.

Certainly no shift as comprehensive as this occurred in the Civil War; few of its soldiers ceased to count certain kinds of combat deaths as murder. But it was also clear that some developed a sense of killing as a craft and of the numbers of dead as an index to their mastery of that craft. Burdette of the 47th Illinois, a volunteer at eighteen, was one who absorbed the harshness of the war's later years. In language unlike that of 1861, he concluded that recruits were paid to kill; that was their "duty"—and their "business." "Killing is the object of war." Thus, when in its last battle of the war his regiment overran a Confederate fort, he proclaimed, "We won it fairly. We are the best killers. . . . That establishes the righteousness of any cause."[32]

Most soldiers departed less sharply from the values of 1861–62. To be sure, they too found increasingly oppressive and sometimes intolerable the conditions of trench war—greater physical hardship, loss of movement, changes in the nature and duration of battle, the use against them of more powerful and impersonal weapons—and more than a few worried that combat had irrevocably changed.

Those of short memory or limited experience reacted by setting the present against the past, mourning the passing of the war's earlier phase and sometimes restoring to it the pristine romance of Fort Sumter days. Author Joseph Kirkland, a Union soldier, would later speak through one of his characters in denunciation of the "fortuitous death by an unseen missile from an unknown hand" and the "simple, mechanical, dull, dogged machine-work" to which "the old art of war" had given way: "no more of the exhilarating clash of personal contest." Blackford found at Petersburg "a mode of warfare strangely differing from the dashing cavalry service on the outposts. Instead of the movement and excitement of rapid marches, sudden attacks, and thrilling personal adventures, alternating with periods of gay social intercourse, I was now thrown into the very jaws of the grim death struggle in the trenches of a vigorously besieged town, and was to begin a strange sort of warfare under ground."[33]

Another reaction, sometimes partner to this lamentation for a spectral past, was the determination to continue to express in one's actions the old values, no matter how altered the conditions of warfare. At Cold Harbor the chief of the Richmond Howitzers' ambulance corps, the "Old Doctor," decided to leave the trenches and seek water at a spring. Alarmed, Stiles "reminded him that it was not quite dark and the sharpshooters would be apt to pay their respects to him." Would he not depart via the "covered way" rather than climbing directly from the trench? He would not: "I can't do it, Adjutant. [The covered way] is dirty; a gentleman can't walk in it, sir." On his return a Union rifleman shot off his thumb at its upper joint.[34]

Some, less disdainful of reality, nonetheless tried to circumscribe its effects, and buttress their own spirits, by attributing reality to enemy contrivance. Hunter insisted that while trench warfare was the last thing to which Southerners should have resorted, it perfectly suited Yankee "habits, tempers and genius." Most, however, unable to ignore the new reality and realizing that those in the opposing trenches enjoyed it no more than they, struggled to confine it within the old framework. Blackford, for example, hated trench life and denounced trench war's most prominent weapon, the mortar (a muzzle-loading cannon of stubby barrel used to throw shells short distances at high angles), almost as if *it* had become *the* enemy, one infinitely more vicious than the Federals.

> These mortar shells were the most disgusting, low-lived things imaginable; there was not a particle of the sense of honor about them; they would go rolling about and prying into the most private places in a sneaking sort of way. They would be tossed over from the trenches of the other side just as if they were balls thrown by hand, not a bit faster did they come, and then they would roll down the parapet into the trench and if the trench was on a slope, down the trench they would roll, the men standing up flat against the sides or flattening themselves on the ground to one side of the shell's path, each moment expecting the deadly explosion of the nasty, hissing, sputtering thing.

It was a narrative of fright, revulsion, anger, and disorientation, but not even the mortar could deny courage its role.

Then when one set of men were passed they would jump up and look down the trench at the track of the shell and shout with laughter at their comrades below whose turn had come to lay low. Then came an explosion, and then two or three dead bodies would be carried by and all go on as before. Very frequently men would pick up these shells and pitch them out of the trench, for which they would receive unbounded applause from their comrades.[35]

Soon, however, Union mortar batteries were "tossing over" 300-pound shells. One that arrived in the night sounding "like a railroad express" landed twenty paces away, providentially failed to explode, but still shook the ground "like an earthquake." In the face of such power, Blackford's attempts to restore the soldier as the war's principal actor, or to reclaim for him a power at least commensurate with that of the weapons being employed against him, became unconvincing even to their author. In a discussion of trench war's resort to mining and underground explosives, he granted that the soldier's earlier powers of adaptation had weakened, that resiliency had grown thin, and that in some cases composure had been lost.

It is very curious how soldiers become so familiar with one kind of danger, to which they have been exposed, as to disregard it almost entirely, and yet become demoralized when danger in a new form presents itself. Our men did not mind musketry and field artillery after the first two or three battles, but when they came under fire from the big guns on the gun-boats below Richmond in 1862, they became nervous at seeing large trees cut off clean and whirled bottom upwards. To this they became accustomed. Then the mortar shells came, at the siege of Petersburg, and in time became familiar to them, but when the explosion at the crater occurred, a veritable panic ensued.

To have the very ground on which they stood blown up under them, without a chance for life or a chance to retaliate, was something so new and so terrible that the bravest turned pale. Every one of them was sure there were two hundred kegs of gunpowder right under his feet, and for days after the explosion not a laugh nor a song was to be heard along the trenches. Anyone familiar with troops can tell the spirit they are in exactly, by walking along the lines, and can catch from the conversation he hears in passing what is on their minds. In this case nothing was talked about but mines: whether a fellow would be killed when he was first lifted aloft, or whether he would know what was going on as he went whirling through the air, and how disagreeable it would be to fall from such a height on the hard ground.[36]

Soldiers sought relief in counteraction, however ineffectual. When a Confederate blacksmith devised an auger that would bore into Petersburg's red-clay soil, the men became convinced that if the holes so produced retained water there was no danger that Union sappers could be creating beneath them a cavern for explosives. "The contrivance took like wildfire. Men sat up all night working at these holes. . . . The men seemed never to tire of sinking [them]." Blackford recognized that the enterprise was desperate: the bore-hole "did not really render the position more secure, but it gave hope . . . and this at that moment was all-important."[37]

No one need doubt the harshness of trench life. After six weeks of it—"sleeping in a pit" and contracting malaria—Blackford, ordinarily the most buoyant of soldiers but in September 1864 fatigued and fevered, was sent home by a Confederate army surgeon. John DeForest noted the same limit of endurance during the siege of Port Hudson: Federal soldiers who had previously done well in open battle nevertheless broke after six weeks in the trenches, that "lazy, monotonous, sickening, murderous, unnatural, uncivilized mode of being."[38]

Both armies realized the toll of trench life at Petersburg and tried to reduce it through the rotation of units. Union policy varied widely—Weld's Massachusetts regiment spent four days in the front-line trenches, two in the support trenches, and then two in rest at the rear; Allen's Rhode Islanders were relieved first after three days and nights at the front, later after two—but few Union soldiers were compelled to remain a week in the trenches without respite. Confederates were less fortunate. By mid-1864 the Northern superiority in numbers had placed such pressure on the Petersburg defenders that the Confederate command could not alternate units, and some regiments passed months in the trenches. When in November 1864 Owen's artillery battalion was ordered from the trenches after six months there, its members greeted the news as a deliverance: "We rejoice in breathing once more the pure air of the woods and fields, and having the pleasure of stretching our limbs without the risk of receiving a rifleman's bullet."[39]

Those were harsh lives indeed, harsher on the Confederate side than on the Union side, but, it should be recorded, seldom touching on either side that order of severity that would come to characterize conditions on the Western front during World War I. Even in the final stages of the Civil War the boundaries of military discipline, however expanded beyond those of 1861, could not always confine soldier attempts to fashion their own relief. Neither discipline nor the enlargement of combat could, for example, completely stifle local truces. Hunter wrote of such instances:

> When the sun came out in fitful gleams and at long intervals, the men would swarm on the parapets, first having established a truce with their friends across the way, whose breastworks fronted theirs some 75 or 100 yards distant. Johnny Reb would get up in the morning and poke his head out of his hollow . . .
>
> Billy Yank! O—B-i-l-l-y—Y-a-n-k!
> Well, Johnny R-e-b?
> Don't shoot! it's a truce. . . .
> All right. . . .
>
> After a good sun-bath and a stretching of limbs the handkerchiefs were taken down and the warning cry of "Rats to your holes!" caused the soldiers of both sides to dodge down out of sight, and then if one poked his head above the works for even a second he would be sure to have an ounce of lead in it.

Truces of a lesser order appeared in one section of the trenches before Atlanta; early each evening Union soldiers halted their fire so that they could listen to concerts offered by a Confederate cornet player. Sometimes Confederate soldiers even slipped away from the Petersburg trenches to take young women riding, walking, or dancing.[40]

Still, neither formal nor informal efforts could balance the disintegrative effects of trench life, especially on Southern soldiers. Hunter put it bluntly: "This mole-like existence was killing the men." Stiles saw the harsh results in those who survived. He and his comrades, who had remained throughout the Petersburg campaign in the quiet and safety of the Confederate artillery reserve, felt guilt as they contrasted their condition with that of those in the trenches:

154

Especially was this feeling intensified when . . . Mahone's division, which had been manning a very trying part of the Petersburg lines, was brought [out]. We thought we had before seen men with the marks of hard service upon them; but the appearance of this division . . . made us realize, for the first time, what our comrades in the hottest Petersburg lines were undergoing. We were shocked at the condition, the complexion, the expression of the men, and of the officers, too, even the field officers; indeed we could scarcely realize that the unwashed, uncombed, unfed and almost unclad creatures we saw were officers of rank and reputation in the army.

That mole-like existence had strained and broken not only men's bodies but their allegiance to many of the ideas with which they had begun the war.[41]

8

Unraveling Convictions

A s Civil War battles revealed by degrees that bravery was no
guarantor of victory, that rifled muskets and defensive works
could thwart the most spirited charge, soldiers sensed the insufficiency of courage and began to move away from many of their
initial convictions.

One of the first tenets to be discarded was the one holding
that exceptional combat courage deserved special protection,
even to the point of suspending efforts to kill the bravest of the
enemy. Indeed, certain commanders had opposed such deference
almost from the outset. Stonewall Jackson always urged special
attention of another sort to the enemy's most courageous soldiers:

> At the battle of Port Republic [June 9, 1862] an officer com-
> manding a regiment of Federal soldiers and riding a snowwhite
> horse was very conspicuous for his gallantry. He frequently ex-
> posed himself to the fire of our men in the most reckless way. So
> splendid was this man's courage that General Ewell, one of the
> most chivalrous gentlemen . . . at some risk to his own life, rode
> down the line and called to his men not to shoot the man on the
> white horse. After a while, however, the officer and the white
> horse went down. A day or two after, when General Jackson
> learned of the incident, he sent for General Ewell and told him
> not to do such a thing again; that this was no ordinary war, and
> the brave and gallant Federal officers were the very kind that must
> be killed. "Shoot the brave officers and the cowards will run away
> and take the men with them."[1]

While Ewell continued to uphold courage as the primary virtue wherever demonstrated, Jackson focused on the way courage bonded enemies, and he wanted no part of anything that might vitiate the combativeness of his troops. He also comprehended, as few did so early in the war, that to obliterate the most courageous of the foe was to demoralize those whose discipline drew on their example.

Other officers, without Jackson's relentless certainty in the matter, moved in his direction as the war went on. An example was the commander of the 8th Alabama at Antietam.

> One incident occurred here which I have always thought was an exhibition of bravery that surpassed even the gallant Frenchman who has been immortalized by Victor Hugo, in the vivid picture he draws in *Les Miserables,* of the destruction of the old guard at Waterloo. When the enemy were scurrying back . . . over the hill which was to give them protection, they were completely demoralized; very few used their muskets as they retreated, but there was one man who never marched out of common-time. He marched as deliberately as if on drill . . . loading while going eight or ten steps, then turning and firing. Again and again he fired as he went up the hill and when he got to the top, all his comrades being out of sight . . . he fired for the last time, and then, turning[,] he slapped his hand on his posterior, to indicate the contempt in which he had us. I am sorry to say I did not at the moment appreciate, as sentiment suggests I should have done, the gallantry of this man. While he was walking up that hillside alone, firing at us and his balls were whistling close by, I shouted to my men, "I will give the man a furlough that will shoot that rascal!" At that time I meant business. The bravest of the enemy were the men I wanted to kill—they set bad examples, and that was no time for sentiment.[2]

That logic soon made targets of the enemy's color-bearers, soldiers whose courage had won them positions of honor as carriers of the regimental standards around which men might be inspired to charge or to rally. By the time of Fredericksburg, a Confederate officer was ordering his men, "Now, shoot down the colors," and by 1865 it had become acceptable practice to direct fire upon color-bearers even as they lay on the ground. ("And how we did keep pouring the bullets into them, the flags for a mark! . . . The flags continued to tumble and rise.") Often every member of the color guard, ordinarily one corporal from each of the regiment's ten companies, was shot down before the battle was over. Early in the war soldiers had coveted such positions. By 1863, though by then additional incentives were offered—in the 20th New York, exemption from guard and picket, company drills and roll call; duty of no more than three hours a day—few any longer volunteered. In such brusque ways, soldiers discovered that a war of attrition left less and less room for concessions to the enemy's courage.[3]

A related casualty was the conviction that courageous behavior imparted battlefield protection. Experience taught the opposite: The cowards either remained at home or found ways to avoid battle; the bravest "went farthest and stand longest under fire"; the best died. In January 1863 General Frank Paxton of the Stonewall Brigade complained: "Out of the fifteen field officers elected last spring, five have been killed and six wounded. . . . In these losses are many whom we were always accustomed to regard as our best men." Three months later he again found it "sad, indeed, to think how many good men we have lost. Those upon whom we all looked as distinguished for purity of character as men, and for gallantry as soldiers, seem to have been the first victims." After thirty days of Wilderness combat, Colonel Theodore Lyman of Meade's staff deplored Grant's strategy: "[T]here has been too much assaulting, this campaign! . . . The best officers and men are liable, by their greater gallantry, to be first disabled."[4]

Those in the ranks noted the phenomenon principally by its result: a decline in the quality of their leadership. John Haskell, an artillery commander in Lee's army, was bitter that those who took such care to protect their own lives, "the dodgers," by virtue of their seniority had been promoted to replace dead or disabled officers who had "taken no pains" to preserve their lives. By such routes soldiers moved far from their original conceptions of ostentatious courage as protection and assurance of victory to the realization that it was instead an invitation to death. A few might attempt to find a new virtue in that reality—Charles Russell Lowell, contemplating the death in battle of Robert Gould Shaw, decided that the best colonel of the best black regiment *had to die,* for "it was a sacrifice we owed"—but most simply felt its demoralization.[5]

Godliness as a protective mantle shared the same decline. For every story in the war's first months about a pocket Bible that had stopped an otherwise fatal bullet, there was in later years a matching tale of the opposite implication—that, for example, of the Union colonel who told his men that the replica Virgin Mary around his neck would protect him, and minutes later was mortally wounded. Hunter said of the Confederate rank-and-file in 1864–65: "The soldiers naturally distrusted the efficacy of prayer when they found that the most devout Christians were as liable to be shot as the most hardened sinner, and that a deck of cards would stop a bullet as effectively as a prayer book."[6]

As convictions about the potency and protectiveness of courage yielded to the suspicion that special courage had become the mark of death, another of the war's original precepts—that the courageous death was the good death; that it had about it some nobler quality reflected, for example, in the smiles of courageous dead and withheld from frowning cowardly dead—also failed the test of observation. As Wilkeson's experiences in the Army of the Potomac taught him, "Almost every death on the battle-field is different." He knew a soldier who had died quickly and whose face had only then become "horribly distorted," suggesting to passers-by a long agony that he had never experienced. The countenances of other dead had been "wreathed in smiles," allowing survivors to assure themselves that their comrades had died happy, but "I do not believe that the face of a dead soldier, lying on a battle-field, ever truthfully indicates the mental or physical anguish, or peacefulness of mind, which he suffered or enjoyed before his death. . . . It goes for nothing. One death was as painless as the other."[7] Despondency sprang from that phrase "It goes for nothing," for the experience of war was teaching him, and so many others, that the rewards of courage were far less significant and the costs far higher than they had imagined and that the individual's powers of control were far feebler than they had supposed.

Doubt that the original equations were still valid sometimes arose in mundane fashion. A Massachusetts soldier noticed that those who persevered to complete arduous marches with the column were often "rewarded" by being placed on guard duty before the stragglers reached camp. Blackford, who like other Confederate cavalrymen was required to furnish his own mount, realized that if one were forthrightly courageous in battle, one's horse was more likely to be killed. From month to month replacements became more and more difficult and expensive to procure, and failure to find one resulted in reassignment to the infantry. "Such a penalty for gallantry was terribly demoralizing."[8]

Though disconcerting, such challenges to the notion that courage permitted the soldier to control his life and death were pinpricks set beside the challenges presented by the failed charge. The rapidity with which great numbers of men were killed at Antietam and the ease with which they were cut down at Fredericksburg and Gettysburg produced gloomy reflection as soldiers contemplated a war that had inexplicably recast its actors as victims. Minds groped to comprehend why courage had failed to secure victory and in the face of such disastrous results began, hesitantly and diversely, to move away from conventional thought and language.

Lieutenant William Wood of the 19th Virginia was one of the 15,000 who made Pickett's charge. Prior to the attack he and his men were ordered to lie down, exposed both to a boiling sun and to the fire of Federal artillery batteries. (A Napoleon cannon could hurl a 12-pound ball a mile.) When they were brought to attention to begin the attack, some of the men immediately dropped of "seeming sunstroke," but for the charge itself Wood had only praise. It was a "splendid array" and a "beautiful line of battle." But it failed: "Down! down! go the boys." As he reached that spot of ground beyond which no Confederate could go, he suffered a sense of personal shame: "Stopping at the fence, I looked to the right and left and felt we were disgraced." The assault's failure bluntly told him that he and his comrades had not done enough, and yet he knew that they had done everything they had earlier been sure would carry the victory. The result was a paralyzing disbelief: "With one single exception I witnessed no cowardice, and yet we had not a skirmish line [still standing]." Courage should have conquered![9]

John Dooley also charged that day, with the 1st Virginia, but his reactions carried him beyond Wood. Those around him who survived the Union shelling, feeling the special impotence that comes to infantry who have no way to respond to a harrowing fire, were "frightened out of our wits." And then the charge: To Dooley it became simply that which opened the "work of death." "Volley after volley of crashing musket balls sweep through the line and mow us down like wheat before the scythe." Only thirty-five of his regiment's 155 men escaped bullets and shells, and

Dooley, with his shattered thighs, was not one of them. "I tell you, there is no romance in making one of these charges," he concluded; "the enthusiasm of ardent breasts in many cases *ain't there*." He realized that the spirit of heroism no longer possessed the men; he mildly regretted its departure, but he had lost confidence that its presence would have reversed the outcome. He had not yet developed any clear vision of why failure came to such charges, but what emerged was a sense of his loss of control. His thoughts had turned from his performance to his survival: "Oh, if I could just come out of this charge safely how thankful *would I be!*" By such rough stages did soldier thought evolve.[10]

Even before the assault at Cold Harbor, soldiers entering their fourth year of war understood perfectly what the result would be. They knew that the Confederates had had thirty-six hours in which to prepare their positions and that by that stage of the war *any* attack under such circumstances was doomed. Charles Wainwright thought it absurd that Grant should simply repeat here the order "which has been given at all such times on this campaign, viz: 'to attack along the whole line.'" On the eve of battle, Union soldiers who had glimpsed some part of the Southern defenses or heard them described by the "news-gatherers" were, Wilkeson reported, depressed: "Some of the men were sad, some indifferent; some so tired of the strain on their nerves that they wished they were dead and their troubles over . . . and though they had resolved to do their best, there was no eagerness for the fray, and the impression among the intelligent soldiers was that the task cut out for them was more than men could accomplish." Indeed, numbers of soldiers wrote their names on small pieces of paper and pinned them to their coats, in a hope, signaling hopelessness, that their bodies would not go unidentified. On June 15, 1864, when Grant's army finally reached the James at a cost of 60,000 casualties, a number equivalent to the size of Lee's army at the outset of the campaign, the Union regular Augustus Meyers felt the "gloomy and depressing effect" of such "awful sacrifices without any advantages." Ira Dodd became convinced that following its attacks in the Wilderness and at Cold Harbor, the Army of the Potomac was never again the same.[11]

Not all soldiers felt compelled to abandon or even to modify early-war views. George Stevens of the 77th New York was one who remained steadfast: "Never was heroic valor exhibited on a grander scale than had been manifested by the Army of the Potomac throughout this long struggle, in which every man's life seemed doomed. [T]heir illustrious valor and never failing courage must sooner or later meet with their reward."[12] But change was afoot. Northern civilians might invoke the courage of the attackers at Cold Harbor as if it continued to constitute a substitute for victory, but soldiers contemplating the deaths of friends, their own narrow escapes, and the seeming uselessness of such charges began to speak of "futile courage" and said no more of "sublime courage."

Swelling conviction of courage's insufficiency bred new doubts about commanders whose virtues encompassed but did not extend beyond bravery. James Nisbet was unhappy when Hood replaced Johnston, for he considered Hood "simply a brave, hard fighter." Thus, in courage's depreciating currency, the ultimate accolade had fallen to faint praise. Hood might possess "a Lion's Heart," but it came to count more that he had "a Wooden Head." On the other side that summer, Theodore Lyman, too, noted changing attitudes toward those diminishing numbers of officers whose impulse was to "dash in": "You hear people say, 'Oh, everyone is brave enough; it is the head that is needed.'"[13]

No longer was courage strong enough to stand alone and thus to serve as its own reward. At the outset both sides had considered medals unnecessary. That notion was akin to the view of some Southern gentlemen and respectable organizers of Union regiments that their own willingness to remain "humble" privates constituted the highest expression of self-effacing patriotism. External signs of virtue or achievement were unimportant, and medals were in any case the insignia of an effete and vainglorious European militarism. But as the war evolved and the centrality of courageous behavior began to erode, agitations arose in both armies for the formal recognition of bravery.[14]

In November 1862 the Confederate Congress authorized the President to bestow medals and badges of distinction on soldiers who had demonstrated special battle courage. Officers were to be cited for individual acts, while the men of each company were to select one of their number for a decoration. Little was done, however. Jefferson Davis was uninterested, and in any case medals were difficult to fabricate in a Confederacy whose resources were being stretched thinner every day. As a substitute of sorts, names were to be inscribed on a Roll of Honor to be read at dress parades, but, given the accelerating tempo of combat, few regiments were able to make time for such a ritual. Fighters increasingly grew to regret that the political leadership seemed simply to assume the Southern soldier's courage and made so little effort to reward extraordinary instances of it. William Owen dined at a Richmond restaurant with English friends, including a Captain Hewitt of the Royal Navy who had won a Victoria Cross at Inkerman. After hearing Hewitt's story, the Confederate complained, "What a pity our boys have no V.C.'s to look foward to! They are doing things every day that deserve decorations."[15]

Regret became vexation in the case of another device that some wished to employ to recognize special courage: promotions for valor. Apparently neither Davis nor Lee permitted them, a stance that raised some anger among the rank-and-file. John Haskell told of two Confederate soldiers who had performed on the battlefield with great bravery. Both had suffered wounds. Their superiors granted them sick leave but sent them off with no word of commendation. When they reached their homes on a stretch of North Carolina coast occupied by Union forces, both took the oath of loyalty and remained out of the war, a loss, Haskell was sure, to be counted against a stingily unappreciative high command.[16]

The situation on the Union side was different but, from the men's perspective, hardly more favorable. Medals and promotions came much more frequently than in the Confederate service—too often for many observers. When the 27th Maine's tour of duty was about to expire just prior to the battle of Gettysburg, President Abraham Lincoln authorized the award of the Medal of Honor to each soldier who would reenlist. Three hundred agreed to remain on duty as "emergency troops," but medals were issued in error to all 864 members of the regiment. The 27th Maine had seen no battle before Gettysburg; its remnant played no role at Gettysburg. Similarly, so many brevet (i.e., honorary) promotions were awarded, Augustus Meyers complained, that they "seemed to lose dignity" and became objects of ridicule. His friends in the ranks began to refer to mules as "brevet horses" and to camp followers as "brevet soldiers." Such awards, moreover, seemed seldom to recognize battlefield bravery. *Field* promotions were almost as rare as in the Confederate Army.[17]

Joshua Chamberlain must rank as one of the Civil War's most stalwart warriors. He fought in at least twenty battles and was wounded six times. On his "day of glory," the bayonet charge into which he propelled his Maine soldiers, their ammunition exhausted, saved Gettysburg's Little Round Top from capture by fiercely fighting Alabamians. General Charles Griffin of the regular army called it a "magnificent sight" to watch him in battle, dashing from one flank to the other, leading assault after assault. Chamberlain's superiors frequently cited his actions in their battle reports and recommended him for promotion to general officer's rank. Yet such recognition did not come until he suffered his fifth wound at Petersburg. In the belief that he was dying and, apparently, that his reputation as a brave soldier required official reinforcement, he asked to be promoted, not for himself but "for the gratification of his family and friends." Grant conferred a battlefield promotion, one of two times he agreed to do so.[18]

Chamberlain was convinced that he had remained unpromoted for so long because he lacked influential friends in Washington, and many others complained that political connections were as nefarious an influence on Union promotions as Southerners thought seniority on their own. The letters of Brigadier General Alpheus Williams reveal graphically the tensions developing between older notions of self-sustaining courage and new desires that others formally acknowledge one's courage. In the Shenandoah Valley campaign of 1862, he remained self-contained: "I court nobody—reporters nor commanders—but try to do my whole duty and trust it will all come out right." He soon began to worry, however, that his accomplishment might require advertisement. He lamented that had he not left the area the day before, he would have been the Union commander during the first battle of Winchester. "I think I could have captured all Jackson's guns and been a major general!"—a selfish thought, he conceded, but the kind prominent in the minds of many around him. Other generals cared little for the common cause. Staff generals "gobble up all the glory." Washington bestowed commands only on its political favorites.

Williams took occasional satisfaction from the tributes paid him from below. When the officers of one of his brigades presented him with a sword, belt, and sash and the enlisted men, hearing of it, offered a gift of their own ("not a usual thing"), he was moved. "You can hardly realize how attached I have become to many of these officers who have been with me through so many trials, privations, and dangers." The love of the men, he professed, "is my chief support and encouragement," to be preferred far above the favors of the government.

Still, he could not renounce his hope of favor. When he was denied promotion, the respect of the men counted for little; in the face of such disappointment, he did not know, he said, whether he could "hold out." He began sending his own battle reports *sub rosa* to friendly editors of hometown Detroit newspapers. He encouraged his officers' efforts to memorialize the President in his behalf. He vowed "a paper war" on Meade until the general finally amended his Gettysburg report to mention Williams's name. ("We . . . lost more men on the morning of July 3rd than the 2nd Division to which he gives the whole credit.") He seemed perpetually angry at correspondents and unable to decide whether they slighted him because they were congenital liars or because other generals had bought them. He grew bitter that another brigadier also passed over for promotion but of lesser military accomplishment than Williams should have been able to resign ("in face of the enemy and within sound of his guns"), go to Washington, play politics, and come away with major general's stars. "I stay and am never thought of."

He was upset too that civilians did not realize that the war was being waged not for Union but to make heroes of "charlatans and braggarts," to the neglect of the truly meritorious.

> People at home can't see why a man's pride and spirit [are] wounded and diminished. Let them work and toil long months under every exposure, doing, in the written judgment of their superiors, their full duty in all respects, and then let them see dozens of sneaks and drivellers put over their heads.

He threatened to resign, professedly because he suspected that "the discouragement and depression the government has put upon me is . . . unfitting me for that zealous and ambitious discharge of duty which is properly due from every man holding the responsible position I do." Finally, Sherman recommended his promotion—but to no avail. Williams blamed those at home and in the Michigan Congressional delegation (Senator Zachariah Chandler in particular), who had done him "greater injustice and personal dishonor" by failing to advance his promotion, and in the end he was compelled to settle for a brevet major generalship.

Alpheus Williams had detested the "low grovelling lick-spit-tle subserving and pandering" to the press and government nec-essary to win promotion, but while never ceasing to denounce such tactics, he had himself employed many of them, at high cost to his pride, his self-respect, and his sense of solidarity with his officers and men. The initial context of his war, that of the in-dividual testing himself, had proved inadequate; courage and duty, he had concluded, could be validated only by formal rec-ognition within both military and civilian spheres.[19]

Another consequence of the new complexity of combat ex-perience following the displacement of the simple courage of 1861–62 was that it allowed distinctions impermissible earlier. With the awareness that the peripheries of battle could be just as trying as combat itself and that the moral nature of the in-dividual determined far less than supposed, those strict defini-tions of the courageous and cowardly began to blur and to merge. In early September 1862, at the outset of Lee's first invasion of the North, Alexander Hunter recorded that there was still "no sign of our commissary wagons and not a mouthful of food had the men that day. Some of our best soldiers were left [behind] on account of sickness, and many began to straggle from ranks to seek in farm-houses along the route something to allay their gnawing hunger. . . . [E]ach one was a serious loss, for we never saw any of them until after the campaign." Soldiers without shoes also fell out, and other straggling could be traced to the weakness of the body—diarrhea, fever, anemia—rather than the weakness of the will.[20] Those remaining in the ranks, all of whom had at least brushed with illness and hunger, thus came to temper their views of those who dropped out. Courage was not always at is-sue. Men could be lost for reasons reflecting no cowardice.

From the shared sense that the rigors of war were broader and the terrors of combat sharper than expected, a readiness to narrow the definition of cowardice arose. Burdette reported that a private in the 47th Illinois was a good soldier in every way but one: Despite all his efforts to "play the man," he ran from every battle! When he later returned, each time with an excuse no one believed, many in the regiment were angry at first, but they came to realize that he measured well against those who feigned illness or exhaustion, stopped to tie shoes during the charge, arranged hospital details, or in other ways avoided or moved themselves beyond the range of charges of cowardice. He marched into every battle. He was brave until blood appeared, and then he fled. "He was beaten in every fight but he went in" every time. "This man was a coward," but "a good coward." Burdette realized that such a formulation begged questions each day growing more difficult: "But who are the cowards? And how do we distinguish them from the heroes? How does God tell?" Uncertain, he agreed that the man should not be punished, joining others whose anger dissipated as they concluded that "God never intended that man should kill anybody." Angered by a soldier who faltered several times during a charge at Fredericksburg, Abner Small pulled him to his feet and called him a coward, but when the man in obvious agony explained that "his legs would not obey him," Small apologized. Soldiers, he concluded, "were heroes or cowards in spite of themselves." Long Bill Blevins of the 21st Georgia knew that his captain was authorized to detail one man as company cook, and he asked for the job: "Captain, I can't stand the shooting, and I'm afraid I might run,—and disgrace my name." The incident was reported without censure. Perhaps soldiers were coming to feel the disdain of one unable to master his fear less than the relief that another had confessed, in actions or words, to the fear that all shared.[21]

By 1864 the new tolerance for men whose behavior would earlier have brought condemnation had achieved informal incorporation in the military justice system. Colonel Rufus Dawes of the 6th Wisconsin was summoned to head the Fifth Corps's examining board. There "cowards met no mercy. They were dismissed and their names published throughout the land, a fate more terrible than death to a proud spirited soldier." But the board broke with the past in acknowledging that the war was now one in which brave men could be overcome by fear for their lives: The "unexampled [Wilderness] campaign of sixty continuous days, the excitement, exhaustion, hard work and loss of sleep broke down great numbers of men who had received no wounds in battle. Some who began the campaign with zealous and eager bravery, ended it with nervous and feverish apprehension of danger in the ascendancy. Brave men were shielded if their records on other occasions justified another [chance], which ordinarily resulted well." Cowards would continue to meet no mercy, but when did a man become a coward? When he faltered a second time? A third time?[22]

Experience that altered soldier definitions of cowardice perforce modified definitions of courage. The most dramatic example was the final dissolution of the previously vital linkage between courage and the charge.

On November 26, 1863, General George Gordon Meade launched an offensive against Lee's Army of Northern Virginia. The Union commander was outmaneuvered, however, and his Army of the Potomac quickly ran up against the Confederates strongly posted in the small valley of Mine Run, Virginia. On November 28, Meade probed Lee's position and prepared a large-scale assault. Meanwhile, Federal rank-and-file had an opportunity to judge for themselves the strength of the defenses. "All felt that it would be madness to assault," Robert Carter of the 22nd Massachusetts said; "I felt death in my very bones all day." George Bicknell of the 5th Maine wrote that there was not "a man in our command who did not realize his position. Not one who . . . did not see the letters [of] death before his vision. . . . [N]ever before nor since had such an *universal* fate seemed to hang over a command." Fortunately, one who agreed was Gouverneur Warren, the commander of the Second Corps; completing a reconnaissance, he reported to Meade that, contrary to his earlier judgment, he considered an attack hopeless. Some members of Meade's staff, thinking perhaps that so much of their planning was going for nothing, insisted that the Confederate works could be carried, but Meade canceled the assault and on December 1 ordered his army back across the Rapidan, a retreat into winter quarters.[23]

Observers quickly characterized Meade's brief campaign as failed, maladroit, and weak-willed, but the Union ranks celebrated their commander's decision as if it were a great victory. "The enemy is too strong! We shall not charge!" "Oh," Bicknell sighed, "such a sense of relief as overspread those men, cannot even be imagined." Lyman praised his superior's courage in ordering withdrawal: Meade had only to "snap his fingers" and there would have been "ten thousand wretched, mangled creatures" lying on the valley's slopes—and praise of Meade for having "tried hard." Earlier in the war audacity in attack had caught much of what men thought important in that word "courage"; now at the close of 1863, to some, courage, turned on its head, had become the will to renounce the charge.[24]

9

The New Severity

Aware of the fragility of their armies, military authorities struggled throughout the war to tighten discipline, but their efforts took on a new intensity in 1863 and 1864 as they sought to counter plummeting soldier enthusiasm for battle.

Change was essential in the matter of officer elections. As part of its reorganization in the spring of 1862, the Confederate Army permitted new field officer elections, with results even more exasperating than commanders had thought possible. Election campaigns seemed to absorb the full attention of numerous units. Challengers promised that if they were elected, the men would be spared exposure to heavy enemy fire and delivered from all rigorous interpretation of the regulations. That was an appealing platform, and many incumbents who had attempted to establish discipline were turned out. Blackford found his captaincy contested by an orderly sergeant who promised the foot-sore company that in exchange for its votes he would secure its transfer from the infantry to the artillery! To him, any solicitation of votes was demeaning, so Blackford simply walked away; he secured an Engineers commission and worked on the construction of a pontoon bridge across the James until called to J. E. B. Stuart's staff.[1]

Clearly the cohesiveness of the army was at stake. Six months later the Confederate government instituted officer examinations, which gradually acquired force. In late 1863 Francis Dawson, an Englishman well connected to the Pegram family and a

member of Longstreet's staff, discovered that the general's rec-
ommendation for his promotion to captain was no longer decisive. Secretary of War Seddon would not exempt him, and he
was subjected to written and oral examinations—questions sent
from Richmond, questions put to him by a three-man board—
before his commission came through.[2]

Still, the Confederacy did not abolish company elections until the last months of the war, and the army's command structure
was never able to control the selection of officers as fully as it
wished. Balloting declined, but how slowly and confusingly the
balance tipped was patent in the case of James Nisbet. In early
1863 he was recommended for promotion to colonel, contingent
upon his ability to raise a new regiment. Returning to Macon,
he advertised in the dailies of the state, scrutinized letters, and
selected applicants, who in turn were supposed to recruit companies or squads. Critical to his effort was his ability to appoint
as officers veterans of proven capability. "The former method of
electing officers could not be relied on at this stage of the struggle," he said. Elections "struck at the very root of that stern discipline, without which new recruits cannot be converted into efficient soldiers." But the Assistant Secretary of War balked on this
point: The law required elections. Adamant, Nisbet carried the
dispute to Jefferson Davis, who, impressed by his temperament,
granted him authority to select the officers of the 66th Georgia.[3]

The Union moved more forcefully on this matter, instituting
officer examinations in July 1861. Although new regiments continued for a considerable time to elect their officers, and state
governors frequently exercised their power to insert their own
candidates, by 1863 balloting had largely given way to advance-
ment by merit, as defined and located by commanders rather
than the men.[4]

Those volunteers in the ranks felt the new grip through the
tightening of indirect pressures and the simple, direct enforcement of long-neglected regulations. After Gettysburg the band
of the 26th North Carolina, whose musicians, Moravians from
Salem, considered it an "independent adjunct" of the regiment
"bound by moral obligation rather than military regulation,"
discovered that General Henry Heth no longer agreed. "Indig-
nant but helpless," they were denied leave and thereafter treated
like conscripts. By 1864 Fifer Bardeen had seen five battles—three large, two "fizzles"—and, remaining curious, had be-

come accustomed to setting out on "little expedition[s] of my own," tours of sightseeing and visiting. He disliked marching by fours, and that too prompted him to go off on his own. He had discovered that he was easily able to escape the unit and "wander about when anything seemed worth looking at." In early 1864 he began to notice efforts to confine him; an order required anyone leaving the regiment to procure a pass from the colonel. Although it is doubtful that he was ever securely caged prior to the mustering-out of the 1st Massachusetts in early summer 1864, in the Wilderness campaign Bardeen did find his movements limited as never before. Earlier he had been able to wander freely, but under Grant, he complained, officers looked at his white diamond corps badge, and if he had strayed from his corps area they made it "unpleasant."[5]

Others experienced more directly the weight of the armies' greater determination to punish malefactors. In 1861 Alfred Bellard, as a three-year enlistee, discovered such pride in his uniform that he wished to "show myself off" to the folks at home, so he took "French leave." Returning to the 5th New Jersey, he told his captain where he had been; the officer did nothing. Two years later, wounded at Chancellorsville and assigned to a Philadelphia hospital for recuperation, he again longed for New Jersey. Told that a fifteen-day absence would be overlooked, he stayed away a month, this time to be greeted on his return with guardhouse incarceration, three weeks of prisoner squad detail, and orders returning him to his regiment.[6]

No longer did rank-and-file solidarity provide protection from discipline as in 1861–62. When the 20th New York calculated that its term of service had expired, a computation disputed by Washington, the men refused to march to the front. They were arrested, all of them, and placed under guard until they agreed to rejoin the fight. A similar dispute in the 2d Maine brought an order from Meade to Chamberlain either to bring the mutineers to heel or to shoot them. Remarkably, Chamberlain succeeded in dispersing the dissidents among the companies of his own regiment, overriding local affiliations in a way unthinkable in the first years of the war. By 1864 officers sometimes ordered regiments to open fire on other units broken in battle and fleeing for the rear and even appointed file-followers with orders to trail assault lines and shoot those of their own regiments who faltered. Many of those orders went unheeded—the attack never became that escape-proof "moving box" of men that Stephen Crane described—but it was significant that officers dared to issue them.[7]

The utmost severity fell not on disputatious or wavering combat veterans but on post–1862 conscripts, substitutes, and bounty soldiers. Wilkeson, a Hudson Valley farm boy not yet sixteen, was "seized" by "the war fever" in mid–1863, long after it had abated in others. Enlisting in the 11th New York Battery, he found himself treated as a convict rather than a volunteer. He was

> . . . promptly sent out to the penitentiary. . . . There, to my utter astonishment, I found eight hundred to one thousand ruffians, closely guarded by . . . sentinels, who paced to and fro, day and night, rifle[s] in hand, to keep them from running away . . . [T]hese recruits gathered around me and asked, "How much bounty did you get?" "How many times have you jumped the bounty?" I answered that I had not bargained for any bounty, that I had never jumped a bounty, and that I had enlisted to go to the front and fight. I was instantly assailed with abuse. Irreclaimable blackguards, thieves, and ruffians gathered in a boisterous circle around me and called me foul names. I was robbed while in these barracks of all I possessed. . . . I remained in this nasty prison for a month. . . . A recruit's social standing . . . was determined by the acts of villainy he had performed, supplemented by the number of times he had jumped the bounty.

Just as the contingent started for Virginia, three bounty men tried to escape and were shot down and killed. In New York City four others attempted to run; sentries shot three and an officer overtook the fourth. "He made no attempt to arrest the deserter, but placed his pistol to the back of the runaway's head and blew his brains out as he ran. . . . That ended all attempts to escape." The contingent remained in the harbor for two days while the officer was tried and acquitted.[8]

Rigor extended to the camp, Wilkeson soon discovered. In that winter of 1863–64 skeleton volunteer regiments were being replenished by those whom he had just learned to think of as "essentially cowardly." "These men had to be heartlessly moulded into soldiers," and thus "[b]reaches of army discipline were promptly and severely punished"—the culprit being tied to the artillery caisson's spare wheel and rotated a quarter turn, or bucked and gagged, or hung up by the thumbs, or tied on the battery wagon's rack. Wilkeson said that this last punishment was "very rarely employed" because it crippled men. No one "could endure the supreme pain inflicted by this torture without screaming. . . . I have heard men beg to be killed rather than to be tied on the rack." Lyman described soldiers of the Ninth Corps who had fled battle made to wear "Coward" placards and to stand atop barrels placed on the Union fortifications at Petersburg, the decision whether theirs was a capital offense apparently left to enemy sharpshooters.[9]

In different ways officers became aware of the new severity of the discipline problem and of the broadened latitude within which they would be permitted to respond to it. In August 1863 Stephen Weld was sent home to attempt to reenlist veterans, with exasperating results. In three weeks of recruiting not a man signed up. Finally, a new draft call and promises of extra state bounties produced a regiment. While still in camp in Massachusetts, however, the men began to desert. En route to Virginia, Weld had to guard both against their desire to escape and their penchant for whisky. In Newark one of his officers became so irate that he shot a civilian liquor seller. In Philadelphia Weld himself lost his temper; he demolished the liquor shop provisioning his men, took the proprietor prisoner, held him handcuffed aboard the train until it arrived in Baltimore, and there shaved his beard and half his head before turning him over to the provost marshal. But Weld had done little more than vent his frustration, and the men continued to find so much drink that in camp he was compelled to break up a whisky-fueled "pandemonium." He ordered those hopelessly drunk strung up by the thumbs. When the worst offender lashed out with a foot, hitting an officer, Weld said to him, "Casey, I will shoot you if you do that again." The private kicked once more, and Weld promptly fired twice, hitting the miscreant's arm and then the bayonet tied in his mouth as a gag. "I meant to kill him, and was very sorry I did not succeed." Thereafter, the trouble abated.[10]

The situation in the Confederate Army was both better and worse. The South was compelled to enact conscription a year earlier than the North, in April 1862, which permitted a smoother and more gradual integration of volunteers and conscripts. Although in the end draftees and substitutes constituted 20 percent of the Confederate forces against 8 percent of the Union Army,[11] Southern soldiers felt much less the stark schism so obvious in Northern units. Cultural heterogeneity, notably the extended social distance between immigrants and native-born, between country and city men, was more pronounced in the North than in the South, and perhaps Southerners' conviction that they were resisting invasion further mitigated cultural dissonance. In any case, unit factionalism was less a problem than in the opposing lines.

On the other hand, the lure of desertion was at first as strong as it was in the Union Army—and subsequently stronger. Resistance to invasion was defense of home, and although Lee's army remained intact, more and more of its soldiers' homes were subjected to the rigors of Yankee raids, campaigns, occupation, and destruction. Hard-pressed families made known, some stridently, some most hesitantly, their need for their men. Influential, too, was the course of the war; while Southerners disagreed regarding its severity, after mid-1863 it was clearly moving against them. Understandably, Confederate military discipline focused on deserters more than on men misbehaving in the ranks.

Military executions accelerated on both sides in 1863. Beatty of the 3d Ohio wrote on April 10, 1863, "A soldier of the [40th] Indiana, who, during the battle of Stone['s] River, abandoned his company and remained away until the fight ended, was shot this afternoon. Another will be shot on the 14th . . . for deserting last fall. . . . Hitherto deserters have been seldom punished, and, as a rule, never as severely as the law allowed." On June 19, Alpheus Williams watched what he mistakenly took to be the Union Army's first executions for desertion; three soldiers were shot as an entire corps looked on. In the same period Colonel James Montgomery apprehended a member of the black 2d South Carolina (U.S.A.) in the act of deserting and, without repercussion, ordered him shot without court-martial. More representative of the new stringency was the fate of a member of the 19th Massachusetts who had "deserted his colors while his regiment was advancing against the enemy. . . . He had come up again to his company on the morning after the fight and had been immediately arrested by his company commander, who sent him to the division provost guard. In the morning at six a drumhead general court-martial was organized and his case was settled in a few minutes. At eight he was dead." Of the Union's 267 reported military executions, 147 were for desertion.[12]

Ella Lonn has noted the same tightening on the Confederate side. "By 1863 . . . commanders [were] found pursuing and arresting [deserters], holding court-martial, shooting them at sight when they resisted, and executing sentence of death upon them." No statistics survive, but Southern executions may well have exceeded those of Federals. On February 28, 1864, twenty-two Confederate deserters were hanged at Kinston, North Carolina, an extraordinary episode military authorities thought justified because the men were taken in Union uniforms. Blackford noted that in the Confederate lines at Petersburg, with desertions mounting as privations increased and reports of family suffering arrived more frequently, "executions were frequent . . . I was passing along the trenches and just as I walked around a 'traverse' I heard a volley of musketry fifty yards distant and . . . saw five men fall into graves dug behind them with the blood spouting from numerous wounds. Then the officer in charge walked up and fired one or two shots from his revolver into the graves at such as were not done for, and then the dirt was shoveled in upon them. Their regiment was on duty in the trenches and these deserters had been sent there for execution."[13]

The repetition of the act began to dull its impact on those who witnessed it. Bardeen continued to think the execution "a serious sight": "In battle men fall all around you, but you don't know who it is going to be or when. To see a man sitting on his coffin and know that the instant the word is given he will pass out of this life into another is solemn"—but his journal entry for December 4, 1863, suggested inurement:

> Pleasant. Our 8 days mail came in. Had 5 letters, 14 papers & 3 bundles. Went over to 1st Div. & saw a man shot for desertion. He belonged to Co. B 124th [New York]. He dropped dead as a nail the first pop. The 3rd Div. changed Camp.[14]

More important was the fact that after 1863 volunteers began to dissociate themselves from those subjected to the most severe forms of military punishment. William Wood of the 19th Virginia, witnessing the execution of a deserter in 1863, still described the man who took six bullets as the "poor unfortunate," but then he added: "The effect was beneficial to other substitutes, whose only object it was to secure the pay and then desert." Union Sergeant Daniel Crotty noted just before the Wilderness campaign that while the shooting of a deserter was "a hard thing to see"—there were tears as the condemned man knelt in prayer—still, "military discipline must have its course." The soldier had deserted his comrades "in the hour of danger" and deserved to die. When the condemned could be further distanced with such labels as "three-time bounty jumper," "foreigner" (immigrant), or "city tough," dissociation became even easier.[15]

Thus, while at the outset of the war common soldiers had been united in their opposition to heavy discipline as a species of officer tyranny, that consensus had disappeared by 1864. No one welcomed the military execution, but the men were divided on its justifiability and its effects on them. For some, it served as the deterrent intended by the high commands. In mid-1862 Sergeant Fay wrote home to Louisiana: "I would give every dollar I possess in the world if this war would end. I could come home in peace. Oh, my children, how I want to see them. When I think of it I feel almost as if I should have come home anyway. But I have seen one deserter shot so I don't think I'll desert." Fay, however, was one of relatively few Confederate soldiers to succeed in burrowing away from combat; those frequently in battle were far less impressed. John Billings recalled that deserter execution "was no uncommon sight in the [Union] army; but it did not seem to stay the tide of desertion in the least."

> How far men were deterred from desertion by witnessing such tragic scenes no one can tell. To no great extent, we think, for the chances of evading recapture were at least ninety-nine out of a hundred in favor of the deserter, and later in the war it is no exaggeration to say that nearly one-fourth of the men on the rolls of the Union army were absent without leave. This fact indicates quite conclusively the utter disregard of consequences shown by these thousands. . . .

Opportunities to get away safely, he added, remained abundant.[16]

Reality offered odds less reassuring than did Billings. Of an estimated 200,000 Union deserters, 80,000 were caught and returned to the army; of 104,000 Confederate deserters, 21,000 were apprehended. Of greater moment, however, were soldiers' changing perceptions: that many more were being shot and that those who died were so repugnant as to make volunteers cautious to avoid associating themselves with such rogues by committing the same offenses. Neither high command solved the problem of desertion—as one might expect, it was epidemic in Confederate forces during the early months of 1865—but both sides had succeeded in fixing in soldier consciousness an element of rigor and severity. Theodore Lyman conceded that many officers willing to expose their own lives in battle remained unwilling to shoot down skulkers, and that "our people can't make up their minds" to adopt such harshness, but by the spring of 1864 he had become convinced that "[p]eople must learn that war is a thing of life or death: if a man won't go to the front he must be shot."[17] Each day the war taught that lesson more forcefully.

At the same time that Stonewall Jackson divined the critical link between courage and discipline and became the first to treat the enemy's courage without emotion—shoot down the bravest, he demanded, and you weaken all of those whose discipline draws on that bravery—he tightened the field leadership of his own commanders by holding them to a discipline of new comprehensiveness and unprecedented rigor. No one had claimed that courage brought with it sagacity in combat, but in the Garnett affair Jackson seemed to insist that it did—or, at least, that misjudgment in battle could be equated with cowardice.

Jackson had devised his plan for the battle of Kernstown (March 23, 1862) on the basis of reports of enemy strength furnished by his chief of cavalry, Turner Ashby. Ashby, however, had been fooled by the Union commander, General James Shields, into thinking Northern forces were far weaker than they were. Consequently, on his first day as one of Jackson's brigade commanders, Richard Garnett found his units overpowered by unsuspected numbers of Federals. To extricate them, he ordered a withdrawal. At that juncture Jackson appeared and commanded a drummer to beat rally instead of retreat. It was too late. Garnett's men surged past Jackson, though some two hundred of them not fast enough to avoid capture. The infuriated Jackson shouted at Garnett that had he only held, Jackson's reserve could have come up and preserved the line. He relieved Garnett of his command, placed him under arrest, and pressed sweeping charges: that the brigadier had not remained with his forces; that he had behaved in unsoldierly fashion; and others, pointing not to an error of judgment but to cowardice.

At the court-martial hearing in August 1862, testimony made clear that Jackson had not acquainted Garnett with his plans for fighting the battle and that the enemy's numbers had indeed been miscalculated. The Adjutant General suggested that Jackson withdraw his charges, a proposal that found support in another quarter: Almost every brigade officer believed that Jackson's reaction had been too severe. Jackson remained obdurate. Although the court adjourned without a decision and the charges were eventually voided, Jackson refused to restore Garnett to his command. In September 1862 he left Jackson's division, still admiring Jackson ("I believe he did me a great injustice, but I know he acted from pure motives."), and was killed nine months later at Gettysburg. Many of those who considered Jackson's conduct unpardonably harsh were nonetheless put on notice that in his reckoning courage was equated only with success, and command error would be ruthlessly defined as a defect in courage.[18]

In other ways too, Jackson was the precursor of the way the war would eventually be fought. His cool courage, his spare personal style, and his battlefield victories exerted a mesmeric hold on his men, permitting him to enforce early a discipline that soldiers would have tolerated from no one else. He responded to the problem of officer departures by simply refusing to accept resignations submitted to him. Taking no leaves himself, he never granted them to others. "General, General, my wife is dying. I must see her." "Man, man, do you love your wife more than your country?" George Pickett chided him for treating wounds and illness as symptomatic of a lack of efficiency, patriotism, or courage: "He places no value on human life, caring for nothing so much as fighting, unless it be praying." To a subordinate who had protested that a certain attack would be "madness: my regiment would be exterminated," Jackson was said to have replied, "Colonel, do your duty. I have made every arrangement to care for the wounded and bury the dead." In court-martial matters, Jackson was, in Ella Lonn's phrase, "one grand exception to the prevailing custom of leniency." He softened no convictions, confirmed every death sentence, and as early as 1862 had ten men shot at one time. He held no enemy in knightly respect.[19]

Following his death at Chancellorsville on May 2, 1863, Union soldiers were assembled to hear their Adjutant General: "In view of the fact that [Stonewall Jackson] was wounded by our division [*sic*] and also as a mark of respect to a gallant Christian soldier the division will receive the announcement [of his death] with uncovered heads."[20] Had Jackson succeeded in removing from Northern ranks a military leader comparable to himself, he would hardly have marked the occasion with such solemn homage. For many on both sides, Stonewall Jackson was the war's highest exemplification of courage. He used the power conveyed by that renown to sever from courage its gentler, more tolerant aspects and, two years before others, to advance a war of utmost stringency.

10

A Warfare of Terror

By 1864 the Civil War had expanded beyond the battlefield to encompass a warfare of terror directed primarily against the civilian population of the Confederacy. The broadened belligerence was not terror by twentieth-century standards—its focus was the destruction of property rather than people[1]—but in contrast with earlier American military practice and popular expectation of the forms that the war would assume and measured by the panic and dismay induced in its victims, it was indeed a warfare of frightfulness. Its appearance signaled less the determination of a few military commanders to interject a new ruthlessness than the climax of a dynamic military–civilian relationship whose evolution began with the first months of the war.

At the outset the armies were most circumspect in maintaining the line separating civil and military spheres. Both sides attempted to prevent soldier foraging. George McClellan abhorred any war that would countenance the depredations he thought the inevitable result of soldiers' roving searches. Militarily, foraging was an indiscipline that would demoralize soldiers and enfeeble their performance. Politically, McClellan regarded it as equally indefensible. It was wrong for individual soldiers to punish civilians within Confederate territory; they were, after all, fellow citizens, and the task of the Union Army was to put down an armed rebellion, not to alienate or impoverish unarmed civilians. McClellan's orders forbade even the burning of fence rails for fuel.[2]

The problem of soldier–civilian conflict occupied Union leaders more extensively than those of the Confederacy because so much of the war was fought across Southern territory, but when the situation was twice briefly reversed, Lee was just as circumspect. On the eve of his invasion of Pennsylvania, he ordered his soldiers to respect private property of all kinds. "The duties exacted of us by civilization and Christianity," his General Order 73 of June 27, 1863, stated, "are not less obligatory in the country of the enemy than in our own. . . . It must be remembered that we make war only upon armed men, and that we cannot take vengeance for the wrongs our people have suffered without lowering ourselves in the eyes of all whose abhorrence has been excited by the atrocities of our enemies, and offending against Him to whom vengeance belongeth, without whose favor and support our efforts must all prove in vain."[3]

Enforcement was as strict as it could be made in a Civil War army. "Our army had daily orders to do no damage," the artillerist Haskell wrote, "and no troops could have passed through the country of their best friends with less harm. I heard of but one act of violence, the murder and robbery of an old man, and the first news we got of it was the sight of the two murderers, hanging by the roadside, having been executed by General Lee's orders." Dooley of the 1st Virginia reported several Southern soldiers shot for plundering farmhouses. The Alabamian Herbert thought that "no army ever respected the rights of noncombatants more rigidly than did ours when in Pennsylvania. Necessary food for men and forage for animals was of course taken, but always by officers who, under order[,] prevented plundering and paid Confederate money, or, at the choice of the parties from whom taken, gave receipts specifying amount and value, that owners might present to their own Government." Casler of the Stonewall Brigade recalled that in crossing to the northern bank of the Potomac, "we thought we would have a fine time plundering in the enemy's country," but marching ranks were carefully maintained by day and guards set out by night. The infantry, he complained, got no more than a few cherries from the trees; Lee was more strict with them in Pennsylvania than in Virginia. On the march Lee had dismounted and pointedly restored to its place a fence rail dislodged by his men.[4]

Critical to the success of Lee's policy was that at this stage of the war most Confederate rank-and-file endorsed it. Many accounts refer to the results with unmistakable pride: "not a fence-rail is disturbed"; "even chickens, milk, and butter were sacred"; orders against straggling and looting were "cheerfully obeyed." Especially persuasive to soldiers on both sides was Lee's characterization of the war as a conflict to be confined to armed men and to the battlefield—that is the place to inflict damage on your enemies, Abner Small of the 16th Maine insisted—a contest between equals, exempting the weak. As Lee's army retreated back to the Potomac, some Confederate soldiers whose rations had been exhausted foraged; hungry, angry, and saddened, they entered homes and took food, but Casler, who had felt so unjustifiably constrained by Lee's orders, seeing two women crying as their last hams disappeared, alerted a general who compelled the soldiers to return their booty. Casler felt good about his role; he was sure that he would never forget the women's tears and their words of thanks.[5]

Well into the war there was considerable advocacy of restraint and considerable effort to remain within official policy, sometimes in ways that from the perspective of 1865 would appear incredible. In Hinman's Sherman Brigade there had been no confiscation through 1861; quartermasters were still giving receipts for the hay they required. In Augustus Meyers's Union division, even fence rails were left undisturbed during the war's first eighteen months. On a Mississippi march in December 1862 the 14th Wisconsin enforced strict orders against foraging with roll calls at every halt and with fines for every pig killed (ten dollars) and for every cartridge missing (fifty cents). In July 1861 the 2d Massachusetts marched from Martinsburg, West Virginia, southwestward into the Shenandoah against the Confederate forces of Joseph E. Johnston:

> While the tents were being packed, while wagons filled the parade ground and luggage encumbered the earth; while there was motion everywhere, as far as the eye could see,—galloping horses bearing orderlies with dispatches, artillery rumbling, and long lines of infantry moving out to the inspiring militia-muster melody of jingling kettledrums, screeching fifes, and roaring bass,—a sharp-featured and sombre person, dressed in the prevailing butternut-colored homespun of Virginia, shying up toward the Colonel of the Second Massachusetts Regiment, demanded a settlement: first for the fence rails we had burned; second for the grass

George B. McClellan said of Confederate opponents in his first campaign of the war, "I would be glad to clear them out of West Virginia and liberate the country without bloodshed, if possible." Throughout the fifteen months in which he later commanded the Army of the Potomac, his tactics remained those of a conservator-general who accorded higher priority to the safety of his soldiers than to the destruction of the enemy.

The most relentless of the early-war generals, Thomas J. ("Stonewall") Jackson
was a commander both of exemplary courage and of a driving insistence that respect
for the enemy's courage not vitiate fierceness in combat. Two years before others,
he advocated a war of utmost severity.

The Union's destroyer-generals, Ulysses S. Grant (*above left*), William T. Sherman (*above right*), and Philip H. Sheridan (*below*), provided in 1864 a military leadership able to employ a warfare of terror as a decisive weapon.

John S. Mosby and members of his 43rd Battalion, Virginia Cavalry, called themselves partisans or rangers but were denounced by Unionists as guerrillas and bushwhackers. Irregular warfare waged in behalf of the Confederacy produced a momentous intensification of Federal soldiers' hostility toward Southern civilians.

George A. Custer, a brevet major general at age twenty-four, entered upon a vendetta with Mosby. Each executed prisoners of war from the other's command.

Soldiers of the 24th Michigan killed during the Battle of Gettysburg, July 1–3, 1863. A mounting sense of peril and loss overtook soldiers as the conflict became a war of attrition. Ultimately, more than 625,000 Union and Confederate soldiers died.

As these Confederate fortifications during the winter of 1864–1865 reveal, Grant's campaign of frontal assaults and flanking movements became at Petersburg a grinding, almost static trench warfare. Here soldiers suffered a final demolition of their original conceptions of how the war would be fought.

On the other side, Union soldiers holding another sector of the 30-mile line of trenches seem to show the fatigue and disenchantment of almost four years of war.

Ruins in Columbia, South Carolina, attest to the accuracy of Sherman's observation that his whole army was "burning with an insatiable desire to wreak vengeance" on the first secessionist state. The result, "a blackened swath seventy miles wide," satisfied the desire for revenge but no longer required, in Robert Gould Shaw's words, deeds of "any pluck or courage."

A Confederate veteran shakes hands with a Union veteran at the 50th anniversary celebration of the Battle of Gettysburg, July 1913. The passage of time enabled participants to forget the hard war of 1864–1865 and to reclaim ideals of courage that they had abandoned by the war's midpoint.

we had trampled down; and third for an extra cost of ploughing in the coming spring, the soil had been trodden down so hard.

Before the regiment marched away the farmer received payment in gold.[6]

In late 1861, catching up with his command at Louisa, Kentucky, James A. Garfield discovered to his sorrow that his men had not kept their hands off the local poultry, pigs, or fences. He assembled the 42d Ohio and told it that he had thought he commanded a regiment of gentlemen. They must cease their depredations and demonstrate to Kentuckians that they had not come to rob and steal; only then would he "believe that I command a regiment of soldiers, not a regiment of thieves." The men were chastened. As late as June 1864—that is, just as he engaged in that destruction of civilian property which "made his name anathema to the people of the Shenandoah Valley" and only days before he burned the Virginia Military Institute at Lexington—General David Hunter continued to punish those of his men who foraged without authorization, a shortage of rations notwithstanding; violators who were noncommissioned officers were reduced to the ranks, and enlisted men were sentenced to carry rails for four hours.[7]

Hunter's compartmentalized restraint was by then aberrant, however, for dominant patterns had shifted long before. From the outset the determination to respect others' property had been contested by two highly practical considerations, and necessity soon triggered a process that would overthrow restraint.

Civil War soldiers suffered serious equipment shortages, on the Confederate side generally more severe than on the Union. The Southern soldiers' cry for shoes was "incessant," but what Ella Lonn called "the most ordinary necessities of the soldier" were often a problem in both armies. Unable to prevent shoe shortages in 1861 and 1862, the Union supply system improved steadily thereafter, but as late as December 1864 there were reports of barefoot Federal soldiers, and spot deficiencies were persistent.[8] That simmering-down process, moreover, left the soldier with less equipment than he needed at certain times. The regulation overcoat was welcome in winter but in warm weather became an insupportable burden to be left at the roadside, on the assumption that another could be gleaned when needed in the fall. Furthermore, it was common practice for units preparing to charge to leave behind their haversacks and sometimes their blankets. Guards were detailed to watch over those kits, but before long soldiers had learned to assume that they would never again see those possessions. They rapidly concluded that they would have to fend for themselves.

The second and more exacting problem involved the soldier's daily food. During the war's first year the distribution of Union rations was riddled with organizational problems—scanty and bad, Abner Small called army food in this period—but it became adequate shortly thereafter. Still, Federals continued to encounter times of short-term hunger. On the other side, citizens of the countryside often invited passing Confederate soldiers in for meals or contributed quantities of foodstuffs, and soldiers sometimes went to work for neighboring farmers in exchange for food. But the Confederate Army's commissary system never functioned as well as its Federal counterpart. Though operating over shorter lines of supply, it lacked both resources and resourcefulness, and in the later stages of the war it seemed to break down completely. The pressure for food felt by the Southern soldier became insistent as early as October 1862. To go a day without food became common experience, and it was not unusual for those marching or fighting to be issued no rations for two days, occasionally three or four. Supplemental purchases were the recourse only of the few. Southern regiments early exhausted the financial resources necessary to draw the sutlers as Union regiments did, but even among the Federals, enlisted men could not often afford the high prices, and officers, under the system left to provide their own rations, sometimes struggled to find food when their pay, like the soldiers', was often delayed for months. The armies thus proved incapable of delivering certain essentials when and where the men required them.[9]

An obvious source of supply was the enemy, and soldiers began making good their deficiencies by picking up the haversacks, equipment, and clothing discarded by retreating opponents. At First Manassas William Wood of the 19th Virginia acquired an overcoat, a canteen, and an oilcloth abandoned by fleeing Federals. "Many good soldiers plundered after a battle," said Nisbet, "to relieve their necessities." Their next resort was to the confiscation of essential items from enemy prisoners of war; blankets, overcoats, haversacks, and caps changed hands in that way. The next step, approached much more hesitantly, was for the soldier to secure what he required from the bodies of enemy dead. Initial repugnance was strong. Blackford "felt a horror" of touching the dead, and Casler explained:

> Now, I am not a moralist, nor capable of moralizing, except in a crude way; but all my moral training caused me to abhor the idea of taking anything from a dead body, except for the purpose of restoring it to the rightful owner, be he friend or foe; and I was greatly shocked when I first learned that such things were done.

Still, necessity prevailed: "But why try to conceal what is well known by all the soldiers of both armies?"[10]

Soon it became a matter of course, for hunger had the power to overcome revulsion. Hinman found that in his Ohio regiment "the precepts of the Bible were, to the average soldier, less potent as a controlling influence than an empty stomach." Confederates dependent on the enemy for food were just as direct. "If there is anything," Carlton McCarthy said, "which will overcome the natural abhorrence which a man feels for the enemy, the loathing of the bloated dead, and the awe engendered by the presence of death, solitude, and silence, it is hunger," a motivator of actions that would later appear "too shameless to mention." Gunner Jellett offered Wilkeson this advice: "Get food, honestly if you can, but get it; and ever remember that we cannot have too much of it in the battery." Discovering that they often had too little of it, soldiers shed their fastidiousness. Confederate infantry soon came to think little of cutting the blood from Union hardtack before eating it. General Richard Taylor lunched "comfortably" from the haversack of a dead Federal soldier, though the recollection was "not pleasant . . . war *is* a little hardening."[11]

The same toughening of sensibility was perceptible in the extension of the soldier's attention from items of necessity to items of interest or value, whether on the bodies of the dead or on prisoners. Enemy prisoners, early in the war deprived of items of outerwear, were later relieved of shoes, rings, photographs, and money. By 1864, Francis Dawson reported, it was "expected" that the soldier would take the money of any man he captured. Of greater sensitivity were the prisoners' packets of letters from home, but captors began to claim those too. That loss was clearly the most painful, for the prisoner was not only denied a source of personal comfort at the outset of an increasingly arduous and often fatal incarceration but suffered the desecration of his most intimate relationships. Soldiers on the line began burning their letters rather than risk their falling into the hands of the enemy—so "no villainous Yankee shall ever . . . gloat in ridicule over the expression of your love." To commandeer such items as well from enemy dead proved easy once soldiers began routinely to search bodies, but that progression simply opened other issues.[12]

It was one matter to take the blankets and overcoats of the dead, but another to desire those of soldiers not yet dead. Hinman watched two shivering Ohio soldiers, their eyes on the blanket covering a wounded Confederate, waiting impatiently for his death. "I wish he would die if he is going to!" The war was moving too fast to retain such niceties. A lieutenant of the Stonewall Brigade discovered that a wounded Northern officer possessed a fine gold watch and told others of his desire to appropriate it as soon as the man died, but a soldier, overhearing, simply went out on the field and took the watch. Accompanying J. E. B. Stuart's cavalry in its ride around McClellan's army in the summer of 1862, John Esten Cooke came on a Northern horseman, a German immigrant, writhing with a bullet in his breast and biting and tearing at the ground. Cooke wished to comfort the stricken man and sent off for water, but "the last I saw of him, a destitute [Confederate] cavalryman was taking off his spurs as he was dying. War is a hard trade."[13]

That practice remained for a long time a matter of special sensitivity. Blackford, who had felt a horror of touching the dead, nevertheless went after the gilt spurs of a fallen Union officer, only to discover that the man was alive, conscious, and fully able to rebuke him. Filled with shame, Blackford turned his face "so that he could not recognize me again" and fled. Still, the experience served to remove him only one step from the looting of the dead. "Though perfectly right and proper to plunder the enemy I always felt reluctant about actually committing the deed, and generally get one of the men to get for me what I wanted."[14]

Others quickly passed beyond scruples of any order. Sam Nunnelly of the Stonewall Brigade proposed to his comrades in the Wilderness battles an excursion over the works to search enemy bodies. "He would risk his life any time for plunder." No one agreed to go along, but, perhaps sensing that his comrades' earlier objections no longer formed a consensus that would restrain him, Sam Nunnelly went out alone and returned with knives, watches, and money—and another precept had been breached. Hinman said of the state of the Sherman Brigade two years earlier that the "demand for something to eat was so imperative as to break down the barriers against confiscation, and these were never again so high and so strong as they had been up to this time in our wanderings. In fact, it was not a great while until they almost wholly disappeared." The need for valuables was assuredly less imperative than for food, and the moral taint on their acquisition never entirely faded. Wilkeson called scavenging soldiers "the battle-field ghouls." The process by which restraint diminished here, however, was of the same nature as in the case of necessities. One of the sights distinguishing the battlefield of 1864–65 from that of 1861 was that in the later period the dead and many of the wounded had their pockets turned inside out.[15]

Such shifts in values opened new realms of action as they proved compelling to wider and wider circles of the war's participants. A soldier had first to persuade himself of the necessity or acceptability of a new practice. Hunger quickly outdistanced moral speculation, but the acquisition of nonessential items often provoked reflection. Some soldiers decided that such things became theirs by the ancient right of conquest. Finding on a battlefield the trunk of a colonel of the 4th Maine, the artillerist Owen took a coat, some tea, and the colonel's underclothing, all appropriated as "spoils of war." Without resorting to so hoary a shibboleth, Casler reached the same conclusion, the appropriateness of rewarding the victor: "It was difficult for a soldier to figure out why a gold watch or money in the pocket of a dead soldier, who had been trying to kill him all day, did not belong to the man who found it as much as it did to anyone else."[16]

Once so persuaded, the soldier might at first act upon his new conviction only when separated from his friends, and surreptitiousness might persist until he was sure that the judgment of his messmates or regimental acquaintances had undergone a similar shift. Hungry men cheering foragers returning with arms or carts laden with food might easily set the process in train.

The next step, persuading field officers to accept the new practices, was not particularly difficult, for they were vulnerable both as men and as officers. Dependent on pay that arrived only fitfully and required to send servants out to forage for food, they too were needful. Moreover, from their command perspective they realized that to be good soldiers their men required adequate food and clothing. Abner Small noticed after Antietam that the 16th Maine's haversacks and overcoats were not sent forward and that men who consequently wore blankets by day and huddled at night in rude shelters constructed of fence rails, cornstalks, and boughs "sank into despondency and uncleanly ways, and sickness and despair." The two facts might not have been related, but officers found in them causal connection and, despairing of army inefficiency, reconciled themselves to the initiatives of the rank-and-file. In any case, many officers recognized in changing practices, whatever their moral unsuitability, a process impossible to arrest. Shortages critical to the men's health and combat performance had to be remedied, one way or another, and once under way the resort to extra-organizational solution could not easily be halted—for example, at the point where the search for necessities melded into the search for valuables. Here officers realized their impotence to impose discipline, and most of them gave it up both because it was another instance of non-combat behavior beyond their reach and because the men's initiative could strengthen combat performance.[17]

The men first attempted to implicate officers in their new practices as beneficiaries. Some of the fruits of foraging appeared in company officers' tents, with no questions asked the only acknowledgment desired. The reward to the men was that officers became intent only on maintaining appearances. In January 1862, disregarding standing orders, Hinman's Ohioans raided Kentucky fences and haystacks. Told about their actions, the colonel rushed about shouting orders to desist but, discovering that the culprits were too numerous to arrest and that "the tide could not be stayed," he laughed and gave up. Riding away, he told those who had not joined the raid that if they wanted straw, they would have to hurry. During the Peninsula campaign of 1862 Berdan's Sharpshooters, still relatively unchanged by war, found their rations exhausted. The men were "put to the desperate strait of risking punishment for violation of orders in killing cattle found in some fields, —and a good many were shot, a steak or roast cut away." Officers attempted to halt the butchering, "or pretended to," "but it was a long time before it ceased." Strong's colonel raged at the men, who were nevertheless fully aware that he was in collusion with their raids on sutlers' shanties and railroad ration cars. Enlisted men could not but be aware that many who spoke stern prohibition privately connived in their depredations.[18]

Such anomalies were not easy for all officers to maintain, and some attempted to escape a sense of hypocrisy by making mockery of their own pronouncements. On the eve of the Vicksburg campaign severe orders against foraging were once again read to the 14th Wisconsin. On the march, the colonel reminded his men of them, but only as an invitation to ignore them. "Boys, you have heard the orders. Now I don't want to see a d—d man touch any of them sheep we just passed, and these hogs, I don't want to see any one touch them. Break ranks!" The men quickly went to work with their bayonets, though one dim-witted soldier, forgetting that with headquarters nearby commanders might still hear what they wished not to see, insisted on using his musket to kill an animal. He was fined ten dollars. The colonel received a fine ham.[19]

Gradually episodes more and more consequential fell within the circle of officer endorsement. When men of the 5th New Jersey asked a Southern store owner if he had tobacco, his reply—that he had none and even if he had, he would not sell it for *their* money—angered them. They searched the shop, found and took the tobacco, tore up fixtures, and carried off other merchandise. The officer closest to the scene received a saddle. The general arrived only in time to save the proprietor's last horse.[20]

While Alfred Bellard's account does not reveal whether the general was privy to the project, plentiful evidence suggests that the men's ability to convert officers to their nonregulation practices carried far up the chain of command. Some officers simply accepted their immobilization. Captain Rufus Dawes of the 6th Wisconsin realized in the autumn of 1862 that because his men were on rations of salt beef and hardtack and because they saw unmistakable expressions of Confederate sympathies in the southern Marylanders on whose roads they marched, he was powerless to prevent the seizure of pigs, turkeys, and chickens; only the ability to enjoy fresh pork remained within his sphere.[21]

Others moved from silent recipients to cheerful co-conspirators. At the start of the Tullahoma campaign in June 1863 the colonel of the 65th Ohio became angry at reports of foraging and ordered his lieutenant colonel to set matters right. The lieutenant colonel in turn sent Hinman to arrest the culprits. Hinman pro-

ceeded to the appropriate company, where he found its lieutenant eating a sparerib. By way of explanation, the lieutenant was
willing to offer only that "it rained pieces of fresh pork this morning, and my boys just held out their gum blankets and caught
'em." Well aware that he could not arrest the entire company,
Hinman reported to the lieutenant colonel, with solemnity one
assumes, this "dispensation of Providence." The lieutenant colonel winked, and the lieutenant later sent Hinman "a nicely-
cooked and fragrant section of pig." No doubt the lieutenant
colonel also dined well.[22]

On another occasion, a Tennessee march, the Ohioans had
only hardtack, and despite the reading of stringent orders and
the posting of guards, the foragers were active. The choice glean-
ings went to the officers, reaching to colonels and brigadier generals. Even they, however, eagerly accepting their portions but
nervous about being found out, continued to lecture the men "in
words of thundering sound" that the orders of some still higher
officer must of course be obeyed, or they would be set to carrying
rails for several hours.[23]

The progression by which the initially unacceptable and even
repugnant were converted to the casually admissible was broad
and powerful, but it did not assuage all guilt, especially in matters of relieving the dead and wounded of their possessions. Here
again orders were strict—after battle, companies were to assign
details to bury the dead and to preserve their effects—but once
more soldiers rapidly became aware that the war was not un-
folding in consonance with their assumptions: No one could count
on the disposal of his remains as regulations prescribed. Soldiers
could too easily imagine themselves the objects of forager
searches, and the thought could demoralize them. To mitigate
the effects on their morale, a new nomenclature offered the refuge of the double standard. Soldiers told themselves that they
were foragers; those on the other side were thieves. *We* take what
we must have "to supply [our] actual needs," "to relieve [our]
necessities"; *they* loot.[24] Or *we* seek souvenirs to send home; *they*
desecrate the bodies of the dead. The resort to such terms broadened, along with recourse to a series of progressively expanding
rationalizations. If a combat soldier does not take that item,
surely a nonfighter will. If a soldier does not, a civilian will. If
one on my side does not, one favoring the enemy will. If I do
not, someone else will.

At the battle of Cross Keys, Virginia, on June 8, 1862, the 6th Louisiana, a part of the Confederate force under R. S. Ewell that fought John C. Frémont's Federal army and compelled its retreat, saw in the outcome an opportunity to loot. Nearby, members of the less-experienced 21st Georgia watched, hesitantly and uncertainly. ("My men had not yet got hardened enough to rob the dead, so they were looking on.") Their irresolution provoked a Louisiana Irishman to defend his activity: "[T]his fellow will not need his watch where he has gone, as time is nothing there, and the burial corps will soon get everything that's left. These [damn] non-combatants get too much already . . . they don't fight for." By the same stages, Garfield's men put behind them their commander's little talk distinguishing a regiment of gentlemen from a regiment of thieves: "In our simplicity we then thought it wrong to confiscate rebel property, but as time moved on and our faces became bronzed, so did our conscientious scruples, and we totally forgot the moral teachings of Colonel Garfield."[25] The Confederacy's Richard Taylor had said it: War *was* a little hardening.

The same dynamic simultaneously carried soldier attention beyond the enemy dead and wounded to the civilian sector, and there it set in train a progression from foraging to looting to destruction. Here too the triggers were hunger and soldiers' compelling need for certain items. Here too initial respect for private property, in most soldiers as deep-seated as respect for the dead, yielded first to what men called necessity and then moved far beyond it.

Seeking food, soldiers on the march with little compunction picked fruit from the trees they passed. Field crops caused some slight hesitation—others had obviously invested in those rows energies not required by apple and cherry trees—but roasting ears were irresistible to those who would otherwise be confined to diets of hardtack and sowbelly. Food in storage, representing as it did civilians' completed labors, often provoked twinges of conscience that would at first yield only to high levels of hunger. Nonetheless, soldiers soon started entering unoccupied homes in their quest for food.

The almost universal assumption was that the flight of the inhabitants showed not a desire to remove themselves from the path of war—soldiers thought all civilians recognized that soldiers bore them no ill will—but sympathy for the enemy's cause. Therefore, food found there could be taken. In the first years of the war that reasoning, and initial soldier aversion to confronting civilians in their own homes, provided an important measure of protection for houses that remained occupied. Charles Wainwright claimed that although first slaves and then Union soldiers had taken items from houses abandoned by Virginians during the Peninsula campaign, in homes where people remained, nothing was touched. By 1864, however, that prohibition too had dissolved.[26]

A related line of approach to the civilian sector opened with several nonfood, nonmilitary items that soldiers also thought essential to their welfare. The cold could be kept at bay by burning farmers' fences or by using their stacked hay. But it was the search for food that thrust the soldier toward a pattern of depredation.

At many points the process was similar to the evolution of attitudes regarding treatment of the dead. There was at first circumspection. In May 1862 Berdan's Sharpshooters, campaigning on the Peninsula, purchased provisions from Virginia farmers—sweet potatoes at two dollars a bushel; eggs at fifty cents a dozen; chickens at seventy-five cents apiece—and paid in gold and silver. There was at first a degree of official rigor. Guards were frequently posted at many of the houses lining the route of march. Then the same gradual relaxation of restraints occurred. One Union soldier noted that he and his friends began to be governed by "circumstances"—only if the henhouse were well-guarded would they ask for or purchase chickens. In Hinman's regiment the embargo on fence rails was rescinded, and the house guards disappeared, except in cases where the owner's loyalty to the Union was verifiable, a rare situation. (The 2d Massachusetts took as its motto the stark call "Lynch Law for Guerillas and No Rebel Property Guarded!") Soon soldiers were loading wagons with corn and hay, indifferent both to farmers' presence and to their remonstrations.[27]

The invasion of the house itself was accelerated by the discovery of unexpected military realities that officers felt compelled them to violate formerly respected lines separating military and civilian spheres. Confronted late in 1861 with numerous measles cases, a Mississippi regimental surgeon persuaded his general to permit the transfer of the sick to houses abandoned by

Kentucky Unionists. Taking possession of another man's home "shocked my feelings very much, but then, I was learning to be a soldier, and this was a part of my military education—such is war!" In a war confined to battlefields, though some might ponder that they were destroying in a moment what others had labored weeks to build, few would hesitate to tear down fences that impeded cavalry or delayed artillery batteries, but the presence in houses of those despised sharpshooters presented a problem of a different order. Snipers expelled from many minds the notion of the sanctity of the home; angry officers ordered houses from which they had been fired upon burned. There was again that expansion of articles soldiers thought themselves justified in appropriating, at its ultimate a matter of sheer looting. Meyers reported the circulation in poker games of large amounts of Confederate money stolen by Union soldiers from homes and even banks. General Jacob Cox watched that process during Sherman's march: "[T]he utmost that discipline can do is to mitigate the evil." Might had come to measure right; "pillage becomes wanton and arson is committed to cover the pillage." "Dante's 'Inferno' could not furnish a more horrible and depressing picture than a countryside when war has swept over it."[28]

Some of the expansion of theft and the intensification of destruction by Federal soldiers were attributable to the frustrations of battle, especially defeats. Thomas Galwey entered Fredericksburg with the 8th Ohio following a river crossing made miserable by Confederate soldiers firing from the town's houses. "Just after passing the bridge we halt near tobacco warehouses. The men pillage them at once." Thereafter Fredericksburg became "a city given up to pillage." Bank safes were blown open, and houses were ransacked of items ranging to sewing machines and even pianos. Many of the men were drunk. For more than an hour officers made no attempt to restore discipline.

In the battle itself Galwey watched the slaughter of the Irish Brigade and other Union units, "the grim and thankless butchery of war" and "an excellent representation of Hell." That night Union soldiers resumed their destruction of the town, though in the course of their subsequent retreat across the Rappahannock provost guards confiscated much of their booty. Galwey himself had pilfered a piece of embroidery and a bedspread; in the almost universal sequence, he threw away the bedspread as soon as it made marching difficult. Reaching their base, he and his comrades found that camp followers had plundered their huts. George Allen of the 4th Rhode Island was one of six or seven Union soldiers who entered a Fredericksburg house. A private sat at the piano and played "really fine music," while the others lay at ease listening. "As he ceases playing, another says, 'Did you ever see me play?' and seizing his rifle, he brings it down full force upon the keyboard, smashing it to splinters." That action signaled other soldiers to destroy the remaining furniture, perhaps in anger that those Confederates on Marye's Heights could not, as they had learned, be so easily demolished.[29]

The greatest impetus to heightened destructiveness arose from Union soldiers' mounting animosity toward Southern civilians. The Federals had assumed that it would be a war pitting soldier against soldier; to the extent that they had considered civilian populations, they thought of them as spectators, distantly supportive of their own soldiers of course, but acknowledging their irrelevance to the decisions combat would render. Within that framework, Northerners were shocked both by the depth of Southern civilian enmity and by the determination to express it.

The beginnings were modest, revealing more than anything else the guileless expectations of young and unsophisticated Federals. Serving guard duty at Maryland's Fort McHenry, members of the 18th Connecticut became so angry when Southern sympathizers came with food and clothing in aid of Confederate prisoners of war but ignored nearby Union sick and wounded that they confiscated the visitors' supplies. Those Berdan Sharpshooters thought "pretty steep" the prices Southern farmers charged for their food, and so did many other Northern soldiers. Upon reflection they concluded, as they would not at home, that high prices were hostile acts. Southern civilians could not be trusted. When Colonel Benjamin Harrison was sent to apprehend a Kentucky doctor suspected of bridge-burning and harboring Confederate officers, the woman who answered his knock was insistent: "Sir, I am a Christian woman. From my childhood I have been taught to speak the truth, and to dread the fate of liars. I tell you once more, Dr. Barnes is not in my house." "I must have him," Harrison said, but the woman invoked chivalry and manners and even deflected Harrison into a debate on infant baptism, complete with an exchange of Biblical quotations. In the end Harrison politely withdrew without pressing his search, to discover later that the doctor had been hiding in the garden. His knightliness had been turned against him to render him ineffectual, and he was thereafter a more obdurate soldier.[30]

Southern civilians behaved in other ways the Union rank-and-file came to deem unpardonable. Women's reactions to their presence produced a special shock. The realization that women would curse them and would spit at the Union flag—or at them—ordinarily brought such surprise and confusion that soldiers could only ignore first instances, but repetitions brought a determination to retaliate. Recalling the silence with which he and other foragers of his Illinois regiment had reacted to a woman's imprecations, Leander Stillwell realized that, had the episode occurred a year later, they would have taken all her hogs and poultry. In Nashville Hinman's Ohioans found that "none were so relentless as the women," and one who spat at the flag discovered that her home was to become a Union hospital. Particularly resented were instances of what Federals regarded as barbarous behavior toward prisoners of war. Wisconsin soldiers captured at Corinth "had been ill treated by the citizens"—a Mississippi woman had spit in a prisoner's face, a special grievance—and when they returned to their unit they became intent on foraging, fence-burning, and house-burning. A Federal soldier was taken in the Vicksburg campaign. When his guard stopped for food at a Meridian residence, the woman of the house, "after heaping all manner of insults upon the prisoner," spat in his face. He later escaped and returned to Sherman's army and to that part of Mississippi. He reminded the woman of their earlier meeting and then burned her home, with all its furniture.[31]

It is not clear that in their sentiments women were markedly more vehement than other Southerners who remained at home, but their reactions to the Federal presence differed most dramatically from Union soldiers' expectations of their deportment. Retaliation was intended to punish not only slaps at the dignity of comrades and country but "unwomanly" behavior, as the Illinois arsonist made clear: "Thus may it be with all who descend from their high pedestal of womanhood and disgrace themselves by spitting upon helpless prisoners."[32]

As Union soldiers abandoned expectations of polite reception, smaller and smaller provocations drew punishing reactions from them. Indiscreet words were sometimes sufficient. When Mississippi plantation owners "boasted" within Garfield's hearing that they would find a way to send their grain to the unoccupied South, he burned it "to make these proud Southerners pay for the war they had started." Indeed, by the time Federals completed their reversal of expectations and came to anticipate animosity, the presence or absence of provocation had become irrelevant. Hinman's regiment began to strip the plantations of those who did no more than balk at taking the oath of allegiance to the United States.[33]

As soldiers expanded the range of actions they considered properly applied to defiant civilians, they severed the connection between their personal standards and their deeds—deeds generated, they were convinced, solely by the obduracy and spitefulness of the enemy population. As Elisha Stockwell of the 14th Wisconsin put it, "We had . . . been brought up not to lie or steal and I despise a thief or liar now. When we foraged, though, we thought of it as a part of war and punishment of the enemy." In that context it became possible for the captain of a Union flotilla, fearing that Confederates had mined the waters of the Rappahannock, to enter a river town, arrest its most prominent citizens, and confine them on the gunboat with which he intended to sail the river, a plan he announced, together with the threat that if one of his crew were injured by a mine, he would burn all nearby houses.[34]

By mid-1863 the desire to inflict punishment on Southerners was moving beyond the army's power to restrain it, a development accelerated dramatically by the appearance of irregular warfare waged in behalf of the Confederacy. Its beginnings, beyond the internecine civilian conflict of border states whose peoples were divided in their loyalties, were from one perspective completely comprehensible. Since Southern conceptions of the war converged on the defense of homeland against foreign invasion, it seemed reasonable—indeed, incumbent—to civilians that they take up arms against those who threatened their own homes. With their muskets in hand, they sometimes acted in small groups generated by the approach of the Yankees, sometimes in previously organized local home guard or militia units.

They made their first significant appearance in the 1862 Peninsula campaign, to that date the Union's farthest penetration into Southern territory; there a number of straggler deaths were attributed to irregulars.[35] Their lack of training, equipment, experience, and leadership ordinarily confined their resistance to ambushes and sporadic forays—a few shots and a hurried retreat.

If their military consequence was negligible, their psychological significance was profound. They imagined themselves valorous defenders of their hearths; the Federals considered them guerrillas. They spoke of their meager attacks as acts of patriotic resistance; those at whom they were directed described them as bushwhacking—and to Federals that was "perhaps the most inexcusable practice in all the Civil War." By their nature, bushwhackers violated many initial combat precepts. They often shot at pickets, a practice soldiers regarded as tantamount to murder. They were not soldiers, and only regular enlistment bestowed the right to kill a soldier. Each was a "cowardly, contemptible battleman who never carried on hostilities unless he was unopposed," "of all created beings [the] most despicable." He was to soldierly combat what lice, fleas, and rats were to prisoner-of-war stockades, and to be dealt with as vermin. Conceiving of irregulars in this idiom, Federals resolved to administer "summary punishment" whenever they could be captured, which, given their stealth, familiarity with the locale, and ability to enlist civilian assistance, was infrequently.[36]

The irregulars acquired higher military consequence when the Confederate Government showed willingness to endorse and support at least one variety of irregular warfare. John Singleton Mosby resigned his commission in a Virginia regiment after a company commander he admired was ousted by vote of the enlisted men. Serving first as a scout for J. E. B. Stuart, he soon sought and after some delay won Richmond's permission to maintain armed struggle in three northern Virginia counties under Union occupation. With authority to establish an independent command and with the official approbation implicit in a series of promotions eventually carrying him to the rank of colonel, Mosby ultimately organized eight companies, an aggregate of between 700 and 800 men. His principal tactics were the ambush and the night attack. He justified such assaults on the grounds that they disrupted the enemy movements of men and supplies and forced the diversion of troops from combat to peripheral areas, but many of Mosby's forays seemed designed simply to sustain his organization. Raids were often pitched no higher than the capture of horses for the use of Mosby's men or the seizure of spoils to be divided among them. On October 13,

1864, on a section of the Baltimore & Ohio west of Harper's Ferry, Mosby and one of his bands halted a passenger train and before burning it relieved two Federal army paymasters of $173,000, a sum subsequently distributed in eighty-four shares. Among such men, Mosby's biographer has conceded, were a number of "cut-throats and freebooters."[37]

The Confederate command was never at ease with Mosby's activities. Stuart, to no avail, urged that he call his companies regulars rather than partisans. Lee several times censured him for raids too obviously aimed at booty and for episodes revealing too emphatically the indiscipline of his forces. The admixture of disdain and envy that Confederate regular regiments felt for par-tisan activity came to constitute a serious morale problem. Fi-nally, the Confederate Congress repealed legislation authorizing independent commands. Nevertheless, Mosby survived; Lee ex-empted his companies from reincorporation on the grounds that Mosby's exploits vitally heartened the South's civilian popula-tion, in whose eyes he was a heroic partisan officer engaged in perfectly legitimate warfare.

The Federals thought otherwise. For them the wrong lay in the relationship between Mosby's men and the local, pro-Con-federate population. Following an action, the raiders ordinarily dispersed, with some of them billeted in their own homes and others returning to sympathizers' farms until the next rendez-vous. Mosby, moreover, continued to recruit locally—his last company was organized in April 1865—and to employ locals as scouts. Although his own contingents were sometimes ambushed, a number of his men captured, and Mosby himself wounded twice, expeditions directed against him ordinarily broke against the rock of local hostility and covert resistance.

The civilian–partisan ties and the frustrations they inflicted on Union commanders angered and inflamed the Federals, who quickly broadened their definition of "enemy" to encompass lo-cal civilians. The same change in perception was occurring else-where as well, for even minor guerrilla activity had a way of intensifying soldier–civilian hostility very quickly. Elsewhere, too, encumbrances were lifted from the assertion of soldier ani-mosity—standing orders against foraging relaxed or enforcement neglected, guards no longer stationed on private property—but the change came with special drama and comprehensiveness in the region Southerners liked to call Mosby's Confederacy.

Unable to suppress a small force of men they saw as cowardly freebooters, Union commanders turned on those they supposed sustained Mosby's resistance. On one occasion Federal officers arrested all the men of Middleburg (on the grounds that many of them *must* have been Mosbyites) and confined its women to their homes. On another occasion, they threatened to burn the town. Campaigns against Mosby expanded to incorporate the internment of partisan families, the execution of perhaps twelve of those Mosby men who could be captured, and the burning of homes, mills, and crops. At one point Grant ordered the incarceration of all Loudon County men under the age of fifty.

Such actions looked, to their targets and to Southerners at large, like measures of savage cruelty without the slightest justification in Confederate tactics. John Esten Cooke defended Mosby as one who was born and bred and continued to bear himself as a gentleman, "a plain unassuming officer of partisans." He was convinced that the Northern depiction of Mosby as a villain was attributable solely to Mosby's military success. He described the scattering of Mosby's men among local families as if it were merely the solution to a minor problem in quartering, a matter of simple logistical convenience.[38] Once again, with the development of a perceptual gulf beyond bridging, alternative vocabularies appeared: The same man might draw as many as a dozen descriptions—bushwhacker; soldier; guerrilla; partisan; murderer; ranger; jayhawker; irregular; and so on. One of the sharpest and ultimately most momentous reflections of the growing disparity was to be found in competing descriptions of the deaths of certain Union soldiers, members of Sherman's army as it marched across Georgia. To one side, they were instances of Union foragers killed by Southern bushwhackers; to the other, they were Yankee looters caught and punished by Confederate irregulars.

Similarly, an incident involving Mosby's men spurred both sides to language indicative of the new distance between them. On September 24, 1864, in response to Grant's instruction that the Shenandoah be made incapable of serving again as a Confederate granary or sanctuary, Sheridan's men began burning barns and crops. On October 7 an engineering officer, Lieutenant John R. Meigs, a member of Sheridan's staff and a friend of the general, was killed by the enemy. Southerners described the incident this way: Meigs, accompanied by two others, had overtaken three of Mosby's men who, wearing "rain oilcloths" over their uniforms, recognized him as a Federal before he realized that they were the enemy. Challenged, he shouted his willingness to surrender but then cocked his pistol and shot at George Martin of the Black Horse Cavalry, who returned fire and killed Meigs. The Northern version was that Meigs, riding inside Northern lines "on a peaceful errand," had come abreast of riders he assumed to be Federals and was simply shot down.[39]

A furious Sheridan ordered the burning of every house within 5 miles of the spot where Meigs was killed, and Custer, who a year earlier had lost one of his orderlies to guerrilla action ("shot down like a dog and stripped of all but his trousers. . . . Habituated as I am to scenes of death and sorrow, I could not help but shed tears over his ignominious end."), was happy to comply. Indeed, Custer had entered upon a vendetta with Mosby, each feeling impelled to match the other's fierceness. Custer executed seven of Mosby's men, one of them hanged and placarded with a sign promising "such is the Fate of All Mosby's Men." Custer remarked, "I mean to return evil for evil until these scoundrels cease their depredations." In reprisal, Mosby compelled twenty-seven Northern prisoners of war to draw lots and then executed five near Custer's headquarters.[40]

Meigs's death sealed a bitterness far beyond that of the commanders. George Sanford protested that Meigs was "given no more chance for his life than any murderer gives his victim"; the episode was "murder—no more, no less." "This sort of work is not war, and is not so regarded in any civilized community. . . . I can scarcely believe now that soldiers of our own blood could be guilty of such crimes." Walt Whitman was convinced that Mosby's guerrillas were "men who would run a knife through the wounded, the aged, the children, without compunction." Confederates were equally outraged in their conviction of the other side's perfidy. Describing Virginia women whose homes were burned as "tearing their hair and shrieking to Heaven in their fright and despair," Henry Kyd Douglas of the Stonewall Brigade accused the Federals of creating "a holocaust upon [Meigs's] tomb." "I try to restrain my bitterness [but] it is an insult to civilization and to God to pretend that the Laws of War justify such warfare."[41]

The polarization of images of the enemy found a hundred echoes here and in other sectors of the conflict. The stance of

Charles Russell Lowell, himself a Union officer in the Valley, exemplified one way in which the debasement of the opposition spurred a new ruthlessness, overtaking, if never quite displacing, gentility. The previous year he had written the Solicitor of the War Department protesting the pillaging and burning of Darien, Georgia, in the course of a raid by Union soldiers: "[I]t is not war, it is piracy." He had later issued to his own command a general order condemning profanity. He continued to consider Mosby "an honourable foe." But by the fall of 1864 Lowell, without apparent distress, had merged his earlier convictions with the practices of Darien in a new gentlemanly synthesis. "I shall probably have to burn other houses," he wrote his wife, "but it will be done with all possible consideration. You must not feel badly." Later, though "I don't think it's pleasant telling you about our work, and I think I shan't any more," he added two concluding judgments: that it was acceptable to burn villages if that put an end to bushwhacking in the area and that there was greater justice in setting fire to the entire valley than in burning parts of it.[42]

It was the season of destruction. The possibility of discourse with an enemy people had passed. Soldiers of Sigel's corps had even earlier signaled that passage. Finding in a Virginia town the bloody clothes of a Federal, they had burned the community and almost hanged its inhabitants, only to discover later that the townspeople had cared in kindly fashion for a Union cavalryman mortally wounded in battle.[43]

The harsher ways of warmaking had begun in the daily experience of common soldiers and had percolated upward through the ranks. The final element in the altered equation, however, exerted its influence in the opposite direction. What was essential to move terror beyond the level of vengeance and vendetta to that of a decisive weapon of war was a new and special quality of military leadership.

In 1861 and 1862 George McClellan acted entirely within the framework of courage's war, for it encompassed all the values he had made central to his life. His religious beliefs were both powerful and complex. He often seemed benumbed by a sense of inadequacy as he faced the enormous work of leading the Army of the Potomac to victory. "I realize now the dreadful responsibility on me—the lives of my men, the reputation of the country, and the success of our cause." "I do not feel that I am an instrument worthy of the great task." "[H]ow small is my ability." "I know how weak I am." But he felt God's presence in his life—"I do not see how any one can fill such a position as I do without being constantly forced to think of . . . the Supreme Being"—and he petitioned Him—"Oh! how sincerely I pray to God that I may be endowed with the wisdom and courage necessary to accomplish the work." He believed that he had received strong divine assurance. It vaulted him above self-doubt. Indeed, his faith sent soaring—far too high, his critics thought—a consciousness of his own powers. "I know that God can accomplish the greatest results with the weakest instruments." "I feel that God has placed a great work in my hands." "God will give me strength and wisdom." "No one else *could* save the country." "I can save the nation."[44]

His devotion to courage was not quite as fervent, but it was still strong and entirely orthodox. During the Mexican War, in which he was slightly wounded, he had been promoted to brevet first lieutenant "for gallant and meritorious conduct in the battles of Contreras and Cherubusco" and to brevet captain for bravery at Chapultepec. Though brevet promotions came to many West Pointers in that war, no young officer emerged with a higher reputation.[45]

Early in the Civil War McClellan was one of many who relished demonstrations of courage as signifying the highest personal qualities and who were often heedless of their military meaninglessness. On April 5, 1862, he wrote his wife, Nell, from Big Bethel, Virginia, that he had seen "a wonderfully cool performance." Pursuing a sheep, three soldiers had come under fire from enemy positions but had persevered, catching and skinning the animal amid the bullets and 12-pound shot. "I never saw so cool and gallant a set of men; they do not seem to know what fear is." Even as army commander, he continued to think of himself as an exemplar of courage to those in the ranks. During the Peninsula retreat he took pains to ensure that he was the last Federal soldier to leave a camp, to cross a bridge, and the like. At Antietam he resorted to that familiar gesture, exposure to enemy fire. In order to uncover Southern positions, he and his staff rode along the entire Union battle line, drawing both the telltale enemy fire and the wild cheers of his own men. Later, he entered combat. Hoping to rally Sedgwick's broken division on the edge of the West Woods, McClellan and his staff galloped into the melée, again provoking shouts, cheers, yells—and a Confederate shelling. "I had to ride in and rally them myself," he wrote home.[46]

McClellan spoke often of honor and duty, and he enjoyed the knightly trappings of command more than most, especially the deference directed to him in the pageantry of large reviews.

No doubt George McClellan wanted fervently, often desperately, to defeat the enemy, but his devotion to courage's war made him above all a conservator. Among the intimidating responsibilities falling to him, he cited first "the lives of my men," then "the reputation of the country" and "the success of our cause"—and nowhere the destruction of the enemy.

His heedfulness to soldier welfare was acute. He wished to win the war, but always in ways as bloodless as possible. Of his first opponents he said, "I would be glad to clear them out of West Virginia and liberate the country without bloodshed, if possible." At the outset of his agonizingly deliberate Peninsula campaign, he wrote: "I do not expect to lose many men, but to do the work mainly with artillery, and so avoid much loss of life." He found painful any casualties beyond his calculation of the minimum deaths required: "In Smith's affair yesterday we lost, I fear, nearly 200 killed and wounded. The object I proposed had been fully accomplished with the loss of about 20, when, after I left the ground, a movement was made in direct violation of my orders, by which the remainder of the loss was uselessly incurred."[47]

He was unable to expel images of war converging on suffering and death. "I am tired of the sickening sight of the battlefield, with its mangled corpses and poor suffering wounded! Victory has no charms for me while purchased at such cost. I shall be only too glad when all is over and I can return where I best love to be." In this he was sincere; rather than celebrate his ouster of Johnston's Confederates from Williamsburg in early May 1862, he mourned, "Had I reached the field three hours earlier I could have gained far greater results and have saved a thousand lives." "Every poor fellow that is killed or wounded almost haunts me! . . . I have honestly done my best to save as many lives as possible." One of his moments of most profound despair—"Truly, God is trying me in the fire"—came when he thought that many of his men, reassigned to John Pope, were needlessly sacrificed by that general at Second Manassas. In the end, McClellan wished "to have it recognized that I have saved the lives of my men and won success by my own efforts," and that "is to me the height of glory." Perhaps it was those views that made him so susceptible to Allan Pinkerton's chronic overestimation of Confederate strength; they licensed the caution integral to McClellan's approach to combat.[48]

The men recognized and applauded his concern for their welfare and safety, of which the ultimate proof was his willingness even to visit the wounded in those terrible hospitals (though one such call produced "the most harrowing day I ever passed"). Soldiers cheered him, called him "Our George," and shouted after him, "Halloo, George! how are you? You are the only one of the whole crowd of generals that is worth a [damn]." McClellan was convinced that they would give their lives for him, that "they love me from the bottom of their hearts." There was no doubt some self-indulgence here, but it was true that the affection in which he was held by those below him was matched only by the exasperation of those above him, whom he treated with arrogance and stupidity. The same man who went to bed knowing that the President of the United States was waiting downstairs to talk with him could in the midst of a critical campaign suspend all normal duties "to give the men a chance to think of all they have gone through."[49]

The conservator's bent also set him in opposition to terror tactics. He detested vandalism on moral grounds (it was wrong for soldiers to punish civilians) and on military grounds (pillage would demoralize his soldiers). In October 1861 he made clear the lengths to which he would go to arrest the development of such practices: "Some of our men have been behaving most atrociously lately in burning houses. . . . I will issue an order to-day informing them that I will hang or shoot any found guilty of it, as well as any guards who permit it. Such things disgrace us and our cause." When Pope, whose Army of Virginia remained in ambiguous command relationship with the Army of the Potomac, issued orders threatening to forage extensively and in certain cases of guerrilla activity to shoot Virginians without civil process and to raze their homes, McClellan was angry at his colleague: "I will strike square in the teeth of all his infamous orders, and give directly the reverse instructions to my army: forbid all pillaging and stealing, and take the highest Christian ground for the conduct of the war."[50]

Other Union commanders prominent during the first half of the war shared many of McClellan's attitudes. In 1861 Rosecrans declined the position of Ohio's chief engineer because "I cannot stay at home . . . duty commands that I should offer my military acquirements to aid in diminishing the loss of life. I must go with our people to the front." Once there, he, like McClellan, stressed meticulous preparation, careful movement, and minimal bloodshed: "No prospect of brilliant victory shall induce me to depart from my intention of gaining success by maneuvering rather than by fighting. I will not throw these raw men of mine into the teeth of artillery and entrenchments if it is possible to avoid it." His Tullahoma campaign masterfully achieved his definition of victory. He outthought and outflanked Bragg, forcing the Confederates to fall back behind the Tennessee River. Though he pleaded with Washington—"I beg . . . that the War Department may not overlook so great an event because it is not written in letters of blood"—such victories were arid. They neither inflicted much loss of life on the enemy nor hastened the end of the war, nor did they offer demonstrations of courage.[51]

George Gordon Meade and particularly Gouverneur Warren also fitted comfortably within the dominant values. Warren was much less colorful than McClellan but equally solicitous of those under him. Lyman called him "certainly the most tender-hearted of our commanders." When he attempted to remain so rather than yield to the new rhythms of the war, the costs of the Wilderness battles nearly broke him: "For thirty days now, it has been one funeral procession, past me; and it is too much!"[52] These were the generals who tried to fight their battles in accord with the precepts of courage. The war did not reward them.

Those who came to power in the Union Army during 1864 and 1865 were imbued far less with the war's initial commandments and in their essential orientation were destroyers rather than conservators. In his actions Ulysses Grant set the pattern, but he was far less contemplative and expressive than Sherman, so it is principally to the junior commander that one must look for the rationale informing their operations.

Neither general fitted easily within courage's constellation. Sherman acknowledged a belief in God, but one who bore little resemblance to the personal deity of others. Where McClellan attributed to God a benevolence offering earthly opportunity, Sherman seemed to find an ill-will constrictive of human actions. Where McClellan looked to God as the promise of the ultimate harmony of all interests, Sherman saw dissonance and a supernatural order that threatened to exploit one's weaknesses. God was to him the dispenser of fate; indeed, only in fate, which ruled life, did the will of God manifest itself. In an unusual and revealing passage, Sherman spoke in dark metaphor: "The antelope runs off as far as possible but fate brings him back. Again he dashes off in a new direction, but curiosity or his Fate lures him back, and again off he goes but the hunter knows he will return and bides his time. So have I made desperate efforts to escape my doom."[53] While others sought to align themselves with God's intentions, Sherman sought flight. Grant, whether being more reticent or having less to reveal, scarcely mentioned religious interests or concerns.

Their views of courage were no more orthodox. Neither thought of himself as an embodiment of courage or attempted to exemplify it for others. Neither was inclined to the heroic gesture; their Civil War records contained none of the individual acts of bravery by which other generals gained the admiration of their men. They were, moreover, much less solicitous of their soldiers than were McClellan and those of his school.

Sherman, who frequently pitched his reflections at the level of social analysis, was obsessed with the problem of discipline. He thought of his soldiers as refractory individualists, of his army as a mob, of society as nearly anarchic, of democracy as a source of severe social weakness. Holding such conceptions, he reacted with minimal emotion to the sights of the battlefield. At First Bull Run, "for the first time I saw the carnage of battle, men lying in every conceivable shape, and mangled in a horrible way; but this did not make a particle of impression on me." What did strike him were the "horses running about riderless with blood streaming from their nostrils, lying on the ground hitched to guns, gnawing their sides in death." At Shiloh he saw scenes "that would have cured anybody of war," but he remained well insulated by his conviction that such sights were intrinsic to war and that the "very object of war is to produce results by death and slaughter," a commonplace today, but not in 1861. He insisted that he felt sympathy for the dead and wounded but, he added, had no time for them.[54]

Ulysses Grant too remained aloof from his men. He was not unfeeling. In 1848 he had attended a Mexican bullfight and had found it "sickening." "I could not see how human beings could enjoy the sufferings of beasts, and often of men, as they seemed to do on these occasions." In the wake of Admiral David Porter's unsuccessful attempt to silence Confederate guns at Grand Gulf, Grant boarded his flagship, which had been struck by an enemy shell. "The sight of the mangled and dying men which met my eye . . . was sickening." Of Champion's Hill he wrote, "While a battle is raging one can see his enemy mowed down by the thousand, or the ten thousand, with great composure; but after the battle these scenes are distressing, and one is naturally disposed to do as much to alleviate the suffering of an enemy as a friend." But Grant's sensitivity seemed to dull as the scale of losses increased. Of Shiloh he wrote,

> I saw an open field . . . over which the Confederates had made repeated charges . . . so covered with dead that it would have been possible to walk across the clearing in any direction, stepping on dead bodies, without a foot touching the ground. On our side National and Confederate troops were mingled together in about equal proportions; but on the remainder of the field nearly all were Confederates. On one part, which had evidently not been ploughed for several years, probably because the land was poor, bushes had grown up, some to the height of eight or ten feet. There was not one of those left standing unpierced by bullets. The smaller ones were all cut down.

Those observations appear to have been employed casually to illustrate Grant's contention that "Shiloh was the severest battle fought at the West during the war." He said of his disastrous charges at Cold Harbor, "This assault cost us heavily and probably without benefit to compensate: but the enemy was not cheered by the occurrence sufficiently to induce him to take the offensive." Ultimately, both Grant and Sherman reduced their concern for combat losses to negligible levels. Grant had become convinced that victory would come to the side "which never counted its dead." During the Atlanta campaign Sherman casually recognized that "I begin to regard the death and mangling of a couple of thousand men as a small affair, a kind of morning dash."[55]

Enlisted men recognized the detachment in both generals.

Wilkeson was struck by Grant's impassivity as the commander watched one of his attacking ranks "smashed . . . to flinders." "He sat impassive and smoked steadily, and watched the short-lived battle and decided defeat without displaying emotion." In contrast to the cheers and salutes that greeted McClellan's approach, rank-and-file demonstrations of enthusiasm for Grant's leadership were rare. Seldom did troops offer him the gestures of affection to which Lee, Jackson, and McClellan had become accustomed. Nor did Sherman become, until well after the war, the "Uncle Billy" whose congeniality won over his veterans. In both generals, soldiers discerned the resolve of destroyers whose efforts to annihilate the enemy were likely to require the annihilation of many of them.[56]

It is impossible to identify precisely the influences that propelled those Union military leaders, all West Pointers, to one stance or to the other, but the patterns of their prewar activity are suggestive. All of the conservators had enjoyed important measures of success. In 1860 McClellan was the president of the eastern division of the Ohio & Mississippi Railroad, at the impressive annual salary of $10,000. Rosecrans, although his business had almost foundered in the 1850s, soon made a profitable venture of his Cincinnati coal-oil plant. Warren, an 1850 West Point honors graduate welcomed into the Engineers' elite, became a topographical engineer-explorer whose work won him a reputation as one of the best of the army's young officers.[57]

In sharp contrast stood Ulysses Grant, almost all of whose 1850s projects in investment, farming, and merchandising buckled in failure. Sherman too knew severe disappointment: lagging promotions; the "dull, tame life" of a commissary captain; and exhausting efforts in banking and finance until the crash of 1857 brought painful indebtedness and the closure of his New York City firm. ("Of all lives on earth," he said, "a banker's is the worst, and no wonder they are specially debarred all chances of heaven.") Sherman's near-bankruptcy and subsequent missteps in law and farming spun him to the edge of nervous collapse. His pessimism was profound, and the imagery in which he portrayed himself stark. "I feel mistrust of everybody and everything." "I look upon myself as a dead cock in the pit, not worthy of further notice." Finally, he sought refuge as superintendent of an insignificant Louisiana military college. Philip Sheridan had been unhappy at West Point. Deficiencies in his social and academic performance had carried him close to expulsion, and his record as a garrison soldier during the 1850s was little better.[58]

Those divergences in accomplishment were important not because they revealed contrasting temperaments or abilities—that was unclear—but because they grew to express themselves in antithetical convictions regarding the efficacy of the individual. The conservator generals entered the Civil War as optimists. They felt great personal empowerment. They viewed combat primarily as a setting for demonstrations of courage and their own military proficiency—within God's Plan of course, but not much restricted thereby. As McClellan said, God was "not wont to aid those who refuse to aid themselves." They comprehended war exclusively as the sum of their own and others' efforts. In short, war was to be what they made of it in their performances upon combat's stage.

Conversely, failure appears to have placed those who were to become the destroyer generals on or beyond the peripheries of many of the conservators' initial precepts. Neither Grant nor Sherman felt any confidence that the individual could master his fate. Thomas Hamer, a man Grant so admired that he expected him to become President, had volunteered for the Mexican War, sickened, and died. Grant decided that had Hamer lived, he would have appointed Grant to a staff position, a favor removing Grant from any possibility of the fame he would achieve. Grant cited the matter "to show how little men control their own destiny." Practically alone in prewar days, Sherman accorded war a separate identity, an intrinsic nature not dependent on its participants' actions. Discussing with a Louisiana friend the approach of war, he had said, "This country will be drenched in blood. . . . You people speak so lightly of war. You don't know what you are talking about. War is a terrible thing. . . . months of marching, exposure and suffering . . . a frightful loss of life and property . . . the demoralization of the people." War was not, as others thought, a test of or contest between values; war was power. He later said that "war, like the thunderbolt, follows its laws and turns not aside even if the beautiful, the virtuous and charitable stand in its path." War was "dark and cruel," a struggle between stronger and weaker.[59] Thus from the outset Sherman held a conception of war as bloody conflict that would inevitably gain a momentum beyond the energy imparted to it by its participants and ultimately an independence of its participants. Here he employed an imagery that would come into general use only during the Great War, one of war as implacable and indifferent, as commanding a nature and a power of its own. Though it left no room for heroic conceptions, Sherman was not repulsed by his vision.

In other ways, too, Grant and Sherman had drifted from conventional values. Grant's *Memoirs* made clear how far he had moved from traditional understandings of courage. Indeed, he turned on their heads actions others deemed courageous and insisted that his own performance of them proved that he was deficient in courage. He believed both that he lacked "the courage to fight a duel" and that most duels were fought "for want of moral courage on the part of those engaged to decline" challenges. He told of journeys he pushed forward, among wolves that frightened him, because he lacked the courage to turn back. He recounted charges he joined and battles into which he thrust his men because he lacked the courage to halt and reconsider—"so I kept right on." That appeared to be, appropriately, a formula for certain failure. If Grant acted in ways others applauded, he told himself he did so only from personal defect; if he did not so act, he would appear cowardly in others' eyes.[60]

One of the peculiar results of Grant's inurement to failure was that it diminished his investment in the system of values others brought to the Civil War and thus provided a detachment making visible and reasonable possibilities hidden or unthinkable to others. When, for example, he confessed his fear, he made no effort to conquer it but simply moved beyond it by concluding that his opponents were just as fearful as he. Expecting far less glory of the war, he was open much sooner to its reality, to "seeing things as they actually were," as Matthew Arnold said of him.[61] Only such a man would have set soldiers laboring on Vicksburg approaches in which he had no confidence, because he thought it better that they work than sit idle and sicken. Only Grant would have sent his soldiers into an attack he thought futile, because he calculated that, if not allowed to try the charge, they would grow impatient in the siege trenches.

In one of his Civil War stories, Harold Frederic described the realization that came in 1864 to those in upstate New York: "A new General was at the head of affairs, and he was going in, with jaws set and nerves of steel, to smash, kill, burn, annihilate, sparing nothing, looking neither right or left, till the red road had been hewed through to Richmond." Ulysses Grant was that general.[62]

As experience upended assumptions about the nature of war, Sherman too seemed to draw power from the sense of powerlessness conveyed by his civilian failures. "Generally," he said, "war is destruction and nothing else." "War is cruelty and you cannot refine it." "You might as well appeal against the thunderstorm as against these terrible hardships of war." Accordingly, against such a force, one no more subject to man's control than natural phenomena, individuals were powerless save to conform. "I have made war vindictively; war is war, and you can make nothing else of it." But that was simply a logician's sleight-of-hand. By subordinating himself, by presenting himself merely as war's agent, Sherman freed himself to wage war in just those ways that made it what he said it was. Sherman said war was hell, and the last years of the Civil War were hellish because he and others made them so.[63]

Sherman cited war's invariable nature, used force that made a shambles of earlier moral restraints (some of which he had espoused), and pleaded his impotence to do otherwise. "Our soldiers," he complained, "are the most destructive men I have ever known," overlooking that his war made it appropriate that they destroy to the utmost. During his advance through South Carolina, he reported that he could do nothing to restrain his army; he forgot his orders to "forage liberally" and his decree of "devastation more or less relentless" if opposition appeared, a condition that, given his description of war's nature, was the flimsiest of deterrents. "Men go to war to kill or to get killed," he said, "and should expect no tenderness"—nor would his war require that they show any. "God help the starving families! I warned them . . . against this . . . visitation and it is at hand," he said, as if he had seen war approaching as a flood, had sounded the alarm—and had no hand on the floodgates. Sherman derived additional justification from a sense of himself as a teacher, instructing others in the nature of war. He wrote of his North Carolina campaign: "Thousands of people may perish, but they now realise that war means something else than vain glory and boasting." Satisfaction, even pride, seemed to resound through his words, "I have taught people what war is."[64]

Sherman had provided a powerful rationale for a warfare of

terror: that frightfulness was the true essence of war and that soldiers had no choice but to align their actions with it. Several corollaries were necessary, however, to broaden the definition of the enemy and to reassure a Northern population that still pictured war differently. Prior to Vicksburg, Sherman had argued in favor of confining warfare to combatants, though more on grounds of discipline than of humanitarian concern: "War at best is barbarism, but to involve all—children, women, old and helpless—is more than can be justified. Our men will become absolutely lawless unless they can be checked." Nevertheless, in defense of his decision to remove Atlanta's remaining civilian population, he did not hesitate to enlarge his definition of the opposition: "[W]ar is war, and not popularity-seeking. If [Atlantans] want peace, they and their relatives must stop the war."[65]

Philip Sheridan made one attempt to return civilians to the spectator's role he thought proper. He calculated that terror directed at the residents of Mosby's Confederacy would force them to separate themselves from partisan activity. If I ravage, he appears to have reasoned, the local people will come to hate the guerrillas whose presence brings me among them. Under Sheridan's harsh pressure, Middleburg citizens did ask Mosby to halt his attacks (probably more to pacify Sheridan than to influence Mosby), but Mosby's refusal brought no weakening of his local support. Sheridan's experiment failed.[66]

More rigid than Sheridan, Sherman had already pushed on to declare that all in the South were irrevocable enemies: "[T]he entire South, man, woman and child, is against us, armed and determined." As enemies, the civilians of the Confederacy risked more than they realized: "A people who will persevere in war beyond a certain limit ought to know the consequence. Many, many people with less pertinacity have been wiped out of national existence." By 1864, that elaboration of the enemy had become a necessity, for it alone could provide justification for the immense destruction of homes, farms, and goods.[67]

Other corollaries proposed that Southerners, civilians and soldiers, were solely responsible for the terror visited on them and, paradoxically, that what befell them was to their ultimate benefit. Again, the reasoning—premised on the enlarged enemy—was relentlessly expansive. If Confederate forces cut Union lines of supply and communication, it was their fault that Union soldiers took everything they found. (And if Federals did not take all they found, what they left behind would surely be used against them.) If Southern farmers burned their forage to deny it to Northern forces, it was their fault that their houses were burned. If Southerners corresponded with those in arms against the North, they were spies. Ultimately, Sherman decided that the costs of the war were "not chargeable to us, but to those who made the war." The rebels "had forced us into war, and . . . deserved all they got and *more.*" Those who started the war, whether they were soldiers, residents of an area of guerrilla activity, or simply Southerners at large, must bear its "natural consequences."[68]

Here was an invitation to a warfare of terror both expansive and increasingly casual. When a telegraph wire was cut and shots were fired at a train, John Beatty took civilian hostages and burned the town of Paint Rock, Alabama. He explained that such action was "the true policy, and the only one that will preserve us from constant *annoyance.*" Veterans would tell of Sherman's ordering a long flanking movement and instructing a subordinate how to report his progress: "See here, Cox, burn a few barns occasionally, as you go along. I can't understand those signal flags, but I know what smoke means."[69]

A final corollary held that such tactics would yield ultimate benefits to both Northerners and Southerners, almost a kindness to the latter. Terror was the fastest road to peace. Sherman argued that "the crueler [war] is, the sooner it will be over." In defense of his destruction of the crops of Loudon County, Sheridan contended that death "is popularly considered the maximum of punishment in war, but it is not; reduction to poverty brings prayers for peace more surely and more quickly than does the destruction of human life." Grant looked upon war as "an aching tooth that cannot be mended. To save greater prolonged suffering, one must bear the more acute but shorter pain of removal. In war the toll of prolonged inactivity is greater than the toll of battle. To conserve life, in war, is to fight unceasingly." Sherman agreed that true mercy lay in hastening the end and in ensuring that the war was made so terrible that the peace would endure. Such was the logic that led him to announce in March 1864, as he prepared for the Atlanta campaign—and Grant for the Wilderness—that "all that has gone before is mere skirmishing. The war now begins."[70]

Union soldiers carried by war's currents from foraging (we need what they have, the reasoning went) to looting (we want what they have; we ought to deprive them of what they have) to destruction (we must punish them by destroying what they have) welcomed such comprehensive and lofty rationales as Sherman's.

Some, like Corydon Foote of the 10th Michigan, who had stolen a plantation family's silver during the march to the sea, wondered perplexedly, "Why does a fellow do things against his own nature?" A few rejected outright the thrust of the war. Sherman's methods horrified Carl Schurz, who found their nearest equivalent in the French destruction of the Palatinate during the seventeenth century and worried that the Union Army would reduce itself to a "band of robbers." Others reacted to particular experiences in ways setting them apart from what was happening around them. The sacking and burning of Darien, Georgia, dismayed Robert Gould Shaw: "I have gone through the war without dishonor, and I do not like to degenerate into a plunderer and a robber. . . . After going through hard campaigning and hard fighting in Virginia, this [wanton destruction] makes me very much ashamed of myself." Rutherford Hayes was so deeply affected by the destruction Banks inflicted on Lynchburg that he emerged, his biographer concluded, "the new and more humane Hayes." He warned his wife against being misled by such catch phrases as "brutal rebels," for "we have brutal officers and men too."[71]

Still, by 1864 most soldiers were inextricably bound to the dynamic of the war and echoed almost all aspects of Sherman's position. Watching Atlanta burn, Michael Fitch agreed that war "is made up of cruelty and destruction." Robert Burdette of the 47th Illinois saw inevitability in the demolition of Southern homes, fences, and railroads: "That's war. Destruction of innocent and useful things. Destruction of everything." Charles Francis Adams's encounter with a Virginia civilian made clear that he too had enlarged his definition of the enemy. Explaining to an "old secesh farmer" why he was taking the last of his corn, Adams told him that "Virginia had brought this on herself and need expect no mercy." Like Sherman, the Illinois officer James Connolly promised to bring down an apocalypse premised on a wildly exaggerated threat of civilian resistance to Federal soldiers: "Everything must be destroyed . . . all considerations of mercy and humanity must bow before the inexorable demands of self-preservation." Charles Lynch of the 18th Connecticut was another who promoted himself from a fighter to an observer of the conflict and thus placed himself above the responsibility of the participant: "I am often reminded that death and destruction follow the path of war." When Alabama farm people, vowing that they were Unionists, begged Federal soldiers not to take their chickens, John Brobst explained in a letter home why the 25th Wisconsin had paid no heed: "But we have no respect of persons down here. They must all suffer alike." Later he wrote home from Georgia: "[T]hat is the way that we carry on the war now, raze, burn, and destroy everything we come to."[72]

That mode of warfare reached its culmination in the march of Sherman's army through South Carolina. For the first of the secession states, Sherman said, his men prepared "the scourge of the war in its worst form"; "the whole army is burning with an insatiable desire to wreak vengeance upon South Carolina." Alpheus Williams reported that his men, "impressed with the idea that every South Carolinian was an arrant Rebel, spared nothing but the old men, women, and children. All materials, all vacant houses, factories, cotton-gins and presses, everything that makes the wealth of a people, was swept away. The soldiers quietly took the matter into their own hands"—with the result "a blackened swath seventy miles wide."[73]

As Sherman's regiments approached Columbia, a Confederate artillery battery appeared and began firing at the Federals. Sherman was angry, for he was sure that his opponents, Beauregard and Hampton, knew that a few shells would have no impact on the military outcome, that they could not prevent Union entry into the city. Amid the smoke of destruction, amid the swirl of pillage, robbery, and violence to which the conflict had come, Sherman invoked with no sign of irony one of the earliest and most preservative precepts of courage's war. To send over those shells, he complained, was "wanton mischief" and an "unnecessary act of war."[74]

11

Unraveling Ties

Nothing could be held constant, Civil War participants discovered. In a conflict waged in its later stages so differently
from its outset, the soldier's basic relationships—with those at
home, with his officers, with his comrades in the ranks—altered
strikingly.

Soldiers continued to cherish notions of "home," but memories did not halt complex changes of attitude toward family,
hometown community, and larger civilian society.

They became convinced, quite accurately, that those at home
did not understand the experience through which they were passing, and they resented, with less justification, that civilian incomprehension. They realized that their prewar and early-war
conceptions of warfare had been unrealistic. Stephen Weld confessed in June 1864: "I never knew before what campaigning was.
I think, though, that all [the Army of the Potomac] have a pretty
fair idea of it now. We have had to march all day and all night,
ford rivers, bivouac without blankets or any covering during rain
and sunshine, and a good part of the time have been half-starved.
. . . Any one who gets through safely may consider himself
lucky." As a matter of elementary logic, he and his comrades
knew that without exposure to the same experiences the home
folks could not make the mental recalibrations that combat had
forced upon soldiers: "I know that no one staying at home can
have any idea of what this army has been through."[1]

Nevertheless, the men grew to resent unchanging civilian allegiance to the precepts with which the war began. On brief furlough, Foote found irritating the reactions of neighbors invited in to hear his story and sought out the only person with whom he felt at home, an invalided veteran. "Gosh, Pop, the rest of 'em can't imagine what it's like down there. No use tryin' to tell 'em, either." "Not much, Cordie. Not much, because most of 'em think they know such a goldern lot more about it than we do!" Fitch objected to a Northern public that enshrined Sherman's march to the sea "in song and poetry as the romance of war." He complained, "The masses prefer the fever of romance to the good health of solid facts." (He forgot that in 1861 he had been equally impervious to the war's "solid facts.") Anger rose especially against those ignorant of combat who continued to impose the burdens of courage on soldiers. In late 1863 Francis Amasa Walker wrote sardonically in anticipation of the next attack, "We aren't doing much just now, but hope in a few days to satisfy the public taste with our usual Fall Spectacle—forty per cent of us knocked over." In his stinging story "Killed at Resaca," Ambrose Bierce portrayed a lieutenant sent to deliver a message to the front. "Vain of his courage," he galloped parallel to the enemy line rather than travel a safe route, and his presence provoked a general battle in which he was killed. When his body was recovered, the narrator found on it a letter from the soldier's lover, expressing forcefully her hope that he was not a coward and urging him to heroic action.[2]

Soldier anger on that count did, however, lose some of its force by its projection upon diverse targets. Some blamed the correspondents, who, while remaining safely beyond the charge, listened to straggler tales, accepted them as authentic, and denied credit to those in the line truly deserving of it; who in their reports falsified the soldier experience with their heroic vocabularies; and who seemed always to be goading the soldiers forward. Galwey of the 8th Ohio complained that "newspaper correspondents have often presented the army as spoiling for a fight, but they have been drawing largely on their imaginations." Robert Carter derided correspondents who reported that "all were anxious for a decisive charge at those impregnable works."[3]

Increasingly, soldiers faulted those who served as the links between military and civilian spheres. Passing the Christian Commission tent one day, Carter and his friends saw a man formerly their teacher. The meeting was congenial only on the surface. The Commission worker "said he liked his place so well that he 'should *stay* and *see the thing out*'; and thereby escape the draft (we mentally added)." He loaded them down with bread and canned peaches, offered to satisfy any deficiencies in their supplies of shirts, stockings, blankets, and towels, and promised to visit them soon.

> We could not help thinking, however, how *generous* and *kind* this class of young men were with all this liberal contribution of goods, which *cost them nothing,* and which they were so *unwilling to march, fight, bleed,* or *sacrifice comfort for.* There were swarms of these *strong-minded well-educated, Christian* young men, who were out with the army simply as clerks and attaches of the different commissions and their departments, who, while spoken of as making the best of soldiers, were rarely in the ranks as actual combatants on the field of battle.

The man had said nothing offensive, and Carter even decided that his generosity with supplies would merit further meetings, but the gap in experience had of itself been sufficient to incite soldier hostility. (Interestingly, soldiers were not alone in their disdain for those who did not approach battle. Nurses, whose positions were only slightly more precarious than those of Christian Commission volunteers, nevertheless scorned others located further from combat; they often developed a contempt for women who remained at home.)[4]

A still more intense anger was directed at civilians who continued to voice the old values and to invoke the 1861 rituals that summoned them. It arose partly out of frustration at the inability to persuade home folks that matters were *not* as they had seemed three years before, and partly out of irritation that soldiers continued to endure ceremonies that only underscored their impotence. From Petersburg Theodore Lyman wrote in 1864:

> There is no shadow of doubt that the body of Southerners are as honestly, as earnestly and as religiously interested in this war as the body of the Northerners. Of course such sentiments in the North are met with a storm of "Oh! How *can* they be?"—"That is morally impossible"—"No one *could* really believe in such a cause!" Nevertheless there is the fact, and I cannot see what possible good can come from throwing a thin veil of mere outcries between ourselves and the sharp truth. . . . The great thing that troubles me is, that it is not a gain to kill off these people—now

under a delusion that amounts to a national insanity. They are a valuable people, capable of heroism that is too rare to be lost.

Sentiment was no different in the opposite trenches. Eggleston observed that only Southern women and stump speakers any longer believed that Confederate soldiers could defeat ten times their number, and he pondered painfully how to explain to civilians that respect for the enemy born of combat.[5]

Just before the Atlanta campaign, an angry James Connolly was dragooned into yet another colors presentation: "I'd rather listen to Bragg's cannonade than to a citizen urging soldiers to stand by their flag." He had not become cynical about Union war aims; to the contrary, the separation of the soldier from civilian attitudes about the war sometimes resuscitated and even sharpened his sense of The Cause. Connolly's devotion to Union expanded as his faith in civilian society's ability to embody that patriotism shrank. He wrote in mid-1863:

> You at home cannot feel the glow of triumph as we do in the field; those of us who looked to the future with high hopes, staked life, reputation, honor, everything in this contest—taking our lives in our hands we went out for what? for money? no; for power? no; for fame? no; only for an idea, for the idea of Union, Freedom, an intangible something always sought for by mankind . . . we have seen our hopes fading one by one . . . our comrades falling one by one . . . we have turned our eyes homeward and there, with heavy hearts, seen those who should bind up our wounds and cheer our drooping spirits, turn their heads against us . . . still we struggled on.[6]

Civilian moral oversight was no longer welcome. Indeed, soldiers now felt able to instruct their elders, for to those like Connolly the army had become the true repository of The Cause. Perhaps they felt that only exalted purpose could begin to justify the terrible losses they had suffered. Here again, however, one encountered an element of soldier self-deception, for Connolly had forgotten that Union and Freedom had interested him little in 1861, that he had had no intention of enlisting until a committee of local respectables had asked him to raise a company for the Union Army. Flattered, and cornered, he had permitted the community to designate his role in the war with little heed to The Cause—"I couldn't decently stay at home when all other boys and young men were going out"—but three years later he did not hesitate to catechize the home folks. He had departed from home firmly resolved to demonstrate his merit to family and friends; now it was the locale whose fitness was on trial. Accordingly, he was pleased with those at home who voted the Republican ticket in 1864: "Ohio, Pennsylvania and Indiana have proven themselves worthy homes of the soldiers they have sent to the field."[7]

Soldiers were antagonized not only by civilian incomprehension of combat and the persistence of civilian early-war sentiment but by their conviction that certain sectors of civilian society had actually begun to work in opposition to soldier interests. Irritation that began with "We do more than they do" escalated from "They do not do as much as they could" to "What they do does us harm" and ultimately to "By what they do they *mean* to harm us." Both Union and Confederate soldiers grew angry at men who remained home, initially at those who dodged military service, subsequently at all who continued to engage in ordinary business activity. Federals, in addition, found even more intolerable the activities of Northern peace advocates.

One might anticipate that soldier antagonism toward service evaders would have been harsher in the Union Army than in the Confederate, for four-fifths of the South's eligible males did serve, against only one-half of the North's. Thomas Livermore wrote: "Substantially the whole military population of the Confederate States was placed under arms." Indeed, several analysts have concluded that too many Southerners became soldiers, to the detriment of the Confederacy's ability to sustain its armies in the field. Soldiers, moreover, were aware of Richmond's vigorous efforts to apprehend evaders; not many escaped the reach of the Bureau of Conscription.[8]

It is therefore surprising to discover such intense animus directed against so small a proportion of the whole. In large measure soldier hostility derived from the fact that legal exemptions were granted to one slaveholder or overseer for every twenty (later fifteen) slaves. Soldiers were convinced that the South's 300,000 slaveholders were underrepresented in the ranks. Defended on grounds of economic productivity and social control, the slaveholder exemption appeared principally to protect the wealthy; thus it incited cries that the conflict was the rich man's war but the poor man's fight. Jesse Reid of the 4th South Carolina was among the aggrieved: "I have come here and left everything that is dear to me on earth to fight and suffer all manner of hardships to protect [the neighbors'] property, not my own [he had none], whilst many of them who have property are still at home with their families—in fact they are the ones as a general rule that stay at home. . . . Will we poor soldiers ever be recompensed for what we are doing? I fear not."[9]

The words of a few made clear the presence of class grievance. Had Southern farmer-soldiers and Northern immigrant-soldiers possessed the education and the habits of expression of the better-heeled, it would probably be discovered that such concerns were more extensive and deep-seated than they now appear. This particular vexation, however, should more accurately be fitted within the Confederate soldier's growing estrangement from civilian society. The tendency among soldiers on both sides, regardless of class, was to attribute their own hardships to the malicious intent of some civilians and the indifference of all others. In late 1862, made unhappy by the large numbers of Confederate soldiers without tents, blankets, or shoes, Paxton complained: "Those of our people who are living at home in comfort have no conception of the hardships which our soldiers are enduring. And I think they manifest very little interest in it. They are disposed to get rich from the troubles of the country, and exact from the Government the highest prices for everything needed for the army."[10]

Northern evaders were far more numerous than Southern stay-at-homes, because the hiring of substitutes and the payment of commutation fees were much more extensive in Union territory. Like many of his comrades, Connolly was both derisive—"the carpet knights at home"—and angry—"the miserable cowardly sneaks at home." Here the New York City draft riots of July 13–16, 1863, proved a critical episode: Federal soldiers united in their vindictiveness toward the rioters. "We are mad with rage," Walter Carter of the 22d Massachusetts wrote. Weld hoped that the Washington government would put down the riots "with a strong hand, and not stop until they have shot or hung every one of the rioters. It is disgraceful, and I only wish that I could be in New York to help kill some of the rascals." Bellard and his comrades were equally impatient and sanguinary: String up the draft rioters and be done with it.[11]

Anger against Northern businessmen rested on grounds comparable to those cited by Confederate soldiers but was far more condemnatory. The link between evasion and business enterprise and injury to the soldier was occasionally expressed directly. When Charles Lynch and his friends of the 18th Connecticut received supplies from a captured Confederate wagon train, they discovered coffee packaged in their home town by, they were sure, profit-hungry businessmen. Carter's characterization of such people, "those ignoble sons who have remained at the rear and reaped the home harvest," was representative. But soldiers more often tied evasion with business activity through their disconcerting realization that after mid-1863 there was at home almost no stigma attached to commutation or substitution and that both had become commercial processes complete with advertising, agents, brokerages, complex financial negotiations, and exchanges of large sums. Those at war easily paired that activity with the shoddy goods scandals involving army contractors in 1861–62, and business enterprise became doubly suspect. The frequency and ferocity with which Union soldiers abused sutlers—tipping over their shanties and wagons, stealing their goods, sometimes beating them—mirrored grievances far beyond immediate irritations.[12]

Those whom Federal soldiers execrated most vigorously were Northern peace advocates. Like others who stayed at home, they were thought to be afraid—"cowardly skunks," James Miller of the 11th Pennsylvania called them. Indeed, privates simply assumed that men at home had joined peace efforts *because* they were cowards. Soldiers arraigned them, as they sometimes did businessmen, for aiding the enemy, but here they moved on to the charge that peace advocacy actually killed soldiers. Beatty was convinced that civilian criticism of the Administration encouraged the rebels, and he argued that only after peace returned should citizens quarrel about the way the war was fought. But whereas Lynch had said of those errant coffee-sellers that those who prolonged the war to enhance profit "should remember that every battle kills a soldier," Beatty indicted the peace party with the utmost directness. On it rested "the blood of many thousand soldiers." That reproach was widely shared in the ranks. Walt Whitman said that in his experience Union soldiers never spoke of Copperheads without a curse and would rather shoot them than rebel soldiers. Indeed, many Federals spoke as if peace proponents constituted an enemy more formidable than the Confederates. James Newton insisted that if only the Copperheads of the North were given whippings, "soon after, we would have peace."[13]

Union soldiers also showed a tendency, appearing as well in Confederate ranks, more and more to characterize their society by its evaders, profiteers, and nonsupporters of the war. Connolly became convinced that "everybody" at home was "scrambling for wealth or for office."[14]

How comprehensive and intense such feelings became as early as Gettysburg was unmistakable in Union soldiers' ruminations on the behavior of Confederate forces in the North. Angry that Pennsylvanians charged high prices for their bread and milk, Julian Hinkley of the 3d Wisconsin "wished a good many times that the rebs could have had a month more among the people of Pennsylvania." One of the Carter brothers scorned as "heavy dogs" the members of the Pennsylvania militia he had encountered: "I wish Lee had got a little further into the state." In mid-1864 Weld hoped "that the enemy would go up into Penn., and transfer the seat of war there. I think that it would have a beneficial effect on our people, and would make them realize the necessity of crushing the enemy in this campaign." Connolly wished that 10,000 Confederate cavalry would raid every Northern state, "burning, robbing and destroying everything in their pathway," and he was pleased when General Jubal Early's Confederate horsemen torched Chambersburg in July 1864: "It gave me pleasure to think of the drunken rebel raiders dancing and howling over the ruin they had wrought."[15]

The quality of those soldier complaints—amorphous or, if crystallized, trivial—suggested the degree to which soldiers had dissociated themselves from the larger society. Connolly earlier remarked that he would like to see what "the North" would do if its territory were invaded by Early's army, as if the North were no longer a collectivity that embraced him. The harshness of soldier proposals mirrored their separation. The ultimate fantasy, appearing with surprising frequency in late 1864, was to have the Union Army itself carry the war to the North. John Brobst said, "We would like to go back and fight northern cowards and traitors [better] than to fight rebels." Such civilians were "the miserablest of all God's creatures," whom Brobst could shoot as easily as he would fire on wolves. Were his father one, he would kill him.[16]

The pressures of campaigning ordinarily contained such antagonism, but when the pressures relaxed, trouble exploded. Sent to Brooklyn on riot duty in July 1863, Galwey's Ohio regiment found no rioters and brawled instead with the police, using belts and brass buckles and leaving a number of opponents seriously injured. One soldier who had nearly killed a deputy sheriff went undetected in a search of the ranks, and "almost all of us were glad of this result, for the police had shown a great desire to interfere with our personnel and to take part with the thieves and confidence men" who victimized soldiers. The end of the war provided many of the expected opportunities for soldier–civilian coalescence, but some as well for the venting of soldier anger. When Robert Strong's Illinois regiment discovered that Chicago had prepared no welcome for its members on their way to downstate homes and that they were expected to make do with rations of wormy crackers and "maggotty" meat, their rage erupted into a beer garden brawl, numerous fights with police, and bayonet charges against groups of Chicago citizens. "It was fun to see them run from those bayonets." General Joseph Hooker advised the Mayor to let the soldiers alone, "or they will burn down your city."[17]

Wrath on this order may ultimately have reflected an isolation from others that soldiers found increasingly oppressive. Given the divergence of experience and thus of attitudes, some weakening of that 1861 soldier–community solidarity was inevitable, but several other wartime developments operated to undermine the identification of unit and locale even faster. Principally to shore up political and popular support of the war, Northern states funneled new men into the war by forming new units. (Old units offered fewer opportunities for new officer appointments and fewer appeals to the prospective volunteer.) Wisconsin alone strove to keep its original regiments filled. Lacking the manpower to maintain such a system, the South was compelled to resort to frequent unit consolidations. Many Confederate companies lost an important measure both of intimacy and of local affiliation. Carlton McCarthy complained that Southern soldiers too often found themselves serving with "all sorts of men from anywhere and everywhere."[18]

The Union Army's problem here came not only from the depletion of its 1861–62 regiments but from the shifting mood at home. Better-heeled Northern communities, pained by the death lists and less anxious than in 1861 to send their own boys to war but threatened with periodic local drafts if their quotas were not met, began to recruit beyond their boundaries. Bounties lured outsiders whose enrollment counted against the town's requirement. From September 1862 to March 1865 Troy, Michigan, met only 30 percent of its quota through the enlistment of local men. Predictably, all of the locals served out their terms, whereas nearly one-half of the outsider recruits deserted.[19] It thus became harder and harder for the locale to continue to think of a particular unit as it had at the outset, just as it became more difficult for soldiers to continue to think of a particular unit as representing their community.

Numerous episodes suggested that by 1864 the dissolution of ties had advanced far beyond the point where structural modifications alone might account for soldier bitterness. Brobst's vow that he would shoot his father should he discover him to be a Copperhead may have been rhetorical, but in Connolly's references to those at home who "shout with fiendish joy as our comrades fell" and to "foes in front of us, foes to the right of us, foes to the left of us, foes behind us, true friends only in our own ranks and in the great heavens above us," anguish was unmistakable. There were expressions of comparable despair on the Confederate side. Eggleston said, "The idea that there was anybody back of us in this war . . . was too ridiculous to be treated seriously."[20]

Ambrose Bierce frequently addressed the isolation of the Civil War soldier and his anger at civilian incomprehension, ingratitude, and unworthiness—and often found it unnecessary to identify whether he was writing of Federals or Confederates. The narrator of "Killed at Resaca," reclaiming from the lieutenant's body the letter that had urged him to that fatally courageous deed, carried it back to its author. But she—a beautiful but "detestable creature"—saw on it spots of her lover's blood, recoiled, and hastily threw it into the fire. Again, in his story "One of the Missing," Bierce sought to demonstrate the soldier's loss of connection with the civilian world. Struck by a shell, a Union soldier lay bleeding and dying in pain, but there came to his mind "[n]o thoughts of home, of wife and children, of country, of glory. The whole record of memory was effaced"—and the man himself was terrified. Here the dying no longer called to those dear to them or framed that last valorous message of uprightness and reassurance.[21]

Still, though they often spoke sharply and sometimes acted angrily, soldiers remained bound by the ambivalence of all their attitudes toward civilian society. There was an ambiguity more profound than that of soldiers who realized civilians could not possibly know the reality of combat and yet became angry that they did not know. Soldiers wanted civilians to know of war. Exhausted by a terrible march, Carter wrote home, "I wished I could have rushed into the house and shown you a poor panting suffering soldier." But at the same time soldiers did *not* want civilians to know. Carter objected to the arrival in camp of a private's wife; visiting the war zone and seeing what soldiers did would, he feared, have a "bad effect on ladies," one "not at all improving of their feminine ideas and graces." That contradiction rested once again in the misfit of expectation and experience. Whether enlisting to defend Union or Southern homeland, soldiers had thought of themselves as fighters against invasive and injurious change, change that their enemies threatened to carry out. They expected that the conditions of life at home for which they risked their lives, and their relationship to that life at home, would remain on the day of their return exactly as they had been on the day they marched to war. But soldiers had themselves changed. Combat had altered them, and so painful had been the changes forced upon them that they wished the home folks to recognize, understand, and sympathize with their experience, but without having that knowledge alter either those at home or their relationships with their soldiers. It was an impossible prescription.[22]

Other ambiguities abounded. If soldiers of 1864–65 resented the women of 1861–62 who had exhorted them to courage, would they feel better about the women of 1864–65 who urged other male family members to remain safely at home? Addressing a letter to the *Tri-Weekly* of his Massachusetts town in early 1864, Carter urged that those at home recognize that the volunteers had done their part, that others should come forward. "The time has gone by for excuses. All who *can*, ought to enlist *now*." In his appeal Carter assumed that women had reversed their early-war attitudes and opposed enlistments.

A wife, sister or sweetheart should not prevail against the dictates of one's conscience. Their cries and entreaties should be of no avail. Let them listen to the mourning of the afflicted ones at home, [former soldiers] who have given up their all to the good of our suffering country, and then blush for shame, that they are such unworthy, recreant daughters of the republic. It is easy for women to cry, "I will not let them go," but there are sons, brothers and husbands in the ranks, and some in the "valley of the shadow of death," that are as dear at home as the precious ones you would keep from duty.[23]

Those conscripts and substitutes who came instead of that "Yeomanry of the North" Carter solicited posed another problem. Soldiers wished the fullest mobilization—Carter hoped that "all the shirkers will have to come"—but at the same time they judged latterday soldiers to be of the most inferior material. Connolly described substitutes as "poor men, cripples, convicts, and the riff raff of society." He thought no better of draftees. Soldiers agreed that all men should be compelled to meet the obligation that the volunteers had earlier accepted, but which of them wished to fight at the side of criminals and scoundrels? The presence of such men would surely bring down on the regiment a heavier discipline, weaken its performance in combat, and even endanger volunteer lives. Draftees and bounty men—"miserable fellows bought with money"—ran from the fight, Lyman attested, leaving "brave, high-toned men, who scorn to shirk their duty [to] be torn with canister and swept away with musketry." Thus the volunteers both envied and despised the slackers. The first set of feelings insisted that slackers be made to risk their lives as did the volunteers; the second set warned that their presence placed volunteers in still greater jeopardy.[24]

Even soldier condemnation of self-serving business activity had a wavering quality, its tone again oscillating between anger and envy. Soldiers were themselves rooted in the business ethic; they esteemed it even while convinced that they had become its victims. Many regretted that the commercial opportunities multiplying at home during the war were being denied them, and a considerable number spent vacant hours fashioning small-scale business schemes that they hoped, usually in vain, would prove operable from within the army.

By the last months of the war such ambiguous attitudes had engendered in soldier minds contradictory images of home. Edward Ripley in one breath spoke as if homesick—"Sunday night around the dining room stove, with its merry outpouring of affection . . . fragrant memories of roast potatoes, and the currant wine Mary used to . . . give us"—and in the next breath of those "croaking, carping, fault-finding 'stay at homes.'" He hoped that the people of Vermont would be haunted by the wrongs that his soldiers had suffered at their hands and that had goaded many volunteers to their deaths. He felt certain that the Union Army had been able to do no better against the enemy because of those "smooth, sleek, respectable citizens" in every community who sold inferior goods to the United States Government. John Brobst denounced home as the refuge of cowards and traitors and yet prized it as offering "all [in] society that is modest and good." Ultimately, home took on the qualities of a dream. Returning from a medical leave, Walter Carter felt as if he were awakening: "My dream is over; I awake to find myself in camp." Robert Gould Shaw was able to secure a leave to return to Massachusetts for his sister's wedding. The gowns, the table cloths, the heated rooms all seemed chimerical. Recalling his pledge to his mother that he would never gamble, Foote decided that such promises had become part of "an unreal world," one he doubted he would ever see again. Here was yet another soldier grievance, that those at home should continue to inveigh against the moral contaminations of army life long after soldier fears had moved far beyond purity to struggle with dismemberment and death.[25]

Perhaps because they found intolerable the prospect of any additional fragility in their lives, many soldiers strove to accommodate opposing images of home. Their efforts ordinarily took the form of a distinction between the home represented by the family and the home represented by home town, national government, and civilian society. They pictured the family home as a small island of warmth, support, and reassurance caught in seas of indifference and neglect or infidelity and betrayal. It was not always easy to make such a separation, to divorce the family from the society soldiers were convinced was unworthy of their sacrifice. James Miller felt embarrassment and rage when he learned that his own brothers had joined other young men in a draft insurance club, contributing sums that would be used to pay the commutation or to hire a substitute for any member who should be drafted. "The Farmington [Pennsylvania] Cowards Mutual Insurance Society," he had bitterly labeled it.[26] But most soldiers appeared to exempt their own families from the anger they directed homeward.

By 1864 that earlier sense of identity between soldiers and

the societies in whose name they had marched to war had been replaced by a sense of soldier disaffection, probably more severe among Federals than Confederates. Southern soldiers could be just as caustic on the failings of the Richmond government and the weaknesses of Jefferson Davis's leadership as Unionists were contemptuous of stay-at-homes or Stanton's War Department, but Confederate soldiers knew that Southern civilians were suffering the harsh exactions of raids, invasion, and occupation, that they were undeniably experiencing the "taste" of war the Federals were so eager to see their own countrymen encounter. Still, some Confederate soldiers acted in ways Southern civilians must have found difficult to distinguish from the behavior of Sherman's men. William Fletcher, in 1864 a member of the 8th Texas Cavalry, with threats of violence and without compunction appropriated the food and firearms of Tennesseans and Georgians: "[O]ne loaded gun in hand would have been more effective than the prayers of all the mothers and the crying and begging of the children." He forced civilians to "trade" their horses. He shot into refugee columns, scattering women and children and the elderly of both races and "enjoying the fun immensely."[27]

Although sustained in both sections, links between soldiers and civilians in North and South had been strained in ways none could have predicted in 1861.

The pattern of the war's final years imposed new stress too on relationships between officers and enlisted men. The intensification of combat; the diminishing resort to officer elections; the arrival of conscripts and substitutes; the increasing severity of discipline; the inclination of officers to seek recognition less in the men's judgment of their courage than in their superiors' readiness to promote them—all seemed to widen distances between the two groups.

Those in the ranks could not escape awareness of growing social separation. Some suspected, not always groundlessly, that it derived simply from snobbery. Accompanied to war by an Irish servant, Charles Wainwright vigorously denounced the Union Army's inclination toward the mixing of classes. He found offensive interclass drinking and the interclass singing of ribald songs. He was disgusted that privates were able to "hobnob" with their captains and that officers and men crowded together in train coaches on "a purely democratic footing." A few Brahmin units had attempted from the beginning to enforce a strict social segregation, and officers had been dismissed from the service for excessive intimacy with their men, for drinking or even eating with them. But the separation drew far less on such class-conscious efforts than on commanders' determination to stifle informality as an impediment to the new disciplinary order they thought essential to the prosecution of the war.[28]

Simultaneously, the men began to feel that higher-ranking officers no longer shared, and were sometimes ignorant of, the increasing onerousness of campaigning. Daniel Crotty was convinced that officers cushioned by high pay and servants lived "like princes" and knew little of the hardships he endured. Carter's complaints were more precise: Officers protected themselves against the cold rain with warming whisky denied the men; officers appropriated for personal use ambulances that should have carried the wounded; officers confiscated unfair shares of the good things sent forward by such organizations as the Sanitary Commission. Soldiers might disagree regarding the degree of blame attaching to officers, but all sensed the new separateness and felt disadvantaged by it. Wilkeson noticed the loss of "the friendly feeling of cordial comradeship between the enlisted men and their officers, which was one of the distinguishing characteristics of the volunteer troops." Bardeen began to feel condescension even in officers attempting to be kind to him; he concluded that even close friends would find that shoulder straps built barriers.[29]

Those same tendencies doubtless ran in the Confederate Army. No longer were Southern officers and men sleeping and eating together "on terms of entire equality." Carlton McCarthy thought that in organizing their own messes officers wished to assert their superiority. They might thereby gain in dignity, but at high cost: the weakening of "the bond of brotherhood" and "the loss of personal devotion as between comrades." Alexander Hunter's indictment of the results read as if written by a Union footsoldier:

> The officers above the rank of captain knew but little of the hardships of war from personal experience. They had their black cooks, who were out foraging all the time, and they filled their masters' bellies if there was fish or fowl to be had. The regimental wagons

carried the officers' clothes, and they were never half-naked, lousy, or dirty. They never had to sleep upon the bare ground nor carry forty rounds of cartridges strapped around their galled hips; the officers were never unshod or felt the torture of stone-bruise.[30]

Still, the impression persists that the gulf was narrower in the Southern army than in the Northern. (The Virginian John Dooley even argued that the common experience of combat—notably, one imagines, the leveling effect of its deprivations and hardships—*lessened* distances between members of Southern social groups.) Federal forces possessed the resources to establish extensive distinctions and the manpower to enforce them; the Confederate Army did not. Indeed, the Union Army extended the pattern of separation far beyond military areas, and this rear-echelon discrimination became a source of special bitterness to some Northern soldiers. Crotty wrote sourly of war zone distinctions: the Long Bridge across the Potomac closed after First Bull Run to enlisted men but not to officers ("Oh, yes, the officers could pass and bask in the sunshine of luxury, but the poor soldier could lie down by the roadside and die from want."), and the water sources on the Peninsula and at Gettysburg reserved for the use of officers. But the experiences of a twenty-day furlough after Antietam provoked his highest wrath. He discovered Washington restaurants that offered officers and men separate and unequal dining facilities; boats and trains that reserved their best accommodations for officers; and sentinels whose sole duty was to enforce such separation. Not until he reached Harrisburg, traveling westward, did he again feel as good as an officer.[31]

Aggravating soldiers' initial egalitarian resistance to differential treatment was the fact that officer perquisites seemed to multiply just as their justification seemed to the men weaker than ever. In 1863 and 1864, particularly in the wake of the terrible casualties of the Wilderness battles, they contended with a painful sense of their own expendability; a common response was to blame officers as those whose orders sent soldiers to their deaths but who, as a group, remained in comfort and safety. Crotty caught this sentiment in his complaint that officers led soldiers to battle but seldom stayed, and in his invocation of a poem that seemed to reach fifty years into the future: "All quiet along the Potomac. . . . /Not an officer lost—only one of the men." The same order of suspicion rose from George Allen's accusation of July 1863 that "this war had not lasted *long* enough to suit some people. Not enough money had been made out of it. Not enough military reputation had been acquired by some shoulder-strapped authority. Not enough blood had been spilt to satisfy some one."[32]

Soldiers occasionally gave vent to such feelings. During a post-Fredericksburg review, when the colonel gave the signal for Galwey's Ohio regiment to cheer General Ambrose Burnside, the ranks remained resoundingly silent. There were as well instances of solidarity against officers built on foundations utterly different from those of 1861–62. In early 1863 a French Canadian recruit serving in the 4th Rhode Island received in the mail a civilian suit whose purpose, many realized, was to facilitate his desertion. Ordinarily, such a person, a "foreigner," would have elicited little sympathy, but "such was the state of feeling in the regiment at that time that no blame was attached to any one who was smart enough to get away." Not even the orderly sergeant bothered to alert an officer to prevent the man's escape.[33]

Such sharp cleavages were rare, however, for at play were other influences softening the estrangement of volunteer soldiers from their officers. The first bore on those who entered the ranks from 1863 onward, those latterday bounty recruits, draftees, and substitutes whom the volunteers recognized as different from themselves. They would continue to complain, as Crotty did, that privates were "degraded with punishment not fit for an Indian savage" or, as Carter did, that common soldiers were executed for crimes that brought down on officers dismissal from the service or, at most, several months' imprisonment, but volunteers silently conceded that if the latecomers were to be made into reliable soldiers, they would require exactly that strong hand of discipline that volunteers so resented when applied to themselves. (This was the context in which soldiers continued to denounce military executions but began to make exceptions when the condemned were bounty jumpers.) Perhaps with both regret and some pride, Wilkeson granted that latterday soldiers lacked' the "moral qualities" to which officers were able to appeal in the 1861–62 volunteers. On the Confederate side, too, Eggleston acknowledged the inferiority of the newly arrived soldiery: "[C]onscription brought in a good deal of material which was worse than useless." He despised them as cowards but, like the Union volunteers, could not locate practical grounds on which the volunteers might continue to enjoy a discipline more lenient than that applied to late arrivals in the same unit. Thus, he proclaimed, the Confederate Army had learned "the value of un-questioning obedience" and the duty "to listen and obey."[34]

There was exaggeration here—the latter phrase came just as jarringly to most soldiers' ears in 1864 as it had in 1861—but both armies had come to accept a new stringency in discipline. Lucius Barber of the 15th Illinois became furious when, as an exchanged prisoner of war, he was held at Castle Williams on Governor's Island in damp and filthy casements that "would shame a hog pen." In close confinement with him were recruits, furloughed men, and Confederate prisoners. Deserters and bounty jumpers were in custody on the floor above. It was a disgrace, Barber complained, that the government did not distinguish between such categories of persons. But he objected principally to the treatment meted out, not to all Federals, but to him and other "good soldiers" who had fought and suffered in rebel stockades: "Can this be a nation's gratitude?" During the Wilderness campaign provost guards followed Union columns and drove the laggards with fixed bayonets ("——you!—You— . . . get up, will you? By——, I'll kill you if you don't go on, double-quick!"), a practice that would have incited men to violent protest in 1861–62. The loss of solidarity within the ranks made increasingly rare the common front against officer imposition.[35]

The second factor muting soldier–officer discord was the brutal reality that by 1864, with so many officers dead on the battlefield, significant numbers of privates had themselves become officers. Shoulder straps did create differences, but as long as both the issuer of commands and the recipient remembered that they had not long before marched shoulder to shoulder, the one was likely to modulate his orders and the other to temper his resistance. The caste differences characteristic of the few regular army units (whose desertion rates, not coincidentally, were strikingly higher) seldom developed among the volunteers. Occasionally a soldier would fiercely differentiate between "them" and "us" and speak of the army's command structure as if it were his primary antagonist, but he was likely to be one of the soldiers involved in detached duty or prisoner exchanges, which left him without the protection of his regiment. Seldom did soldiers speak of their own units in that fashion. Often those most critical of officers exempted their own lieutenants and captains. Even the acidic Crotty had praise for his regiment's field officers. For each incident manifesting a common front against officers, there were others to suggest some continuing congruence of interest between volunteers and their officers. In Dooley's 1st Virginia, volunteers who feared the inexperience of the conscripts joined *with* officers in urging the new arrivals not to elect one of their own to a command position.[36]

Still, an awareness of the limits of change should not obscure the fact that basic change had occurred. In the first months of the war soldiers and officers had joined in their shared respect for courage, a force that had proved more cohesive than the stresses of discipline had been divisive. By 1864, however, that early willingness to view officers as other men of courage bound fewer and fewer soldiers. Affinity was diminishing, and formal discipline was gaining strength.

Feeling themselves drawn apart from those at home, from later arrivals in their own ranks, and, in lesser degree, from their officers, volunteer soldiers on both sides experienced a troubled sense of isolation, which they attempted to relieve by tightening bonds between themselves. In all wars there is in units subjected to rigorous campaigning and suffering high casualties a propensity for shrinking circles of survivors to strengthen their ties— "the camaraderie of misery," Ernie Pyle called it[37]—but the Civil War offered its soldiers particular inducements. The changing nature of combat weakened drastically the original soldier conviction that at the center of war stood the confident individual. On the contrary, this war had demonstrated its power to punish all soldiers far more severely than any personal deficiency could possibly penalize the single soldier. In short, private concerns regarding one's courage or cowardice began to yield to the collective experience, and soldiers became more concerned with survival than with any private triumph of values.

Another set of concerns also intensified comradeship. However emotionally unprepared, soldiers had marched to war expecting to kill. They had not, however, expected to steal, burn, and destroy, and the unease they felt on those counts drew them closer to others who had acted identically. Far more intense than casual home town friendship, comradeship offered support in combat that the soldier of 1861 would have denied he would ever require; a compensation for the emotional support of the home folks that seemed surprisingly less relevant; and a reassurance that, though he was acting in ways that would have been abhorrent three years before, he had not become an evil person.

The mess became the focus of comradeship. Early-war arrangements employing company cooks had not worked, and the armies gave soldiers permission to establish their own messes of from three to eight or even ten men. Those were not rigid units—later recruits might be granted admission after they had been taunted, hazed, and tested in battle—but there was a strong basis of affinity implicit in the soldier's selection of his own messmates, a rapport likely to be cemented by combat experience. Bell Irvin Wiley called messes the armies' "little families," and within them many soldiers developed emotional attachments of a quality unknown to them before or after. "Cut off as he is from all the allurements of the world, the charm of social life, the fascination of money-making, all the endearing joys of home," Alexander Hunter wrote of the Confederate soldier, "he has to look for happiness in the kindness and good will of his comrades. Their joys and sorrows are his; he learns to look upon them as brothers; there is no sacrifice that he will not make for them; no trouble that he will not cheerfully take. Fellowship becomes almost a religion."[38]

Telling themselves that others could no longer understand how soldiers were acting in war (and, even less, how the war was acting on soldiers), men began to speak of the mess as home, of their group as a family, and of their comrades as brothers. The strength of such ties found its most dramatic demonstration in the determination of some soldiers to return to the war when nothing save comradeship impelled them to do so. Those were cases, extraordinary to be sure, of furloughs cut short, of extensions unapplied for, of subterfuges employed to thwart doctors' refusals to release the sick or wounded. Hunter said, "No greater pleasure is known to the soldier than the warm welcome extended him after a long absence, by his comrades."[39]

Comradeship was not ordinarily a gateway to a new relationship with the army. Some turned to the company or regiment—the soldier who had not distinguished himself, Fitch believed, came to depend on "the fame of his organization"—but most could not fully invest themselves in units they were compelled to share with those contemptible conscripts. As for the army at large, a few soldiers employed expressions of twentieth-century tonality—"the mysterious solidarity of the mighty compelling organisation," the merger of the "individual consciousness into the composite consciousness of a regiment"—but such statements appeared infrequently. Comradeship, moreover, while a condition owing much of its power to affect, was doubtlessly also one of practicality. No one denied its advantageousness as a combat insurance policy, a soldier's commitment to aid stricken comrades on the understanding that others would similarly assist him. Nevertheless, Civil War soldiers discussed much more frequently comradeship's emotional affiliations. To them, it was a refuge in a day when previously important links with others within and beyond the armies were weakening or disappearing. In reality, the soldier had nowhere to turn save to his friends in the ranks, for the experience of combat had isolated him from the patterns of civilian life in ways that army discipline could not.[40]

Despite the intensification of combat and the acceleration of terror tactics, the character of the connection between Federal and Confederate soldier adversaries altered less than any of those relationships described above. Several issues threatened to engender bitterness, but each time front-line soldiers located elsewhere the source of villainy and absolved of responsibility the fighters of the other side. Indeed, from that growing sense of their own isolation, soldiers seemed to denounce all parties to the war except the enemy in combat.

The treatment of prisoners of war, under military jurisdiction in both North and South, seemed sure to harden enmity. More than 30,000 Federal soldiers died in Confederate prisons or camps (a mortality rate of 15.5 percent) and almost 26,000 Southerners in Northern facilities (a 12 percent mortality).[41] During the war distant reports of great numbers of deaths produced less impact than the sight of wretched returnees, young men captured who when exchanged appeared to have been made old by utmost misery. Soldiers and civilians on both sides were enraged at what they deemed purposeful mistreatment, but while civilians sprang from the issue to a denunciation of the opposing cause and all its adherents, soldiers almost always exempted from blame those directly across the lines. In their view, the evil lay with other, nonfighting soldiers, with enemy civilians, or with the enemy government.

James Nisbet of the 66th Georgia was captured at Peachtree Creek on July 22, 1864, and sent north for fourteen months' imprisonment on Johnson's Island, near Sandusky, Ohio. His treatment by Union soldiers near the front was considerate, but that on the island was shameful. The home guards of the 128th Ohio were "absolutely brutal" and, he charged, killed and wounded prisoners who failed to extinguish their lights by 9:00 P.M. But Nisbet seemed angriest that his guards did not share the combat soldier's perception of the opponent: "To admire gallantry, in a foe, or to admit that he was honest in battling for what he held to be right, was beyond anything they could conceive." His only satisfaction came when the 128th, sent to pursue the Confederate raider John Morgan, was captured, paroled, and returned to Johnson's Island minus its weapons, to the delighted jeers of the prisoners.[42]

Rice Bull of the 123d New York was taken at Chancellorsville when Southern forces overran his position. He was immediately robbed by Confederates, whom he called "stragglers and skulkers" and whom he was pleased to report were soon rounded up by provost guards. From that point "the Johnnies," even those from units that had lost heavily in that battle, "treated us with kindness and with consideration for our feelings." At an assembly point, another Union prisoner sang "Home, Sweet Home" and Federals and Confederates alike became tearful. Southern civilians who came to view the prisoners, however, did not share their soldiers' "kindly feelings," for their comments evinced hatred and their questions were derisive, until a Confederate soldier who had befriended Bull and had returned four times to aid him told one of his persecutors, "You just keep quiet, old man, don't you see these are wounded men? You have no right or business to insult them."[43]

When Lucius Barber of the 15th Illinois was captured in October 1864, members of the 6th Mississippi, "a noble looking set of men," treated him "civilly." "I found amongst them some brother masons, and the strong bonds of fraternal love which permeates our order were held sacred by those arrayed in arms against us." Later, another Mason trusted him to go without a guard to fill canteens. The Alabama militia, however, treated them "more like brutes than men" before they were deposited in Andersonville, of which they had long held "a horrid dread." Fear was justified, for there they joined Federal prisoners who were "confined in loathsome dungeons, or foul pens, starved, sick, meeting with nothing but injury and insult." The prisoner experience threatened to demolish all soldier precepts of courage and cowardice, with one exception—the worthiness of the battlefield opponent: "[W]henever we fell into the hands of veteran soldiers who had fought us bravely on the battle-field, we received all of the kind and considerate attention due a prisoner of war, but whenever we were in charge of militia or that class of persons who, too cowardly to take the field, enlisted in the home guard, we were treated in the most outrageous manner."[44]

All denounced their incarceration—it was the occasion for the bitterest words of wartime and postwar periods—but seldom was the indictment extended to the combat opponent. Indeed, it might be argued that such contrasting treatment tightened the bonds between battlefield adversaries.

The advent of a warfare of terror seemed even more likely to intensify the animosity of soldier for soldier. Confederates, after all, knew that their own families had been or might become its targets. No doubt feelings ran deep on that score. Nisbet remarked of Sherman's Georgia offensive, "Throughout this whole campaign the regulations of Civilized Warfare and the teachings of humanity, were trampled under foot by the Federals—with open brutality." Thomas Key was incensed at the shelling of Atlanta and the subsequent forced evacuation of its civilians by Union occupiers. But once again blame did not fix itself at the level of the combat soldier, though he might very well have been burning Southern homes. It remained focused instead on individuals deemed to be of a malignant and surpassing evil. As survivors of Southern prisons would fasten the deaths of fellow prisoners on Captain Henry Wirz, the commandant of Andersonville—"an emissary of Satan," "this devil in human shape"—or on a small group of Confederate political leaders—"a pitiless cabal," "the clique of ambitious statesmen . . . responsible for the terrible sufferings that befell the unhappy captives"—so did Southern soldiers confine responsibility for terror warfare to individuals, principally Sherman. Key thought it sufficient to describe the bombardment of Atlanta as Sherman's "cruel piece of cowardice." "*He* shelled the women and children of Atlanta for five days" and then, to cover "*his* cruel and ungentlemanly conduct," he forced the evacuation. One required no further explanation. The problem was one of personal malevolence. Sherman was a heartless man.[45]

Neither terror warfare nor prisoner deaths significantly altered battlefield relations. The informal truces of the enlisted men remained a problem for both high commands. The same Nisbet who had charged that Yankees in Georgia trampled "the teachings of humanity" described, with no sense of contradiction, soldiers' determination to cease shooting each evening to listen to musicians standing atop the opposing works and to mingle "fraternally" with the enemy whenever opportunity could be created. Even amid the fierce combat of the Petersburg lines, the unofficial truce persisted. Those who continued to kill one another in battle often felt less estrangement from their victims than from those in whose behalf they had gone to fight.[46]

12

Disillusionment

Forced to absorb the shocks of battle, to remodel combat behavior, to abandon many of the war's initial tenets, to bear discipline of an order intolerable not long before, to rationalize a warfare of destruction, and to come to terms with changes in their relationships with commanders, conscripts, and civilians, soldiers suffered a disillusionment more profound than historians have acknowledged—or the soldiers themselves would concede twenty-five years later. The intensification of ties with comrades and the maintenance of respect for enemy combatants were ultimately defensive reactions by soldiers who were alarmed that the war's experience was isolating them from those beyond battle and were turning for support to those who knew battle as they did. Neither, however, could offset the effects of their separation from the foundations of their prewar lives.

Disillusionment, here defined as the deeply depressive condition arising from the demolition of soldiers' conceptions of themselves and their performance in war—a void of disorientation, Robert Wiebe has called it—is not an easy state of mind to detect or to verify in large groups. One must therefore rely on inferences from broad indications that general moods, transient earlier, became more intense and enduring and that soldiers testified to the gravity of those moods in new language, images, and conclusions regarding the war. The attempt to establish such disillusionment is meant to suggest not that it had an unrecognized military influence on the course of the war but rather that disregard of it in post-1865 considerations of the significance of the war would become a matter of great social consequence.

It is possible to take the contrary position that the war that changed soldiers itself provided the means of immunizing soldiers against the full force of that change. Cognizant of what was happening to them, soldiers called it "hardening" and recognized it as essential to their ability to remain in the ranks. "The dread and sickening loathing created by many a corpse on a battlefield," Washington Davis said, "is by familiarity and constant view transformed into a stoical indifference. Were this not so, the awful carnage of some battles would have made deserters of thousands of soldiers." Indeed, some felt satisfaction that the war was toughening them. The infantryman occasionally drew a dry pleasure from a description of himself as "a callous old soldier, who has seen too many horrors to mind either good or bad."[1]

Difficulties arose, however, as the process continued to extend itself, and hardening merged with coarsening. When William Blackford passed surgeons' tables for the first time and lost his stomach in "ecstasies of protest," he was anxious to put such reactions behind him. While still "unused to such incidents," he had found the battlefield "a dismal sight," but he began to harden and was soon able to examine the results of battle in a manner "interesting and instructive." "I made it a point . . . to ride over the battlefields immediately after the firing ceased, and acquired much valuable information in this way. You see exactly where the best effects were produced, and what arm of the service [infantry or artillery fire] produced them, for there lies the harvest they have reaped." Later he inspected the bones of a Federal soldier he believed he had killed: "But such is war! . . . it made me feel a little queer to see that skull grinning at me . . . and yet his bullet might have placed me in a similar position." Though he continued to consider the groans and prayers of the wounded "not agreeable," he began to find "something soothing" in the sight of so many of the enemy suffering on the field.[2]

Some annealing was essential, but the evolution of the soldier often moved beyond it to a gratuitous malevolence. Two episodes recounted by Frank Wilkeson suggest the pitch of hardness common in the Petersburg lines during the final year of the war.

> Thickly scattered among the trees, and grouped at the edge of the open field, in the shade, were those cowards, the "coffee boilers."

241

Gangs of officers' servants and many refugee negroes were [also] there. Pack-mules loaded with pots, frying-pans, gripsacks, and bags of clothing stood tied to trees. White-capped army wagons . . . stood at the edge of the woods. The drivers . . . were drinking coffee with friendly "boilers," and they were probably frightening one another by telling blood-curdling tales of desperate but mythical battles they had been engaged in . . . I could almost smell the freshly made Rio and the broiled bacon. It was as though a huge pic-nic were going on in the woods. The scene angered me. I knew that the "coffee-boilers" were almost to a man bounty-jumping cowards, and I wanted the camp broken up. [Here Wilkeson's battery passed to the rear to replenish its ammunition and on its return attracted the enemy's attention.] I saw the Confederate gunners spring to their cannon. I looked at the camp of the "coffee boilers." They were enjoying life. I leaned forward and clasped my knees with [an] excess of joy as I realized what was about to occur. . . . Clouds of smoke shot forth from the redoubt, and out of these, large black balls rose upward and rushed through the air, and passed, shrieking shrilly, close above us, to descend in the camp of the "boilers." It was a delightful scene. I hugged my knees and rocked to and fro and laughed until my flesh-less ribs were sore. [L]arge trees . . . fell with a crash among the frying-pans and coffee-pots. Teamsters sprang into their wagons . . . and ran for the rear. Men, clad and armed as soldiers, skurried as frightened rabbits, hid in holes, lay prone on the earth. . . . Through the dust and smoke and uproar I saw men fall, saw others mangled by chunks of shell, and saw one, struck fairly by an exploding shell, vanish. Enormously pleased, I hugged my lean legs, and laughed and laughed again. It was the most refreshing sight I had seen for weeks.

That afternoon the battery quartermaster-sergeant, goaded to desperation by the taunts of the artillery privates, nerved himself with whiskey and came to the battery to display his courage. The Confederate sharp-shooters had attacked us about noon, and our works were hot. I, snugly seated under the earthworks, looked at this representative of the staff with all the intense dislike privates have for the gold-laced officers. I was wicked enough to wish that he would get shot. He swaggered up and down behind the guns, talking loudly, and ignorant of the danger. I, with high-beating heart, looked eagerly at him, hungrily waiting for him to jump and howl. I was disappointed. A sharp-shooter's bullet struck him on the throat. It crashed through his spine at the base of the brain, and he neither jumped nor howled—simply fell on his back dead.

Even the practical jokes played on comrades could become harsh. Robert Strong described one of the "pranks" contrived by Sherman's men during the South Carolina campaign. When soldiers fell asleep leaning against pine trees, the top branches would be set afire, and hot pitch, running down the trunks, would "glue" soldiers to burning trees.[3]

Combat soldiers followed several lines of reasoning in the attempt to explain what had happened to them. Sherman's argument that harshness was the essence of war and that the soldier could act in no other fashion won wide currency. Contemplating the expulsion of Southern civilians from their homes, Theodore Upson decided that it was "pretty tough . . . but it is war." Sherman had said that war was hell, and "I think that it is." Another popular attitude was one best expressed by Mary Livermore, who herself worked to develop an endurance of the sights of battlefield and hospital. As she conceived it, hardening was a merciful process productive of "a temporary stoicism." In that light, the soldier might think of the war simply as thrusting his true, peacetime nature into a state of suspension. Again Upson agreed. In a letter discussing the vices of camp life, he assured those at home that the soldiers' "better-selves" were "lying dormant" and that once soldiers returned to civilian life, their "roughness" would fall away.[4] Neither hardening nor the ideas supporting it, however, sufficed to persuade all that they were as powerless as Sherman implied or that the results were as transient as Livermore promised. Some felt threatened by the momentum of the process, dreaded its effects, and tried to draw lines against actions they feared were corrupting. Berry Benson of the 1st South Carolina decided that looting was (as McClellan claimed) "a species of demoralization," and he long resisted taking anything from Federal corpses or captives—until in the spring of 1865 he confiscated a prisoner's boots to replace his own worn-out and ill-fitting pair.[5] Nevertheless, most soldiers, intent on self-preservation and ill-equipped to resist the war's impetus, conformed to the actions of those around them.

Charles Francis Adams pondered his reaction to the sight of a wounded Southern officer: "The poor fellow was lying in the snow at the foot of the tree, shot through the abdomen and now and again writhing in pain. . . . [H]ow could I look on him wholly without feeling? And yet I did just that. No one who has not felt it knows what a brutaliser war is!" John DeForest grew to regard extended soldiering as productive of soldiers who became "bloodhounds held in leash." Two stretcher bearers brought a fatally wounded soldier off the field, dug his grave, then sat and smoked, heedless of the soldier's gasps "in the agonies of death." When he died, they roughly tipped him into the hole and went back for the next. Watching, George Allen of the 4th Rhode Island concluded with regret:

> By being accustomed to sights which would make other men's hearts sick to behold, our men soon became heart-hardened, and sometimes scarcely gave a pitying thought to those who were unfortunate enough to get hit. Men can get accustomed to everything; and the daily sight of blood and mangled bodies so blunted their finer sensibilities as almost to blot out all love, all sympathy from the heart, and to bring more into prominence the baser qualities of man, selfishness, greed, and revenge.[6]

Not everyone worried about such matters. Many accepted coarsening as blithely as Wilkeson, but a significant number were troubled by the cost of the emotional callus necessary to endure life in war. Their yearning for something softer was evident in the songs they asked to hear. "The Battle Hymn of the Republic" may have reflected Northern popular attitudes when it appeared in the *Atlantic Monthly*'s February 1862 issue, but soldier preferences began to shift soon thereafter. Nurse Woolsey noticed in mid-1863 that soldiers were singing it less often than "When This Cruel War Is Over." The historian Dixon Wecter called that song "the war's supreme ditty of heartbreak." "A depressing song . . . it was sometimes banned by local provosts marshal in the interests of group morale." "Tenting Tonight," with its longing for peace, rivaled it as *the* soldier song of 1863, and in 1864 the mood darkened further with "Just Before the Battle, Mother," probably the Union Army's most frequently sung song. There were reports that it and others like it—"Rock Me to Sleep, Mother," "Home, Sweet Home," "Do They Miss Me at Home?"—provoked quivering lips, tears, and even sobbing in soldier audiences. The only late-war song that retained any jauntiness was "When Johnny Comes Marching Home," "the touchstone," Wecter wrote, "of happy days to come."[7]

There was another set of concerns that no soldier could treat lightly. At its heart was the soldier's feeling that he had become less an actor in war than an object caught in a process moving forward in ways that would inexorably encompass his own disaster. If soldier attitudes could be compressed into phrases, then "We won the battle and our bravery was glorious" or "Though we were defeated, our bravery was sublime" might reflect the war's early period, and "The battle was terrible but redeemed by the soldiers' wonderful gallantry" its midpoint. But by 1864 soldiers were talking as if nothing could relieve combat of its tragic aspects or provide returns commensurate with its costs. Letters from the Wilderness no longer exulted or lamented over the outcomes of particular battles. Each fight seemed simply the next stage of that fearful process. Thought focused not on victory and defeat—Grant's victories were more costly than Lee's defeats—but on the soldier's diminishing hope of evading or delaying his own destruction.

Here the development of greatest impact was the decimation of the regiments. That notion of simmering down possessed a sad pertinence beyond the winnowing of equipment and beliefs: It applied equally to the weeding of men. Interestingly, some soldiers expressed gratification at its early results. Alexander Hunter felt pride that the Army of Northern Virginia's initial disease and combat deaths had "purified [it] of all the delicate and broken-down, the sick as well as the cowards and skulkers." Robert Strong thought that his regiment, thinned by the departure of dead and wounded and by the flight of the cowardly to the teamsters and ambulance corps, was then "made up of the best material." Of the 105 young men who had left Chicago, the thirty-five who remained were "as tough as gristle." Alpheus Williams was pleased that the Army of the Potomac had been "simmered down to the very sublimation of human strength and endurance." But such feelings could scarcely persist beyond the point where soldiers realized that the process did not halt when it achieved that "sublimation" and that the survival of the best of them was no more likely than that of any of the others. Soon the congratulatory note disappeared from Williams's reaction: "Deaths, wounds, sickness, and discharges are rapidly reducing us to a skeleton army."[8]

Here, as individuals, no matter how spirited, courageous, and healthy, came to realize their own vulnerability to simmering down, the diminution of the regiment became ominous. Paul Steiner has estimated that without replacements Civil War regiments disappeared in about three years—after mid-1861, the usual term of enlistment in the Union Army—and, as noted, recruits were ordinarily organized into new regiments rather than assigned to keep existing regiments up to strength. Bruce Catton placed the strength of the average regiment in the latter stages of the war at between 200 and 300 men. Almost 300 Union regiments suffered at least 130 battle deaths and fatal woundings, and forty-five regiments lost between 200 and 295—to which figures must be added twice those numbers for those succumbing to disease. Yet to many soldiers this terrible shrinkage to 20 or 30 percent of the unit's original strength was made even more oppressive by their consciousness of *who* had been lost.[9]

Volunteers watching the regiment dwindle to the size of a battalion, then a company, and sometimes a platoon were acutely sensitive to the disappearance of those with whom they had come to war. Michael Fitch began his service as a sergeant with the 6th Wisconsin. Of his company's original complement of ninety-two, fifty-two were killed or wounded, and when he returned in early 1865 to visit the company, then a part of a newly consolidated regiment, he recognized no more than a half-dozen faces. "All of the other members of the company then present were strangers to me." Of the eight Southerners who had formed Berry Benson's mess, three were killed in action and the other five wounded. In the war's final stages it seemed to him that he rarely saw a Confederate soldier who had not been wounded. Hinman realized that the six regiments of the Sherman Brigade, in which more than 7,000 officers and men had served, could summon to duty in 1865 no more than 1,200—and that one-third of the survivors bore wounds. Losses on such a scale made soldiers painfully aware of the dwindling and sometimes disappearance of certain categories of soldiers. LeGrand Wilson noted with regret that day in the Wilderness when his Mississippi regiment lost the last of the field officers who had come with it to Virginia in 1862. Of the thirty-four officers who had mustered in with Oliver Wendell Holmes's 20th Massachusetts—the Harvard Regiment—only two were still present when it mustered out four years and ten days later.[10]

Among those who remained, the common reaction was fear that one was being abandoned. "I am losing all my old army friends," Carter wrote from the Wilderness. Following a battle in which his men, caught in a Confederate fire that wounded him and seemed to "knock over" everybody, Stephen Weld appeared obsessed by the thought that "[e]veryone is being killed that I know." Perhaps it was in that frame of mind that Alpheus Williams—conscious of the loss of his officers (as early as Second Bull Run he had written home, "Not a field officer is here! All killed or wounded!"), of the deaths of many friends ("sudden and painful partings and . . . friendships swept away by hundreds in an hour of bloody battle"), and of the departures of remaining friends (when in mid-1864 the last of his Detroit friends left the service, he lamented that "I shall have no one about me from home")—felt such deep isolation: "I sometimes get so *lonely* when surrounded by thousands."[11]

As hopefulness drained away, the sequel was likely to be the thought, "I am next." Carter told his family, "Many wrote yesterday and today are dead. I hardly dare to write you of my safety, lest I am a dead man before the vain assurance reaches you." During Sherman's march, General Williams one day went out to inspect rebel fortifications blocking his path. Several hours later a twenty-year-old member of his staff proceeded to the same spot and was "brought back to my quarters a corpse." Williams was deeply agitated; so many men had been struck down near him, he thought it a miracle that he had escaped. "Accustomed as I have been for three years to like scenes, I know of no similar event as the death of this brave and beautiful boy, which has so long and so deeply impressed me," perhaps because he was aware that one could not count on the recurrence of miracles. Captain Andrews of the 8th Infantry asked James Wilson if the general knew where he could obtain a bugle mouthpiece: "Oh, I merely want to be considered as belonging to the band, which, you know, remains behind the fighting line and carries off the wounded. This is the only berth in this army where a man's life is worth a cent. Nearly everybody I know has been killed or wounded, and if this campaign [Sherman's Georgia campaign], with its senseless assaults of entrenched positions and its ceaseless tributes of blood and death, is to continue much longer, my turn is sure to come soon, and I want to avoid that if I can honorably do so." Wilson appointed the captain his aide-de-camp.[12]

The willingness of Union soldiers to accept black units on grounds that blacks could stop Confederate bullets as well as white soldiers has been seen as sharply racist, no doubt with some justification, but it should be said that white receptivity was based less on any contemplation of blacks as substitutes for themselves than as others who would share their fate. All soldiers had become cannon fodder. Charles Russell Lowell did not "want to be shot till I've had a chance to come home." The unknown was not whether but when one would be killed. (His wish was not granted.)[13]

A sense of the inevitability of one's own death was often accompanied by a fear, no less oppressive, of anonymous death. It was not principally the prospect of death that brought disillusionment—most soldiers continued to draw reassurance from conceptions of Christian afterlife—but soldiers who had been unable to foresee the impersonal aspects of Civil War combat could not come to grips with impersonal death. Many had witnessed scenes like that of the smokers waiting to tumble the dying soldier into his grave. They came to fear that they too would die alone, an apprehension that mounted as their circle of comrades contracted. They worried too that the manner of death, and perhaps even the fact of death, would go unreported to those they loved and that their remains would be desecrated. On those counts Thomas Key spoke forthrightly: "It is dreadful to contemplate being killed on the field of battle without a kind hand to hide one's remains from the eye of the world or the gnawing of animals and buzzards."[14]

In the course of the war there had been occasional attempts to ensure that bodies would be identified. Soldiers pinned name slips on their tunics prior to such battles as Fredericksburg and Cold Harbor. Paxton always carried with him, as identification, one of his wife's letters. A headquarters circular reaching the Sherman Brigade in mid-1863 recommended that soldiers have their names and regiments printed on the arm—and a brief flurry of business fell to India-ink tattoo artists. But despite the men's apprehension, no systematic attention was given the matter, perhaps because of the equally widespread suspicion that to prepare for death was to invite death. One could always hope for the best—that the dying soldier would be comforted by a friend; that his family would be told by letter, with perhaps even a lock of hair enclosed; that he would receive burial; that his grave would be marked with a piece of cracker box and his name carved with knife or written with pencil—but, as the soldier knew, the odds were poor. Despite those name papers, only 2,487 of the more than 15,000 bodies buried in the national cemetery at Fredericksburg were identified. Clara Barton's postwar investigation led her to conclude that of 315,555 Northern soldier graves, 143,155—45 percent—were marked "unknown" and that there had been 43,973 other soldier deaths for which there were no known graves.[15]

Those were not matters of which soldiers spoke or wrote easily, but there were hints that for some death had become omnipresent. Sitting on the bank of the Rapidan high above Germanna Ford watching the crossing of the Army of the Potomac's Fifth and Sixth Corps on May 4, 1864, Theodore Lyman imagined that each of the soldiers destined to die in Wilderness combat had already been marked and was wearing a large badge. In that same spring Abner Small of the 16th Maine climbed Virginia's Cedar Mountain, the site of an earlier battle, in an almost mystical anticipation of escape from war.

Another day, the chaplain, Captain Conley, and I rode to the signal station on Cedar Mountain. I felt a sudden lightening of heart as we went up. For a moment I was happy in the foolish and wonderful certainty that where we were going there would be no war nor memory of war, no troubling dreams, no dread of returning to the land of agony. A little higher, and we should be rising lightly into a region that we had never quite ceased to hope might be above us. I almost saw the glow of it brightening. Perhaps it was only sunlight among the trees. When we got to the top of the hill there was nothing but the signal station and the view.

Away on every side spread a broken country, shaggy with forest and thicket, creased with many watercourses . . . I saw it green and smiling with spring; and I looked away, because it was grinning with dreadful ghosts. The chaplain didn't see any ghosts. He was pointing out the beauties of nature. [The far-off Wilderness] was lovely with the careless innocence of nature; yet I remembered that in lonely hollows under those trees lay horrors of charred bones and rotting flesh. Only last spring we were at Chancellorsville. [Now] I was there again; it was dreadfully quiet; from under a haggard pine a grey and sunken face was staring at me emptily. I started, and heard the chaplain rattling on.[16]

Because, beyond common anxieties, Confederate soldiers bore the incubus of defeat, it might be surmised that theirs was the greater burden of disillusionment. Some of the evidence points to this. The news of Richmond's fall almost shattered John Dooley; it was "the most affecting intelligence I ever received."

"I feel bewildered, crushed, by the sudden, fearful fall. Never before have I felt so desolate, so prostrate, so helpless." He was distraught that "whole seas of blood and treasure" had been poured out to no avail. As the war ended, he concluded that worldly desires brought only remorse and he spoke with sorrow of his earlier decision to delay entry into the priesthood. But what was surprising was not that Confederates were further depressed by the military tide running against them but that Union soldiers were so little buoyed by it. "The winner," Burdette concluded, "has to pay for his winnings about as much as the loser pays for his losses."[17]

So powerfully absorptive had the experience of war become that it appeared to smother even victory in combat's daily costs. Rice Bull's 123d New York was a part of Sherman's army as it moved from Atlanta to Savannah in twenty-six days—"an enjoyable march." Though in the Carolinas Bull and his comrades encountered storms, mud, floods, and swamps, resistance remained negligible and their work of destruction went largely unhindered. Still, the note of triumph was missing.

> The next afternoon on our way to the picket line I saw fifteen unburied Confederate soldiers lying where they had fallen. It was not a pleasant sight to me, even though these men had been our enemies. I thought when I saw them, of the sorrow and grief there would be in fifteen homes somewhere; and for what had these young lives been sacrificed? . . . There should be some way to settle political differences without slaughtering human beings and wearing out the bodies and sapping the strength of those who may be fortunate enough to escape the death penalty.

Men who could no longer see in combat an experience that would purify and strengthen individual character and who felt themselves living under "the death penalty" were no longer sure of the bases of celebration.[18]

In the Eastern armies especially, military outcomes were further obscured by a sense that fighting had acquired the quality of endlessness. Some Confederates had discovered very early that battlefield success held far less decisiveness than they had assumed. At the end of 1862 Paxton already felt that "[o]ur victories . . . seem to settle nothing; to bring us no nearer the end of the war. It is only so many killed and wounded, leaving the work of blood to go on with renewed vigor." Twenty months later, in the

wake of Wilderness battles that seemed to him only bloodlet-
tings, Lyman had been similarly oppressed by the war's inter-
minability: "I get so mad and bothered. For, when we have no
good chance, or almost none, when our best undertakings fall
through, I lose confidence in each move, and, when I hear the
cannon, I look for nothing but our men coming back and a beg-
garly report of loss of prisoners. It is not right to feel so, but I
can't help it." When at last Lee surrendered and Stephen Weld's
sister chided him for his "want of enthusiasm" for the end of war,
he tried to explain to her that he simply could not comprehend
that the war was over. Lee, he said, had come to haunt him and
his comrades as a ghost haunts children; they had begun to live
with the conviction that they would fight for the rest of their
lives. Even in Sherman's army, with its power, mobility, and
habit of success, there were some afflicted with dread of the endlessness of the conflict. General Grenville Dodge prepared to resign when the Atlanta campaign persuaded him that "[b]lood
enough has been shed to establish empires in the old world. Still
the rebels stand up[,], bleeding[,] ready to receive more."[19]

While in most the belief that the war had become boundless
cast the future in darkest tones—Paxton concluded in 1862 that
the future "seems to hold for us an inexhaustible store of suffering"—in extreme cases it appeared to deprive soldiers of their
very sense of a future. By 1864–65 Lee's soldiers had ceased to
save money or to make plans for their postwar lives, George Eggleston reported, because "there really seemed to be no future."
"I remember the start it gave me when a clergyman, visiting
camp, asked a number of us whether our long stay in defensive
works did not afford us an excellent opportunity to study with a
view to our professional life after the war. We were not used to
think of ourselves as possible survivors of a struggle which was
every day perceptibly thinning our ranks." In ways that could
not have contrasted more starkly with their initial conception of
war as a series of opportunities to achieve exalted personal goals,
they had ceased to think of themselves even as survivors; for many
the future had become "a blank."[20]

Reflecting the sense of victimization by war, soldier letters
contained new images that had little in common with those of
1861. One set spoke to feelings of helplessness and bitterness at
the seeming inevitability of death in combat. Following fights at
Perryville and Murfreesboro, John Beatty reported in early 1863

that he and his comrades had for the first time realized what battle was: It was to men what an arctic wind was to autumn leaves. In 1862 Charles Francis Adams had celebrated his first experience under fire—"I would not have missed it for anything . . . the sensation was glorious. . . . Without affectation one of the most enjoyable days I ever passed"—and his initial exhilaration with army life had brought anguished envy to his diplomat-aide brother Henry. Three years later Charles Adams was a physical ruin of 130 pounds to whom the conflict then seemed comparable to a beautiful fruit that, when bitten, turned to ashes: War "was for me a Dead Sea apple." Another set recast combat itself in images of butchery. Weld wrote from the Army of the Potomac at the end of the Wilderness battles: "The feeling here in the army is that we have been absolutely butchered, that our lives have been periled to no purpose, and wasted. [T]hose high in command, such as corps commanders and higher officers, still . . . have time and again recklessly and wickedly placed us in slaughter-pens. I can tell you, Father, it is discouraging to see one's men and officers cut down and butchered time and again, and all for nothing." At the same time, Oliver Wendell Holmes, Jr., began to speak of battle losses as "the butcher's bill."[21]

Such currents subjected religious conviction to severe strain. High levels of religious interest persisted through the winter of 1863–64 in Confederate regiments and in some Federal units. James Nisbet of the 66th Georgia reported that those were the months in which a "revival . . . was conducted in almost every Division, and the interest was intense." In its winter quarters across the lines, Walter Carter's Massachusetts regiment erected a chapel for its prayer meetings and "quite a religious interest developed." But the intensity of 1862–63 revivalism soon slipped away, as attrition warfare began to absorb minds and exhaust bodies.[22]

Combat, now almost continuous, crowded out occasions previously allowing and prompting religious observance. At first there had been no more than an awareness that army Sundays seemed unlike home Sundays. An Illinois surgeon with Sherman's army, E. P. Burton, traced in diary entries the slippage from week to week. "But little like Sunday again—." "Another Sabbath has seemed but little like the Sabbath." "For some reason or other . . . this has seemed the least like Sunday since being in the service. No preaching of any kind and but little chance for me to get out alone in a meditative mood. This eve soon after candle light I went into Nelson[']s room after some cough sirup and before the day occurred to me I proposed a game of checkers. Of course *I* retracted as soon as I thought." "The hallowed Sabbath is disturbed not only by the usual camp noise, but by the sacking of this town [Acworth, Georgia]." Burton had entered the army only nine months before. Many with longer service had much earlier ceased to think of Sunday activities as anomalous; by mid-1864 they no longer had any thought to give to the Sabbath. As John Billings of the 10th Massachusetts Artillery recognized, in the Wilderness "holy associations were lost sight of in the unceasing activities of war." Even Christmas became a casualty. "We know it only in name," Michael Fitch sadly wrote.[23]

Chaplains no longer wielded the influence that could vigorously demand religious observance. James Kidd reported that the chaplain of the 9th Michigan Cavalry was "not at all fitted for the hardships and exposure . . . and it was as much as he could do to look after his own physical well-being, and the spiritual condition of his flock was apt to be sadly neglected." Indeed, in the field, Chaplain Greeley was less a spiritual guide than a child "to be watched by the men." Many chaplains returned home; others had grown to prefer boarding with neighborhood civilians to sleeping among the men. Some who remained, it was true, continued to perform useful and sometimes difficult services— cheering the sick; visiting hospitals; writing letters for the disabled and the illiterate; distributing mail; carrying the men's pay home to families—but their activities seemed to move more and more to the peripheries of soldiers' lives. Privates continued to praise the "fighting parson," but he became a rarity; few clerics wished to see Wilderness combat a second time. As Carter put it, in the Union Army "clergymen with fighting propensities were few and far between."

Abner Small attended a service conducted by the brigade's chaplains on the eve of the battle at Chancellorsville. "They were eloquent in their appeals to patriotism, and pictured in glowing colors the glory that would crown the dead and the blazons of promotion that would decorate the surviving heroes. They besought us all to stand firm, to be brave; God being our shield, we had nothing to fear." Suddenly Confederate shells landed among the worshipers. "'Whoosh!' . . . 'Crash!' . . . The explosions . . . the screams of horses, and the shouted commands of officers were almost drowned out by the yells and laughter of the men as the brave chaplains, hatless and bookless, their coat-tails streaming in the wind, fled madly to the rear over stone walls and hedges and ditches, followed by gleefully shouted counsel: 'Stand firm; put your trust in the Lord!'"[24]

As chaplains worked to keep comfortable the conditions of their own lives, the men became less and less respectful of those who were frequently away and who when present enjoyed officer privileges. Thomas Galwey of the 8th Ohio charged that "the chaplain of our regiment continued sitting idly in his saddle with one of his saddle bags full of bottles of Jamaica ginger while men were prostrated and dying of sunstroke." Hinman recorded that when members of the Sherman Brigade began throwing away their testaments—"Bibles and blisters didn't go well to-gether"—the protests of the chaplain were easily ignored because "he had a horse to ride." Other parsons whose aloofness from camp and combat inclined them to retain civilian outlooks also ran afoul of soldier attitudes. Theodore Lyman was contemptuous of a minister he met on the Petersburg front: "He was like all of that class, patriotic and one-sided, attributing to the Southerners every fiendish passion; in support of which he had accumulated all the horrible accounts of treatment of prisoners, slaves, etc., etc., and had worked himself into a great state." In few instances did the figure of the chaplain appear prominently in the latter pages of soldier narratives of the war.[25]

In truth, soldiers were moving away from chaplains as rapidly as they charged that chaplains were drifting away from them. Combat could no longer be fitted easily within Christian precepts, and in men impelled to resolve that tension, religious ordinances could be suppressed as the daily experience of war could not. In 1864–65 fighting, many lost or at least suspended a significant measure of their early-war piety. Alexander Hunter claimed:

> Among "Lee's Miserables" devotional exercises languished, except in a few favored localities. It is hard to retain religion on an empty stomach; a famine-stricken man gains consolation from no creed. The Johnnies had been fighting now nearly four years and they had gone through so much that many of them honestly thought, as one ragged sinner rather profanely put it, "they had such a hell of a time in this country that the good Lord would not see them damned in the next."

He argued that it would be wrong to think of the Confederates as a pious army, for although the South had been "a deeply religious section" in 1861 and although Lee and Jackson's examples had in 1862 stimulated "a devout feeling" and conversions "by the thousands," the "deep, intense, religious fervor soon changed to indifference; and I certainly saw nothing and heard nothing of an out-door prayer-meeting or a conversion among the cavalry during the last year of the war." Devoutness had been undermined by the hardening processes of the war (especially, Hunter thought, the soldier's removal from women's influence) and by habituation to death. "At the beginning of the war every soldier had a Testament in his pocket; three years later there was not a half dozen in each regiment."[26]

Corresponding experience on the other side provoked comparable but perhaps less intense reactions, for the institutional incorporation of religion had never proceeded as far in the Union Army as it had in the Confederate. Contrasts between 1861 and 1864 practices were thus more muted, but many Federals too felt tenets of faith slipping away. In ways scarcely contemplated three years before, Carter found himself questioning whether Christian sensibilities, rather than fortifying and preserving the soldier in combat, did not in reality "unfit" a man for war.[27]

The drift from religious faith should not be exaggerated. It remained a powerful influence. There were few renunciations of belief in God, or even expressions mistrusting God's control of the evolution of the war. Carter's condemnation of Grant as a butcher and his horror at such enormous numbers of dead soldiers were profound, but the persistence of a religious framework still capable of assimilating such reactions ("*What* a gathering of souls before God," he exclaimed of bodies piled thick.) mitigated some bitterness and despair. The dread sights of the hospital ("everything had an air of butchery about it") could still be deflected by setting them within such thoughts as Carter's, that "the dawn of the great hereafter will behold those slaughtered heroes, resurrected and beautiful." Confederates continued to find within God's Plan explanations of their military defeats. They, not God, were wanting. Frank Paxton concluded, "We have a just cause, but we do not deserve success. . . . Fasting and prayer by such a people is blasphemy, and, if answered at all, will be by an infliction of God's wrath, not in a dispensation of his mercy." As late as mid-March 1865 William Poague of the

Stonewall Brigade found a religious refuge from the despondency that the Confederacy's collapse inflicted on others: "The ground of my composure" was the persistence of belief in God's will, encompassing even the possibility that "He will overrule all so that that shall be done which will be best for this people."[28]

Still, the slow crumbling of 1861 certainties was unmistakable as soldiers manifested their drift toward skepticism not in shouted profanation but in muted questions that many put only to themselves. Following a hospital tour in which he had seen several harrowing gangrene cases, Alpheus Williams was deeply troubled. He pondered whether the enemy, the leaders of the Confederacy, might have become the tools of God: Those "human heads and arms . . . working for our destruction . . . I suppose . . . are but instruments of divine will, though why He should use those who most blaspheme his authority, it is hard to imagine. I have seen dark times, but none where before I could not see some superior intellect that might probably be brought to our safety." Joshua Chamberlain's doubts focused not on the nature of a God who would employ the ungodly to cut down the faithful but on the verity of that conviction that soldiers were doing the work God intended them to do. By the time of Five Forks, the battle in which his exertions to halt a Union retreat brought him both another wound and the hurrahs of opposing armies, the carnage perplexed him and he was no longer sure that by killing rebels he and his men continued to execute God's will. Was it God's command that we heard or must we now "forever implore" his forgiveness?[29]

Some in the ranks were equally troubled. Hamlin Coe of the 19th Michigan had been sustained by the credo of courage through two years of war. He had been confident of God's support and protection: "I . . . trust in Him who wields the destiny of all." He had been spared in battle, he was convinced, by "the guidance of Him who protects us all." Though he prayed that the war would cease, he did not doubt God's support of the Union cause: "God protect the right and when the strife is ended, may it be in accordance with His will." But by mid-1864 combat had eroded his convictions, and in his account of one of Sherman's Georgia battles he revealed doubts about God's mandate as troubled as Chamberlain's:

> It was dreadful for a few hours. Many a poor fellow fell, and we gained nothing but a little ground. . . . The sun set clear and

bright, too lovely for the scenes about us, but such are the horrors of war. Will God forgive men for such work is a question I often ask myself, but I receive a silent reply and utter my own prayers for the safety of my poor soul and my country.[30]

Few soldiers returned home professed skeptics, but neither had the war permitted its participants any easy retention of their prewar certainties. Gone was that untroubled confidence that faith would extend the mantle of God's sanctification over all their activity. It was indeed difficult to see God's hand in combat and to remain convinced that it was driving the war forward in order that good might ensue.

Finally, numbers of Civil War soldiers were compelled to suffer an experience, the prison camp, that seemed as ruinous as combat and, especially for those confined in Andersonville, sealed their disillusionment with the war.

Imprisonment had its own evolution and in its early stages was far from oppressive. Alexander Hunter had been captured at Antietam, paroled promptly by his Federal captors, and within forty-eight hours marched back to Confederate lines; he had then returned to his home to wait "a few weeks" until Southern officials notified him that he had been duly exchanged and might return to the war. Captured in the first Peninsula campaign, Stephen Weld was confined in Richmond—after a fashion. Prisoners were able to steal out at night through a hole in a fence and walk about the city. Confederate officers held at Camp Chase strolled the streets of Columbus, Ohio, in uniform and registered at the best hotels. Attending sessions of the Ohio Senate, they were sometimes invited to sit within the bar. They enjoyed the services of black servants.[31]

Such leniency, however, itself became one of two spurs to a new severity. Neither high command could tolerate a prisoner system so lax that in order to escape combat field troops would purposely surrender and in order to escape captivity prisoners would pledge allegiance to the captor's side, enter his army, and desert at the first opportunity. Nor could either administration resist for long the temptation to employ prisoners as levers in disputes with the enemy government by threatening retaliatory steps against prisoners of war if black soldiers were committed to combat, if guerrilla forays persisted, or if terror tactics were employed. The embroilment of the prisoner issue in countless other controversies—and, to be sure, in endless disputes over the administrative processes necessary to operate a system that both sides discovered could no longer be left to the individual's word of honor—brought the exchange cartel to collapse. When the Union suspended officer exchanges in May 1863 and within months the exchange of enlisted men broke down, strict incarceration became the rule; by 1864 the prison had become a source of trauma for many of those 408,000 soldiers imprisoned rather than paroled in the field.[32]

The experience repeated many of the shocks of combat. Prisoners were stunned to discover how tenaciously death dogged them—and so far beyond the battle. Wilkeson watched Confederate prisoners at Elmira, New York, die "as sheep with the rot." A Southern surgeon placed the number of prisoner deaths at Andersonville between late February and late September 1864 at 9,479, nearly one of every three confined within "this gigantic mass of human misery." Ultimately, 13,000 died there, in conditions more appalling than those of the roughest battlefield. At Andersonville there were severe deficiencies in the provision of food, shelter, and medical attention—whether the result of Confederate intent or the exhaustion of Confederate resources would be argued as long as Civil War veterans remained alive. No one, however, denied the effects. Frank Bailey of the 6th Pennsylvania Reserves watched fellow prisoners "shut out from all earthly sympathy, surrounded by scenes of horror and disgust, in the hands of merciless, unrelenting captors" dying "like dogs." The disposition of the dead was no more ceremonious than on the battlefield. Barber reported: "It is very shocking to human feelings the way the dead are disposed of. They are piled up in a wagon like so much wood, taken to holes dug for them and piled in, with no respect for decency or humanity." At Andersonville the omnipresence of death became more than the long campaign's spectral presence: It was reality. "There was no time of day," Barber wrote, "but what we could see some dead men lying around camp while scores of others were dying." Again soldiers encountered powerful forces binding them in helplessness. Bailey described "the slow, sure wasting away of mind and body; as though one were cast into a deep, dark pit, surrounded by dead and dying victims, whose emaciated bodies, despairing countenances, decaying forms and grinning skeletons marked the progress of death's victory." "It is plain to me," Ransom said, "that all will die." When he learned that his family had been told he was dead, he felt no alarm, anger, or indignation: "Perhaps it is just as well . . . for them to anticipate the event a few months."[33]

If prisons repeated and often intensified the shocks of battle, they also introduced new ordeals that prisoners ultimately found harsher than combat. Lucius Barber recorded his arrival at Andersonville: "Our feelings cannot be described as we gazed on these poor human beings. . . . No wonder that stout hearts, who had faced death in a thousand forms on bloody fields with unblanched cheek and flashing eye, should now give up and groan in anguish and despair!" He had seen battle misery at its worst, but combat "would be a blessing indeed, compared to the dark despair which here engulfed us." "[T]he worst that I had ever seen was paradise compared to what here met vision."[34]

One of the results hardest to accept was the destruction of comradeship. If a soldier had been captured with others of his unit, there was at least a foundation for cooperative action, but, as Barber observed, "if one was captured alone, put with strangers and became sick, it was ten chances to one that he would die unattended by any human being." Men called one another only by prison camp nicknames. Often even comrades could not help one another. "No matter how the heart was wrung with sympathy for others, no material help could be imparted." Worse, the survival of the individual sometimes depended on his willingness to do injury to others. Life in Andersonville, Bailey concluded, was "necessarily selfish." The scarcity of food pitted prisoner against prisoner. Desperate soldiers fought one another, Ransom reported, "just like so many snarly dogs, cross and peevish" or "like so many hungry wolves penned up together." Some stole from others or won preferential treatment by informing on others. Often the sick were stripped of clothing and other belongings before they died. Religious sensibility seemed almost to disappear. Ransom observed that "very many . . . who have heretofore been religiously inclined . . . throw off all restraint and are about the worst." Men retained testaments primarily as reminders of home, and prayer diminished. Ransom wrote in surprise of a messmate: "He prays; think of that." "The worst side of human nature becomes visible," Bailey observed. "The weak were a prey to the strong, stealing was carried on without limit, and deeds of lawlessness were of hourly occurrence." "The animal predominates," said Ransom. Entering the compound with supplies of meat and bread and offering them in exchange for enlistments, Confederate recruiting officers did not hesitate to make explicit the reality of the prisoners' situation: "[T]o remain here is to *starve* and *die* . . . to desert is to *live*."[35]

Another factor worked to create fragmentation at Andersonville. Had the food been distributed equitably, it would not have sufficed, especially in periods of Andersonville's highest numbers. (In August 1864, 33,000 were incarcerated there.) But that situation, dire of itself, was rendered tragic when actual control of the prisoner compound fell to loose bands of bounty-jumpers and soldier-criminals, who proceeded to impose a reign of terror. Only in July were the volunteers able to effect an organization of their own, to arrest and try the thugs, and, with the camp administration's blessing, to hang six of the worst. Prisoner-of-war experience had come far from those sightseeing excursions in Richmond and Columbus streets.

So bereft did some feel amid those conditions that they thought they were going mad. Men whose writings show them to have had great personal resources were drawn to suicide. In imprisonment Francis Amasa Walker suffered "a period of nervous horror such as I had never before and have never since experienced, and memories of which have always made it perfectly clear how one can be driven on, unwilling and vainly resisting, to suicide. I remember watching the bars at my window and wondering whether I should hang myself from them. I had not the slightest wish or purpose to do so; but I felt as if I were being pushed on by some unseen force in the direction of insanity." Made desperate by what they found at Andersonville and "in utter despair at such a prospect of existence," three members of Bailey's squad stepped over the "dead line" in invitation to guards to shoot them down.[36]

Those who survived often carried an unmistakable physical stamp. Walt Whitman watched in disbelief the return of Union prisoners: "[T]he sight is worse than any sight of battlefields, or any collection of wounded, even the bloodiest. . . . Can these be *men*—these little, livid brown, ash-streaked, monkey-looking dwarfs? Are they really not mummied, dwindled corpses? . . . Probably no more appalling sight was ever seen on this earth." Perhaps the stamp of the experience on the mind was even more enduring, for it drew some of the most fervid passages in the memoir literature of the war. Twenty years later Bailey recalled his imprisonment as "a long, dark night of lingering horror." In what was done to prisoners of war, "we felt our manhood crushed to the very earth."[37]

A moment of critical importance in the Civil War has been viewed by others as evidence of soldier dedication and resolve. In late 1863 and early 1864, 140,000 Union rank-and-file, 30,000 of them soldiers in the Army of the Potomac, signed up for additional three-year terms of service. It was a momentous development, signifying the Federal army's ability to retain a volunteer nucleus. Had those men departed on the expiration of their enlistments in the summer and fall of 1864, the Union could have continued to prosecute offensive warfare only with the greatest difficulty.

The volunteers' willingness to reenlist has been portrayed in positive terms—they took pride in the proffered title of veteran volunteer; they were determined to see the conflict through to its end; they responded to a patriotic impulse. Some of the volunteers themselves later wrote in apparent corroboration of such analyses. Hinman thought it a "wonder" that in Sherman's army "so large a number who had marched and fought and suffered so long, and *knew what war was*, should be willing to sign for 'three years more.'" He was certain that courage and patriotism had led them to do so. "The great impelling force" was their resolve "to stand by 'Old Glory' until the rebellion was conquered." Lucius Barber agreed: "I had a strong desire to see the end and nothing but absolute physical debility would prevent it." But among the men ran a more powerful counter-current, suggesting that a spirit of another kind informed the great reenlistment, a spirit of disillusionment and desperation rather than hopefulness and resolution.[38]

The mechanics of the reenlistment process were crucial to its results. Federal soldiers often scoffed at Washington policy as it touched on their lives, but even they might have subsequently agreed that there was an unusual shrewdness at play here. The army command required soldiers to make their decisions six months to a year prior to the expiration of their 1861 enlistments, and in order to retain their services it offered a series of inducements. The first was a $400 bonus, immensely appealing ("the munificent bounty") to privates receiving $13 a month and persuaded that everyone except the soldier had made profit from the war. The second was the government's promise that if three-quarters of a regiment reenlisted, its organizational integrity would be maintained, a provision attractive to those increasingly drawing on comradeship as their principal support. The third was an offer to bestow on those who remained in the service the title "veteran volunteer," a measure whose attractive power rested in its ability formally to distinguish the 1861–62 volunteers from the 1863–64 conscripts and bounty soldiers. The final inducement was the promise of an immediate thirty- to thirty-five-day furlough at home. Sherman regarded that last provision as "very unmilitary," but he agreed that it was "politic." Indeed, it was decisive.[39]

The debate among the men, climaxing during the Christmas season of 1863, was waged not between the ardent and the unenthusiastic but between greater and lesser pessimists, with those of greatest foreboding urging reenlistment. To them the consideration crowding out all others was the period just ahead; few thought that they would survive those days separating them from the expiration of their current tours. That they could come through the jeopardy of 1864 spring and summer campaigning intact was inconceivable. They thus argued with heavy emotion that given the likelihood of their deaths, a reenlistment furlough would at least allow them to see their families again. George Bicknell of the 5th Maine even dared to hope that a month at home might restore to him the possibility of a future:

> Many of the men had been away from home for two years and a half. . . . Thirty-five days' furlough! It seemed almost an age. So long did it seem in prospective, that one might have almost thought, from the action and conversation of some of the men, that there was a possibility of the war being actually over before [the furlough] could expire. The news spread like lightning. Reenlist? Yes. What tempted those men? Bounty? No. The opportunity to go home. . . . Oh, if they could only see home again, they were ready to risk anything and everything. The theme was up on all lips. It was reenlistment—furlough—home.

Even in Sherman's army, Elisha Stockwell of the 14th Wisconsin noted, "the furlough was the big inducement." Soldiers, Captain

Brewster of the 65th Ohio reported, resolved to hazard "three years more of hell" in exchange for "thirty days of heaven— home."[40]

Those who opposed reenlistment urged that volunteers would do better to complete terms already five-sixths expired and then return home "for good" as men "free in conscience." (It was significant that neither side any longer was concerned that civilians might rebuke soldiers who left the war; all thought it sufficient to say to those at home, "For three years we have done all this; go thou and do likewise.") An opponent of reenlistment, Carter sniped at those volunteers who, though earlier censorious of "damned two hundred dollar recruits," were now loudly desirous of their own bounties, but he granted that the point of greatest leverage against his stance lay elsewhere: "I will not re-enlist for three years, just to get a furlough home." His was a principled position, but its proponents could not promise survival until that "big furlough," and here Carter was compelled to concede his opposition's principal point. "What may happen before then, we cannot tell; we can only claim the present . . . by snatching an hour from the contemplated future." Many thought that future too menacing to contemplate and resolved to snatch any hour of respite from the war.[41]

Where it could, the Union Army mixed its inducements with an assortment of pressures. Once the reenlistment drive began, no furloughs of other kinds were granted. Colonels entreated their men to reenlist. Prominent citizens arrived from home to add their voices. Occasionally key soldiers were singled out for special persuasion. Carter's decision, it was known, was likely to carry five comrades with him; he was offered a lieutenancy first by the adjutant and subsequently by the governor of his state. There were threats of arrest aimed at soldiers speaking too forthrightly against extension and menacing suggestions that units not reenlisting might find themselves serving unusually unpleasant or dangerous duty. Those who chose to serve out their terms were to be called, most unfairly, "non-veterans."[42]

Other pressures came from soldiers who had already chosen to reenlist and were preparing for their furloughs. Those in the 64th Ohio "unmercifully" chided soldiers staying behind. John DeForest reported that his Connecticut veterans laughed at the "remarkably large proportion" of those refusing to reenlist who were shortly thereafter killed in battle—"a humorous bit of di-

263

vine vengeance." Nonveterans might eventually repay such attentions—Bicknell noted that weeks later, on the day of the veterans' return, "[t]here was sorrow on many a poor fellow's face as he reflected that he had rebound himself, and that possibly he had seen his home for the last time"; "The whole camp seemed gloomy for days"—and the nonveterans would ultimately be the first to march from camp for the last time, but the presenting fact was the necessity to watch their reenlisted comrades depart for home, and for some that proved unbearably painful. Among Hinman's Ohioans:

> At the last moment three or four of our non-veteran squad "weakened;" the temptation to go home was too strong for them to resist. Fearing that it might be everlastingly too late, they asked eagerly if they would be permitted to re-enlist [and] hastily gathered up their belongings and followed the flag.

Among Allen's Rhode Islanders, "at [the] last many [of those who had before been 'strenuous opposers' of reenlistment] changed their minds, for the temptation to see home and wife and little ones was too great for them."[43]

Thus the war had brought many soldiers to recommit themselves to combat as the only way that they might briefly escape it. The more profound their pessimism regarding chances of their survival, the greater the impetus to reenlist.

On July 29, 1861, a thirty-two-year-old New York Congressman had stood in the House of Representatives to speak of a war then in progress only four months:

> [War] is not a question of valor, but a question of money; . . . it is not regulated by the laws of honor, but by the laws of trade. I understand [that] the practical problem to be solved in crushing the rebellion of despotism against representative government is, who can throw the most projectiles? Who can afford the most iron or lead?[44]

Soldiers who read Roscoe Conkling's words must have found wanting both the speaker and the speech, for not only was he a man of robust appearance and formidable physique who, with a high commission his for the asking, had decided not to enter the army, but his remarks challenged the bases of their own participation in war. The four years that followed, however, would reveal to them the brutal reality behind Conkling's words.

The change in soldier perspective between 1861 and 1865 was never a matter of smooth or all-embracing sequences. Some soldiers, probably those least equipped and least inclined to record their reactions, may have entered the war with a feeble allegiance to courage's values. Others, holding to them tightly whatever the stresses of combat, may have survived the war with their dedication to courage—and even knightliness—largely undamaged. But experience cost many soldiers their conviction that war was "a question of valor."

In April 1865 Captain Rawlins Lowndes of Wade Hampton's staff was ordered to carry to the victorious Sherman the Confederate command's request for a meeting whose outcome could only be the capitulation of all of Joseph E. Johnston's Confederate troops in the Carolinas. While awaiting the Union reply, Lowndes fell into conversation with the Federal cavalry's General Hugh Judson Kilpatrick. Feeling perhaps the humiliation of his mission but still pugnacious, the captain proposed that they not await the outcome of their commanders' discussions, that Kilpatrick, his staff, and 1,500 Union horsemen, armed only with sabers, should immediately meet on the field of battle Wade Hampton, his staff, and 1,000 Confederate cavalry. The charge would determine, four years of combat notwithstanding, the best men.[45] The response of Kilpatrick, whose remorseless belligerence had earned him the nickname "Kill Cavalry," was not recorded, but one suspects that even respect for a defeated foe could not have smothered his laughter.

Epilogue

THE HIBERNATION

What were Union soldiers returning to their homes to say of their war?* Combat had overthrown their original views, while at home initial conceptions of the war, though subjected to stress, had remained the common currency. The home folks thus expected to hear tales of battle in which their soldiers had acted to fulfill the values of 1861. Aware of such expectations, soldiers feared that candid depictions of combat would make them appear cowardly, that graphic descriptions of foraging would make them seem brutish. Moreover, especially after Abraham Lincoln's assassination, civilians regarded the enemy with an anger soldiers did not ordinarily share. From their sons they wished no expositions on the changing nature of combat or its unanticipated arduousness; they wished to know how they had damaged the foe.

Soldiers in any case were reluctant to look back, for at home

---

*Those soldiers on whose reactions I relied in framing preceding chapters of course ceased their letter-writing as they returned home. Most abandoned journal-keeping as well. When some of them later undertook to write autobiographies, they assumed that readers would be interested exclusively in their wartime adventures. They said little of their postwar experiences and opinions, a neglect shared by most twentieth-century biographers of Civil War figures. Because the groundsill evidence is less sturdy, conclusions regarding veteran attitudes, 1865–98, must remain more tentative than those regarding soldier attitudes, 1861–65.

they found difficulty enough in contending with the problems of the present. Many returned in precarious physical condition. Almost all experienced disorientation in various degrees. Some felt that they had returned from another world or another plane of existence. The rules governing their daily lives changed so abruptly as to require almost overnight adjustments. Killing once again became homicide; foraging was again theft, and incendiarism arson. Even language was a problem: Camp talk had to be cleaned up.

Even had they not been surfeited with war and preoccupied with personal problems, even had they wished to tell all, soldiers suspected that it could not have been done. During the war some had become aware of the narcotic effect of intense combat; their perceptions of what they had done from one day of battle to the next shifted, overlapped, and merged, leaving them with blurred memories and blunted emotions. They knew well enough the cumulative impact of extended campaigning, the disillusioning sum of their experience, but many specific actions and particular battles became submerged in a generalized blur. As early as May 1864, Oliver Wendell Holmes, Jr., had realized that the facts of battle "so rapidly escape the memory in the mist which settles over a fought field." On the Fourth of July, 1864, Daniel Crotty reviewed his three years at war and recognized that "now that we have passed through such bloody ordeals, we cannot realize fully that we have experienced such tiresome marches and fearful battles. As we look over the past, to most of us it seems [already] like a dream."[1]

Soldiers once at home became subject to an acceleration of selective memory, that strong psychological propensity to suppress the painful. A few later tried to describe those parts of the process of which they were aware. The Confederate Berry Benson pictured his memory of war "slipping away, down, down, sparkling as it sinks, but ever growing dimmer, dimmer, until I fear that ere I am hardly bemoaning my first grey hairs I shall have to bethink myself to say truly whether I did share in the clash and struggle . . . whether indeed I have seen painted red on the sky the tattered flags of Jackson's battalions."[2]

While forgetfulness worked to efface painful experience, soldiers construed bad memories in a way that smoothed their departure. When they were able to discuss the problem among themselves, soldiers ordinarily did so under a rubric—"Time heals all wounds"—revelatory of their assumptions. In the war, wounds had been suffered by some and not by others; the problems they created were thus the concern of the individuals involved, not of society. The soldier had wished to rid himself of the effects of body wounds as rapidly as possible; the veteran would do everything he could to accelerate the disappearance of mind wounds. Disturbing memories were to be kept to oneself, not to be aired publicly to relieve the sufferer and certainly not to correct public misapprehension of the nature of combat. Thirty-seven years later John Foster, the Indiana soldier who had gone on to become Secretary of State under Benjamin Harrison, told a crowd gathered for the dedication of the Indianapolis Soldiers' Monument that though some might on that occasion experience "the sad recollection of the carnage of battle and the wasting experience of the hospital . . . time has healed the scars of war. We can now look back upon the scene as one only of heroic deeds." No one expressed regret that healing should entail the loss of certain kinds of war memories.[3]

During World War II, Ernie Pyle realized that if he were to convey the war realistically to those at home, he would have to struggle each night to recreate what he had seen of battle during the day and then fix it in his mind. As he lay in his bedroll "thinking and thinking and thinking," "at last the enormity of all those newly dead struck like a living nightmare." He would have to force himself to keep alive the horror of combat. Civil War soldiers saw no reason to attempt such an extraordinary thing; they meant instead to effect a "cure" by ridding themselves of the horror as quickly as possible.[4]

On all counts, then, returned soldiers felt impelled to turn rapidly from the war. Uncertain that they could describe accurately what they had gone through or could speak of such things in ways those at home could understand, they decided to say whatever would cause the least discomfort to themselves and others—little or nothing. Indeed, reticence paid its own dividend: Families and friends considered it heroic modesty. Holmes later elevated it to a civic virtue by proclaiming such reserve an article of the Soldier's Faith: "Having known great things, to be content with silence."[5]

The Wisconsin officer Michael Fitch described how he and his comrades turned their faces from war. Sherman's soldiers, he claimed, were unmoved even by the Grand Review marking the end of the war. They did not bestir themselves to watch the Army of the Potomac parade through the streets of the capital; they were indifferent to the cheers greeting their own maneuvers. "To them this magnificent display [200,000 soldiers, marching sixty abreast] which so impressed the thousands who had not been in the war, was merely the last ordered duty in a long, arduous and deadly struggle in which they had triumphed and from which they were only too glad to get away." Once at home, they wished only to forget the war. They "had then no inclination to study the comparative analysis of the war, or the proper bearing it had upon our country and race." They were "too near to it to see anything but the raw facts. The glitter of gun barrel and sword, the red carnage of the field, the terrible echoes of . . . artillery, were yet close realities. . . . At the muster out . . . the nerves of the soldiery had not recovered from [the] tremor of the battle charge." "For a great many years after the war, I paid little attention to it." "I do not for a moment delude myself with the idea that this epoch was the most important in my life. It was not." The average soldier "thought only of how he could best take up the pursuits of peaceful industry."[6]

Stephen Weld was "reluctant to reminisce about his army days" and was unwilling to publish his war journals. William McKinley would rarely speak of the war. "He preferred to forget the trying days and nights, the hunger and personal discomfort, the danger, and above all, the agony for which the war stood." Abner Small would say little about it except that it had given him bad dreams. In shaving off the military mustache "nourished in blood," Holmes began an extended retreat from the martial. He was a war hero whose demeanor surprised those entertaining him during a tour of England in 1866: He was "as little military as need be, and, like Coriolanus, not baring his wounds . . . for public gaze." He would not read of the war or observe the anniversaries of its battles. Robert E. Lee helped to set the same pattern for Confederate soldiers returning to a shattered economy and to the ruined homes and farms that would hold them imperatively to the "pursuits of peaceful industry." Lee did not read books on the war and seldom even read newspapers. "I do not wish to awaken memories of the past." As late as 1877, veterans were disinclined to include in biographical directories information regarding their Civil War experience.[7]

Only with former comrades-in-arms would Abner Small

sometimes discuss old campaigns. Here was a disposition, shared by many others, that set limits on veteran willingness to give the war experience any collective dimension in the early postwar years. Attempts at higher organization fared badly. The most important veterans' group—the Grand Army of the Republic—appeared in 1866, the result not of the desires of infantrymen but of the inspiration of an army chaplain and a Union major and the organizing efforts of former high-ranking Federal officers, notably John Logan. It produced a brief flurry of activity, perhaps in reflection of soldier hopes that such an organization could preserve wartime comradeship, and then waned rapidly. By 1868 one-third of its posts were inactive. Ten years later, it could count few more than 30,000 members. Throughout the 1870s, less than 2 percent of Union veterans responded to Logan's urgings that they organize. The same pattern prevailed in the South, with results even more modest. In 1870 Generals Pickett and Early founded the Society of the Army of Northern Virginia; most of its chapters soon became skeletons. Not until 1889 would a regionwide federation of Confederate veterans appear. The historian Mary Dearing has called 1865–80 "the quiescent years" of veteran organization; she might as easily have styled them the moribund years.[8]

One of the prices exacted by the mere maintenance of veterans' organizations during that period was the willingness to say nothing of the hard war of 1864–65. At the outset the GAR set several goals: to win for veterans jobs and government payments equalizing wartime bounties; to secure financial aid for dead soldiers' widows and orphans; and, in a move that aligned it with civilian anger, to continue to work to suppress treason. The leadership understood that if its aims were to be achieved, the soldiers' war would have to be made a public issue, whatever veterans' reluctance, and—in ways significant for the development of veteran influence—that it would have to be discussed in a particular way. Logan realized that to speak of the war in images disturbing to the public would raise opposition, while a congenial characterization might advance GAR aims.

> To keep the scenes of war with all its horrors vivid before the [public] mind, without some still more important motive, would hardly meet with the approval of this intelligent age. It was to keep constantly before the mind the *cost* of liberty, and the *price* paid for the suppression of rebellion, and the preservation of a free and

independent Government; to keep forever green the hallowed memory of the heroic dead, who had fallen to save their country from disunion and dishonor.[9]

Shorn of their circumlocutions, such phrases meant that society would reward only veterans whose claims were based on the war of courage that civilians continued to think their soldiers had fought.

The mood of the country reinforced the veteran inclination to pay as little heed as possible to the memories of war. Though there were periodic eruptions of anger incited by politicians who waved the Bloody Shirt, they broke only briefly the dominant war-weariness. Within wide bounds, Americans were willing and even anxious to thrust into shadow all things martial. That reaction did not derive from disillusionment with war. No demythologizing of the soldier and of combat took place at that time, nor did any renunciation of war as a social experience, as occurred following the Great War. But there was a pervasive sense of the war as loss. Northerners and Southerners counted their dead.

At the close of the war, Mary Livermore received offers to publish an account of her wartime experiences. She refused, she said, because people continued to suffer the anguish of bereavement and wished to forget the war. Here she understood the public temper better than those publishers who were responsible for a brief flurry of war books in 1866 but soon discovered that their expectations of public interest were misplaced. The 1870s saw the publication of fewer Civil War novels than any other decade. Popular magazines published little on the war. Between 1869 and 1873, *Harper's* printed two Civil War articles, and between 1869 and 1876, the *North American Review* carried only one.[10]

Public uninterest reflected itself too in the nation's neglect of its military structure. Though reorganized following the war, Northern militias soon faltered. Only twelve states kept units in operation, and in many of them records maintenance was the principal activity. Only in Massachusetts and Connecticut was there interest sufficient to support summer camps. Ordnance supplied by the federal government was often given away or simply lost. In 1871 a group distressed by the neglect of military affairs, especially the decline of marksmanship, established the

National Rifle Association; for a number of years it remained a barely viable organization.[11]

Reduced by demobilization to a ghost of its wartime force, the regular army was further diminished by Congressional enactments cutting its authorized strength to 37,000 in 1869 and to 27,000 in 1874. Seldom could it count more than 19,000 soldiers on active duty. No doubt the citizenry wanted a skeleton military, for its wartime links to the army had been broken by developments beyond the demobilization of Civil War volunteers. The use of the army to enforce Reconstruction policies was anathema to white Southerners and increasingly troubling to many Northerners. The army's subsequent relocation to the Western frontier brought an end to that criticism but threatened oblivion. A woman said of New Englanders whom she visited after years in the West, "Why, one-half of them do not know the uniform and could not distinguish an officer of the Army from a policeman!" Disdain for professional soldiers revived. Many postwar recruits were drawn from the urban poor; some were fugitives from justice, and others were newly arrived immigrants. The annual turnover ranged from 25 to 40 percent, and desertion rose as high as 32 percent. "The Regular Army, Oh," a popular ditty produced by the New York comedy stage team of Harrigan and Hart in 1875 and adopted in self-deprecation by Plains army units, commented on the caliber of the soldiery:

> We had our choice of going to the army or to jail,
> Or it's up to the Hudson River with a cop to take a sail;
> So we puckered up our courage and with bravery we did go,
> And we cursed the day we marched away with the
> Regular Army, oh! . . .

> We were captured by the Indians and brought [in front
> of the chief],
> Says he, "We'll have an Irish stew," the dirty Indian [thief].
> On the telegraphic wire we skipped to Mexico,
> And we blessed the day we marched away from the
> Regular Army, oh!

Officers, too, were linked unfavorably with urban America in the minds of farmers and townspeople who were beginning to feel threatened by the growth of the cities. West Pointers were again considered class-ridden snobs who waved the epaulettes of their fancy uniforms "in the fashionable circles of metropolitan society." Although few civilians were aware that the regular army maintained four black regiments (officered by whites), those who were deemed them a dangerous social experiment. In the view of a handful of Eastern humanitarians, soldiers were those who did too much, principally in the mistreatment of Indians. To most Americans, they were men with "no snap," poker-playing, whisky-swizzling loafers who did too little.*[12]

Soldiers thus found that, when any heed was paid them, they were treated "with condescension if not contempt." The *Army and Navy Journal* complained: "The name soldier, as [people at large] use it, seems to be a synonym for all that is degrading and low, and whenever they meet a person bearing it they cannot forbear showing their contempt." In 1878, when wounds sustained fighting Indians would not heal and Captain Charles King returned to Wisconsin on sick leave, people on the streets of Milwaukee reacted to his uniform with "impudent and jeering comment." Businessmen were no less mean-spirited: "Well, old fellow, how do you manage to kill time out in the Army—nothing but play poker and drink whiskey?" When Andrew Carnegie exclaimed in 1881 that to him "the real glory of America lay in the fact that she had no army worth the name," he deftly caught the mood of his society in the fifteen years following the war.[13]

The strength of that temper could be measured by the popular reactions it visited on those who challenged it. Joshua Chamberlain had been deeply affected by his experience of combat, twenty battles and six wounds. During and after the war he struggled to locate the constructive purposes he desperately hoped underlay the work of destruction. "War! nothing but the final, infinite good, for men and God, can accept and justify human work like that!" "Fighting and destruction are terrible but are sometimes agencies of heavenly rather than hellish powers." Following two terms as Governor of Maine, he accepted the presidency of Bowdoin College and thought he saw there an opportunity to put the lessons of the war to worthy ends. Military

---

*The formative years of Frederick Winslow Taylor, the well-known industrial engineer and father of the time-and-motion study, coincided with the period of Hibernation. In his handbook for industrial managers he arraigned the slow pace of the workers, due to "loafing" and "marking time," as "the greatest obstacle" to the attainment of proper standards of factory efficiency. Taylor repeatedly referred to the problem as "soldiering."

exercise would build student character, instilling a discipline no longer to be found elsewhere in the society.

In 1872, aided by an officer seconded by the War Department, he formed the all-male student body into four infantry companies, adopted the West Point uniform, established drill schedules, and required saluting beyond duty periods. His innovations provoked a revolt. Insisting that there were better sources of manhood and discipline than drill, the college newspaper charged Chamberlain with attempting to erect a "military depotism." Students objected to the uniforms they were required to purchase. Petitions circulated. Groans began issuing from the ranks. Denunciations appeared on chapel walls. A Napoleon cannon was dismounted. Finally, late in the 1872–73 school year, when from the ranks came a raucous and, to some, shocking eruption of shouting and profanity, the faculty responded by suspending the entire junior class. That step incited its members to vow that they would never drill again and brought sophomores and freshmen to their support. Against that alliance Chamberlain moved decisively. He sent home all three classes and pursued them with letters demanding that they promise to resume drill or be expelled. At that juncture outraged parents and local public opinion (which, though not sympathetic to all student methods, supported student opposition to drill) combined to pressure the college trustees to decree that drill be made optional. An investigating committee appointed by the governing board reprimanded Chamberlain for acting as if he were a military commander rather than a college president. The "Drill Revolt" had triumphed. In the fall term four students elected drill. Several years later Chamberlain, drained of vigor, resigned. He had learned that whatever the lessons of the war, in the 1870s tolerance of military methods in civilian spheres was not one of them.[14]

Though there was abroad in American society much sentiment reinforcing the demobilized soldier's inclination to let the martial past slip away and to banish military influences from peacetime lives, otherwise that 1861 sense of unity with community was not restored. Born of extraordinary and untransmittable experience, the solitariness of the veteran persisted. Many had assumed, with Theodore Upson, that the "roughness" of war would fall away, leaving veterans once again like others, but their consciousness of separation endured. Ambrose Bierce drew the differences too sharply with his notion of two worlds, that of the veteran and that of the civilian, "untested, insulated from the quintessential experience of violence and death" and without "an inkling of the soldier's austere trade." But the differences did exist. Perhaps Bruce Catton caught more accurately the degree of separation: The veteran had "lost something; if not life itself, then the dreams or illusions of youth which once seemed to give life its meaning. He has come down to earth ahead of time. [Veterans] shared an understanding other folk did not have. Like Adam, they had been cast out of the enchanted garden, leaving innocence behind"—and in the 1860s there was more innocence to be lost.[15]

THE REVIVAL

About the year 1880 American interest in martial matters began to revive. Civil War books became popular. The circulation of the *Century* nearly doubled when, between 1884 and 1887, that magazine ran its series "Battles and Leaders of the Civil War." Militias in almost every state found new support and began programs of expansion. Many fraternal orders established military branches. The earliest was the Odd Fellows which in 1885 organized its soldierly auxiliary, the Patriarchs Militant. By 1897 such bodies counted perhaps 250,000 brothers devoted to camping, drilling, and parading in uniforms of spectacular ornamentation. The membership of the GAR jumped from 30,000 in 1878 to 146,000 in 1883, then to 233,000 in 1884 and to 320,000 in 1887. In 1890—at 428,000 members—it touched its crest. Its Columbus encampment of 1888 attracted 40,000 veterans and 60,000 family members, friends, and interested citizens. A subsequent Washington encampment drew 250,000.[16]

Commemoration of the war began first to influence and then to fuse with public ritual in both sections of the country. Ladies' memorial associations, organized in the South during the years of Hibernation, principally to solemnize those lost in the war, began a remarkable expansion of activity beyond graves-keeping and Memorial Day observances. During the 1880s and 1890s, with their fairs, raffles, picnics, dances, annual church services, and monument campaigns, Southern women moved to the center of community ceremony. They rode a wave of public enthusiasm set in motion by that set of ideas, the Lost Cause, which found much romance in the life of the antebellum South and much courage in the soldiery of the Confederacy. They were at first joined, and ultimately overborne, by newly established local veterans' groups whose own causes—reunions, statues and monuments, museums, Memorial Day (with emphasis on parades and speeches rather than cemetery sorrow), battle reenactments—sometimes paralleled women's interests but often extended the reach of martial influences. Especially expansive following the founding of the regionwide United Confederate Veterans in 1889, they urged fellow Southerners to offer veterans both respect and political preferment; to honor the Confederate flag; to name their sons after Southern combat heroes; and in many other ways to revivify their awareness of the war.[17]

In countless Northern towns, the GAR post became a focus of community activity. Its parades, fireworks displays, reviews, and receptions became fixtures of small-town life, and under its aegis Memorial Day and the Fourth of July became increasingly martial occasions. By 1890 veterans' organizations in both North and South often enjoyed a social influence commensurate with that of school and church.

A parallel development was a new burnish on the reputation of the regular army. Here the key figure was Captain Charles King, who between his disability retirement in 1879 and 1914 wrote or contributed to seventy-two books, including thirty-eight novels of the West and nine on the Civil War. As he benefited from the martial revival, he also imparted to it direction and intensity. For a quarter-century he was one of America's most popular authors; twenty-seven of his Western stories reached two or more editions. Though he wrote execrably—his plot turns were seldom credible and his character depictions invariably shallow—the message of his books registered powerfully. The United States Army, he insisted, was not a foreign body; whether in its ethnic components, its class composition, or its organizational temper, it was safely American. Though its soldiers represented an "array of nationalities," it possessed the power to convert the "scum" and to tincture the whole "with the clearheaded individuality of the American." King also maintained that the army was not class-ridden. On the Plains no commander wore Civil

War buttons, stars, or epaulettes; one could not distinguish General George Crook, a man of untrimmed beard and "little fuss," from his privates.

Finally, King's books held that the regulars were fighting in the West a war that their countrymen refused to recognize. "Indian warfare is, of all warfare, the most dangerous, the most trying, and the most thankless. Not recognized by the high authority of the United States Senate as war, it still possesses for you the disadvantages of civilized warfare, with all the horrible accompaniments that barbarians can invent and savages execute. In it you are required to serve . . . without favor or hope of reward." From the struggle against the Plains Indians new soldier heroes were emerging. In story after story the protagonist proved himself not only an exemplar of manliness, knightliness and courage in battle ("this knightly soldier . . . this brilliant, gallant officer . . . this Bayard without fear, without reproach") but a person of impeccable moral sensibilities. A "gentle-hearted man," he sorrowed over a comrade's coffin, "mingling his tears with those of that comrade's lonely little one"; he never spoke ill of a man behind his back or failed to hold "a woman's name as sacred." Contemporary critics applauded Charles King for the realism of his writing.[18]

As the Civil War was incorporated in public ritual and the reputation of soldiering rose, participation in war became an important mark of merit. Honor attached itself less to courageous or cowardly conduct, battles won or lost, causes preserved or destroyed than to one's simple presence in the war. Survival, too, by whatever circumstances actually achieved, became a source of pride. Veterans experiencing some return of confidence told themselves that it could not have been mere chance, that they must have possessed certain worthy attributes or acted in certain meritorious ways that accounted for their survival. As community ritual magnified the war, the war began to magnify all those who had fought and lived.

The fact that they shared participation and survival helped to accelerate the reconciliation of former Union and Confederate soldiers. Although there had never been much animosity between opposing enlisted men, at war's end feeling between some general officers had run high. A number of tempering influences, however, soon appeared. The West Point tie proved compelling; the reunions of the United States Military Academy Association of Graduates coaxed back and won over a number of former Confederate field commanders. Postwar arguments over the war's strategic and tactical movements also proved ameliorative, for generals who contested with colleagues to win credit withheld from them or to escape charges of malfeasance leveled against them sometimes solicited the testimony of commanders who had opposed them in the disputed encounters. Funeral gatherings provided strong public signals of reconciliation. When Grant died in 1885, John Gordon, Joseph E. Johnston, Fitzhugh Lee, Wade Hampton, and Simon Buckner attended services for the man who fifteen years before had praised Confederate bravery in the war and had toured the South. Many felt the poignancy in 1891 when Johnston succumbed to pneumonia said to have been contracted while standing hatless in the raw cold at Sherman's funeral.[19]

Former enlisted men had fewer opportunities and less need to effect public reconciliation. Soldier visits to battlefields, increasing dramatically in the 1880s and 1890s, brought encounters with former enemies as did, on a larger scale, joint observances of such battle anniversaries as that of Gettysburg in 1893. In 1882 the GAR had its national encampment in Baltimore, for the first time among people whose sympathies had rested with the opposition in 1861–65. Confederate veterans marched with Union contingents. In 1895 the GAR convened in Louisville, the heart of another border area, and rank-and-file reconciliation, though not complete, touched its apogee.[20]

The merging of veteran interests, important in itself, was but one of the aspects of the larger reunification of the sections. After 1880 the power of the Bloody Shirt to resuscitate wartime hostilities declined sharply. Concepts of the New South disseminated by Henry Grady and Henry Watterson heralded the desire of some Southerners to invite Northern investment, indeed to emulate the North's industrialization. (The "plaster of profit," the Northern novelist Albion W. Tourgee suggested, would heal the sores of war.) Correspondingly, the elaboration of the Lost Cause proved almost as appealing to Northerners as to Southerners, for many of the former, troubled by the decline of small-town communities wrought by urbanization and industrialization, felt the empathy of a people confronting a "disappearing civilization" of their own. Of less power was the appearance of a new common enemy. Charles King's characterization of the Plains Indians was ambivalent, but it tended to incite rather than inhibit action against them. Indians were portrayed as strong enough and malevolent enough to menace whites—hungry-eyed and merciless savages, they subjected prisoners to "fiendish torture," mutilated corpses, and dug up cadavers to claim their scalps; love of war and rapine was their "ruling passion." But Indians were also weak enough and degenerate enough to merit that oblivion to which King wished to consign them; they were a people of "innate sloth and restlessness," beggars and skulkers. King's stories fixed in the minds of white Northerners and Southerners images of a new enemy, leaving less room for the old enemies of 1861–65. In the pages of the popular story weeklies Confederate and Union officers combined to fight Indians in perfect harmony.[21]

In the 1880s and 1890s the militarization of thought, activity, and style touched veterans of the countryside and the city, veterans poor and rich, obscure and renowned.

Hamlin Garland's father, a Midwestern farmer whose years of army service had become "his most moving, most poetic experience," wore on all special occasions the regulation blue coat with the veteran's bronze button in its lapel. A faithful member of the GAR, he attended all meetings of the local post. He asked his son to accompany him to Chicago for a Grand Review—cities intimidated him—and once aboard the train hailed every old soldier as "Comrade." In Chicago, "he was like a boy on Circus Day." He gloried in the parade; its phalanxes seemed to him "fragments of a colossal dream—an epic of song and steel." He became tearful at the sight of tattered banners.[22]

The portrait of the veteran-father to which Sherwood Anderson so often turned in his books showed a man whose life centered on martial memories and on the opportunities they afforded in small-town Ohio. Irwin Anderson was "a responsible craftsman," the manufacturer and merchant of fine harness, the employer of one or more assistants—until his business failed in the early 1880s. Thereafter he worked sporadically, wandering, painting houses or signs, hanging paper, doing odd jobs. Most of his days were spent "veteranizing"—telling stories of his courage in a Civil War cavalry troop; attending GAR meetings; taking roles in GAR plays; performing in GAR talent shows; marching in GAR Fourth of July and Decoration Day parades. Sometimes the father exasperated his son: "by the fire at evening, through fast day and feast day, at weddings and at funerals . . . again and again endlessly, everlastingly this flow of war words." Sometimes he disgusted his son—when, for example, he spent scarce funds for a new suit and went off to a GAR convention or dismissed the son's criticism of his debts with, "You don't understand the heart of a soldier." Sometimes he touched his son's sympathy. How, Sherwood Anderson asked, was his father to have known "that after the war he was to marry and have many children, that he would never be a hero again, that all the rest of his life he would have to build on [those] days, creating in fancy a thousand adventures that never happened." In one way the father impressed the son: The war conveyed in his stories became "that universal, passionate, death-spitting thing."[23]

Such lives suggested how the military revival licensed veterans to employ their positive memories of the war in compensation for the insufficiencies of their civilian lives. Wartime camaraderie might be employed as a palliative for peacetime feelings of isolation; combat excitement for peacetime boredom; the life-and-death issues of war for civilian inconsequentiality; the constant movement of campaigning for peacetime immobility. Such useful counterbalances may not have lifted from the veteran his sense of solitariness, but they surely eased its burden. Bruce Catton has described how veterans appeared to him as a small boy: They were

> . . . men set apart. . . . They were pillars, not so much of the church (although most of them were devout communicants) as of the community; the keepers of its patriotic traditions, the living embodiment . . . of what it most deeply believed about the nation's greatness and high destiny. They gave an especial flavor to the life of the village. Years ago they had marched thousands of miles to legendary battlefields, and although they had lived half a century since then in our quiet backwater all anyone ever thought of was that they had once gone to the ends of the earth and seen beyond the farthest horizon.

Though they remained "men set apart," their separation had been granted public recognition and their estrangement elevated to civic virtue.[24]

280

Economic hardship was not a requisite for the martial revivification of one's life. Following combat service with Cleveland's Hibernian Guards, Thomas Galwey earned three degrees, found a succession of jobs in education, publishing, and law, and became a successful attorney for the City of New York. He was apparently a gentle man. He refrained from fighting; he wrote letters critical of deer hunters. His family wondered how he had ever fired a rifle. Nevertheless, he assumed and delighted in the manner of the soldier. He carried a sword-cane and "marched" everywhere. On Sundays he took his children to visit Grant's Tomb, and on Decoration Day he attended every parade. He relished the salutes of streetcar conductors. Addressed as "Captain" or "Captain Brevet" or "Captain Tom" or "Little Cap," he became so protective of the honor that he worked to expose others who were called "General" or "Major" without having participated in the war.[25]

At a point on the social spectrum as far as possible from failure and obscurity, no one demonstrated better than Oliver Wendell Holmes, Jr., the compelling power of the social climate to alter both style and attitude regarding the war. In combat twenty years earlier, he had undergone severe disillusionment. He had grown weary of such words as "cowardice," "gallantry," and "chivalry." He had described Fredericksburg as "an infamous butchery in a ridiculous attempt." He had referred to the results of battle as "the butcher's bill." In May 1863 he had prayed that he might lose a foot in order to escape a return to combat, and a year later, in the last days of the Wilderness campaign, he had feared that battle's "terrible pressure on mind and body" was pushing him toward insanity. He had finally resigned his commission, prior to the end of the war, because he no longer thought it a duty to serve. By 1885, however, the war of 1864–65 had largely departed from his consciousness. He again cultivated the military mustache, just as Charles King's stories were reasserting its importance as a sign of character. He installed his sword and regimental colors above the mantel in his study. In processions of Supreme Court Justices, he habitually turned to an ex-Confederate associate and gave him a military salute. He began to observe war anniversaries, even those of battles in which he had been wounded.

In public addresses he exalted unquestioning faith and obedience to command as the hallmarks of the true soldier: "[I]n the midst of doubt, in the collapse of creeds, there is one thing I do not doubt . . . and that is that the faith is true and adorable which leads a soldier to throw away his life in obedience to a blindly accepted duty, in a cause which he little understands, in a plan of campaign of which he has no notion, under tactics of which he does not see the use." Man's destiny was battle, and his faith would trample under foot "the cynic force with which the thoughts of common-sense will assail [him]." "War, when you are at it, is horrible and dull," he told the Harvard graduating class of 1895. "It is only when time has passed that you see that its message was divine. . . . For high and dangerous action teaches us to believe as right beyond dispute things for which our doubting minds are slow to find words of proof. Out of heroism grows faith in the worth of heroism." The Civil War, he told fellow veterans, had allowed soldiers to see "with our own eyes, beyond and above the gold fields, the snowy heights of honor." "Through our great good fortune, in our youth our hearts were touched with fire."[26]

No one indicted the war more fiercely than Ambrose Bierce. His 1875 article "What I Saw of Shiloh" described how an Illinois company, refusing to surrender, had been shot down and their bodies consumed by a woods fire: "Some were swollen to double girth; others shriveled to manikins. . . . their faces were bloated and black or yellow and shrunken. The contraction of muscles which had given them claws for hands had cursed each countenance with a hideous grin. Faugh! I cannot catalogue the charms of these gallant gentlemen who had got what they enlisted for." But even Bierce felt the hard war slipping away:

> O days when all the world was beautiful and strange; when unfamiliar constellations burned in the Southern midnights, and the mocking-bird poured out his heart in the moon-gilded magnolia; when there was something new under a new sun. . . . Is it not strange that the phantoms of a blood-stained period have so airy a grace and look with so tender eyes?—that I recall with difficulty the danger and death and horrors of the time, and without effort all that was gracious and picturesque?

He grasped the process. A part of him deplored the change it was working; another part did not want it halted. During the Spanish–American War he closed an article on Chickamauga, then a training camp, with a passage that would have drawn applause from every Memorial Day gathering in the nation:

> To those of us who have survived the attacks of both Bragg and Time, and who keep in memory the dear dead comrades whom we left upon that fateful field, the place means much. May it mean something less to the younger men whose tents are now pitched where, with bended heads and clasped hands, God's great angels stood invisible among the heroes in blue and the heroes in gray, sleeping their last sleep in the woods of Chickamauga.

In the new century Bierce's fascination with battle sites intensified. Just before his disappearance in Mexico, he revisited five of the fields—the "Enchanted Forest," "this Dream-land—my Realm of Adventure"—over which he had fought a half-century before.[27]

Not even the few who worried that the polish being applied to an old war might make attractive a new one could remain immune to broadening military influences. Nurse Clara Barton, who founded the American Red Cross in the hope that it would serve as the "bit in the mouth, the curb on the neck of the war horse," honored battle anniversaries, wore her military decorations, spoke at veterans' reunions, accepted election as GAR national chaplain, and spoke in military phraseology, all of it in the heroic mold. In the 1890s Francis Amasa Walker opposed jingoism and criticized teachers whom he accused of imbuing students with bloodthirstiness—the GAR program to establish military instruction in schools had not suffered Chamberlain's failure—but at the same time Walker wrote the history of his Civil War corps ("intense enthusiasm" in every line), participated vigorously in veteran organizations, employed military expressions, and appeared to fancy himself the commanding officer of the Massachusetts Institute of Technology. He was addressed as "General Walker," not "President Walker."[28]

The most ironic example of the reconceptualization of war is offered by William Tecumseh Sherman. During early postwar years he had been one of the few prominent Americans to speak candidly of the war of 1864–65; he was perhaps the most caustic critic of the kind of conflict he had done so much to develop. War, he repeated, was an awful game demanding destruction and death; military fame was to suffer one of those deaths and then to have your name spelled wrong in the newspapers. In 1880 he spoke his most famous formulation to 5,000 GAR veterans gathered in Columbus: Though there might be "many a boy here today who looks on war as all glory . . . it is all hell. You can bear this warning voice to generations yet to come. I look upon war with horror." Nevertheless, Sherman began to build nostalgic memories of the march through Georgia; commanding his columns, he concluded, had been "the highest pleasure of war." Such perceptions continued to mount in his mind until war had climbed far from hell. In 1890 he addressed veterans of the Army of the Tennessee:

> Now my friends, there is nothing in life more beautiful than the soldier. A knight errant with steel casque, lance in hand, has always commanded the admiration of men and women. The modern soldier is his legitimate successor and you, my comrades, were not hirelings; you never were, but knight[s] errant transformed into modern soldiers, as good as they were and better. Now the truth is we fought the holiest fight ever fought on God's earth.

Just a year before his death, Sherman portrayed the war in terms of a knightliness that he had held in contempt thirty years before.[29]

How are the militarization of social thought and the purification of memory, forces of great consequence in the 1890s, to be explained?

No doubt the passage of time did heal many wounds of memory. No doubt it was important that American society institutionalized the heroic aspects of the war and omitted from its postwar ceremonies any reference to war's fear or futility; community ritual celebrated all wounds as evidence of courage and enshrined all deaths as efficacious deaths. But the change that began in 1880, so powerful in the lives of so many, must have had another impetus as well.

In the 1865–90 period the economy of the United States underwent remarkable change. Rapid industrial expansion created social consequences as profound as its economic effects. It awarded to its principal beneficiaries a new wealth far beyond the resources of Americans at large. It established industrial leaders as new models of social success.

On several counts those developments agitated veterans. They did not much like those who grew to such power and prominence. None of the magnates had been soldiers. J. Pierpont Morgan, John D. Rockefeller, and Andrew Carnegie had hired substitutes. Veterans were also aware that while they themselves had served, speculators at home had built the foundations of great wealth. Phillip Armour's first great strike had come when he sold pork short in 1864. Jay Gould, Jay Cooke, Jim Fisk, and Collis Huntington had established or multiplied their fortunes while soldiers fought. So it was with a combination of anger and envy that veterans regarded the financial and social success of such people. Carlton McCarthy spoke indignantly of those who had stayed out of the war to make money—skulkers, "the able-bodied bomb-proofs"—and twenty years later were more admired and courted than the veteran with an arm or leg missing. "How 'big' they are now!"[30]

Even if veterans had been able to ignore new standards of success inflated by the accomplishments of the magnates, many of them realized that they had not achieved the goals they had set for themselves two decades earlier. The "pursuits of peaceful industry" had not always proved as remunerative as they had anticipated, and they sought explanations. One took the form of a conviction that while nonparticipation had given the magnates a head start, participation had continued to hobble soldiers even after they were able to join the race. As Rice Bull put it:

> Looking back now I realize, far more than I did then, how unprepared we were to meet the life conditions that faced us, not alone from wounds or broken health but from the greater reason that our long absence during the years of life when we would have fitted ourselves by education and experience for a successful effort were years gone. Many faced the future with the handicap of physical weakness, ignorance and lost opportunities.[31]

Prodded by the GAR, society offered veteran preference in civil service hiring and veteran pensions, but those were refuges from the competition that dominated the culture. They were at best, many veterans felt, consolation prizes that American society held out to its losers.

Efforts to dispel such conclusions imparted a poignant defensiveness to the statements of veterans. William Ripley told Vermont high school students that veterans should not be compared with other competitors, that they were subject to different standards only they could comprehend: "These old soldiers are not all pure gold, it is true; there are perhaps a few, a very few, whom we would make over again, and in a different mould if we could; but let no man who has never been a soldier judge him who has." Other veterans not only denied the worthiness of the winners but denounced the rules of the game and angrily asserted their superiority to both:

> The veteran soldiers are the aristocracy of the land. I do not refer to the distinctions which society may try to make supreme, or the glitter with which misers of gold may seek to dazzle the people. I mean by aristocracy, the heroes who have proven the best men in the land—the dauntless hearts, without whose valorous devotion, we would not have to-day a Union, or the world a home for liberty. . . . No matter, comrades, if a veteran soldier may be poor in purse, humble in position, perhaps, somewhat ignorant (for hundreds of thousands gave years of their school days to war duties), he has proved the possession of immortal and self-sacrificing courage. He has recorded himself by his deeds as immensely superior to the devotees of fashion, or the worshippers of gold.[32]

Now it was the present that receded—veterans nodded as Sherman spoke of "the gloom of ordinary humdrum existence"— and Civil War service that became luminescent. "At the time of my discharge," Enos Vail wrote, "I thought little of my work for the Union, but as the years went by and I talked with other veterans, we began to appreciate the priceless service the boys of '61-'65 had rendered." Another said at a veterans' campfire: "Do you know, comrades, I sometimes think that we didn't really appreciate, at the time, the grandeur of what we were permitted to do in the war for the preservation of liberty." Battlefield visits had a special power to enhance wartime accomplishment. When Robert L. Drummond returned to a Gettysburg reunion,

> . . . I was myself startled . . . to hear *my own voice* breaking the almost painful stillness with "Comrades of the 111th New York Infantry," and *realized* that I was actually speaking these words upon the *World's Greatest Battlefield* and to men who in the strength of their young manhood really lay behind that same wall upon which I stood, with their eyes strained, every sense quickened, their fingers upon the triggers of their Springfield Rifles, watching the advance of the Flower of the South and while so watching . . . admiring, still anxiously, painfully, waiting for the

ominous word "FIRE," which was to blast the hopes of a People and because of their deadly aim and splended resistance would bring to nought the bravest, most courageous and daring assault that the World ever has known.

Such routes led many veterans to conclude that combat had been the most important chapter of their lives.[33]

The veteran's reconceptualization of the war was one expression of a larger social process that also drew on the fear of business hegemony. Many Americans unconnected with veterans worried that business power would overturn basic social relationships and replace traditional values. The revival of military spirit was in significant measure the result of their resistance to a society that threatened to measure all things "by dollar-mark standards" and their search for some alternative way by which they might define what it meant to be an American.[34]

Some of their explorations moved in the direction of patriotism. There were in the years 1880–98 several surges of American nationalism that were in no way responses to threats or challenges from overseas. Veterans applauded; as Bruce Catton said, "With them, patriotism was automatic, something one simply takes for granted, something that comes into a person along with the air he breathes . . . it was an unspoken, compelling attitude of mind." Here Confederate veterans would yield nothing to ex-Unionists. George Cary Eggleston explained that Southerners, believing in secession as a Constitutional right, had been as truly and purely patriotic as Northerners; they had differed only in their judgment of what constituted the duty of the patriot. If, however, some Northerners balked at the notion of the attack on Sumter as an expression of American patriotism, it was still possible to locate other bases more appropriate to common celebration—the American Revolution, for example. Northern and Southern veterans met one another for the first time at the centennial celebration of Bunker Hill in 1875. A year later *Scribner's* described George Washington as "the great rebel of his day."[35]

Another alternative to Americanism construed as business endeavor was a definition based on race. New England Brahmins in particular proposed that the American essence resided in racial qualifications. John C. Ropes maintained that the great battles of the Civil War engendered pride not only in country but in Anglo-Saxonism, and many such urgings appeared in the 1890s.[36]

Neither race nor patriotism proved capable of drawing lines as veterans wished. The magnates, most of them of Anglo-Saxon backgrounds, retorted tellingly that nothing fortified national strength more than industrial development. The formulation that emerged, while incorporating elements of love of country and racial pride, relied principally on military values to offset the selfishness attributed to businessmen. To many Americans in the late 1880s and the 1890s, the soldier, as the spirit of antimaterialism, became the incarnation of Americanism.

Such a formulation tapped several older sources of anti-business sentiment. New England and Southern elites had long been disdainful of industry. During the war the Bostonian Francis Parkman had railed against those who permitted "the pride of a good bargain" to dislodge "the pride of manhood." Sidney Lanier coupled trade with bohemianism [!] as the sources of evil. John Esten Cooke was confident that "the blood flows faster and much more gloriously through the veins [in war] than in trade." Professional military officers, too, particularly in the years of Hibernation, had defined themselves in contradistinction to business values, with their "genial, wholesouled qualities" set against the "selfish ideas" of the moneymakers. In 1887, when the Cleveland Administration proposed to return captured battle flags to Southern states, Sherman complained that the Adjutant General, the Secretary of War, and the President had never known "the blood and torture of battle" or "captured a flag"; they appraised regimental colors only at their "commercial value." Finally, sparks of the volunteers' wartime animosity against business enterprise remained to be rekindled in veterans. As a protest against the change wrought by industrialism, the martial enthusiasm of the 1890s stood not far below the agrarian revolt of the Populists.[37]

The most influential expression of the vision of soldierly qualities as the antidote to business materialism was Edward Bellamy's novel *Looking Backward*. Its utopian society of the year 2000 dispensed with merchants and bankers, buying and selling. It organized itself as an industrial army whose members' wages were those of honor rather than money. The book's nineteenth-century visitor was impressed: "By making honor the sole reward of achievement you have imparted to all service the distinction peculiar in my day [1888] to the soldiers." Bellamy himself confessed "an admiration of the soldier's business as the only one in which, from the start, men throw away the purse and reject every sordid standard of merit and achievement. The very conditions which [his Nationalist movement] promises—that is to say, security as to livelihood, with duty and the love of honor as motives—are the actual conditions of military life." Bellamy's protagonist in *Looking Backward* found in the military parade an admirable expression of those conditions: "Here at last were order and reason, an exhibition of what intelligent co-operation can accomplish . . . it was their perfect concert of action, their organization under one control, which made these men the tremendous engine they were."[38]

Veterans who sunned themselves in the revival of military spirit spoke as if soldier life and business life represented separate and opposed sets of values. They failed to comprehend, or to concede, that the war and its aftermath had helped prepare a way for the dominance of business.

The ultimate methods of the war had done much to undermine moral standards and to elevate success achieved through power.[39] Veterans complained that businessmen "broke the rules," but as soldiers they themselves had transgressed against the standards of behavior to which they subsequently held businessmen. Sherman's profligate use of soldiers as instruments was not unrelated to the way Carnegie used, and used up, workers in his mills. The magnate's celebration of his ability to exercise power over others was little different from Sherman's.

As it did for others, Civil War experience engrained in Oliver Wendell Holmes, Jr., a "reverence for men of action." Soon after peace returned, he had traveled to Concord to call on his "revered master," Emerson. The sage, however, "aired transcendental ideas about life and death, conscience and duty" that bored and disgusted the visitor, for Emerson had not, as Holmes had in war, crossed "the threshold of reality." Thereafter the businessman, admirable in his fierceness and power, replaced the philosopher as the object of Holmes's admiration. He respected particularly the energy and daring of men like railroad builder James J. Hill, "one of the greatest forms of human power." "Business in the world is unhappy, often seems mean, and always challenges your power to idealize the brute fact—but it hardens the fibre and I think is more likely to make more of a man of one who turns it to success."[40]

In another way there evolved a symbiosis with business unacknowledged by ex-soldiers: The veteran organization developed its own vital economic aspects. The GAR built a pension machine with a network of clerks, claims agents, attorneys, and lobbyists. Civil service preference created a comparable jobs machine. A GAR entertainment circuit provided such touring acts as "The Drummer Boy of the Rappahannock," who, as late as 1916, offered small-town audiences programs of war songs, anecdotes, jokes, drum rolls, patriotic addresses, and battle reenactments. Individuals too—from Irwin Anderson and his touring magic lantern show to blind veterans employed to sell Civil War books door to door—adapted the war to commercial ends. With the growth of advertising, some veterans even offered product endorsements. An 1890 Georgia publication included a picture of a Union soldier, John Conway of Loudon, Ohio, sitting on the ground, leg extended with knee bandaged and right arm in a sling, against a backdrop of battle:

> I was wounded in the leg at the battle of Stone['s] River, December 31st 1862. My blood was poisoned from the effects of the wound, and the leg swelled to double its natural size, and remained so for many years. The poison extended to my whole system, and I suffered a thousand deaths. Nothing did me any good til I took SWIFT'S SPECIFIC, which took the poison out of my blood, and enabled me to feel myself a man again. S.S.S. is the only remedy for blood poison.

Although many of the margins of veteran life had been commercialized, veterans—the Galweys, the Garlands, the Andersons, even Oliver Wendell Holmes, Jr.,—became increasingly dependent on their sense of themselves as soldiers still, soldiers whose values transcended the dominant business ethos.[41]

The social forces revivifying the martial past ultimately moved beyond their antibusiness impulse to depreciate the value that Americans attached to peace.

The problem had begun during the war, for the patterns of struggle had injected poison into both Northern and Southern perceptions of peace. Because through much of the conflict the Confederate war aim, independence, could have been realized simply through the return of peace, peace advocacy became suspect in the North. Federal soldiers were certain that the efforts of the peace party cost the lives of thousands of their comrades; the enemy at home seemed more despicable than the enemy in the field. In the South, peace had seemed to stand at Appomattox hand-in-hand with capitulation. The war thus linked peace either with cowardice and disloyalty or with defeat and alien occupation.

An equally profound impact of the war was that its trauma created a receptivity to the notion that war was life itself, or at least that war was the apt metaphor for the processes of life. The Social Darwinian tenet that life was struggle became persuasive to many, especially in military and academic circles. William Church, the editor of the *Army and Navy Journal,* premised his appeals for the expansion of the military services on the conviction that "life is a struggle for supremacy, and . . . the contests of the battlefield are but the intensified expression of antagonisms that are ever active in human societies, that are indeed the divine means for advancing man beyond the state of his primitive ancestor." Admiral Stephen Luce was another who was convinced that strife was the law of existence: Every man was at war first with himself and then with his neighbors. War thus derived not from human institutions subject to modification and amelioration but from an ordinance by which God worked out the destinies of nations. One of the period's most renowned academics, Yale's William Graham Sumner (for whom a wealthy patron had provided money to hire a substitute) built a structure of sociological analysis atop the assumption that conflict was fundamental to life, that war would always exist inside and around men.[42]

But if life was inevitably war, why should peace suffer a decline in public estimation? Because, it was claimed, business materialism had captured peace, and too many people were living life as if it were not struggle. Peace was thus blamed for that erosion of fundamental values felt by so many Americans. Selfishness, ennui, and spiritual disintegration became the hallmarks of peace.

Ambrose Bierce began to contrast the "glad" days of the war with the "contracting circle" of peacetime boredom and spiritual decline. Holmes referred to the United States as "this snug, over-safe corner of the world." Hayes found "largeness of the human spirit" only in his comrades of the 23d Ohio and complained that courage, generosity, and sacrifice had been lost in peace. Peace, said Sumner, was at times self-seeking: "Men sometimes go into raptures about the blessings of peace when peace is selfishness, when men look with indifference upon wickedness and injustice so long as it does not touch themselves. . . . They sigh over war when war only proves that there is a cause or an idea for which men are ready to die, and that they have a deeper horror of false-hood than of bloodshed." All of those threads were spun together in the indictment of Captain H. C. Taylor, president of the Naval War College. Nations that practiced too long the arts of peace, he taught, grew enfeebled and corrupt. Religion declined and "race decadence" accelerated. Peacetime ease "has in it some-thing more degrading for the human race than [war's] simple savagery." Taylor echoed the conviction of the English art critic and social prophet John Ruskin: Peace was bound with sensual-ity, selfishness, and, remarkably, even death. Here Luce ex-tended the thought: Without war, Greece had subsided into aes-theticism; without war, Rome had found luxury more destructive than the sword. Nations that suspended the "battle of life" per-ished.[43]

The solution was to be found in a return to war. Sardonically, Bierce favored it on the grounds that war—or famine or pestil-ence—would stop people from cheating. Henry Adams also ap-proved of it:

> If war made men brutal, at least it made them strong; it called out the qualities best fitted to survive in the struggle for existence. To risk life for one's country was no mean act even when done for selfish motives; and to die that others might more happily live was the highest act of self-sacrifice to be reached by man. War, with all its horrors could purify as well as debase; it dealt with high motives and vast interests; taught courage, discipline, and a stern sense of duty.

Luce went even further: "War is one of the great agencies by which human progress is effected." It stimulated national growth, solved otherwise unsolvable domestic problems, and even purged the nation of undesirable "humors." Again follow-ing Ruskin's lead, Taylor insisted that no art was possible except that based on battle. To numbers of Americans in the 1890s war seemed the remedy for the problems of peace.[44]

The peace movement was unable to reverse or even to blunt the impact of such thought. Many of its members had come out of traditional peace churches and were without experience of war. One of its leaders, Alfred Love, "had always been a peace man; it was as natural to him as to take the air into his lungs. He could not but see that a peaceful condition was best for us all; the amiable and affectionate feelings of the heart, and all the facilities for being at peace would not have been given to us, were it not intended that we should be at peace." Veterans fiercely resented a position, so effortlessly achieved, that war was wickedness.[45]

Peace advocates neglected serious consideration of the combat experience. Continuing to emphasize the licentiousness of military life, they concentrated on the camp images of drinking, gambling, and sexual temptation, just as King's books were dispelling them. They also injured themselves with tactics that leapt from the denunciation of war to the disparagement of soldiers. Love, who had "positively refused" to serve in the war, objected to addressing soldiers by their military titles: "I do not want to call anyone by a name which signifies a man-killer, or one skilled in destroying human beings." Peace actions were often highly symbolic. At the Philadelphia Centennial much was made of three swords, purchased by peace advocates and then presented to a manufacturer able to turn them into a plow and pruning hooks. The Universal Peace Union and the Women's Christian Temperance Union attempted to establish the third Sunday in December as an International Peace Day, but their efforts were unavailing. There were programs of greater substance and sophistication—notably the campaign to persuade nations to sign arbitration treaties—but seldom did the peace movement succeed in penetrating the patterns of American daily life as had the activities of the GAR and the United Confederate Veterans.[46]

Veterans, along with many others, remained contemptuous of peace efforts. When a peace congress wired the GAR, "We congratulate you on a peaceful encampment. As veterans can you not add your protest against war, that there may never more be another war encampment," the reply was, "Your congratulations reciprocated. The Grand Army of the Republic is determined to have peace, even if it has to fight for it."[47]

One trace of an earlier social climate—a sense of war as loss—did persist, though how much due to peace efforts and how much to residual memory of the war was unclear. Through the 1880s it retained sufficient strength to mute advocacy of war for its own sake; even in 1896–98 some war partisans felt compelled to argue that because Spanish actions against Cubans constituted war, American belligerency was necessary principally to reestablish peace. Nevertheless, by 1890 references to war as loss or terror were becoming perfunctory. Each censorious expression—"war is wrong, absolutely immoral"; "war is cruel and brutal"; "war is certainly a great evil"; "war is horrible"; "war is hell"—seemed no more than a ritual bow sure to be followed by "but," as glorification in the concrete overwhelmed condemnation in the abstract. In 1898 Carl Schurz detected that "a resort to war is on every possible occasion spoken of not only by the miscreants . . . but even by otherwise rational and respectable persons, with a flippancy as if war were nothing more serious than an international yacht-race or football match." When Hamlin Garland asked the young Stephen Crane how, without experience of combat, he knew about war, he blithely replied that his knowledge came from the football field, that the opposing team was the enemy and the psychology of the game the same as that of war.[48]

Those ultimately called upon to translate the burgeoning military spirit into action were the sons, those of the next generation who had listened to the stories and speeches, read the patriotic texts, learned the flag salute, entered the essay contests, and attended the parades and school assemblies. "Over all of us in 1898," Carl Sandburg wrote, "was the shadow of the Civil War and the men who fought it to the end."[49]

After 1890 veterans knew precisely what they wanted to tell their sons about war. They had come to think of themselves as models for the battles of life and of war, and they expected their sons to become the custodians of their war—or at least of the valor and nobility in which they then thought of their war. Washington Davis spoke of the Sons of Veterans, founded 1881: "How will the boys feel with a knowledge of fathers' deeds that the whole world admires and pronounces unequaled? Can they help being proud of the honor of being sons of such sires? Can they do anything collectively, as well as individually, to prove themselves worthy descendants of those heroes?" Robert Drummond told the students of Hamilton College: "[B]efore you lies the battle of Life, and in Technology, and in Law, in Medicine and in Business, there are regiments, brigades and divisions to be commanded and one of the questions is, who shall command them? *[A]re you able to meet the emergency . . . are you willing to pay the price?*" Sons were also made aware of their debt. "Are you shaping your lives," Drummond asked, "so that someone will pay tribute to you as I do to 'the companions of my boyhood?' . . . You are in full possession of the heritage purchased by their blood. Shall the purchase price . . . be forgotten, or . . . depreciated?"[50]

Challenges were often accompanied by insinuations of filial ingratitude, flaccidity, and deficient patriotism. "Lying on your sick bed," Drummond chided, "you have asked, maybe impatiently, to [have] your pillows [changed]; these [soldiers] had no pillows to change" or mothers there to change them. "Some of you feel that your lot is not cast in sunny places, but are unmindful . . . that they [Union prisoners of war] were treated like *dogs* because of their loyalty to the flag that *you*, perhaps, have never learned to love." To a Vermont audience William Ripley made clear the qualifications for such a love: "[N]o man can really love [the flag] till he has marched under it, fought under it, suffered under it, and seen his comrades die under it." If in 1864–65 the war had seemed intolerable to many soldiers, by the 1890s veterans were using the war both to escape from an unrewarding present ("How willingly," said Carlton McCarthy, the veteran "closes his eyes to the present to dream of camp-fire times.") and to reproach their sons for the defects of the present.[51]

It was no coincidence that many young men who had never seen war and who lived in a society subjected to no external threats or even provocations should begin to feel themselves and their generation vaguely deficient and that, in response, should pursue war as if obsessed. Stiles and a friend agreed to a young acquaintance's request for a day's walking tour of the Seven Days battlefields:

> Rainsford caught the plan [of battle] instantly. Going over it in detail with him, upon the very spots, and climbing the very slopes up which Lee's legions had rushed to the charge, he was thrilled

295

to almost savage excitement, yelling like a rebel infantryman, his giant frame and his grand face absolutely inspired. In his martial ecstasy he threw his great arms about us . . . declaring he . . . could never forget us now, and that to have lived in and been a part of those days and those battles was enough to lift men forever to heroic stature and character.

Some of those who would become the most renowned of the post-war generation—Theodore Roosevelt, Richard Harding Davis, Stephen Crane—were convinced that combat was an experience both desirable and essential. Even Finley Peter Dunne, creator of the ever skeptical Mr. Dooley, was persuaded that "the good reporter, like the good soldier, must look upon war as the supreme adventure in the great drama called Life." No war exceeded the Spanish–American War in initial martial enthusiasm.[52]

The values young men carried to war in 1898 were again those of 1861. Though he would become the exemplar of the Spanish–American War as a war of courage, Theodore Roosevelt was only one of thousands who felt impelled to test himself in combat. Manliness again permeated approaches to action, as recruits sought constantly to do "the manly thing." Indeed, Roosevelt may have defined manliness more rigorously than had Civil War volunteers; while the latter had seen in several "feminine qualities" possible sources of male sympathy and sensitivity, Roosevelt equated them only with weakness. The luster of the charge was undiminished. Interwar military journals had confirmed the propriety of Grant's offensive tactics, and the soldiers of 1898 conceived of combat exclusively in terms of the charge; they never thought to do otherwise. Combat was again to be individualized experience. Roosevelt would later say to Bierce, "Do you know, as I rode up San Juan Hill upon a very memorable occasion, I held firmly before my eyes the vision of a lone horseman—oh, you know the man! the man in your story, 'A Son of the Gods,' who went forward to reconnoiter, to find if the enemy were concealed behind a ridge!" The notion of Noble Death survived undiminished. Richard Harding Davis would write of a sergeant's death in the first Cuban skirmish: "God could not have given him a nobler end; to die, in the forefront of the first fight of the war, quickly, painlessly, with a bullet through the heart, with his regiment behind him, and facing the enemies of his country." Those at home again spoke of soldier wounds as "honorable scars." Fourteen Americans would die of fever for every one struck down in combat, but that was one of many realities that the soldiers of 1898 would have to discover themselves.[53]

The picture of war that the sons carried to Cuba was false because their fathers' memories had become false to the war of 1864–65. Around their camp fires veterans reminded one another how the "explosion of a shell was frequently followed by the crack of a joke, and a bullet or a bayonet produced more fun than fear; yet neither were ever so close that they left no time for a prayer." Men overtaken by the infirmities of age recalled how "tough and hard" they had become by the end of the war, "brought down to solid fighting weight by long service in the open field." A "terrible blow" across the face with a musket, leaving a soldier with "a slight black spot under each eye" next morning, "would have laid . . . up [a civilian] for a month." Men increasingly dependent on others were sure that they had controlled the course of their war: "[B]ehind the war of musketry was a war of mind. Each bullet and each bayonet was guided by a thought and an inspiration." The Confederate veteran Carlton McCarthy recalled, "The emotions are never so stirred as [in war]. Imagination takes her highest flights, poetry blazes, song stirs the soul, and every noble attribute is brought into full play . . . the building of a noble character [is worth] all the toil and sacrifice of war." The Union veteran William Ripley asked high school students to remember "how grandly" the soldiers of the Civil War had died.[54]

To Bruce Catton, growing up in Benzonia, Michigan, in the first years of the new century, the veterans of the Civil War "seemed to speak for a certainty, for an assured viewpoint, for a standard of values that did not fluctuate" and for "the continuity of human experience."[55] So did they speak to all Americans in 1900. Civil War veterans had become symbols of changelessness—but only by obliterating or amending an experience of combat so convulsive of their values that it had for a time cut the cord of experience.

Dramatis Personae

Abbott, Henry L. The son of a distinguished Boston family, he was born in 1842 and educated at Harvard, graduating with the class of 1860. An officer in the 20th Massachusetts, he saw hard fighting at Fredericksburg and Gettysburg. Union soldiers regarded him as an exemplary commander and often cited his courage in battle, his refusal to take furloughs, his hesitation to accept promotion, and his efforts to warn his men against profanity, gambling, and drinking. At age twenty-two he was killed in the Wilderness on May 6, 1864. He was promoted posthumously from major to brevet brigadier general.

Allen, George H. A baker by trade, he became a corporal in the 4th Rhode Island in September 1861. After unusual duty as marines assigned to naval vessels operating off the Carolinas, he and his comrades participated in many major battles of the Army of the Potomac. In Petersburg's Battle of the Crater, two hundred men of the 4th advanced; while seventy-five were wounded, captured, or killed, Allen ran to make his escape. He was one of a minority of the 4th who agreed to reenlist in early 1864, and when in October those whose terms had expired marched home, taking the 4th's colors with them, he accepted with great reluctance incorporation in the 7th Rhode Island. He was mustered out in mid-July 1865.

Barber, Lucius W. A soldier in the ranks of the 15th Illinois from May 1861 to September 1865, he shared that unit's misadventures in the Western theater. Disgusted with tours guarding railroads and skirmishing with elusive guerrillas ("Most anything was more tolerable than this harassing life."), in October 1864 he was captured with

298

his whole regiment. After a mercifully brief stay in Andersonville, he was included on the sick-exchange list through the intervention of sympathetic Confederates anxious to aid a brother Mason, and he was able to rejoin Sherman's army in South Carolina for the last months of the war. He died in 1872 at age thirty-two, the victim of consumption he believed he had contracted as a prisoner of war.

Bardeen, Charles W. A disobedient and boisterous boy after the death of his father and the remarriage of his mother, he enlisted in the musicians' corps of the 1st Massachusetts at age fourteen. Though unable to master an even drum roll, he learned to play the fife. He witnessed the fighting at Fredericksburg, Chancellorsville, Gettysburg ("the greatest experience of my life"), and in the Wilderness and escaped both wounds and serious sickness, although he was not always spared the hospital work musicians were ordered to perform when their regiments went into battle. In 1864–65 he attended Lawrence Academy in Groton, Massachusetts; enrolling at Yale, he was one of the two members of his regiment who went to college following the war. He subsequently settled in Syracuse, where he became a vigorous participant in veterans' activities.

Beatty, John. Born near Sandusky, Ohio, in 1828, he was working as a businessman and banker when he resolved to answer Abraham Lincoln's first call for volunteers. Becoming lieutenant colonel and then colonel of the 3rd Ohio, he was with the regiment at Perryville, "the long-looked-for battle" in which two-hundred of the unit's five-hundred men were killed or wounded. He was unable to reverse the flight of his panicked brigade at Stone's River. Increasingly disillusioned and homesick for his wife and children, he resigned his commission in January 1864. He served in Congress from 1868–1873 but gave his principal postwar efforts to business ventures and writing, publishing three novels between 1883 and 1904. He died in 1914 at age eighty-six.

Bellard, Alfred. Born in England, he was an eighteen-year-old carpenter's assistant when he joined the 5th New Jersey in August 1861. Throughout the war he weekly sent home long letters accompanied by skilful drawings of camp life and combat. A private whose comments on himself and others were caustic and whose behavior was often refractory, he remained skittish of combat: "Soldiering agrees with me, but I do not agree with soldiering. There is a little too much risk for me." Working after the war as an engraver and a florist, he died in a soldiers' home in 1891.

Blackford, William W. Born in 1831, he lived in New Granada (Colombia) while his father—a Lynchburg, Virginia, editor—served as American Consul there (1841–45). Following two years of study at the University of Virginia, he worked as a civil engineer and mine operator. He was one of five brothers who served in the Confederate Army. He served as a cavalry lieutenant, J. E. B. Stuart's adjutant, and an engineer major and lieutenant colonel often in or near battle, yet he suffered his only wound on a cavalry raid in Pennsylvania. Service in the Petersburg trenches, however, exacted a heavier toll; acquaintances did not recognize him when he returned home. Recovering to resume his career as an engineer, he lived until 1905.

Brobst, John F. Joining the 25th Wisconsin from Gilmanton, a small frontier farm community near the Mississippi, he and his friends were sent to Minnesota to fight Sioux and only 4½ months later to Kentucky to fight Confederates. A young and sensitive soldier given to wide swings of mood, he served through the Vicksburg and Atlanta campaigns. Discharged in June 1865, one of the five-hundred survivors of a regiment originally enrolling twice that number, he returned to Gilmanton, married a woman not yet sixteen, worked as a farmer and stockman, and lived until 1917.

Bull, Rice C. Following grammar school and several years of farm work in northeastern New York State, he enlisted in a local company that became part of the 123rd New York. He was wounded and captured by Confederates at Chancellorsville. A corporal, he fought throughout Sherman's Atlanta and Carolinas campaigns. Following the South's surrender, as his regiment marched over the Chancellorsville battlefield on its way to Washington for the Grand Review and he stood on the spot where he had been wounded, he "felt a great sense of gratitude to God" that he had survived. He became a civic leader of Troy, New York—a banker, railroad organizer, officer of the Presbyterian church—and died in 1930 at age eighty-seven.

Burdette, Robert J. Stretching to meet the height requirement of 5'3", he managed to enlist in the ranks of the 47th Illinois. He fought in more than a score of battles in the West and marched with Sherman to the sea. After the war he became the pastor of the Temple Baptist Church of Los Angeles.

Carter, Robert G. One of four sons of an editor-politician whose work took him from Maine to Massachusetts, Robert Carter joined the

22nd Massachusetts in August 1862 and participated as a private in many of the battles of the Army of the Potomac. In 1870 he completed studies at West Point. Ultimately he became a captain in the 4th United States Cavalry and the recipient of a Congressional Medal of Honor for gallantry in action against the Comanches. His three brothers also saw action in the Civil War: Eugene Carter, an 1861 West Point graduate, fought with the 8th U.S. Infantry; Sergeant Major Walter Carter with the 22nd Massachusetts; and Sergeant John Carter with the 1st Massachusetts Horse Artillery. All survived combat.

Casler, John O. Born near Winchester, Virginia, in 1838, as a young man he spent several years in Missouri before returning to Virginia, abandoning the shoemaker's trade, and enlisting as a private in the Stonewall Brigade's 33rd Virginia. Reliable in combat, he was chronically given to "devilment" devised to relieve the monotony of camp life. Painfully conscious that he was almost the sole survivor of his company, in late 1864 he employed chicanery to secure a transfer to the cavalry. Captured in February 1865, he was charged with being a guerrilla and subjected to severe imprisonment at Fort McHenry, Baltimore. After the war he lived in Oklahoma, where in the late 1890s he became the commanding officer of that state's division of the United Confederate Veterans.

Chamberlain, Joshua L. Born in Brewer, Maine, in 1828, educated at Bowdoin College, and prepared at Bangor Theological Seminary for a career as a Congregational missionary, he was teaching at Bowdoin when in August 1862 he accepted a lieutenant colonelcy in the 20th Maine. A fierce fighter, he won the Congressional Medal of Honor for the bayonet charge into which he propelled his men at Gettysburg, preserving the Union's critical position at Little Round Top. He sustained several wounds and in the Wilderness was the beneficiary of "miraculous" surgery. At Appomattox the Federal high command chose him to receive the surrender of the Confederate infantry. After the war he was governor of Maine, president of Bowdoin, and commanding officer of the state militia. In 1913, a year before his death, undergoing a mystical experience at a Gettysburg reunion, he felt himself being drawn within "a radiant fellowship of the fallen."

Connolly, James A. Born in Newark in 1843, he was at the time of Sumter a lawyer practicing in Charleston, Illinois. Elected major of a local unit townspeople had asked him to recruit, he saw combat in most of the important battles of the West as a line officer, a regimental commander, and a divisional staff officer. He accompanied Sherman's army during its Georgia and Carolinas campaigns. At once attracted and repelled by his experience of war, he seemed to whirl daily between duty and homesickness, between the excitement and danger of combat, between anger at the Southern people and remorse at the injury done them by his own troops. A state legislator and member of Congress following the war, he died in 1914.

Cooke, John E. Born in 1830 into a Winchester, Virginia, family in comfortable circumstances, he long debated whether to become a writer or follow his father into the law. His romantic novels of the 1850s won him a high reputation in and beyond the South. A gunnery sergeant at First Bull Run and later a captain on J. E. B. Stuart's staff, he remained in Confederate service until Appomattox; no writer saw more of the Civil War. He was burdened throughout his life by an emotional volatility that not even deep religious conviction could calm. He both denounced war as a brutish business and acclaimed it as the ultimate adventure, but the latter conception dominated his writings, frequently at the cost of historical accuracy. For twenty years following the war, he lived as a country gentleman and worked to complete an oeuvre of almost thirty books. He died of typhoid in 1886.

Cox, Jacob D. So nominal was his position as brigadier general and so moribund the skeleton Ohio militia he commanded that he never wore a uniform prior to the Civil War. Yet his rank and the influence the organization was assumed to reflect qualified him for an equivalent appointment in the Union Army. Entrusted at first with the independent command of several Ohio and Kentucky regiments in the West Virginia campaign, he was soon ordered to incorporate his forces into Rosecrans's army. Although he later participated in Sherman's Atlanta campaign and won promotion to major general, his standing derived from his political influence rather than leadership in combat. He built a varied and successful postwar career as governor of Ohio, secretary of the interior under Grant, railroad president, congressman, and president of the University of Cincinnati.

Crotty, Daniel G. An Irish immigrant who settled in Grand Rapids, he joined the 3rd Michigan at eighteen and fought in Union ranks from First Bull Run to Appomattox. When in 1864 the number of those of the 3rd willing to reenlist proved insufficient to maintain that regiment, he joined the 5th Michigan as a color sergeant. He survived grim combat at Chancellorsville, in the Wilderness, and in other Eastern battles and less dangerous riot-control duty in New York City and Troy. Nothing that happened to him in war diminished his resistance to officers' prerogatives or his anger at displays of wealth and influence.

Custer, George A. Born in rural Ohio in 1839, he spent part of his childhood in Monroe, Michigan, the hometown of Libbie Bacon, whom he would marry in 1864. Following his graduation from West Point, his exuberance and aggressiveness as a Union cavalry officer won him renown and promotion to brevet brigadier at twenty-three, brevet major general at twenty-four. Sentimental yet relentless, he survived the war and died spectacularly at the Little Big Horn on June 25, 1876. Libbie Custer died in 1933.

Dame, William M. Born and reared in Danville, Virginia, he was a student in the town's military academy when the war began. His father, the minister of the Episcopal church, and his mother, whose father and grandfather had been Revolutionary soldiers, balked at their son's enlistment at sixteen, but he overcame their opposition and joined the Richmond Howitzers as a private. A gentleman's unit in which the mock burial of a pet crow once brought forth "two brilliant eulogies in English," an original ode in Greek, and an original oration in Latin, it was hardly an effete band; it fought in every important battle in the East from First Bull Run to Appomattox. Dame, of a warm and resilient temperament, in 1869 realized a purpose conceived during the war—to enter the ministry. For more than forty years he served as rector of Baltimore's Memorial Church (Episcopal).

Dawes, Rufus R. Though born in Ohio, he came to identify with Wisconsin while attending the state university at Madison. At the outbreak of war he raised a company, accepted election as its captain, and led it in fighting with the 6th Wisconsin of the famous Iron Brigade, the only all-Western brigade in the East. Heavily engaged from Second Bull Run to Petersburg, the 6th, with Dawes as its colonel, lost a higher percentage killed than all except nine other Union regiments. Losses at Antietam led Dawes to write to his mother, "Our splendid regiment is almost destroyed." His fall from a horse while on furlough ("a great piece of good fortune") permitted his resignation upon expiration of the regiment's enlistment in August 1864. Married in January 1864, he became the father of Charles G. Dawes, a future vice president. He served as a congressman in the 1880s and died in 1899.

DeForest, John W. A privileged background—an old American family
of Huguenot extraction, a father who was both a wealthy businessman and a judge—offered him unusual opportunities: European travel, an extended stay with a brother working as a missionary in Syria, the leisure to write books on a variety of subjects during
the 1850s. In late 1861, at age thirty-five, he recruited a company
and became a captain in the 12th Connecticut. He fought in the
West under Butler, Banks, and Sheridan, spending a total of forty-
five days under fire and returning in December 1864 with a "totally
ruined constitution." For three years he worked with the Freed-
men's Bureau as a military-government officer. He subsequently
managed only a bare living from his writing. His books, most notably *Miss Ravenel's Conversion*, contained some powerfully real-
istic passages, but their effects remained muffled by a romantic
framework that DeForest never abandoned. His inheritance exhausted, he lived in a New Hampshire railroad hotel from 1890 to
1903 and died in 1906.

Dodd, Ira S. A New Jersey soldier, he fought with his regiment in several of the battles of the Army of the Potomac beginning in late
1862. At the time of Chancellorsville—May 1863—he was a sergeant. He survived the war and thirty-three years later published
a poetic and reflective memoir of his military experience.

Dooley, John. Born of Irish immigrant parents who built in Richmond
a family of wealth and social standing, he enlisted in the 1st Virginia after attending Georgetown College. Though elected a lieutenant in April 1863, he had little opportunity to exercise command: he was severely wounded in Pickett's Charge at the climax
of the battle of Gettysburg, and captured and imprisoned for eighteen months in the Johnson's Island prison camp. Paroled in February 1865, he was afflicted by what he saw of the Confederacy's
disintegration. In September 1865 he returned to Georgetown as a
Jesuit novice, but he sickened in 1868 and died five years later, prior
to his ordination.

Eggleston, George C. Though born in southeastern Indiana, when relatives invited him to visit Virginia in 1857 he discovered in the South
"a dream life of exquisite perfection." He entered Richmond College with the aspiration of becoming a "literary lawyer." Of an im-
petuous and romantic temperament, he was quick to join the Confederate Army; he served on J. E. B. Stuart's staff and fought with
the Nelson (Virginia) Light Artillery through the Wilderness and

Petersburg campaigns. His battery surrendered at Appomattox. His memoirs provoked Northern opposition when they appeared in the mid-1870s, but they later became popular enough to   port the publication of four editions.

Fay, Edwin H. Born in rural Alabama in 1832, he went north, to his parents' native section, to obtain a Harvard education. In 1861, as the headmaster of a boys' school in Minden, Louisiana, and the owner of several slaves, he became a soldier only reluctantly. An orderly sergeant in the Minden Rangers, a cavalry company, he saw some combat but far more patrol, scout, and escort duty. Despite his blustery rhetorical attacks on the enemy, he was a delicate and timid soldier who constantly maneuvered to leave Confederate service. In 1864 he became an engineer officer whose principal duty was crop collection. A month before Appomattox he continued his efforts to purchase an additional slave. In the 1880s he became Louisiana's state superintendent of education. He died in 1898.

Fitch, Michael H. Appointed first sergeant of a company raised in the town of Prescott in northwestern Wisconsin, he remained for a year with the 6th Wisconsin as it fought with the Army of the Potomac. Then he transferred to the West as a lieutenant and adjutant in the 21st Wisconsin. After a tour as a divisional staff officer, he returned to command the 21st during the Atlanta campaign—reporting that Sherman's army was "completely worn out, like a superannuated dray horse"—and the march through the Carolinas. He was discharged as a lieutenant colonel in June 1865. Of the ninety-two members of his original hometown company, twenty-seven had been killed or had died of wounds, twenty-five others had been wounded but had survived, and eight had deserted.

Galwey, Thomas F. Although he was born in 1846 to an Irish family living in London, by 1851 his home was a farm located on the extension of Cleveland's Euclid Avenue. At fifteen he joined the Hibernian Guard Company and the 8th Ohio as a private. He fought with them in the East from the West Virginia campaign of 1861 to Petersburg in 1864. At Antietam, 28 of the 32 in the company were hit; at Gettysburg, 103 of the 216 in the regiment were killed or severely wounded. Highly critical of the assistance Masons gave brother Masons in the opposing army ("How little faith can be put in men who are bound to one another by secret ties?"), he later met with Confederate Fenians across the Rappahannock. Promoted to first lieutenant at seventeen, he was induced by poor health to leave the army a year later in July 1864. Following the war he enjoyed a successful career in New York City, most prominently as city attorney. He died in 1913 at age sixty-seven.

Herbert, Hilary A. Born in 1834 in a South Carolina village whose academy his father served as principal and his mother as assistant principal, until his family moved to Alabama in 1846 he lived on a plantation that worked between fifteen and thirty slaves. He was educated at the University of Alabama (until expelled for leading a revolt of the sophomore class) and the University of Virginia. In 1860 he joined the local militia and was elected second lieutenant. During the war, as commanding officer of the 8th Alabama, he fought with Lee's Army of Northern Virginia at Second Bull Run, at Gettysburg—there his regiment suffered half of its 420 casualties—and in the Wilderness. Severely wounded in the latter battle, he was promoted to colonel and retired as disabled. A successful Montgomery lawyer after the war, he served in the House of Representatives from 1877 to 1893 and, as chairman of the Naval Affairs Committee, built a national reputation as an advocate of naval modernization and expansion. At the end of his tenure as secretary of the navy in Cleveland's second administration, the United States Navy had become the world's sixth largest. He died in 1919.

Hinman, Wilbur F. An Ohioan, he grew up in Berea, near Cleveland, and there attended Baldwin University. He joined the 65th Ohio in the autumn of 1861 and served as an orderly sergeant through many important battles of the West. He was wounded at Chickamauga. A perceptive observer, he wrote of the high command's failure to commit his regiment to battle at Perryville, "The truth is that the art of conducting war on such a prodigious scale was as yet unlearned." Of the 65th's ten orderly sergeants, one was killed, two died of disease, four were discharged as disabled, one deserted, and two, Hinman and another, survived to receive promotion to lieutenant. After a Texas tour of duty that infuriated the men, the 65th was discharged in late December 1865. It had marched, Hinman calculated, 3,315 miles.

Holmes, Oliver W., Jr. Growing up in the shadow of a father renowned as a physician, poet, teacher, and writer, he graduated from Harvard in the class of 1861. He served as an officer in the 20th Massachusetts, sustaining five wounds before resigning his commission in 1864. Deeply affected by his experience of war, he used it to frame his thought as writer and jurist. Bored with courtroom work, he immersed himself in legal scholarship; the results gave a powerful impetus to new notions of the law as the creation less of logic and precedent than of experience, economic interests, and social necessities. After twenty years on the Massachusetts Supreme Judicial Court, the last three as chief justice, he was appointed to the United States Supreme Court by President Theodore Roosevelt. There the quality of his opinions enhanced an already formidable reputation. He died in 1935 at the age of ninety-four.

Hunter, Alexander. Born into a propertied family—his father was a United States Navy officer who owned land in Virginia and the District of Columbia—Hunter interrupted studies at Virginia College, Alexandria, to enlist as a private in the 17th Virginia. After combat at First Bull Run, in the 1862 Peninsula campaign, and at Second Bull Run, two-thirds of the forty-six survivors of the regiment's original complement of eight-hundred were killed or wounded at Antietam, and Hunter was captured for a second time. In the spring of 1863 he transferred to the Virginia Black Horse Cavalry—Robert E. Lee endorsed his request—and there he was captured on a scout and wounded in a skirmish. He survived both the Wilderness and Petersburg campaigns and recorded feelingly the demoralization of the Southern soldiery in the war's final stages.

Key, Thomas J. Born in Tennessee in 1831 and raised in Mississippi, he worked on a newspaper from age fifteen to nineteen, attended LaGrange College for two years, and returned to journalism by purchasing the newspaper that earlier had employed him. After establishing a pro-slavery journal in Bleeding Kansas, he moved to Arkansas and became a member of the state legislature. In 1862, moved by a mission in which he brought home the body of a cousin killed in combat, he enlisted in the Confederate Army, and he rose grade-by-grade from private to captain of artillery. When, almost two years later, he at last won permission to visit his wife behind enemy lines, he went sadly, for he had heard that she was dying of consumption. Instead, he discovered at home that she was weak with mourning; she had been told ten months earlier that he had been killed in battle. After the war he became the publisher of the *Southern Agriculturist.* He died in 1908.

Livermore, Mary A. Of New England origins, at the outset of the Civil War she was living in Chicago with her husband, a Universalist clergyman and the editor of a weekly. Experience in church work and a strong Unionist sentiment—previously of no significance to her, the national banner became the "holy flag"—led her to organize relief work on behalf of Federal soldiers. In 1862 she and Jane Hoge organized the Chicago branch of the Sanitary Commission. Subsequently appointed a national director, she visited battlefields, inspected military hospitals, carried messages between families and their soldier relatives, and traveled widely to establish aid societies and raise funds for medical supplies. Her greatest accomplishment was the organization of Chicago's Northwestern Sanitary Fair in October 1863. She became a dedicated chronicler of women's role in the war.

Lyman, Theodore. Born into a prominent New England family in 1833, he was educated privately and at Harvard. In 1863, following his marriage and an extended stay in Europe, he joined Meade's staff as a volunteer aide. Though he spent much of his time as a protocol officer overseeing the visits of foreign observers, he was occasionally under fire. (He "wasn't going to get behind trees, so long as old George G. [Meade] stood out in front and took it.") From a position equidistant from that of Union soldiers and their generals, he became a sensitive and discerning commentator on events that passed before him. In the 1880s he served in the United States House of Representatives.

McCarthy, Carlton. Though of an educated and genteel background, he thought it his patriotic duty to serve in the Richmond Howitzers as a simple private. Enlisting in July 1861, he remained in Confederate service through most of the principal battles of the Army of Northern Virginia and surrendered at Appomattox. In the war's final months, after his battery had been compelled to abandon its cannons, he and his comrades fought as infantry. His brother, a Confederate captain, was killed at Cold Harbor.

Mosby, John S. Of small frame but pugnacious temperament, he was expelled from the University of Virginia and jailed in the early 1850s because of a shooting incident. When the war began he exchanged his law practice for a lieutenancy in J. E. B. Stuart's cavalry. His affinity for dangerous scouting missions led to his organization of the controversial Partisan Rangers, irregulars who fought and raided in three northern Virginia counties occupied by Union forces. Ultimately a colonel, he was captured twice and wounded at least three times. Ulysses Grant's postwar support won him various government posts, including the Hong Kong consulship (1878–85), but Mosby's endorsement of Republican candidates cost him his popular standing in the South. Wishing, in his last years, that he had fallen in the war, he died in 1916.

Newton, James K. An eighteen-year-old teacher in a one-room school, he decided in 1861 to leave the town of DePere to enlist in the 14th Wisconsin. He fought at Shiloh, Vicksburg, Red River, and Nashville. In 1865 he was promoted to lieutenant: "Quite an honor, isn't it? I don't know as I feel any better for it tho." He later taught at Oberlin College and died in 1892.

Nisbet, James C. A Georgian born in 1839, he graduated from Oglethorpe College in 1858. As war approached, he became the organizer of a local unit that became part of the 21st Georgia. A captain, he participated in battles from the Shenandoah Valley to Fredericksburg. In late 1863 he became the colonel of a unit, the 66th Georgia, that he had returned home to recruit. During the Atlanta campaign he was captured and imprisoned for more than a year on Johnson's Island, near Sandusky, Ohio. He died in 1917.

Owen, William M. A native of New Orleans, he joined that city's Washington Artillery in 1861. As battalion adjutant and then in such positions as artillery commander and as chief of staff to a Confederate general, he was primarily a staff officer whose duties were various and whose opportunities were extensive. Returning to the Washington Artillery for six onerous months in the Petersburg trenches, he was wounded in the cheek by a Union sharpshooter. As a lieutenant colonel in the last days of the war, he was assigned command of an infantry brigade shrunken from 3,000 to 250 men. Though a soured courtship in Richmond had led him to resolve "to throw my life away in battle with the Yank," he survived to return to New Orleans, where he later became inspector general of the Louisiana national guard and a leader in veterans' affairs.

Paxton, Elisha F. A Virginian born in 1828, he was educated at Washington College and Yale before taking a law degree at the University of Virginia. Elected a lieutenant in the Stonewall Brigade's 27th Virginia, he became aggrieved at Stonewall Jackson's repeated refusals to grant him a winter furlough, and he unsuccessfully attempted to resign. In June 1862 he failed of reelection as major; he admitted that he had been "rather rigid" with the regiment. Following a tour of duty on Jackson's staff, he returned to the brigade as brigadier general commanding. Introspective and deeply religious, he alternated between a cheerful acceptance of the circumstances in which the war had placed him and a pessimism bordering on anguish. He was killed at Chancellorsville at age thirty-five.

Poague, William T. Born into a rural middle-class Virginia family, he graduated from Washington College in 1857 and briefly practiced law in Missouri before enlisting in the Rockbridge Artillery of Lexington, Virginia. Elected a second lieutenant, he rose to the command of the battery and the battalion and was several times cited for bold and skilful handling of artillery pieces. Forthright and judicious, he became in postwar years a founder of schools, a Virginia legislator, and the treasurer of the Virginia Military Institute. He died in 1914 and was buried in the Lexington cemetery that holds the remains of Stonewall Jackson.

Reed, William H. A Sanitary Commission worker stationed in Washington, he helped to organize the reception of wounded soldiers arriving from Virginia battlefields. On visits to the front, he moved among the casualties taking last messages, writing letters, supplying nourishment, arranging transport or burial. He retained his self-assurance: the work was "hard, exhausting . . . sometimes discouraging, and always sad," but "every day we were made stronger for duty by the [wounded soldiers'] beautiful revelations of character."

Reid, Jesse W. A cotton mill worker from age eleven or twelve and after his marriage a stone worker, he moved with the local militia into the 4th South Carolina. A private, he remained modest ("Please pass over all errors, as I have never studied grammar a day in my life, and am by no means a learned man.") and skeptical of soldiering at the behest, he suspected, of the wealthy ("I mean to do what fighting I have to do as soon as possible and get back home to Dixie."). Discharged in 1862 after fighting at First Bull Run and on the Peninsula, he was recalled when the Confederate Congress raised the draft age to forty-five. After delaying as long as possible his return to service, he survived the war as a recruiter and member of an engineer unit.

Ripley, Edward H. Born in Center Rutland, Vermont, in 1839, he was a medical student at Union College when the Civil War began. He enlisted as a private in the 9th Vermont, but his ability to recruit others quickly brought him a captain's commission. Captured at Harper's Ferry and after his exchange confined to inactive theaters, he did not return to combat until the fall of 1864. Twice wounded, he became a brigadier general at age twenty-five. After the war he worked as a banker, hotelier, and railroad and steamship company operator; he also served as a Vermont legislator. He died in 1915. His brother, William Y. W. Ripley, won a Congressional Medal of

Honor for bravery while a lieutenant colonel in a regiment of United States Sharpshooters.

Ropes, Hannah. Born in Maine in 1809, she married a school principal, bore four children, and separated from her husband after thirteen years of marriage. A feminist, she urged women to engage in activities beyond the home, for marriage was "the debasing crime of legalized prostitution, for the sake of a home and temporary companionship." An abolitionist and a nurse, she served the anti-slavery forces in Bleeding Kansas in the mid-1850s. During the Civil War she was appointed matron of the Union Hotel Hospital, Georgetown, and there she died of typhoid pneumonia in January 1863.

Shaw, Robert G. Born in Boston in 1837, the son of a family prominent in the Revolution, the China trade, and civic activity, he was educated in Europe and at Harvard. Abandoning his studies in his junior year to join an uncle's mercantile firm in New York City, he discovered that he disliked business ("I am a slave now."). With the coming of war, he joined the 7th New York as a private, but he soon accepted a commission in the 2nd Massachusetts, serving as a line officer and a member of the brigade staff. In early 1863 he accepted the command of the 54th Massachusetts, the first black regiment raised in the North. His presentiment that he was to be killed was borne out in the Union attack on Battery Wagner in Charleston harbor on July 18, 1863. Emerson celebrated his courage in a poem. In 1897 the Shaw Memorial, the work of sculptor Augustus Saint-Gaudens, was unveiled on Boston Common.

Sheeran, James B. Born in Ireland in 1819, he worked as a tailor and a schoolteacher in New York, Pennsylvania, and Michigan. He married and became the father of two children, but following the death of his wife he was ordained a Catholic priest of the Redemptorist Congregation. While serving a New Orleans church, he joined the 14th Louisiana as chaplain. An ardent Confederate, he urged captured Union soldiers to "ask yourself in the presence of God, if in fighting for your perjured President, you are fighting for the Constitution of your country." He saw frequent combat, much of which troubled him, but he continued to serve. A dispute with Sheridan regarding his ministrations to Southern wounded behind Union lines brought him two months' imprisonment. Following the war, he worked as a parish priest in New Jersey until his death in 1881.

Small, Abner R. Enlisting in the 16th Maine with hometown friends, he was appointed regimental adjutant when he soon proved himself a successful recruiter. He first saw combat at Fredericksburg and found great relief in the results: "I had passed unscathed through the Valley of the Shadow, and was no longer a slave to the fear that at first had nearly overpowered me." His regiment was routed at Gettysburg, and he was again sent home to recruit. At Petersburg he was captured and was confined in prisons in Virginia and North Carolina. Although weighing only 90 pounds when exchanged in February 1865, he recovered sufficiently to accept command of the regiment in April 1865.

Stiles, Robert. The son of a Georgia-born Presbyterian minister posted to churches in New York and Connecticut, Robert Stiles graduated from Yale in 1859 and attended Columbia Law School until he could no longer tolerate the post-Sumter atmosphere of the North. Traveling south with his father and two brothers, he enlisted as a private in the Richmond Howitzers. He fought in the Peninsula, at Gettysburg and Fredericksburg, and, as an engineer officer and captain of artillery, in the Wilderness and at Petersburg. He was a deeply religious man who often prayed with his men. Promoted to major, he was captured in the war's final weeks and was imprisoned in Ohio until he finally consented to take the oath of allegiance. "I sadly turned my back upon the only great thing in my life, and dropped into the undistinguishable mass of 'The People.'"

Stillwell, Leander. Born in 1843 on the Illinois farm "of a simple, backwoods people," he enlisted in the 61st Illinois in 1861. Appointed corporal by a friend serving as sergeant, he fought at Shiloh and Vicksburg and then endured bouts of sickness and monotonous months of railroad-guard duty and insignificant combat after his regiment was "switched off" into Arkansas. He was commissioned a second lieutenant after Appomattox. Though he went out to cut and shock corn on the morning after his return home, he did not remain a farmer. Following study in Albany, he began to practice as an attorney.

Strong, Robert H. A nineteen-year-old northern Illinois farm worker, he became a private in the 105th Illinois, a regiment that atypically remained on extended garrison duty in Kentucky and Tennessee and did not enter combat until the spring of 1864 (though many of its members had earlier succumbed to illness). Strong was under fire daily for a month during Sherman's Atlanta campaign. When illness brought confinement to hospital that threatened to deny him participation in the march to the sea, he deceived his doctors and returned to the front. Mustered out in Chicago on June 13, 1865,

312

he immediately returned home, where for a long time he found it hard to sit on a chair or sleep in a bed because he had become accustomed to sitting and sleeping on the ground. He later moved to Arkansas in the hope of relieving the effects of the arthritis contracted during the war.

Wainwright, Charles S. The son of a Hudson Valley landowning family, he was a well-educated and widely traveled gentleman never forgetful of his social standing. Failing to raise his own regiment, he joined the 1st New York Artillery as a major in October 1861. Accompanied to war by an Irish servant, he fought with the Army of the Potomac for three years and was promoted to colonel. The indiscipline of the volunteers appalled him: "What a totally unmilitary, unexact people we are!" The absence of social restraint was equally painful: he judged that of five hundred Union officers attending a dinner in Meade's honor, thirty were "actual gentlemen," a hundred others "had pretensions," and the rest "were little better than street blackguards." He lived in New York City, Washington, and Europe until his death in 1907.

Walker, Francis A. Born in 1840 and raised in Boston in the family home next to the Holmeses', he graduated from Amherst in the class of 1860. He joined the 15th Massachusetts as a sergeant major, soon became a captain in the 7th Massachusetts, and by the end of the war had risen to brevet brigadier general. He participated in the severe fighting of McClellan's army during the Seven Days; he was wounded at Chancellorsville, captured in the Wilderness, and held in Libby Prison, Richmond. His health broken, he resigned from the army in January 1865. His varied postwar activities included posts as editorial writer, chief of the Bureau of Statistics, superintendent of the Census, commissioner of Indian Affairs, Yale professor, and president of the Massachusetts Institute of Technology. Active in veterans' affairs, he authored a history of the Second Corps and served as president both the Military Historical Society of Massachusetts and the Massachusetts Commandery of the Loyal Legion. He died in 1897.

Weld, Stephen M. The son of a Brahmin family established in New England in 1632, he entered Harvard at fourteen and graduated with the class of 1860. He participated in the campaigns of the Army of the Potomac from the Peninsula to Petersburg as a staff officer and a regimental commander. He was wounded once and captured twice. After the war he overcame several business failures resulting from floods, the frauds of others, and his own miscalculation, finally to make a success of a cotton brokerage. Confident and opinionated even as a young man, he gave expression to a softer side in a love of flowers. He died in 1920.

Wilkeson, Frank. In 1863, at the age of fifteen, he ran away from his father's Hudson Valley farm and in Albany enlisted in the 11th New York Battery. He fought as a cannoneer in the battles of the Wilderness, Spottsylvania, and Cold Harbor and remained with the Army of the Potomac through the opening stages of the Petersburg campaign. Caustically critical of the Union high command—"I had had enough of marching and fighting—enough of seeing good men's lives squandered in assaults against earthworks"—in late June 1864 he accepted a lieutenancy in the regular army's 4th Artillery. With one of its sections he was sent to Elmira, New York, to stand guard over Confederate prisoners. At war's end he resigned his commission and returned home.

Williams, Alpheus S. Born in Connecticut in 1810 and educated at Yale, he became a prominent citizen of Detroit in the 1840s and 1850s: attorney, probate judge, bank president, and newspaper owner. Long service in the local militia brought appointment as Brigadier General of Volunteers in August 1861. A vigorous participant in the Antietam, Gettysburg, and Atlanta campaigns, he was disappointed by what he considered the stagnation of his military career; only in 1865 did he become a brevet major general. During Reconstruction a military administrator in Arkansas and later the American minister to San Salvador and a member of Congress, he died in 1878. An equestrian statue on Detroit's Belle Isle honors him; his biographer reports that both man and horse appear weary.

Wilson, LeGrand J. Five years after his birth in Tennessee in 1836, his family and its forty slaves moved to Mississippi. Following medical study in Philadelphia in 1858–59, he joined the Alcorn Rifles of the 1st Mississippi. When his regiment was captured at Fort Donelson, he escaped by walking away. At home he recruited a replacement company that elected him its first lieutenant. He subsequently transferred from the line and served as regimental surgeon in the Wilderness and Petersburg campaigns. A sensitive and sympathetic man, he was a steadfast Presbyterian.

Notes

INTRODUCTION (*pp. 1–3*)

1. Donald, 121.

CHAPTER 1. Courage at the Core (*pp. 7–16*)

1. McCarthy, 208.
2. (Georgian) Nisbet, 299; (Texan) Fletcher, 76; Webster, 559; Porter, 250; Sanford, 181. See also Peskin, 120. James A. Garfield congratulated his men on their victory at Middle Creek, Kentucky: "Soldiers of the Eighteenth Brigade! I am proud of you. . . . With no experience but the consciousness of your own manhood, you have driven [the enemy] from his stronghold."
3. Stiles, 110.
4. Jesse Reid, 24; Fay, 34; Poague, 66.
5. Custer, 95.
6. Hunter, 53; Stiles, 142–43; Dunaway, 35.
7. Poague, 140; Hinman, 357.
8. Sheeran, 6; Burdette, 47; Eggleston, *Rebel's*, 197.
9. Webster, 374. Among the examples offered are duty as obedience to princes, magistrates and laws; obedience, kindness, and respect to parents; fidelity to friends; reverence to God. Weld, 300.
10. Webster, 559. Emphasis in original. Beaty, 95.
11. Holmes, Jr., *Touched with Fire*, 27.
12. Pickett, 73, 75.
13. Douglas, 259–60.
14. Edward Ripley, 31–84.
15. Dunaway, 98, 101–4.
16. Monroe, 75, 79, 81–86.

315

17. Custer, 139.
18. Mary Livermore, 663; Munroe, 89.
19. Cox, I: 271–72, 280.
20. Eggleston, "Old Regime," 615; Beaty, 161; Howe, 10; Osterweis, *Romanticism and Nationalism*, 26.
21. Eggleston, *Rebel's*, 123.

CHAPTER 2. Courage from Battlefield to Hospital (*pp. 17–33*)

1. Moran, x, 61, 63–64. Eisenhower quoted in Lee Miller, 400. Steinbeck, 138; James Jones, 62, 150.
2. Russ, 280–81; Herr, 66; O'Brien, 65.
3. Moran, xi, 4, 147; Dollard, 9, 12, 71; Steinbeck, xvii; Lee Miller, 275, 413; Duncan, 68; Herr, 27.
4. Porter, 249.
5. (Ashby) Poague, 14; (Stuart) Haskell, 19–20; (Jackson) Blackford, 79.
6. Robert Strong, ix.
7. Lewis, 213; Stiles, 96–97; Meyers, 226–27.
8. Wilkeson, 185; Burke Davis, *Civil War*, 143.
9. Burdette, 51; Hinman, 430.
10. Dame, 133–35.
11. Barnard, 219; Wilkeson, 149–50; Wellman, 331.
12. Robert Strong, 27; Carter, 386.
13. Bull, 56; Bardeen, 106; James T. Miller to William J. Miller, June 8, 1863, Miller Papers; Bull, 115.
14. Herbert, "Grandfather's Talks About His Life Under Two Flags," 204–5, Herbert Papers.
15. Stillwell, 269; Cooke, 487; Wallace, 201; Dooley, 38; Robert Strong, 17; Porter, 250.
16. Paxton, 19–20.
17. Connolly, 263; Casler, 291; McCarthy, 208.
18. Gould, 38; Wiley, *Johnny Reb*, 331; Dunaway, 71; Wiley, *Billy Yank*, 303; Stillwell, 267–68; Crane, 197–98.
19. T. Harry Williams, 7, 19; Robert M. Cross, "Joshua Lawrence Chamberlain," senior essay, Bowdoin College, 1947, 30, in Chamberlain Papers; James Miller letter (note 13 above); Wallace, 150.
20. Stiles, 197.
21. *Ibid;* Cross, "Chamberlain," 21; (Eggleston's brother) McCarthy, 103; Sanford, 266.
22. Holmes, Jr., *Speeches*, 58; Reed, 148.
23. Hannah Ropes, 33, 71.
24. Freeman, vi, 35.
25. Reed, 24, 66, 185.

26. Whitman, 173; Mary Livermore, 325; (no display) Whitman, 191; (coward) Blackford, 122; George Stevens, 252.
27. Whitman, 173–74; Mary Livermore, 192–94, 196–97.
28. Fay, 32; Jesse Reid, 29; Dodd, 67; Reed, 25; Woolsey, 128–30. See also Porter, 250.
29. Barnard, 221; Johnson, 132; Sievers, 224–25; Dame, 81; Bent, 102; Alcott, 36.
30. Weld, 335–36; Quintard, 110; George Stevens, 221; Newton, 151.

CHAPTER 3. Courage as the Cement of Armies (*pp. 34–60*)

1. Dooley, xvii, 33–38. Emphasis in original.
2. Catton, *Reflections*, 52: "Discipline was incurably loose."
3. Grant, II: 552.
4. McCarthy, 8; Herbert, "Grandfather's Talks About His Life Under Two Flags," 112, Herbert Papers; Washington Davis, 218; Fitch, 30.
5. Sherman, *Home Letters*, 209, 211, 212.
6. Bent, 164; Perkins, 82; McCarthy, 115. In their intractability Civil War soldiers were heir to a long tradition of poor discipline. See Fred Anderson, *A People's Army: Massachusetts Soldiers and Society in the Seven Years' War* (1984) and Charles Royster, *A Revolutionary People at War: The Continental Army and American Character, 1775–1783* (1979).
7. Wilkeson, vii.
8. Logan, 47; Upson, xvii; Bull, 118. Not all units were local units. Regular Army regiments drew from a larger compass, as did some special organizations. Berdan's Sharpshooters drew one of its regiments from New York, Michigan, New Hampshire, Vermont, and Wisconsin and the other from Minnesota, Michigan, Pennsylvania, Maine, Vermont, and New Hampshire. See Charles Stevens, 4. Ironically, the regiment whose composition was perhaps most "national," and even international, was the first black fighting unit recruited in the North, the 54th Massachusetts, whose men were drawn from Massachusetts, Pennsylvania, New York, Ohio, Indiana, Missouri, Illinois, Michigan, and Canada. See Burchard, 85. (Friends) Hinman, 273; Dodd, 99; Catton, *America Goes to War*, 52–53.
9. Richard Taylor, 125–26; Gerber, 46, 48, 50, 54, 55. Another "degradation," in the view of Alexander Hunter and his friends, was the policing of camp areas, work fit only for the city scavenger. Many of the men "were placed in the guard house for refusing to work in such capacity." Hunter, 46. See also Thornton, Chap. 4 *et passim*.

10. McCarthy, 29; Eggleston, 32.
11. Dooley, 164; Lonn, 15.
12. Sherman, *Memoirs*, I: 339.
13. Peskin, 92.
14. Sherman, *Sherman Letters*, 118; Eggleston, 32.
15. Nisbet, 45; Paxton, 92.
16. Beatty, 71–82.
17. O'Connor, *Sheridan*, 16.
18. Logan, 48; Allen, 13.
19. Owen, 20–21; Paxton, 25.
20. Chamberlain, "Abraham Lincoln, Seen from the Field in the War for the Union," 13, Chamberlain Papers.
21. McCarthy, 39.
22. Casler, 41.
23. Small, 8, 199; Jimerson, 277; Palfrey, 22, 28.
24. Cooke, 127; Beatty, 139–40.
25. Stiles, 115.
26. Trefousse, 117; Richard Taylor, 153–54; Nisbet, 46. See also Kidd, 97–98.
27. Trefousse, 138.
28. Richard Taylor, 130–31. Emphasis in original.
29. Blackford, 32; Cox, II: 31.
30. Stiles, 66.
31. Catton, *Stillness at Appomattox*, 312–13; O'Connor, *Sheridan*, 228.
32. Burdette, 160; Hinman, 791.
33. Casler, 47; Lonn, 35.
34. Douglas, 130; Sievers, 218–19, 281.
35. Casler, 204–5; Harry Hall, 81; Dawson, 87; Vail, 29; Cox, I: 127.
36. Johnson, 63–64.
37. Hinman, 252, 262, 273. Emphasis in original. Casler, 73.
38. Hinman, 272. Emphasis in original. McCarthy, 51.
39. Nisbet, 173–74; Robert Strong, 152–53.
40. Bardeen, 44–45, 294; LeGrand Wilson, 28; Robert Strong, 87–88.
41. Vail, 89–90.
42. Casler, 101.
43. *Ibid.*, 102; Washington Davis, 216–24. Emphasis in original.
44. Bellard, 187–88.
45. Fay, 33; Whitman, 121; Robert Strong, 85; Billings, *Hardtack and Coffee*, 152; Vail, 113.
46. Casler, 193–94.
47. Washington Davis, 262–64; Robert Strong, 90–92.
48. Washington Davis, 224; Bellard, 188; Hinman, 225–26, 229.
49. Herbert, "Grandfather's Talks About His Life Under Two Flags," 105–6, 137–38, Herbert Papers.

50. Meyers, 254: "The fear of the contempt of his comrades is even more powerful a factor than discipline in keeping a timid or nerveless soldier in the ranks during battle."
51. George Stevens, 221.
52. Beatty, 223; Hunter, 123.
53. Hunter, 123.
54. Allen, 231, 239–40; Carter, 346–48. Emphasis in original.
55. Galwey, 143–45.
56. Paxton, 74: "Such spectacles witnessed in the quiet of the camp are more shocking than the scenes of carnage upon the battle-field. I am sick of such horrors." Bardeen, 288.
57. Casler, 114; Quintard, 83–86.
58. Washington Davis, 29; Harry Hall, 25; Mary Livermore, 559. There were suggestions that some court-martial officers voted death sentences on the assumption that the President would exercise leniency. See Dawes, 145–46.
59. Fay, 150–51: "I know . . . I shall not let down another fence preparatory to a charge but shall be at the head of it certain." Eggleston, 39.

CHAPTER 4. The Uses of Courage (*pp. 61–79*)

1. Stiles, 167; Fay, 35.
2. Hunter, 317; Catton, *Glory Road*, 66. Shakespeare's *Julius Caesar*, II, ii, line 32: "Cowards die many times before their deaths;/The valiant never taste of death but once."
3. Bruce, 74–75.
4. George Stevens, 173; Whitman, 38–39; Harwell, 21.
5. Wallace, 54–55, 60; Sanford, 192.
6. Stiles, 95–96.
7. Cooke, 126; Stiles, 98.
8. Stiles, 149–51; Burdette, 192. For the extension of this conception into the civilian sector, see Freeman, 67, 73. Of the battle raging at Fredericksburg, "We can only hope and pray that the God of battles may speed the right." When the disastrous results were known, "All will be yet over-ruled for good; the Almighty has, I believe, a hand in this war, and he hath his own ends to accomplish."
9. Hammett, 39–40.
10. McCarthy, 7; Gould, 27. Three-quarters of the Union forces were born in the United States, and many others had spent most of their lives here. Charles Francis Adams *et al.*, I: 79; Edward Ripley, 34–35; Washington Davis, 52. Emphasis in original.
11. DeForest, 91; Pickett, 30–31.

12. Bridges, 273; Eggleston, 30, footnote; Holmes, Jr., *Speeches*, 1, 2; Gerber, 57–58.
13. Catton, *Reflections*, 46; Barrett, 21; Galwey, 147; Robert Strong, 117.
14. Bellard, 83; Bardeen, 59; Casler, 303. One gains the impression, and no more than that, that those least certain of their own courage were those most likely to express hatred of the enemy.
15. Blackford, 211; Fay, 100; Wellman, 254.
16. Wilkeson, 113–14.
17. Bull, 130; Robert Strong, 123, 125.
18. Quintard, 57.
19. Owen, 168; Douglas, 80.
20. Dodd, 156; Forbes, 18. See also Lyman, 106: "These men are incomprehensible—now standing from daylight to dark killing and wounding each other by thousands, and now making jokes and exchanging newspapers! You see them lying side by side in the hospitals, talking together in that serious prosaic way that characterizes Americans. The great staples of conversation are the size and quality of rations, the marches they have made, and the regiments they have fought against. All sense of personal spite is sunk in the immensity of the contest." For an opposing interpretation, see Handlin, 143.
21. Grant, I: 271.
22. Washington Davis, 94; Burchard, 110.
23. Beatty, 30; Dunaway, 86–87.
24. Robert Strong, 61; Bardeen, 49, 50, 57, 62–63, 165; Galwey, 52; Alpheus Williams, 330; Hinman, 235.
25. Herbert, "Grandfather's Talks About His Life Under Two Flags," 154, Herbert Papers.
26. Poague, 16, 39; Taylor, 58, 70; Weld, 194.
27. Gray, 51.
28. Vail, 117; Nisbet, 154; Stillwell, 62; Rosser, 9; Bull, 56; Hinman, 456; Dawes, 91; Burke Davis, *Civil War*, 210.
29. Sajer, 234–35; Gray, 55.
30. Richard Taylor, 74; Kinsley, I: 128 and (Kearny) I: 45; Lewis, 223.
31. Foster, 43–44; Dawes, 91; Robert N. Cross, "Joshua Laurence Chamberlain," senior essay, Bowdoin College, 1947, 30, in Chamberlain Papers; Poague, 7.
32. Dodd, 17; Connolly, 158; Poague, 7; Edward Ripley, 250; Alpheus Williams, 62; Wilkeson, 70; Hunter, 252; Kinsley, I: 128.
33. Peskin, 170; Cox, I: 405, II: 8–9, 112; Porter, 249–50; Poague, 11.
34. Bruce, 357; Burdette, 167.
35. Werstein, 179, 204.
36. Beatty, 154–58; Wallace, 145.

37. Charles Stevens, 41.
38. T. Harry Williams, 308; Whitelaw Reid, I: 347.
39. Bierce, "A Son of the Gods," *Collected Writings*, 24–29.
40. Morris, 654.

CHAPTER 5. Courage and Civilian Society *(pp. 80–110)*

1. Hinman, 33.
2. Poague, 3–4; Stiles, 51; Hunter, 18, 22–23, 194. "Defense of the hearthstone" was a powerful propellent to combat, but, when combined with a constricting localism, it could pose serious military problems for Confederate commanders. A significant number of Southerners believed that defense of home meant defense of one's own home. Thus pro-South Kentuckians flocked to Johnson's army when it arrived to campaign but scattered (some of them to become guerrillas) as soon as it again turned south. See Lonn, 16, 63–64.
3. Cox, I: 4–5; Foner, 11–39. See also Jimerson, 35, 39; Brobst, 15. Emphasis added.
4. Clifford, 138–39; Whitman, 227.
5. See Catton's view (*Reflections*, 4–5) that slavery caused the Civil War but that most of those who fought did not care about slavery. Whitman, 54–55.
6. Dawes, 161–62; Howe, 109.
7. Peskin, 87; (Meade) Lonn, 135; Billings, *Hardtack and Coffee*, 150–51, 154; Richard Taylor, 72.
8. Alpheus Williams, 54. Emphasis in original. Palfrey, 28.
9. Hannah Ropes, 96–99.
10. Dooley, 110; LeGrand Wilson, 90; Bardeen, 7, 81.
11. Sievers, 170. Emphasis in original. Newton, 74.
12. Dunaway, 15; Adelaide Smith, 24; Hinman, 61; Edward Ripley, 47–48.
13. Mary Livermore, 372, 375; Owen, 9; Edward Ripley, 167; McCarthy, 11–13; Mary Livermore, 283–84.
14. Reed, 168; Woolsey, 144, 148.
15. Dodd, 41–43; Billings, *Hardtack and Coffee*, 25–26.
16. John Jones, I: 33; Richard Hall, 125; Casler, 305; Hunter, 645–46; Kay and Campbell, 69.
17. Langford, 13, 25, 30, 35–36.
18. Casler, 358.
19. Joseph Kirkland, 11–12, 16–17, 52, 143, 249, 305 ff.; Doughty, 207.
20. Wilkins, 37, 40–41, 46.
21. Roper, 153, 161–63, 216; Morris, 38–40.
22. Munroe, 53; Casler, 304–5.
23. Casler, 309; Lonn, 49, 110.

24. Fay, 86.
25. *Ibid.*, 92, 156, 244, 284, 315, 325, 328–29, 424.
26. Woolsey, 142–43; McCarthy, 167.
27. Burchard, 71, 73–75.
28. Casler, 311; Mary Livermore, 143; Dodd, 205–6.
29. Dodd, 206; Mary Livermore, 141, 646–47.
30. Mary Livermore, 660–61. Emphasis in original.
31. Custer, 92, 97, 142, 231.
32. Dodd, 205; Peskin, 211; Sievers, 246. Emphasis in original. Key and Campbell, 161; Custer, 91, 99, 114.
33. Mary Livermore, 410–11, 414–15, 419, 428, 450–53.
34. Keegan, 296; Gross, 24.
35. Reed, 56; George Stevens, 2, 149, 196; Logan, 127.
36. Weld, 189–190. Emphasis added. Not all participants were oblivious to the incongruities. See Lyman, 247: "The use of the word 'annoy' is another military eccentricity. When half the men are killed or wounded by the enemy's riflemen, an officer will ride pleasantly in to the chief of artillery, and state that the battery is a good deal 'annoyed' by sharpshooters." Even such mild demurrers, however, were rare.
37. Paxton, 61; Ropes, 68, 71, 101–2, 128; Allen, 78, 81, 361.
38. Herbert, "Grandfather's Talks About His Life Under Two Flags," 140, Herbert Papers.
39. Woolsey, 150–51. Emphasis added.
40. Leah Strong, 27–29.
41. Nisbet, 80. In four years of service Nisbet could not recall meeting "an avowed infidel" in the Southern ranks (p. 81). Confederates often pointed out that their Constitution invoked the Deity, while that of the United States did not.
42. *Ibid.*, 52–53; George Stevens, 9; Bull, 113; Mary Livermore, 632; McClellan, *McClellan's Own Story*, 445. McClellan, Dawes added savagely, "didn't inaugurate forward movements on any other day of the week either." Dawes, 24; Paxton, 59.
43. Carpenter, 27; Douglas, 88; Stillwell, 66; Newton, 65; Bull, 54.
44. Coe, 123; Dame, 68–69. Emphasis in original.
45. Nisbet, 85; Poague, 141. Emphasis in original.
46. Poague, 140; Dame, 179–82.
47. Poague, 140; Key and Campbell, 77.
48. Casler, 146.
49. Burr, 19–22.
50. Robert Strong, 26; Stillwell, 59; Weld, 198.
51. Key and Campbell, 77.
52. Carpenter, 20; Quintard, 121.
53. Paxton, 59–60, 82; Connelly, 94; Fishwick, 207; Peskin, 125.

54. McKinley, 283; Paxton, 80; Ambrose, 25.
55. Sheeran, 71–72.
56. Custer, 80, 155; Hannah Ropes, 27.
57. Mary Livermore, 445–46.
58. Hannah Ropes, 113; Woolsey, 144. Emphasis in original. Key and Campbell, 155–57.
59. Mary Livermore, 167, 686; Hannah Ropes, 112–13; Alcott, 41–42.
60. Stiles, 219.

CHAPTER 6. Unexpected Adversaries (*pp. 113–133*)

1. Dawson, 7–8; Owen, 49; Robert Strong, 3.
2. Allen, 15–16.
3. Tate, 117; Brobst, 53–54; Charles Stevens, 79–80; McCarthy, 21–22.
4. Steiner, vii; Long, 710–11. Southern battle deaths are estimated at 94,000 and disease deaths at 164,000, a ratio of 1:1.75, but there is growing scholarly sentiment that Southern deaths, especially in the latter category, have been underestimated.
5. Galwey, 8; Steiner, 8, 12.
6. Hinman, 42, 245; Fox, 5. Also see Newton, 22.
7. Fay, 54.
8. George Stevens, 1, 74–75, 117; Lyman, 11.
9. Dwight is quoted in Steiner, 38. Peskin, 127, 138–39.
10. Hunter, 279–80; Bardeen, 39.
11. Dooley, 60; Beatty, 180, 269; Wainwright, 279; Dawes, 27; George Stevens, 183–85.
12. Beatty, 132; Reid, 44; George Stevens, 11; Vail, 53.
13. Fay, 34; Emerson, 252; Stillwell, 35–37; Hunter, 441; Brooks, 13.
14. Beatty, 238.
15. Adelaide Smith, 129; Billings, *Hardtack and Coffee*, 139–40; Vail, 108; Sheeran, 38.
16. Casler, 98–99; Hinman, 159.
17. Bardeen, 86, 163, 290.
18. Upson, 38. There is evidence that in some respects Confederate camps remained more genteel than Union camps. See Benson, 89. While a prisoner, Berry Benson was surprised at the "immense amount of cursing and blackguarding I heard going on everywhere" in Federal encampments. Dawes, 203–4; Sievers, 170, 226, 230.
19. LeGrand Wilson, 206.
20. Upson, 38, 41, 42, 102–4, 148, 153.
21. DeForest, 80. Emphasis in original. Paxton, 15; Sherman, *Memoirs*, II: 130; Grant, I: 446, 449, 455.

22. Vail, 50; Charles Stevens, 26; Bull, 35–36; Hinman, 391; Wilkeson, 39; Mary Livermore, 641–42; DeForest, 7; Reid, 40–41.
23. Frederic, "The War Widow," *Major Works*, II: 195.
24. Stillwell, 56; Higginson, 260; Sheeran, 19, 43–44. See also Dooley, 23.
25. Long, 711; Alpheus Williams, 130, 133; Bull, 68; Burr, 118–19.
26. Richard Hall, 128; Crotty, 45; Weld, 139.
27. Trefousse, 122, 126; Burchard, 125; Charles Francis Adams *et al.*, I: 288; Weld, 43; Wilkeson, 126.
28. Mumford, 14; Robert Strong, 18; Carter, 325; LeGrand Wilson, 110; Bull, 20; Robert Strong, 204; Dooley, 3.
29. Munroe, 49–50; Crotty, 45; Bardeen, 237; Peskin, 118–19.
30. Dooley, 112; Sheeran, 88; Robert Strong, 74; LeGrand Wilson, 133; Munroe, 50; Whitman, 103.
31. Adelaide Smith, 100; Lonn, 158; Beatty, 253. Beatty described the inability to stop and help wounded friends as "the most painful recollection" of those in battle.
32. Hunter, 550–51; Dooley, 107, 111, 117; LeGrand Wilson, 118.
33. Weld, 303–4; Robert Strong, 39.
34. Sherman, *Memoirs*, II: 407. See also Key and Campbell, 157, and Edward Ripley, 110.
35. Owen, 45.
36. Bull, 23–25.
37. Hannah Ropes, 113, 115–16. Emphasis in original.
38. Reed, 143, 145.
39. Mary Livermore, 286–87,
40. *Ibid.*, 302.
41. Hunter, 348.
42. Small, 26.

CHAPTER 7. Sword and Shovel (*pp. 134–155*)

1. Galwey, 92.
2. U. S. Grant, I: 95.
3. Meyers, 234; Dunaway, 16–17.
4. Grossman, 72; Robert Strong, 32; Upson, 157–58. Unwilling at first to acknowledge the increase in firepower, Southern officers cursed their men as cowards for running from Union skirmishers armed with repeaters.
5. Galwey, 42.
6. Fitch, 208.
7. Cox, II: 223, 242–43.
8. Sherman, *Memoirs*, II: 72; Cox, II: 277.
9. Sherman, *Memoirs*, II: 91–92; Cox, II: 277.
10. Lyman, 170; Bartlett, 82–83; Bardeen, 127; Beatty, 263.

11. Bardeen, 128; Newton, 148.
12. Bull, 41; Lyman, 19, 70; Robert Strong, 30.
13. Weld, 355.
14. Howe, *Shaping Years*, 96–97.
15. Nisbet, 154.
16. Sherman, *Memoirs*, II: 53; Lyman, 107–8.
17. Douglas, 102; Sheeran, 75.
18. James Wilson, II: 229–30.
19. Custer, 63; Stiles, 67, 260; Sanford, 265–66.
20. Dawes, 57–58; McCarthy, 115.
21. Hinman, 165–66, 369; Owen, 81, 175, 195; Bull, 123; Hunter, 530; Sherman, *Memoirs*, II: 45, 55, 397. Lyman reported (p. 137) in June 1864 that Northern cavalry, dismounting, were throwing up breastworks and fighting behind them.
22. Stiles, 347. At Spottsylvania Poague's artillery unit also experienced for the first time fighting from an entrenched position (p. 91). Hood, 131. Emphasis in original. Wainwright, 258–59.
23. Dame, 141–42. Emphasis in original.
24. Cox, II: 282; Stiles, 285, 347; Wainwright, 259.
25. George Stevens, 73; Hinman, 370.
26. Carter, 459; Stiles, 290; Weld, 343.
27. Cooke, 510–12; Fitch, 360; Allen, 273, 279; Billings, *Tenth Massachusetts Battery*, 264. See also Haskell, 72.
28. Wilkeson, 97; Owen, 336–37.
29. Wilkeson, 120–21, 136–38.
30. James Wilson, I: 219; DeForest, 144.
31. Bierce, "One of the Missing," *Collected Writings*, 32.
32. Pyle, 217; Burdette, 27, 205–6.
33. Joseph Kirkland, 83; Blackford, 260–61.
34. Stiles, 291–92.
35. Hunter, 687; Blackford, 263–64.
36. Blackford, 268–69.
37. *Ibid.*, 269–70.
38. *Ibid.*, 274–75; DeForest, 144.
39. Weld, 344; Allen, 276–77; Haskell, 71; Owen, 353–54.
40. Hunter, 686–87; Nisbet, 303; Owen, 354.
41. Hunter, 687; Stiles, 311.

CHAPTER 8. Unraveling Convictions (*pp. 156–168*)

1. Hunter, H. McGuire, *The Confederate Cause and Conduct in the War Between the States,* as quoted in Stiles, 245–46.
2. Herbert, "Grandfather's Talks About His Life Under Two Flags," 147–48, Herbert Papers.
3. Dunaway, 57–58; Benson, 183; Vail, 89.

4. Dodd, 251; Paxton, 70, 78; Lyman, 148.
5. Haskell, 56–57; Emerson, 288–89.
6. Washington Davis, 80; Hunter, 685.
7. Wilkeson, 197, 199–200.
8. Carter, 335–36; Blackford, 203.
9. Wood, 45–46.
10. Dooley, 103–8. Emphasis in original.
11. Lyman, 142–43; Wainwright, 405, 411; Wilkeson, 127; Meyers, 320; Dodd, 239.
12. George Stevens, 358, 360.
13. Nisbet, 305; Lyman, 139.
14. McCarthy, 29; Cox, I: 14; Lord, 229.
15. Nisbet, 141–42; Owen, 305.
16. Hunter, 577; Haskell, 59.
17. Lord, 229; Mitchell, 7–9. In 1916 a board of review struck all 864 names from the rolls of the Medal of Honor; Meyers, 308.
18. Robert N. Cross, "Joshua Lawrence Chamberlain," senior essay, Bowdoin College, 1947, 20, 22, 25, 31, in Chamberlain Papers; Wallace, 126, 134–35.
19. Alpheus Williams, 64, 66, 96, 98, 131, 135, 162–63, 203, 255, 271, 288–89, 317, 331–32, 342, 348–49, 356, 379, 389–90.
20. Hunter, 268, 270.
21. Burdette, 101–8; Abner Small, 70–71; Nisbet, 64.
22. Dawes, 299–300.
23. Carter, 375; Bicknell, 287–88. Emphasis in original. Lyman, 56; Galwey, 177.
24. Bicknell, 287; Lyman, 57–58, 273.

CHAPTER 9. The New Severity (*pp. 169–179*)

1. Blackford, 62–63, 69.
2. Dawson, 111–13.
3. Nisbet, 185–88. See also Blackford, 251. Beginning in early 1864 elections were no longer tolerated in newly formed units.
4. McPherson, 171.
5. Harry Hall, 60–61; Bardeen, 103, 166, 273, 294, 307.
6. Bellard, 8–10, 232–33.
7. *Ibid.*, 210; Wallace, 68–69; Crane, 35. Lyman reported that, during a bayonet charge ordered by Emery Upton, "Some of the men, who faltered, were run through the body by their comrades." Lyman, 109.
8. Wilkeson, 1–2, 8, 13, 17.
9. *Ibid.*, 30–34; Lyman, 243.
10. Weld, 257, 259–62.
11. McPherson, 181–83.

12. Beatty, 185; Alpheus Williams, 216; Burchard, 115; Galwey, 219.
13. Lonn, 58–59; Blackford, 280.
14. Bardeen, 287–88.
15. Wood, 42; Crotty, 123–24; Billings, *Hardtack and Coffee*, 161–62.
16. Fay, 61; Billings, *Hardtack and Coffee*, 157, 161.
17. Long, 714; McPherson, 468; Lyman, 117.
18. Burke Davis, *Stonewall*, 169–70, 449; Chambers, I: 474; Vandiver, 207, 210, 212.
19. Paxton, 16; Douglas, 236; Pickett, 27; Bardeen, 191; Lonn, 59–60.
20. Bardeen, 190.

CHAPTER 10. A Warfare of Terror (*pp. 180–215*)

1. Sherman acknowledged his army's many acts of pillage and violence, but he insisted that no murder or rape occurred. Sherman, *Memoirs*, II: 182–83. Cox conceded the "tendency of war to make men relapse into barbarism . . . when an army is living in any degree upon the enemy's country," as was Sherman's army in Georgia, but he "almost never heard" of instances of criminal personal assault. Cox, II: 233–34. Lloyd Lewis's work supported claims of only two cases of rape in which Sherman's soldiers were implicated in 1864–65. Lewis, 452–53. See also Leonard, 18–19.
2. Wainwright, 60–61.
3. Owen, 241.
4. Haskell, 48; Dooley, 97; Herbert, "Grandfather's Talks About His Life Under Two Flags," 169, Herbert Papers; Casler, 168, 170; Douglas, 245; Hunter, 416–17; Dawson, 92.
5. Owen, 240, 242; Small, 17; Casler, 178.
6. Hinman, 78; Meyers, 217; Stockwell, 52–53; Burchard, 40.
7. Peskin, 104; Long, 516; Lynch, 64.
8. Lonn, 7, 8, 129–30.
9. Small, 52; Lonn, 9.
10. Wood, 5; Nisbet, 185; Isham *et al.*, 409; Blackford, 45; Casler, 89.
11. Hinman, 229; McCarthy, 67; Wilkeson, 45; Casler, 208; Richard Taylor, 77. Emphasis in original.
12. Isham *et al.*, 409; Dawson, 122; Fay, 43.
13. Hinman, 148; Casler, 208; Cooke, 169.
14. Blackford, 45, 107–8.
15. Casler, 209; Hinman, 255; Wilkeson, 67.
16. Owen, 44; Casler, 89.
17. DeForest, 97; Small, 44, 48, 49, 50.
18. Hinman, 83–84; Charles Stevens, 43; Robert Strong, 59–61; Billings, *Hardtack and Coffee*, 234.
19. Stockwell, 61–62.
20. Bellard, 172.

21. Dawes, 22–23.
22. Hinman, 392–94.
23. *Ibid.*, 123–24.
24. *Ibid.*, 229; Nisbet, 185.
25. Nisbet, 94–95; Peskin, 106.
26. Billings, *Tenth Massachusetts Battery*, 277; Casler, 176; Wainwright, 61–62.
27. Charles Stevens, 82; Hinman, 121–22, 128–29, 220, 254, 328; Washington Davis, 169; Billings, *Hardtack and Coffee*, 37.
28. LeGrand Wilson, 37–39; Burdette, 148–49; Meyers, 285; Cox, II: 233–34.
29. Galwey, 57–66; Allen, 175.
30. Lynch, 9; Charles Stevens, 82; Sievers, 202–7.
31. Stillwell, 111; Hinman, 114; Stockwell, 52; Barber, 137.
32. Barber, 137.
33. Peskin, 144; Hinman, 254.
34. Stockwell, 54; Reed, 40–41.
35. Meyers, 214.
36. Washington Davis, 157–58; Foster, 100; Hinman, 828.
37. Virgil Jones, 14.
38. Cooke, 103–4, 108, 111, 113.
39. Hunter, 670; Casler, 239–40; Sanford, 302–3.
40. Kinsley, I: 178–79, 226–27; Virgil Jones, 111.
41. Sanford, 302–3; Whitman, 240; Douglas, 315–16.
42. Emerson, 265–67, 301, 313, 332, 353.
43. Alpheus Williams, 244.
44. McClellan, *McClellan's Own Story*, 60, 83, 85, 172, 402, 568. Emphasis in original.
45. McClellan, *Mexican War Diary*, 4; Eckenrode and Conrad, 9.
46. McClellan, *McClellan's Own Story*, 307, 468–69, 606; Hassler, 282–83.
47. McClellan, *McClellan's Own Story*, 59, 310–11.
48. *Ibid.*, 354, 398, 408, 567.
49. *Ibid.*, 172, 405, 442, 455.
50. *Ibid.*, 167, 463.
51. Lamers, 23, 28.
52. Lyman, 147.
53. Sherman to Ellen Sherman, February 21, 1860, quoted in Detzler, 27.
54. Sherman, *Home Letters*, 208, 222, 227.
55. U. S. Grant, I: 175, 355–56, 475–76, 521; Lewis, 271–72, 379.
56. Wilkeson, 92–93; Meyers, 209, 255, 320.
57. Eckenrode and Conrad, 16; Lamers, 18; Emerson Taylor, 8–9, 43.
58. Lewis, 77, 87, 95, 102, 110.

59. U. S. Grant, I: 103; Lewis, 138, 352, 417.
60. U. S. Grant, I: 59–60, 77, 110–11, 352, 417.
61. Arnold, 27.
62. Frederic, "The War Widow," *Major Works*, II: 184.
63. Sherman, *Memoirs*, I: 278; Lewis, 415–16, 420.
64. Sherman, *Home Letters*, 214, 260, 283, 342; Lewis, 244, 269, 462; Sherman, *Memoirs*, II: 175.
65. Lewis, 269; Sherman, *Memoirs*, II: 111.
66. Virgil Jones, 232.
67. Sherman, *Sherman Letters*, 162; Lewis, 335.
68. Sherman, *Memoirs*, I: 278; II: 28, 260; Sherman, *Sherman Letters*, 230. Emphasis in original. Lewis, 442, 496.
69. Washington Davis, 211; Beatty, 108–9. Emphasis added.
70. Lewis, 330; O'Connor, *Sheridan*, 197; Jesse Grant, 25; Sherman, *Home Letters*, 287, 310.
71. Foote, 214; Trefousse, 148; Burchard, 110; T. Harry Williams, 194, 203.
72. Fitch, 233; Burdette, 151; Charles Francis Adams *et al.*, I: 292; Connolly, 324; Lynch, 86; Brobst, 46, 103.
73. Lewis, 486; Sherman, *Memoirs*, II: 227–28; Alpheus Williams, 373, 387.
74. Sherman, *Memoirs*, II: 279.

CHAPTER 11. Unraveling Ties (*pp. 216–239*)

1. Weld, 302.
2. Foote, 170–71; Fitch, 239; Munroe, 68; Bierce, "Killed at Resaca," *Collected Writings*, 40–45.
3. Galwey, 80; Carter, 374.
4. Carter, 480. Emphasis in original. Hannah Ropes, 122.
5. Lyman, 187. Emphasis in original. Eggleston, 45.
6. Connolly, 106–7.
7. *Ibid.*, 14, 16, 282.
8. Thomas Livermore, 10, 18; Randall, 262.
9. Reid, 13.
10. Paxton, 62.
11. Connolly, 238, 253; Carter, 337; Weld, 244; Bellard, 232.
12. Lynch, 67; Carter, 484; Murdock, x.
13. James Miller, "Introduction to Correspondence," Miller Papers; Lynch, 67; Beatty, 220; Whitman, 147; Newton, 128.
14. Connolly, 255.
15. Hinkley, 91; Carter, 326; Weld, 334; Connolly, 253–54.
16. Connolly, 238; Brobst, 93.
17. Galwey, 137; Robert Strong, 215–17.

18. McCarthy, 37–38.
19. Prentiss, 42, 45.
20. Connolly, 107; Eggleston, 41.
21. Bierce, "Killed at Resaca," 45, and "One of the Missing," 107, both *Collected Writings;* Wilkeson, 205.
22. Carter, 383, 446.
23. *Ibid.*, 377–78. Emphasis in original.
24. *Ibid.*, 378; Connolly, 212; Lyman, 177–78.
25. Edward Ripley, 194–95, 203; Brobst, 110, 144, 147; Burchard, 56, 68; Foote, 57, 73.
26. James Miller, "Introduction to Correspondence," Miller Papers.
27. Fletcher, 104, 109, 110.
28. Wainwright, 14, 277–78, 302; Weld, 273; Burchard, 38.
29. Crotty, 151; Carter, 353, 413, 454; Wilkeson, 30; Bardeen, 165.
30. Eggleston, 33; McCarthy, 36–37; Hunter, 517.
31. Dooley, 150–51; Crotty, 25, 58, 77–78, 91.
32. Crotty, 155, 169; Allen, 210. Emphasis in original.
33. Galwey, 74; Allen, 188–89.
34. Lyman, 208–9; Crotty, 169; Carter, 348; Wilkeson, 35; Eggleston, 49–52.
35. Barber, 189; Lyman, 157–58.
36. Carter, 376; Fitch, 275; Cox, I: 166; Stockwell, 113; Crotty, 151, 176–77; Dooley, 89.
37. Lee Miller, 400.
38. Billings, *Hardtack and Coffee,* 202–3; Hinkley, 64; Wiley, *Billy Yank,* 340; Hunter, 517.
39. Hinman, 782; Wood, xi; Dodd, 103; Bull, 94; Robert Strong, 78–79; Stillwell, 154–55; Hunter, 517.
40. Fitch, 284; McCarthy, 37; Dodd, 49–50, 61, 151.
41. Long, 715.
42. Nisbet, 312–13, 328–29.
43. Bull, 63, 73, 82.
44. Barber, 160–61, 163–67.
45. Key and Campbell, 100, 108. Emphasis added. Washington Davis, 118; Isham *et al.*, 485–86.
46. Nisbet, 300.

CHAPTER 12. Disillusionment *(pp. 240–265)*

1. Washington Davis, 302; Lyman, 263.
2. Blackford, 28, 44, 55, 74.
3. Wilkeson, 166–68, 172–73; Robert Strong, 183.
4. Upson, 133; Mary Livermore, 328.
5. Benson, 65, 186.
6. Charles Francis Adams *et al.*, I: 260; DeForest, 73; Allen, 278–79.

7. Woolsey, 113; Dawson, 109; Wecter, 157; Jimerson, 332; Reed, 140; Mary Livermore, 641; Adelaide Smith, 112.
8. Hunter, 276; Robert Strong, 207; Alpheus Williams, 231, 252.
9. Steiner, 8; Catton, *America Goes to War*, 63; Fox, 3, 122.
10. Fitch, 26–27, 275; Benson, 7–8; Hinman, 727–28; LeGrand Wilson, 169; Bruce, 445–49.
11. Carter, 403; Weld, 298; Alpheus Williams, 111, 342, 348. Emphasis in original.
12. Carter, 297; Alpheus Williams, 356–57; James Wilson, I: 426–28.
13. Emerson, 357.
14. Key and Campbell, 182.
15. Paxton, 8; Hinman, 380–81; Allen, 181; Ross, 87.
16. Lyman, 180; Small, 129.
17. Dooley, 176–77, 199; Burdette, 207.
18. Bull, 231–32.
19. Paxton, 58; Lyman, 225; Hirshson, 104.
20. Paxton, 63; Eggleston, 95–97.
21. Beatty, 138; Edward Kirkland, 30–31; Weld, 318; Holmes, Jr., *Touched with Fire*, 117.
22. Nisbet, 269; Carter, 380.
23. Burton, 23, 32, 34, 40. Emphasis in original. Billings, *Tenth Massachusetts Battery*, 223; Fitch, 182.
24. Kidd, 56; Carter, 480; Small, 85.
25. Galwey, 129; Hinman, 78; Lyman, 230.
26. Hunter, 685–86.
27. Carter, 480.
28. *Ibid.*, 428, 456. Emphasis in original. Paxton, 82; Poague, 153.
29. Alpheus Williams, 219–20; Wallace, 149.
30. Coe, 123, 131, 141, 154.
31. Hunter, 294, 306, 313; Weld, 127; Hesseltine, 48–49.
32. Lonn, 158; Long, 715; Barziza, 91; Fitch, 237; Hesseltine, 76–77.
33. Wilkeson, 225; Isham *et al.*, 449, 456; Washington Davis, 93, 112; Barber, 169, 171; Ransom, 59, 94.
34. Barber, 167–68.
35. Washington Davis, 112, 114; Barber, 169; Drummond, "Recollections," 27; Ransom, 10, 39, 60, 62, 65, 68, 99, 202. Emphasis in original.
36. Munroe, 93–94; Washington Davis, 108.
37. Whitman, 216. Emphasis in original. Washington Davis, 125.
38. Catton, *Stillness at Appomattox*, 33–36; Hinman, 473–74, 476. Emphasis in original. Barber, 130.
39. Allen, 249; Sherman, *Memoirs*, I: 405.
40. Bicknell, 296; Stockwell, 67; George Stevens, 299; Hinman, 474, 476.
41. Allen, 249; Carter, 376, 488.

42. Stearns, 28, 32; Carter, 382; Barber, 143.
43. Hinman, 478, 489; DeForest, 231; Bicknell, 296; Allen, 249.
44. Jordan, 37.
45. Wellman, 180–81.

EPILOGUE (*pp. 266-297*)

1. Holmes, Jr., *Touched with Fire*, 23; Crotty, 146.
2. Benson, 199.
3. Foster, 182.
4. Pyle, 152–53, 217.
5. Holmes, Jr., *Speeches*, 65.
6. Fitch, 13–14, 344–45.
7. Weld, xxiv; McKinley, 274; Small, viii; Howe, *Shaping Years*, 8, 229; Edmund Wilson, 753–54; Fishwick, 134; Prentiss, 53.
8. Small, viii; Logan, 145, 148; Buck, 237; Bushong, 299: "The society [of the Army of Northern Virginia] went on record favoring the formation of similar groups in each Southern state. These, in turn, were to be authorized to establish sub-associations, which were expected to collect the muster rolls and names of all ex-Confederate soldiers, living and dead. After this material had been assembled, it was to be forwarded to the state organization and from it to the general association. . . . After a few years, due partly to the general disorganization of all Southern state institutions after the war, they declined in popularity and were barely able to maintain a skeleton staff to carry on their work." Dearing, 185.
9. Washington Davis, 240. Emphasis in original.
10. Mary Livermore, 7; Lively, 21; Connelly, 67.
11. Riker, 44; Hill, 121–22; Tucker, 294.
12. Utley, 15–16; Knight, 220, 222; Bigelow, 1; Loesser, 164, 167–69; F. W. Taylor, 30–35.
13. Utley, 22; *The Army and Navy Journal*, January 13, 1883, p. 526, quoted in Knight, 221; Knight, 221–22; Alderson, 101.
14. Wallace, 172, 201, 234–40; Richard L. Chittim, "A Letter from Bowdoin," a speech delivered to the Town and College Club, Brunswick, Maine, April 16, 1971, 10, 12, in Chamberlain Papers; Hatch, 134, 138; Robert N. Cross, "Joshua Lawrence Chamberlain," senior essay, Bowdoin College, 1947, 61–66, in Chamberlain Papers. I am grateful to Professor Chittim for his advice regarding the Drill Revolt.
15. Upson, 104; Aaron, 188 (Aaron's paraphrase of Bierce); Catton, *Reflections*, 159.
16. Osterweis, *Lost Cause*, 43–44; Carsten, 50–51; Dearing, 317, 432. See also Davies, Chap. 2.

17. Robert L. Rodgers, "Report of the Historian," 4–5, 14–17, 21, in Barnsley Papers.
18. Knight, 8, 17, 20; King, *Crook*, 7, 111, 152, 154–55, 158; King, *Colonel's Daughter*, 9, 407.
19. Hughes, 309–10; Francis Smith, 7–8; Tucker, 308; Lewis, 652.
20. Buck, 238–40; Wall, *Watterson*, 220–21.
21. Olsen, 29; King, *Crook*, 30, 33, 123; Knight, 228, 229; King, *Starlight Ranch*, 95, 218, 232; Noel, 104.
22. Garland, 204–6.
23. Schevill, 5, 7, 8–9; Anderson, *Story Teller's Story*, (veteranizing) 6–7; Anderson, *Memoirs*, (veteranizing) 78, (suit) 156; Anderson, *Tar*, (never a hero again) 29; Anderson, *Windy McPherson's Son*, (heart of soldier) 20, (war words) 21–22, (death-spitting thing) 21.
24. Catton, *Morning Train*, 190.
25. Galwey, 237, 238, 239, 241, 246, 247, 251, 255.
26. Bowen, 178, 380; Holmes, Jr., *Touched with Fire*, 79, 121, 122, 149–50; Howe, 155; Knight, 82; Bent, 270; Holmes, Jr., *Holmes-Pollock Letters*, I: 64; Holmes, Jr., *Speeches*, 11, 58, 59, 62, 63.
27. Bierce, "What I Saw of Shiloh," *Collected Works*, I: 261–62, 269; Bierce, "A Little of Chickamauga," *Collected Works*, I: 278; McWilliams, 319, 320.
28. Ross, 110, 122, 130, 132, 150–51, 162, 164, 171, 177; Munroe, 263–65, 268–69, 366–67, 376, 388, 404.
29. Lewis, 457, 515, 635, 636, 647.
30. Harbaugh, 225; Wall, *Carnegie*, 190; McCarthy, 35.
31. Bull, 249.
32. William Ripley, Memorial Day Address, 1895, Rutland (Vermont) High School, Ripley Papers; Washington Davis, 375.
33. Sherman, "Camp-fires," 502; Vail, 152; Washington Davis, 370; Robert L. Drummond to Juliet LeRoy Mangum, July 4, 1913, Mangum Papers. Emphasis in original.
34. Frederic, "Marsena," *Stories of York State*, 173.
35. Catton, *America Goes to War*, 69; Eggleston, 56; Dearing, 220; Osterweis, *Lost Cause*, 37.
36. John Ropes, 778, 785.
37. Farnham, 281; Starke, 104; Cooke, 503; Sherman, *Sherman Letters*, 375.
38. Bellamy, 120, 322; Morgan, 321.
39. For a forceful expression of the position that the war eroded moral values, see Mumford, 12–13: The "very method of warfare upset . . . the ideals and rational purposes for which it was fought, leaving greed, arrogance, and vindictiveness piled up behind the bodies of the dead heroes. . . . War does not bring the martial virtues into the subsequent peace: it merely prepares a richer soil for the civilian's vices."

40. Howe, *Shaping Years*, 249. See also Bowen, 289. Wecter, 156. See also Biddle, 35–36; Howe, *Proving Years*, 111.

41. Catton, *Morning Train*, 214–16; Anderson, *Story Teller's Story*, 25–26; Anderson, *Tar*, 205–6; *History, Confederate Veterans of Fulton County, Georgia*, 3, Barnsley Papers.

42. Bigelow, 189; Luce, 677–79, 681, 683; Starr, 48, 144–45, 485.

43. McWilliams, 35–36; Holmes, Jr., *Speeches*, 62–63; T. Harry Williams, 5; Starr, 145; H. C. Taylor, 183–84; Luce, 673, 677.

44. O'Connor, *Bierce*, 176; Henry Adams, iv, 277; Luce, 672; H. C. Taylor, 183.

45. Love, 4.

46. Leonard, 35; Earhart, 262, 271; Love, 5–6.

47. J. H. Goulding, "Origin and History of the G.A.R.," *The Vermonter Magazine* 10 (April 1905): 283, Ripley Papers.

48. H. C. Taylor, 182, 183; Luce, 680; McCarthy, 213; Williamson, 216; Elson, 334; Schurz, 219; Berryman, 78. I am grateful to Mr. Ed Burns of United Press International for directing me to the Berryman reference.

49. Sandburg, 409.

50. Washington Davis, 322; Drummond, "Personal Reminiscences of Prison Life During the War of the Rebellion," an address delivered at Hamilton College, February 22, 1901, 7, Mangum Papers. Emphasis in original.

51. Drummond, "Personal Reminiscences of Prison Life During the War of the Rebellion," address delivered at Hamilton College, February 22, 1901, 14–15, Mangum Papers. Emphasis in original. William Ripley, Memorial Day Address, 1899 (?), Vergennes, Vermont, Ripley Papers; McCarthy, 194.

52. Stiles, 91–94. Dunne quoted in Downey, 131.

53. Langford, 199; O'Connor, *Bierce*, 260; William Ripley, Memorial Day Address.

54. Washington Davis, 15, 79; McCarthy, 213; William Ripley, Memorial Day Address, 1896.

55. Catton, *Reflections*, xv; Catton, *Morning Train*, 193.

Bibliography

Aaron, Daniel. *The Unwritten War: American Writers and the Civil War.* New York: Knopf, 1973.

Adams, Charles Francis; Henry Adams; *et al. A Cycle of Adams Letters, 1861–1865.* Ed. Worthington C. Ford. 2 vols. Boston and New York: Houghton Mifflin Company, 1920.

Adams, Henry. *History of the United States of America.* 9 vols. New York: C. Scribner's Sons, 1889–1909.

Alcott, Louisa May. *Hospital Sketches.* Boston: J. Redpath, 1863.

Alderson, Bernard. *Andrew Carnegie: The Man and His Work.* New York: Doubleday, Page & Company, 1909.

Allen, George H. *Forty-Six Months with the Fourth R.I. Volunteers, in the War of 1861 to 1865.* Providence: J. A. & R. A. Reid, Printers, 1887.

Ambrose, Stephen E. *Upton and the Army.* Baton Rouge: Louisiana State University Press, 1964.

Anderson, Sherwood. *Sherwood Anderson's Memoirs: A Critical Edition.* Ed. Ray Lewis White. Chapel Hill: University of North Carolina Press, 1969.

———. *A Story Teller's Story: A Critical Text.* Ed. Ray Lewis White. Cleveland: Press of Case Western Reserve University, 1968.

———. *Tar: A Midwest Childhood—A Critical Text.* Ed. Ray Lewis White. Cleveland: Press of Case Western Reserve University, 1969.

———. *Windy McPherson's Son.* London: J. Cape, 1923.

Arnold, Matthew. *General Grant.* Ed. John Y. Simon. Carbondale: Southern Illinois University Press, 1966.

Barber, Lucius W. *Army Memoirs of Lucius W. Barber, Company "D",*

15th Illinois Volunteer Infantry. Chicago: The J. M. W. Jones Stationery & Printing Company, 1894.

Bardeen, Charles W. *A Little Fifer's War Diary.* Syracuse, N.Y.: Printed by the author, 1910.

Barnard, Harry. *Rutherford B. Hayes and His America.* Indianapolis: The Bobbs-Merrill Company, 1954.

Barnsley, George S. Papers. Southern Historical Collection, University of North Carolina Library, Chapel Hill.

Barrett, Orvey S. *Reminiscences, Incidents, Battles, Marches and Camp Life of the Old 4th Michigan Infantry in War of Rebellion, 1861 to 1864.* Detroit: W. S. Ostler, 1888.

Bartlett, Asa W. *History of the Twelfth Regiment, New Hampshire Volunteers in the War of the Rebellion.* Concord: I. C. Evans, Printer, 1897.

Barziza, Decimus E. U. *The Adventures of a Prisoner of War, 1863–1864.* Austin: University of Texas Press, 1964.

Beatty, John. *Memoirs of a Volunteer, 1861–1863.* New York: W. W. Norton & Company, 1946.

Beaty, John O. *John Esten Cooke, Virginian.* New York: Columbia University Press, 1922.

Bellamy, Edward. *Looking Backward, 2000–1887.* Boston and New York: Houghton, Mifflin & Company, 1889.

Bellard, Alfred. *Gone for a Soldier: The Civil War Memoirs of Private Alfred Bellard.* Ed. David H. Donald. Boston: Little, Brown, 1975.

Benson, Berry. *Berry Benson's Civil War Book: Memoirs of a Confederate Scout and Sharpshooter.* Ed. Susan W. Benson. Athens: University of Georgia Press, 1962.

Bent, Silas. *Justice Oliver Wendell Holmes: A Biography.* New York: The Vanguard Press, 1932.

Berryman, John. *Stephen Crane.* New York: William Sloane Associates, 1950.

Bicknell, George W. *History of the Fifth Regiment Maine Volunteers.* Portland, Me.: H. L. Davis, 1871.

Biddle, Francis. *Mr. Justice Holmes.* New York: Charles Scribner's Sons, 1942.

Bierce, Ambrose. *The Collected Works of Ambrose Bierce.* 12 vols. New York and Washington: The Neale Publishing Company, 1909–12.

——. *The Collected Writings of Ambrose Bierce.* New York: The Citadel Press, 1946.

Bigelow, Donald N. *William Conant Church and the Army and Navy Journal.* New York: Columbia University Press, 1952.

Billings, John D. *Hardtack and Coffee*. Boston: G. M. Smith & Company, 1888.

———. *The History of the Tenth Massachusetts Battery of Light Artillery in the War of the Rebellion*. Boston: The Arakelyan Press, 1909.

Blackford, William W. *War Years with Jeb Stuart*. New York: C. Scribner's Sons, 1945.

Bowen, Catherine D. *Yankee from Olympus: Justice Holmes and His Family*. Boston: Little, Brown & Company, 1944.

Bridges, Leonard H. *Lee's Maverick General, Daniel Harvey Hill*. New York: McGraw-Hill, 1961.

Brobst, John F. *Well, Mary: Civil War Letters of a Wisconsin Volunteer*. Ed. Margaret B. Roth. Madison: University of Wisconsin Press, 1960.

Brooks, Aubrey L. *Walter Clark, Fighting Judge*. Chapel Hill: The University of North Carolina Press, 1944.

Bruce, George A. *The Twentieth Regiment of Massachusetts Volunteer Infantry, 1861–1865*. Boston and New York: Houghton, Mifflin & Company, 1906.

Buck, Paul H. *The Road to Reunion, 1865–1900*. Boston: Little, Brown & Company, 1937.

Bull, Rice C. *Soldiering: The Civil War Diary of Rice C. Bull, 123rd New York Volunteer Infantry*. Ed. K. Jack Bauer. San Rafael, Calif.: Presidio Press, 1977.

Burchard, Peter. *One Gallant Rush: Robert Gould Shaw and His Brave Black Regiment*. New York: St. Martin's Press, 1965.

Burdette, Robert J. *The Drums of the 47th*. Indianapolis: Bobbs-Merrill Company, 1914.

Burr, Agnes R. *Russell H. Conwell and His Work: One Man's Interpretation of Life*. Philadelphia: The John C. Winston Company, Publishers, 1926.

Burton, Elijah P. *Diary of E. P. Burton, Surgeon, 7th Reg. Ill., 3rd Brig., 2nd Div. 16 A.C.* Des Moines: The Historical Records Survey, 1939.

Bushong, Millard K. *Old Jube: A Biography of General Jubal A. Early*. Boyce, Va.: Carr Publishing Company, 1955.

Carpenter, John A. *Sword and Olive Branch: Oliver Otis Howard*. Pittsburgh: University of Pittsburgh Press, 1964.

Carsten, Oliver M. "Work and the Lodge: Working-Class Sociability in Meriden and New Britain, Connecticut, 1850–1940." Doctoral dissertation, University of Michigan, 1981.

Carter, Robert G. *Four Brothers in Blue*. Austin: University of Texas Press, 1978.

Casler, John O. *Four Years in the Stonewall Brigade.* 2nd ed. Girard, Kans.: Appeal Publishing Company, 1906.

Catton, Bruce. *America Goes to War.* Middletown, Conn.: Wesleyan University Press, 1958.

———. *Glory Road: The Bloody Route from Fredericksburg to Gettysburg.* Garden City, N.Y.: Doubleday, 1952.

———. *Reflections on the Civil War.* Garden City, N.Y.: Doubleday, 1981.

———. *A Stillness at Appomattox.* Garden City, N.Y.: Doubleday, 1953.

———. *Waiting for the Morning Train: An American Boyhood.* Garden City, N.Y.: Doubleday, 1972.

Chamberlain, Joshua Lawrence. Papers. Bowdoin College Library, Brunswick, Maine.

Chambers, Lenoir. *Stonewall Jackson.* 2 vols. New York: W. Morrow, 1959.

Clifford, Deborah P. *Mine Eyes Have Seen the Glory: A Biography of Julia Ward Howe.* Boston: Little, Brown, 1979.

Coe, Hamlin A. *Mine Eyes Have Seen the Glory: Combat Diaries of Union Sergeant Hamlin Alexander Coe.* Ed. David Coe. Rutherford, N.J.: Fairleigh Dickinson University Press, 1975.

Connelly, Thomas L. *The Marble Man: Robert E. Lee and His Image in American Society.* New York: Knopf, 1977.

Connolly, James A. *Three Years in the Army of the Cumberland: The Letters and Diary of Major James A. Connolly.* Ed. Paul M. Angle. Bloomington: Indiana University Press, 1959.

Cooke, John E. *Wearing of the Gray.* Ed. Philip Van Doren Stern. Bloomington: Indiana University Press, 1959.

Cox, Jacob D. *Military Reminiscences of the Civil War.* 2 vols. New York: C. Scribner's Sons, 1900.

Crane, Stephen. *The Red Badge of Courage.* New York: D. Appleton & Company, 1895.

Crotty, Daniel G. *Four Years Campaigning in the Army of the Potomac.* Grand Rapids, Mich.: Dygert Brothers & Company, Printers, 1874.

Custer, George A. *The Custer Story: The Life and Intimate Letters of General George A. Custer and His Wife Elizabeth.* Ed. Marguerite Merington. New York: Devin-Adair, 1950.

Dame, William M. *From the Rapidan to Richmond and the Spottsylvania Campaign.* Baltimore: Green-Lucas Company, 1920.

Davies, Wallace E. *Patriotism on Parade: The Story of Veterans' and*

Hereditary Organizations in America, 1783–1900. Cambridge, Mass.: Harvard University Press, 1955.

Davis, Burke. *Our Incredible Civil War.* New York: Holt, Rinehart & Winston, 1960.

———. *They Called Him Stonewall: A Life of Lt. General T. J. Jackson, C.S.A.* New York: Rinehart, 1954.

Davis, Washington. *Camp-Fire Chats of the Civil War.* Chicago: Lewis Publishing Company, 1888.

Dawes, Rufus R. *Service with the Sixth Wisconsin Volunteers.* Ed. Alan T. Nolan. Madison: State Historical Society of Wisconsin, 1962.

Dawson, Francis W. *Reminiscences of Confederate Service, 1861–1865.* Baton Rouge: Louisiana State University Press, 1980.

Dearing, Mary K. *Veterans in Politics: The Story of the G.A.R.* Baton Rouge: Louisiana State University Press, 1952.

DeForest, John W. *A Volunteer's Adventures.* Ed. James H. Croushore. New Haven: Yale University Press, 1946.

Detzler, Jack J. "The Religion of William Tecumseh Sherman." *Ohio History* 75 (Winter 1966): 26–34, 68–70.

Dodd, Ira S. *The Song of the Rappahannock.* New York: Dodd, Mead & Company, 1898.

Dollard, John. *Fear in Battle.* New Haven: Institute of Human Relations, Yale University, 1943.

Donald, David H. *Liberty and Union.* Boston and Toronto: Little, Brown & Company, 1978.

Dooley, John E. *John Dooley, Confederate Soldier, His War Journal.* Ed. Joseph T. Durkin, S.J. Washington: Georgetown University Press, 1945.

Doughty, Howard. *Francis Parkman.* New York: Macmillan, 1962.

Douglas, Henry K. *I Rode with Stonewall.* Chapel Hill: University of North Carolina Press, 1940.

Downey, Fairfax. *Richard Harding Davis: His Day.* New York: Charles Scribner's Sons, 1933.

Drummond, Robert L. Papers. Southern Historical Collection, University of North Carolina Library, Chapel Hill.

Dunaway, Wayland F. *Reminiscences of a Rebel.* New York: The Neale Publishing Company, 1913.

Duncan, Donald. *The New Legions.* New York: Random House, 1967.

Earhart, Mary. *Frances Willard: From Prayers to Politics.* Chicago: University of Chicago Press, 1944.

Eckenrode, Hamilton J., and Bryan Conrad. *George B. McClellan: The*

Man Who Saved the Union. Chapel Hill: The University of North Carolina Press, 1941.

Eggleston, George C. *A Rebel's Recollections*. New York: Hurd & Houghton; Cambridge, Mass.: The Riverside Press, 1875.

———. "The Old Regime in the Old Dominion." *Atlantic Monthly* 36 (November 1875): 603–16.

Elson, Ruth M. *Guardians of Tradition: American Schoolbooks of the Nineteenth Century*. Lincoln: University of Nebraska Press, 1964.

Emerson, Edward W. *Life and Letters of Charles Russell Lowell*. Boston and New York: Houghton, Mifflin & Company, 1907.

Farnham, Charles H. *A Life of Francis Parkman*. Boston: Little, Brown & Company, 1901.

Fay, Edwin H. *"This Infernal War": The Confederate Letters of Sgt. Edwin H. Fay*. Ed. Bell I. Wiley. Austin: University of Texas Press, 1958.

Fishwick, Marshall W. *Lee After the War*. New York: Dodd, Mead, 1963.

Fitch, Michael H. *Echoes of the Civil War as I Hear Them*. New York: R. F. Fenno & Company, 1905.

Fletcher, William A. *Rebel Private, Front and Rear*. Beaumont, Tex.: Press of the Greer Print, 1908.

Foner, Eric. *Free Soil, Free Labor, Free Men*. New York: Oxford University Press, 1970.

Foote, Corydon E. *With Sherman to the Sea: A Drummer's Story of the Civil War, as Related by Corydon Edward Foote to Olive Deane Hormel*. New York: John Day Company, 1960.

Forbes, Edwin. *A Civil War Artist at the Front: Edwin Forbes' Life Studies of the Great Army*. Ed. William F. Dawson. New York: Oxford University Press, 1957.

Foster, John W. *War Stories for My Grandchildren*. Cambridge: Printed for private circulation by the Riverside Press, 1918.

Fox, William F. *Regimental Losses in the American Civil War, 1861–1865*. Albany, N.Y.: Albany Publishing Company, 1889.

Frederic, Harold. *The Major Works of Harold Frederic*. 5 vols. New York: Greenwood Press, 1969.

———. *Harold Frederic's Stories of York State*. Ed. Thomas F. O'Donnell. Syracuse, N.Y.: Syracuse University Press, 1966.

Freeman, Julia W. *The Boys in White: The Experience of a Hospital Agent in and Around Washington*. New York: Lange & Hillman, 1870.

Galwey, Thomas F. *The Valiant Hours: Narrative of "Captain Brevet," an Irish-American in the Army of the Potomac.* Ed. W. S. Nye. Harrisburg, Pa.: Stackpole's, 1961.

Garland, Hamlin. *A Daughter of the Middle Border.* New York: Grosset & Dunlap, 1926.

Gerber, John. "Mark Twain's 'Private Campaign.' " *Civil War History* 1 (March 1955): 37–60.

Gould, Benjamin A. *Investigations in the Military and Anthropological Statistics of American Soldiers.* New York: Hurd & Houghton, 1869.

Goulding, J. H. "Origin and History of the G.A.R." *The Vermonter* 10 (April 1905): 281–82.

Grant, Jesse R. *In the Days of My Father, General Grant.* New York and London: Harper & Brothers, 1925.

Grant, Ulysses S. *Personal Memoirs of U. S. Grant.* 2 vols. New York: C. L. Webster & Company, 1885–86.

Gray, Jesse Glenn. *The Warriors: Reflections on Men in Battle.* New York: Harcourt, Brace, 1959.

Gross, Theodore L. *Thomas Nelson Page.* New York: Twayne Publishers, 1967.

Grossman, Julian. *Echo of a Distant Drum: Winslow Homer and the Civil War.* New York: Harry N. Abrams, 1974.

Hall, Harry H. *A Johnny Reb Band from Salem.* Raleigh: The North Carolina Confederate Centennial Commission, 1963.

Hall, Richard S. *Stanley: An Adventurer Explored.* London: Collins, 1974.

Hammett, Hugh B. *Hilary Abner Herbert: A Southerner Returns to the Union.* Philadelphia: American Philosophical Society, 1976.

Handlin, Oscar. "The Civil War as Symbol and as Actuality." *Massachusetts Review* 3 (Autumn 1961): 133–43.

Harbaugh, William H. *Power and Responsibility: The Life and Times of Theodore Roosevelt.* New York: Farrar, Straus & Cudahy, 1961.

Harwell, Richard B. *The War 1861–1865 as Depicted in Prints by Currier and Ives.* Columbus, O.: Nationwide Insurance, 1960.

Haskell, John C. *The Haskell Memoirs.* Ed. Gilbert E. Govan and James W. Livingood. New York: Putnam, 1960.

Hassler, Warren W. *General George B. McClellan, Shield of the Union.* Baton Rouge: Louisiana State University Press, 1957.

Hatch, Louis C. *The History of Bowdoin College.* Portland, Me.: Loring, Short & Harmon, 1927.

Herbert, Hilary Abner. Papers. Southern Historical Collection, University of North Carolina Library, Chapel Hill.

Herr, Michael. *Dispatches.* New York: Knopf, 1977.

Hesseltine, William B. *Civil War Prisons: A Study in War Psychology.* Columbus: The Ohio State University Press, 1930.

Higginson, Thomas W. *Cheerful Yesterdays.* Boston and New York: Houghton, Mifflin & Company, 1898.

Hill, Jim Dan. *The Minute Man in Peace and War: A History of the National Guard.* Harrisburg, Pa.: Stackpole Company, 1964.

Hinkley, Julian W. *A Narrative of Service with the Third Wisconsin Infantry.* Madison: Wisconsin History Commission, 1912.

Hinman, Wilbur F. *The Story of the Sherman Brigade.* Alliance, O.: Printed by the author, 1897.

Hirshson, Stanley P. *Greenville M. Dodge, Soldier, Politician, Railroad Pioneer.* Bloomington: Indiana University Press, 1967.

Holmes, Oliver Wendell, Jr. *Holmes–Pollock Letters: The Correspondence of Mr. Justice Holmes and Sir Frederick Pollock, 1874–1932.* Ed. Mark De Wolfe Howe. Cambridge: Harvard University Press, 1941.

———. *Speeches.* Boston: Little, Brown & Company, 1918.

———. *Touched with Fire: Civil War Letters and Diary of Oliver Wendell Holmes, Jr., 1861–1864.* Ed. Mark De Wolfe Howe. Cambridge: Harvard University Press, 1946.

Hood, John B. *Advance and Retreat: Personal Experiences in the United States and Confederate States Armies.* New Orleans: Published for the Hood Orphan Memorial Fund, 1880.

Howe, Mark De W. *Justice Oliver Wendell Holmes: The Proving Years, 1870–1882.* Cambridge: Belknap Press of Harvard University Press, 1963.

———. *Justice Oliver Wendell Holmes: The Shaping Years, 1841–1870.* Cambridge: Belknap Press of Harvard University Press, 1957.

Hughes, Nathaniel C. *General William J. Hardee: Old Reliable.* Baton Rouge: Louisiana State University Press, 1965.

Hunter, Alexander. *Johnny Reb and Billy Yank.* New York and Washington: The Neale Publishing Company, 1905.

Isham, Asa B.; Henry M. Davidson; and Henry B. Furness. *Prisoners of War and Military Prisons.* Cincinnati: Lyman & Cushing, 1890.

Jimerson, Randall C. "A People Divided: The Civil War Interpreted by Participants." Doctoral dissertation, University of Michigan, 1977.

Johnson, Charles F. *The Long Roll.* East Aurora, N.Y.: The Roycrofters, 1911.

Jones, James. *WWII.* New York: Grosset & Dunlap, 1975.

Jones, John B. *A Rebel War Clerk's Diary at the Confederate States Capital.* 2 vols. Philadelphia: J. B. Lippincott & Company, 1866.

Jones, Virgil C. *Ranger Mosby.* Chapel Hill: The University of North Carolina Press, 1944.

Jordan, David M. *Roscoe Conkling of New York: Voice in the Senate.* Ithaca, N.Y.: Cornell University Press, 1971.

Keegan, John. *The Face of Battle.* New York: Viking Press, 1976.

Key, Thomas J., and Robert J. Campbell. *Two Soldiers: The Campaign Diaries of Thomas J. Key, C.S.A., December 7, 1863–May 17, 1865, and Robert J. Campbell, U.S.A., January 1, 1864–July 21, 1864.* Ed. Wirt A. Cate. Chapel Hill: The University of North Carolina Press, 1938.

Kidd, James H. *Personal Recollections of a Cavalryman with Custer's Michigan Cavalry Brigade in the Civil War.* Ionia, Mich.: Sentinel Printing Company, 1908.

King, Charles. *Campaigning with Crook, and Stories of Army Life.* New York: Harper & Brothers, 1890.

———. *The Colonel's Daughter, or, Winning His Spurs.* Philadelphia: J. B. Lippincott Company, 1904.

———. *Starlight Ranch, and Other Stories of Army Life on the Frontier.* Philadelphia: J. B. Lippincott Company, 1890.

Kinsley, D. A. *Favor the Bold.* Volume 1: *Custer: The Civil War Years.* New York: Holt, Rinehart & Winston, 1967.

Kirkland, Edward C. *Charles Francis Adams, Jr., 1835–1915: The Patrician at Bay.* Cambridge: Harvard University Press, 1965.

Kirkland, Joseph. *The Captain of Company K.* Ridgewood, N.J.: Gregg Press, 1968.

Knight, Oliver. *Life and Manners in the Frontier Army.* Norman: University of Oklahoma Press, 1978.

Lamers, William M. *The Edge of Glory: A Biography of General William S. Rosecrans, U.S.A.* New York: Harcourt, Brace, 1961.

Langford, Gerald. *The Richard Harding Davis Years: A Biography of a Mother and Son.* New York: Holt, Rinehart & Winston, 1961.

Leonard, Thomas C. *Above the Battle: War Making in America from Appomattox to Versailles.* New York: Oxford University Press, 1978.

Lewis, Lloyd. *Sherman, Fighting Prophet.* New York: Harcourt Brace, 1958.

Lively, Robert A. *Fiction Fights the Civil War.* Chapel Hill: The University of North Carolina Press, 1957.

Livermore, Mary A. *My Story of the War.* Hartford: A. D. Worthington & Company, 1890.

Livermore, Thomas L. *Numbers and Losses in the Civil War in Amer-*

343

ica, 1861–65. 2d ed. Boston and New York: Houghton, Mifflin & Company, 1901.

Loesser, Arthur. *Humor in American Song.* New York: Howell, Soskin, Publishers, 1942.

Logan, Mary S. *Reminiscences of the Civil War and Reconstruction.* Ed. George Worthington Adams. Carbondale: Southern Illinois University Press, 1970.

Long, Everette B. *The Civil War Day by Day: An Almanac, 1861–1865.* Garden City, N.Y.: Doubleday, 1971.

Lonn, Ella. *Desertion During the Civil War.* New York and London: The Century Company, 1928.

Lord, Francis A. *They Fought for the Union.* Harrisburg, Pa.: Stackpole Company, 1960.

Love, Alfred. *A Shaker Meeting.* Mt. Lebanon, N.Y.: Publisher unknown, 1891.

Luce, S. B. "The Benefits of War." *North American Review* 153 (December 1891): 672–83.

Lyman, Theodore. *Meade's Headquarters, 1863–1865: Letters of Colonel Theodore Lyman from the Wilderness to Appomattox.* Ed. George R. Agassiz. Boston: The Atlantic Monthly, 1922.

Lynch, Charles H. *The Civil War Diary, 1862–1865, of Charles H. Lynch, 18th Conn. Vol's.* Hartford: Case, Lockwood & Brainard Company, 1915.

McCarthy, Carlton. *Detailed Minutiae of Soldier Life in the Army of Northern Virginia, 1861–1865.* Richmond: J. W. Randolph & English, 1888.

McClellan, George B. *McClellan's Own Story.* New York: C. L. Webster & Company, 1887.

————. *The Mexican War Diary of George B. McClellan.* Ed. William S. Myers. Princeton, N.J.: Princeton University Press, 1917.

McKinley, William. "A Civil War Diary of William McKinley." Ed. Howard Wayne Morgan. *Ohio Historical Quarterly* 69 (July 1960): 272–90.

McPherson, James M. *Ordeal by Fire: The Civil War and Reconstruction.* New York: Knopf, 1982.

McWilliams, Carey. *Ambrose Bierce: A Biography.* New York: A. & C. Boni, 1929.

Mangum, Adolphus W. Papers. Southern Historical Collection, University of North Carolina Library, Chapel Hill.

Meyers, Augustus. *Ten Years in the Ranks, U.S. Army.* New York: Arno Press, 1979.

Miller, Charles M. *An Armed America: Its Face in Fiction*. New York: New York University Press, 1970.

Miller, James T. Papers. James S. Schoff Civil War Collection, William L. Clements Library, University of Michigan, Ann Arbor.

Miller, Lee G. *The Story of Ernie Pyle*. New York: Viking Press, 1950.

Mitchell, Joseph B. *The Badge of Gallantry*. New York: The Macmillan Company, 1968.

Moran, Charles McM. W. *The Anatomy of Courage*. Boston: Houghton Mifflin Company, 1967.

Morgan, Arthur E. *Edward Bellamy*. New York: Columbia University Press, 1944.

Morris, Edmund. *The Rise of Theodore Roosevelt*. New York: Coward, McCann & Geoghegan, 1979.

Mumford, Lewis. *The Brown Decades: A Study of the Arts in America, 1865–1895*. New York: Harcourt, Brace & Company, 1931.

Munroe, James P. *A Life of Francis Amasa Walker*. New York: H. Holt & Company, 1923.

Murdock, Eugene C. *One Million Men: The Civil War Draft in the North*. Madison: State Historical Society of Wisconsin, 1971.

Newton, James K. *A Wisconsin Boy in Dixie: The Selected Letters of James K. Newton*. Ed. Stephen E. Ambrose. Madison: University of Wisconsin Press, 1961.

Nisbet, James C. *Four Years on the Firing Line*. Chattanooga, Tenn.: The Imperial Press, 1914.

Noel, Mary. *Villains Galore: The Heyday of the Popular Weekly*. New York: Macmillan, 1954.

O'Brien, Tim. *If I Die in a Combat Zone*. New York: Delacorte Press, 1973.

O'Connor, Richard. *Ambrose Bierce: A Biography*. Boston: Little, Brown & Company, 1967.

———. *Sheridan the Inevitable*. Indianapolis: The Bobbs-Merrill Company, 1953.

Olsen, Otto H. *Carpetbagger's Crusade: The Life of Albion Winegar Tourgée*. Baltimore: Johns Hopkins Press, 1965.

Osterweis, Rollin G. *The Myth of the Lost Cause, 1865–1900*. Hamden, Conn.: Archon Books, 1973.

———. *Romanticism and Nationalism in the Old South*. New Haven: Yale University Press, 1949.

Owen, William M. *In Camp and Battle with the Washington Artillery of New Orleans*. Boston: Ticknor & Company, 1885.

Palfrey, Francis W. *In Memoriam: H.L.A.* Boston: Printed for private distribution, 1864.

Paxton, Elisha F. *The Civil War Letters of General Frank "Bull" Paxton, CSA, a Lieutenant of Lee and Jackson.* Ed. John G. Paxton. Hillsboro, Tex.: Hill Junior College Press, 1978.

Perkins, Jacob R. *Trails, Rails and War: The Life of General G. M. Dodge.* Indianapolis: The Bobbs-Merrill Company, 1929.

Peskin, Allan. *Garfield: A Biography.* Kent, O.: Kent State University Press, 1978.

Pickett, George E. *Soldier of the South: General Pickett's War Letters to His Wife.* Ed. Arthur Crew Inman. Boston and New York: Houghton, Mifflin Company, 1928.

Poague, William T. *Gunner with Stonewall.* Jackson, Tenn.: McCowat-Mercer Press, 1957.

Porter, Horace. "The Philosophy of Courage." *The Century Magazine* 36 (June 1888): 246–54.

Prentiss, Dale. "Troy, Michigan, in the Civil War Draft." Senior honors thesis, University of Michigan, 1981.

Pyle, Ernest T. *Here Is Your War.* New York: H. Holt & Company, 1943.

Quintard, Charles T. *Doctor Quintard, Chaplain C.S.A. and Second Bishop of Tennessee.* Ed. Arthur H. Noll. Sewanee, Tenn.: The University Press, 1905.

Randall, James G., and David H. Donald. *Thè Civil War and Reconstruction.* 2d ed. Boston: Little, Brown, 1969.

Ransom, John L. *John Ransom's Diary.* New York: P. S. Eriksson, 1963.

Reed, William H. *Hospital Life in the Army of the Potomac.* Boston: William V. Spencer, 1866.

Reid, Jesse W. *History of the Fourth Regiment of S.C. Volunteers.* Greenville, S.C.: Shannon & Company, Printers, 1892.

Reid, Whitelaw. *Ohio in the War: Her Statesmen, Generals and Soldiers.* 2 vols. Cincinnati: R. Clarke Company, 1895.

Riker, William H. *Soldiers of the States: The Role of the National Guard in American Democracy.* Washington, D.C.: Public Affairs Press, 1957.

Ripley, Edward H. *Vermont General.* Ed. Otto Eisenschiml. New York: Devin-Adair, 1960.

Ripley, William Young. Papers. William R. Perkins Library, Duke University, Durham, N.C.

Roper, Laura W. *FLO: A Biography of Frederick Law Olmsted.* Baltimore: Johns Hopkins Press, 1973.

Ropes, Hannah A. *Civil War Nurse: The Diary and Letters of Hannah Ropes.* Ed. John R. Brumgardt. Knoxville: University of Tennessee Press, 1980.

Ropes, John C. "The War as We See It Now." *Scribner's Magazine* ix, 6 (June 1891): 776–88.

Ross, Ishbel. *Angel of the Battlefield: The Life of Clara Barton.* New York: Harper, 1956.

Rosser, Thomas L. *Addresses of Gen'l T. L. Rosser at the Seventh Annual Reunion of the Maryland Line, Academy of Music, Baltimore, Md., February 22, 1889, and on Memorial Day, Staunton, Va., June 8, 1889.* New York: The L. A. Williams Printing Company, 1889.

Russ, Martin. *The Last Parallel: A Marine's War Journal.* New York: Rinehart, 1957.

Sajer, Guy. *The Forgotten Soldier.* New York: Harper & Row, 1971.

Sandburg, Carl. *Always the Young Strangers.* New York: Harcourt, Brace, 1953.

Sanford, George B. *Fighting Rebels and Redskins.* Ed. E. R. Hagemann. Norman: University of Oklahoma Press, 1969.

Schevill, James. *Sherwood Anderson, His Life and Work.* Denver: University of Denver Press, 1951.

Schurz, Carl. "About War." *Harper's Weekly* 42 (March 5, 1898): 219.

Shaffer, W. A. Papers. Southern Historical Collection, University of North Carolina Library, Chapel Hill.

Sheeran, James B. *Confederate Chaplain: A War Journal.* Ed. Joseph T. Durkin, S.J. Milwaukee: Bruce Publishing Company, 1960.

Sherman, William T. "Camp-Fires of the G.A.R." *North American Review* 147 (November 1888): 497–502.

———. *Home Letters of General Sherman.* Ed. Mark De Wolfe Howe. New York: C. Scribner's Sons, 1909.

———. *Memoirs of General William T. Sherman.* 2 vols. New York: D. Appleton & Company, 1875.

———. *The Sherman Letters.* Ed. Rachel Sherman Thorndike. New York: C. Scribner's Sons, 1894.

Sievers, Harry J. *Benjamin Harrison: Hoosier Warrior, 1833–1865.* Chicago: H. Regnery Company, 1952.

Small, Abner R. *The Road to Richmond.* Ed. Harold A. Small. Berkeley: University of California Press, 1939.

Smith, Adelaide W. *Reminiscences of an Army Nurse During the Civil War.* New York: Greaves Publishing Company, 1911.

Smith, Francis. *West Point Fifty Years Ago: An Address Delivered Before the Association of Graduates of the U.S. Military Academy,*

West Point, at the Annual Reunion, June 12, 1879. New York: D. Van Nostrand, 1879.

Starke, Aubrey H. *Sidney Lanier: A Biographical and Critical Study.* Chapel Hill: The University of North Carolina Press, 1933.

Starr, Harris E. *William Graham Sumner.* New York: H. Holt & Company, 1925.

Stearns, Amos E. *The Civil War Diary of Amos E. Stearns, A Prisoner at Andersonville.* Rutherford, N.J.: Fairleigh Dickinson University Press, 1981.

Steinbeck, John. *Once There Was a War.* New York: Viking Press, 1958.

Steiner, Paul E. *Disease in the Civil War: Natural Biological Warfare in 1861–1865.* Springfield, Ill.: C. C. Thomas, 1968.

Stevens, Charles A. *Berdan's United States Sharpshooters in the Army of the Potomac, 1861–1865.* St. Paul: The Price-McGill Company, 1892.

Stevens, George T. *Three Years in the Sixth Corps.* Albany, N.Y.: S. R. Gray, 1866.

Stiles, Robert. *Four Years Under Marse Robert.* New York and Washington: The Neale Publishing Company, 1903.

Stillwell, Leander. *The Story of a Common Soldier of Army Life in the Civil War, 1861–65.* Eire (?), Kan.: Franklin Hudson Publishing Company, 1920.

Stockwell, Elisha. *Private Elisha Stockwell, Jr. Sees the Civil War.* Ed. Byron R. Abernethy. Norman: University of Oklahoma Press, 1958.

Strong, Leah A. *Joseph Hopkins Twichell, Mark Twain's Friend and Pastor.* Athens: University of Georgia Press, 1966.

Strong, Robert H. *A Yankee Private's Civil War.* Ed. Ashley Halsey. Chicago: H. Regnery Company, 1961.

Tate, Allen. *Stonewall Jackson: The Good Soldier.* New York: Minton, Balch & Company, 1928.

Taylor, Emerson G. *Gouverneur Kemble Warren: The Life and Letters of an American Soldier, 1830–1882.* Boston and New York: Houghton, Mifflin Company, 1932.

Taylor, Frederick W. *Shop Management.* New York: Harper & Brothers, 1919.

Taylor, H. C. "The Study of War." *North American Review* 162 (February 1896): 181–89.

Taylor, Richard. *Destruction and Reconstruction.* New York: D. Appleton & Company, 1879.

Thornton, J. Mills. *Politics and Power in a Slave Society: Alabama, 1800–1860.* Baton Rouge: Louisiana State University Press, 1978.

Trefousse, Hans L. *Carl Schurz: A Biography.* Knoxville: University of Tennessee Press, 1982.

Tucker, Glenn. *Hancock the Superb.* Indianapolis: Bobbs-Merrill, 1960.

Upson, Theodore F. *With Sherman to the Sea.* Ed. Oscar O. Winther. Bloomington: Indiana University Press, 1958.

Utley, Robert M. *Frontier Regulars: The United States Army and the Indian, 1866–1891.* New York: Macmillan, 1973.

Vail, Enos B. *Reminiscences of a Boy in the Civil War.* Brooklyn, N.Y.: Printed by the author, 1915.

Vandiver, Frank E. *Mighty Stonewall.* New York: McGraw-Hill, 1957.

Wainwright, Charles S. *A Diary of Battle: The Personal Journals of Colonel Charles S. Wainwright, 1861–1865.* Ed. Allan Nevins. New York: Harcourt, Brace & World, 1962.

Wall, Joseph F. *Andrew Carnegie.* New York: Oxford University Press, 1970.

———. *Henry Watterson, Reconstructed Rebel.* New York: Oxford University Press, 1956.

Wallace, Willard M. *Soul of the Lion: A Biography of General Joshua L. Chamberlain.* New York: T. Nelson, 1960.

Webster, Noah. *An American Dictionary of the English Language.* Springfield, Mass.: G. and C. Merriam, 1861.

Wecter, Dixon. *When Johnny Comes Marching Home.* Boston: Houghton Mifflin, 1944.

Weld, Stephen M. *War Diary and Letters of Stephen Minot Weld 1861–1865.* 2d ed. Boston: Massachusetts Historical Society, 1979.

Wellman, Manly W. *Giant in Gray: A Biography of Wade Hampton of South Carolina.* New York: C. Scribner's Sons, 1949.

Werstein, Irving. *Kearny the Magnificent: The Story of General Philip Kearny, 1815–1862.* New York: John Day Company, 1962.

Whitman, Walt. *Walt Whitman's Civil War.* Ed. Walter Lowenfels. New York: Knopf, 1960.

Wiley, Bell I. *The Life of Billy Yank: The Common Soldier of the Union.* Indianapolis: Bobbs-Merrill, 1952.

———. *The Life of Johnny Reb: The Common Soldier of the Confederacy.* Indianapolis: Bobbs-Merrill, 1943.

Wilkeson, Frank. *Recollections of a Private Soldier in the Army of the Potomac.* New York and London: G. P. Putnam's Sons, 1886.

Wilkins, Thurman. *Clarence King: A Biography.* New York: Macmillan, 1958.

Williams, Alpheus S. *From the Cannon's Mouth: The Civil War Letters of General Alpheus S. Williams.* Ed. Milo M. Quaife. Detroit: Wayne State University Press, 1959.

Williams, T. Harry. *Hayes of the Twenty-Third.* New York: Knopf, 1965.

Williamson, Harold F. *Edward Atkinson: The Biography of an American Liberal, 1827–1905.* Cambridge, Mass.: The Riverside Press, 1934.

Wilson, Edmund. *Patriotic Gore: Studies in the Literature of the American Civil War.* New York: Oxford University Press, 1962.

Wilson, James H. *Under the Old Flag.* 2 vols. New York and London: D. Appleton & Company, 1912.

Wilson, LeGrand J. *The Confederate Soldier.* Ed. James W. Silver. Memphis: Memphis State University Press, 1973.

Wood, William N. *Reminiscences of Big I.* Ed. Bell Irvin Wiley. Jackson, Tenn.: McCowat-Mercer Press, 1956.

Woolsey, Jane S. *Hospital Days.* New York: D. Van Nostrand, 1870.

Index

Abbott, Henry L., 44, 84, 298
Abolitionists, 82, 131
Abraham Lincoln Brigade, 18–19
Adams, Charles Francis, Jr., 65–66, 118, 126, 214, 243, 252
Adams, Henry, 65, 252, 292
Agassiz, Ida, 89
Alcott, Louisa May, 28, 32, 109–10
Allen, George H., 58, 114, 130n, 153, 194, 231–32, 244, 264, 298
American Revolution, 287
Anderson, Irwin, 279–80, 290
Anderson, Sherwood, 279–80
Andersonville, 71, 237–38, 257, 258–61
Andrew, John A., 93
Anglo-Saxonism, 287
Antietam (Md.), battle of, 8, 15, 32, 35, 66, 70, 73–74, 110, 125, 126, 136, 140, 157, 160, 188, 202–203, 257; see also Sharpsburg
Appomattox Court House (Va.), 147, 291
Armour, Phillip D., 285
Armstrong, Johnston, 55
Arnold, Matthew, 210
Ashby, Turner, 20, 21, 70, 177
Atlanta, campaign of, 136, 141, 143, 145, 154, 207, 212, 213, 214, 219, 238, 251

Bailey, Frank, 258–59, 259–60, 261
Ball's Bluff (Va.), battle of, 12, 62–63, 83, 140
Banks, Nathaniel P., 214

Barber, Lucius W., 233, 237–38, 258, 259, 261, 298–99
Bardeen, Charles W., 23–24, 51, 59, 68, 72, 85, 121, 126, 127, 138, 170–71, 175, 230, 299
Barton, Clara, 248–49, 283
Beatty, John, 41, 44–45, 57, 71–72, 77, 118, 119–20, 138, 149, 174, 213, 222, 251–52, 299
Beauregard, Pierre G. T., 15, 117, 215
Bellamy, Edward, 288–89
Bellard, Alfred, 52–53, 68, 171, 188, 220, 299
Belmont (Mo.), battle of, 71
Benson, Berry, 243, 246, 267
Bicknell, George W., 168, 262, 264
Bierce, Ambrose, 78, 149, 217, 225, 275, 282–83, 291–92, 296
Big Bethel (Va.), battle of, 202
Billings, John D., 53, 84, 120, 176, 253
Black soldiers, 2, 68, 93, 247–48
Blackford, William W., 46, 150–51, 151–53, 159–60, 169, 175, 185, 186, 241, 300
Blevins, William, 167
Bragg, Braxton, 93, 205, 283
Brobst, John F., 82, 215, 223, 225, 228, 300
Buckner, Simon B., 278
Buell, David, 24–25
Bull, Rice C., 24, 69, 73, 103, 123, 125, 131, 139, 143, 237, 250, 285, 300

Bull Run (Va.); *see also* Manassas
  first battle of, 36, 206, 231
  second battle of, 247
Burdette, Robert J., 22, 65, 76–77, 150,
  166–67, 214, 250, 300
Burnside, Ambrose E., 46, 118, 136, 232
Burton, E. P., 252–53

Camp life, 117–24
Carnegie, Andrew, 273, 285, 289
Carnes, William W., 69
Carter, Eugene, 301
Carter, John, 301
Carter, Robert, 58, 127, 168, 217–18, 222,
  226–27, 230, 232, 246, 247, 253, 255,
  263, 300–301
Carter, Walter, 220, 228, 252, 301
Casler, John O., 26, 47, 48, 52, 53–54,
  59, 68, 91, 93, 105, 120–21, 181,
  182, 185, 187, 301
Catton, Bruce, 46, 67, 246, 275, 280,
  287, 297
Cause, The, 80–82, 219
Cedar Creek (Va.), battle of, 46–47, 78
Cedar Run (Va.), battle of, 52
Chamberlain, Joshua L., 25, 27–28, 43,
  63, 75, 77, 163–64, 171, 256,
  273–74, 283, 301
Champion's Hill (Miss.), battle of, 207
Chancellorsville (Va.), battle of, 62, 65,
  75, 103, 106, 125, 127, 138, 171,
  178, 237, 249, 253
Chandler, Zachariah, 165
Chantilly (Va.), battle of, 74
Chaplains, 93, 103, 120, 253–54
Chapultepec (Mexico), battle of, 202
Charges, 21, 136–38, 139, 160–62, 168,
  296
Cheatham, Benjamin F., 32
Cherubusco (Mexico), battle of, 202
Chickamauga (Ga.), battle of, 22, 46,
  138, 282–83
Christian Commission, 28, 217–18
Church, William C., 291
Churchill, Winston S., 18
Coe, Hamlin A., 256–57
Cold Harbor (Va.), battle of, 129, 136,
  143, 145, 146, 147, 148, 151, 161,
  162, 207, 248
Comradeship, 234–36, 259, 270, 280
Conkling, Roscoe, 264–65
Connolly, James A., 26, 214, 219–20,
  221, 223, 225, 227, 301–302
Contreras (Mexico), battle of, 202

Conway, John, 290
Conwell, Russell H., 105–106
Cooke, Jay, 285
Cooke, John E., 11, 15, 25, 64, 147, 186,
  199, 288, 302
Corinth (Miss.), campaign of, 117, 143,
  195
Courage
  as assurance of success, 61–62
  as bond between enemies, 65–70
  in the charge, 21; *see also* Charges
  and combat deaths, 124–26, 127–28
  in conservator-generals, 202–203
  in destroyer-generals, 206, 210
  as discipline, 34–60, 177
  and disease, 116–17
  and disposal of bodies, 126–27
  and emotion, 73–79
  exhibitions of, 44–47
  in hospital, 28–31, 130–33
  as insulation against battlefield
    trauma, 61, 64–65
  in Korean War, 18
  as limitation on violence, 71–72
  meaning in Civil War, 17, 19–20
  modifications in meaning, 166, 168
  in Spanish-American War, 296
  as special protection, 68–70, 156–58
  as substitute for victory, 61, 62–64,
    162
  test of, 7, 20, 21–23, 25–26
  in Vietnam War, 18, 19
  in World War I, 17–18
  in World War II, 18, 19
  and the wounded, 128–30
Cowardice, 7, 8, 10, 18, 21, 23, 25–26,
  31, 75, 166–67
Cox, Jacob D., 15, 76, 82, 137, 145, 193,
  213, 302
Crane, Stephen, 26, 172, 294, 296
Crater, battle of the (Petersburg, Va.),
  68
Crook, George, 277
Cross Keys (Va.), battle of, 191
Crotty, Daniel G., 126, 127, 175–76,
  230, 231, 232, 233, 267, 302–303
Currier and Ives, 63
Custer, Elizabeth ("Libbie"), 9, 95, 108,
  303
Custer, George A., 9, 44, 74, 95, 108,
  142, 200, 303

Dame, William M., 22, 32, 103–104,
  104–105, 144, 303

Davis, Jefferson, 38, 56, 137, 162, 163, 170, 229
Davis, Lemuel C., 88
Davis, Rebecca, 88
Davis, Richard H., 88, 296
Davis, Washington, 241, 294–95
Dawes, Rufus R., 73–74, 75, 83, 118, 121, 167, 189, 303
Dawson, Francis, 113, 169–70, 185
Dearing, Mary K., 270
Death
  anonymous, 248–49
  in combat, 124–26, 127–28
  euphemisms for, 98–99
  honorable, 12
  nineteenth-century acquaintance with, 29
  the soldier's, 12
  sweet, 109, 159
Decatur (Ga.), battle of, 137
DeForest, John W., 66, 123, 124, 149, 153, 243–44, 263–64, 304
Desertion, 90–92, 174, 176–77
Dewey, Dan, 90
Discipline, 43
  and courage, 34–60, 177
Disease, 115–17
Dodd, Ira S., 31, 70, 75, 86, 93, 95, 161, 304
Dodge, Grenville M., 37, 251
Dollard, John, 18–19
Donald, David H., 3
Dooley, John E., 34, 35, 39, 85, 127, 128, 129, 160–61, 181, 231, 234, 249–50, 304
Douglas, Henry K., 13, 200
Drummond, Robert L., 286–87, 295
Dunaway, Wayland F., 14, 26, 72
Duncan, Donald, 19
Dunne, Finley P., 296
Duty, 7, 10–11, 16, 89, 92, 203
Dwight, Wilder, 117

Early, Jubal A., 46–47, 50, 104, 223, 270
Egalitarianism, 36, 37, 38–39, 48, 50, 231
Eggleston, George C., 10, 15, 28, 38, 40, 60, 67, 219, 225, 232–33, 251, 287, 304–305
Eisenhower, Dwight D., 18
Elections of officers, 40, 169–70, 229
Emerson, Ralph W., 289

Enemy
  initial images of, 65–66
  subsequent relationship with, 66–71, 236–39
Ewell, Richard S., 141, 156–57, 191
Executions, 58–59, 174–77
Ezra Church (Ga.), battle of, 137

Fair Oaks (Va.), battle of, 116
Falling Waters (W.Va.), battle of, 14
Fay, Edwin H., 9, 31, 53, 59–60, 62, 92, 116, 176, 305
Fay, Sarah, 92
Fear, 23–25
Fearlessness, 17, 18, 19, 20, 44
Fenians, 305
Fisk, James, 285
Fitch, Michael H., 136, 147, 214, 217, 235, 246, 253, 268–69, 305
Five Forks (Va.), battle of, 77, 256
Fletcher, William A., 229
Fogle, Jake, 105
Foner, Eric, 82
Foote, Corydon E., 214, 217, 228
Forbes, Edwin, 70
Fort Pillow (Tenn.), battle of, 68
Fort Stedman (Petersburg, Va.), battle of, 82–83
Fort Sumter (Charleston, S.C.), battle of, 80, 81, 82, 150
Foster, John W., 268
Frederic, Harold, 124, 210
Fredericksburg (Va.), battle of, 62, 63–64, 66, 74, 99–100, 119, 136, 143, 157, 160, 167, 193–94, 248, 281
Freeman, Julia W., 29
Frémont, John C., 45, 191

Galwey, Thomas F., 58, 72, 115, 134, 136, 193–94, 217, 224, 232, 254, 281, 290, 305–306
Garfield, James A., 40, 76, 84, 95, 107, 117, 127–28, 183, 191, 195–96
Garland, Hamlin, 279, 290, 294
Garnett, Richard, 177–78
Geary, John W., 51
Gettysburg (Pa.), battle of, 8, 13, 23, 25, 39, 45, 62, 65, 66, 68, 72, 73, 76, 83, 100, 121, 122, 126, 127, 128, 129, 136, 144–45, 160, 163, 164, 170, 178, 223, 231, 278, 286–87
Godliness, 7, 8–10, 16, 65, 76, 83, 84, 102–10, 116, 127, 158–59, 201–202,

Godliness (*cont.*)
205–206, 209, 248, 252–57, 259,
280, 297
Gone With the Wind, 115
Gordon, John B., 278
Gould, Jay, 285
Grady, Henry, 278
Grand Army of the Republic, 270–71,
275, 276, 278, 279, 280, 283, 284,
285, 290, 292
Grand Gulf (Miss.), battle of, 207
Grant, Ulysses S., 12, 20, 36, 71, 104,
123, 135, 136, 145, 147, 149, 158,
161, 164, 199, 205–10, 213, 245,
255, 278, 296
Gray, Jesse Glenn, 73, 74, 75, 78–79
Griffin, Charles, 164

Halleck, Henry W., 117
Hamer, Thomas, 209
Hampton, Wade, 23, 68, 215, 265, 278
Hardee, William J., 141
Harlowe, Calvin, 82–83
Harper's Ferry (W.Va.), battle of, 13, 66
Harris, Thomas, 38
Harrison, Benjamin, 32, 48, 54, 85, 95,
121, 194–95, 268
Harrison's Landing (Va.), battle of, 100
Haskell, John C., 158, 163, 181
Hayes, Rutherford B., 22–23, 27, 31,
118, 121, 214, 292
Herbert, Hilary A., 24–25, 36, 55–56,
72, 99, 181, 306
Heroic vocabulary, 98–102, 110
Herr, Michael, 18, 19
Heth, Henry, 170
Higginson, Henry, 89
Higginson, Thomas W., 124–25
Hill, Daniel H., 34, 44, 46, 67, 142
Hill, James J., 289
Hinkley, Julian W., 223
Hinman, Wilbur F., 49–50, 55, 72, 73,
121, 123, 143, 145–46, 182, 185,
186, 187, 188, 189–90, 192, 246,
254, 261, 264, 306
Hoke, Jacob, 14–15
Holmes, Oliver W., Jr., 12, 16, 28, 37,
67, 83, 246, 252, 267, 268, 269,
281–82, 289–90, 292, 306–307
Holmes, Oliver W., Sr., 32
Honor, 7, 11–15, 16, 32, 203, 277
Hood, John B., 68, 99, 137, 144, 145,
162

Hooker, Joseph, 106, 119, 224
Hospitals, 28–31, 130–33
Howard, Oliver O., 106–107, 133
Howe, Samuel G., 82
Howells, William D., 128
Howze, George, 122
Hunt, Henry J., 70
Hunter, Alexander, 57–58, 62, 81, 88,
119, 133, 151, 154, 159, 166,
230–31, 234, 235, 245, 254–55, 257,
307
Hunter, David, 183
Huntington, Collis, 285
Hugo, Victor, 157

Ide, John S. M., 77–78
Indians, 272, 273, 277, 279
Indiscipline, 36, 37, 41, 43, 48–54, 84
Individualism, 36–37
Irregular warfare, 2, 196–201

Jackson, Thomas J. ("Stonewall"), 9, 13,
20, 21, 42, 44, 48, 52, 64, 66, 74,
103, 104, 141, 156–57, 164, 177–79,
208, 255
Johnston, Joseph E., 137, 141, 145, 162,
182, 265, 278
Jones, James, 18

Kearny, Philip, 21, 74, 77
Keegan, John, 97
Kennesaw Mountain (Ga.), battle of, 8,
106, 136
Kernstown (Va.), battle of, 177
Key, Thomas J., 95, 105, 106, 109, 238,
248, 307
Kidd, James H., 253
Kilpatrick, Hugh J., 265
King, Charles, 273, 276–77, 279, 281,
293
King, Clarence, 89–90
Kirkland, Joseph, 89, 150
Knightliness, 7, 15–16, 195, 203, 265,
277, 284
Korean War, 18, 19

Lanier, Sidney, 288
Last messages, 83, 87, 225
Lee, Fitzhugh, 278
Lee, Robert E., 9, 21, 22, 27, 34, 35, 39,
62, 74, 103, 107, 118, 136, 141,
142, 163, 168, 181, 182, 198, 208,
223, 245, 251, 255, 269

Lincoln, Abraham, 39, 59, 80, 81, 90, 95, 96, 126, 163, 266
Livermore, Mary A., 30–31, 95–97, 98, 109, 132–33, 243, 271, 307–308
Livermore, Thomas B., 220
Local truces, 67, 154, 239
Locale as source of soldiers' identity and support, 36
Logan, John A., 37, 270–71
Longstreet, James, 34, 49
Lonn, Ella, 39, 174–75, 178, 183
Love, Alfred, 293
Lowell, Charles R., 63, 119, 158, 201, 248
Lowndes, Rawlins, 265
Loyal Publication Society, 63
Luce, Stephen, 291, 292
Lyman, Theodore, 116, 138, 139–40, 158, 162, 168, 173, 177, 205, 218–19, 227, 249, 251, 254, 308
Lynch, Charles H., 214–15, 222

Manassas, second battle of, 99, 125, 126, 204; *see also* Bull Run
Manliness, 7, 8, 16, 67, 277, 296
Martin, George, 200
Masons, 118, 237, 299, 305
McCarthy, Carlton, 7, 26, 36, 37, 38–39, 43, 86–87, 142, 185, 224, 230, 285, 295, 297, 308
McClellan, George B., 34, 102–103, 107, 133, 143, 145, 180, 201–205, 205–206, 208, 209, 243
McKinley, William, 108, 269
Meade, George G., 84, 165, 168, 170, 205
Medals, 162–63
Meigs, John R., 199–200
Mexican War, 124, 135, 202, 209
Meyers, Augustus, 161, 163, 182, 193
Middle Creek (Ky.), battle of, 127
Military courtesy, 51
Miller, James T., 24, 222, 228
Milroy, Robert H., 76
Mine Run (Va.), campaign of, 168
Missionary Ridge (Tenn.), battle of, 73, 75, 138
Mitchell, Margaret, 115
Montgomery, James, 174
Moran, Charles, 18
Morgan, John H., 237
Morgan, John P., 285
Mosby, John S., 197–201, 212, 308

Mumford, Lewis, 126
Murfreesboro (Tenn.), 93, 251

Napoleon Buonaparte, 62
Napoleon cannon, 160, 274
Nashville (Tenn.), battle of, 107
National Rifle Association, 272
Nelson, Allison, 52, 54
New Hope Church (Ga.), battle of, 136
Newton, James K., 85–86, 103, 139, 222–23, 309
Nightingale, Florence, 29
Nisbet, James C., 73, 140, 162, 170, 184, 237, 238, 239, 252, 309
Northwestern Sanitary Fair, 95–97, 98, 109
Norton, Charles E., 63
Nunnelly, Sam, 104, 186–87

Olmsted, Frederick L., 90
Opdycke, Emerson, 22
Ovendorf, John, 51
Owen, William M., 130–31, 143, 153, 163, 187, 309

Page, Thomas N., 97
Palfrey, John, 63
Parkman, Francis, 288
Parsons, Charles C., 69–70
Paxton, Elisha F., 25–26, 40, 107, 108, 123, 158, 221, 248, 250, 251, 255, 309
Peace advocacy, 222–23, 290–94
Peachtree Creek (Ga.), battle of, 137, 237
Pelham, John, 44, 64
Peninsula, campaign of the (1862), 64, 77, 81, 116, 145, 188, 192, 196, 202, 203, 231, 257
Peninsula, campaign of the (1864), 75, 104
Perryville (Ky.), battle of, 44, 69, 251
Peters, Lewis, 31
Petersburg (Va.), siege of, 27, 128, 140, 146–55, 164, 173, 175, 218, 239, 241–42, 254
Phillips, Wendell, 82
Picket duty, 72
Pickett, George E., 13, 66, 178, 270
Pickett's charge, 129, 136, 160–61
Pinkerton, Allan, 204
Poague, William T., 10, 75, 76, 81, 104, 105, 255–56, 310

Polignac, Charles, 45
Polk, Leonidas, 141
Pope, John, 204
Port Hudson (La.), siege of, 149, 153
Port Republic (Va.), battle of, 156
Porter, David, 207
Porter, Horace, 20, 25, 76
Prisoners of war, 12–14, 14–15, 236–38, 257–61
Pyle, Ernie, 19, 149–50, 234, 268

Quintard, Charles T., 32, 59

Ransom, John L., 259, 260
Red Badge of Courage, The, 26
Reed, William H., 28, 29–30, 31, 87, 132, 310
Reid, Jesse W., 119, 124, 220–21, 310
Ring, John, 105–106
Ripley, Edward H., 13, 75, 86, 130, 227–28, 310
Ripley, William Y. W., 77–78, 285–86, 295, 297, 310–11
Rockefeller, John D., 285
Roosevelt, Theodore, Jr., 78, 90, 296
Roosevelt, Theodore, Sr., 90
Ropes, Hannah, 28, 29, 84–85, 108, 109, 131, 311
Ropes, Henry, 76
Ropes, John C., 287
Rosecrans, William S., 49, 76, 78, 123, 205, 208
Rosser, Thomas, 73
Ruskin, John, 292

Sabbatarianism, 102–103, 108–109, 252–53
Sajer, Guy, 74
Sandburg, Carl, 294
Sanford, George B., 63–64, 200
Sanitary Commission, 28, 30, 90, 230
Schurz, Carl, 45, 126, 214, 294
Scott, Walter, 15–16
Seddon, James A., 170
Sedgwick, John, 141
Selma (Ala.), campaign of, 141
Seven Days, battles of the, 295–96
Sharpsburg (Md.), battle of, 35; *see also* Antietam
Sharpshooting, 72, 147–49, 173, 193
Shaw, Robert G., 71, 92–93, 126, 158, 214, 228, 311
Sheeran, James B., 108, 120, 125, 126, 128, 141, 311

Shenandoah campaign (1862), 164
Shenandoah campaign (1864), 199
Sheridan, Philip H., 14, 41, 46–47, 76, 78, 199–200, 208–209, 212
Sherman, William T., 2, 8, 36–37, 39, 40, 50, 74–75, 122, 123, 130, 136, 137, 141, 143, 145, 165, 205–15, 238–39, 243, 262, 265, 278, 283–84, 286, 288, 289
Sherman's march, 217, 247, 250, 284
Shields, James, 177
Shiloh (Tenn.), battle of, 54, 106, 117, 126, 143, 206, 207, 282
"Simmering down," 113–15, 116, 183, 245
Skinner, Josephine, 32
Small, Abner R., 44, 133, 167, 182, 184, 188, 249, 253–54, 269–70, 311–12
Smith, Edmund K., 14
Smith, Orlow, 50
Social Darwinism, 291
Society of the Army of Northern Virginia, 270
Sons of Temperance, 121
Sons of Veterans, 294
Spanish-American War, 282, 296–97
Spottsylvania Court House (Va.), battle of, 104–105, 138–39, 141, 142, 143
Stanley, Henry M., 87–88, 126
Stanton, Edwin McM., 229
Steinbeck, John, 18, 19
Steiner, Paul, 115, 245–46
Stevens, George T., 32, 116, 119, 145, 161–62
Stiles, Robert, 27, 61–62, 64, 81, 143–44, 145, 146, 151, 154–55, 295–96, 312
Stillwell, Leander, 25, 73, 75, 106, 119, 124, 195, 312
Stockwell, Elisha, 196, 262
Stone's River (Tenn.), battle of, 10, 77, 78, 93, 138, 174, 290
Strong, Robert H., 23, 69, 126–27, 128, 129–30, 188–89, 224, 243, 245, 312–13
Stuart, James E. B. ("Jeb"), 9, 16, 20, 44, 46, 197, 198
Sumner, William G., 291, 292

Taylor, Frederick W., 273n
Taylor, H. C., 292–93
Taylor, Richard, 38, 45–46, 84, 185, 191
Taylor, Zachary, 38
Tests
of command, 44–45, 47

of courage, 20, 21–23, 25–26
of manhood, 8, 27
Thomas, George H., 22
Torbert, Alfred, 44, 142
Tourgee, Albion W., 278
Trench warfare, 146–47, 150–55
Truces, 67, 68, 239
Tullahoma (Tenn.), campaign of, 123, 205
Twain, Mark, 16, 38, 67, 101
Twichell, Joseph H., 101–102

United Confederate Veterans, 276, 293
Universal Peace Union, 293
Upson, Theodore F., 33, 121, 122–23, 243, 274–75
Upton, Emory, 108

Vail, Enos B., 49, 73, 119, 120, 286
Vance, Zebulon B., 91
Vicksburg (Miss.), campaign of, 12, 45, 123, 139, 148, 189, 195, 210, 212
Vietnam War, 18, 19

Wainwright, Charles S., 118, 144, 145, 161, 192, 229–30, 313
Walker, Francis A., 14–15, 90, 127, 217, 260, 283, 313
Warren, Gouverneur K., 168, 205, 208
Washington, George, 287
Watterson, Henry, 278
Webster, Noah, 8, 11
Wecter, Dixon, 244
Weld, Stephen M., 11, 32, 98, 105, 126, 129, 140, 146, 153, 173, 216, 220, 223, 245–47, 251, 252, 257, 269, 313–14
West Point, 117, 208, 272–73, 278

White House Landing (Va.), battle of, 100
Whitman, Walt, 28, 30, 53, 63, 82–83, 128, 200, 222, 260
Wiebe, Robert, 240
Wilderness (Va.), campaign in the, 14, 125, 127, 128, 138, 147, 149, 161, 167, 171, 175, 205, 213, 231, 233, 245, 246, 249, 252, 253, 281
Wiley, Bell I., 235
Wilkeson, Frank, 23, 37, 69, 126, 147–48, 149, 159, 161, 172–73, 185, 187, 208, 230, 232, 241–42, 244, 258, 314
Williams, Alpheus S., 72, 125, 164–66, 174, 215, 245, 247, 256, 314
Williamsburg (Va.), battle of, 101, 116, 126, 127, 203
Wilson, James H., 141–42, 148–49, 247
Wilson, LeGrand J., 51, 128, 129, 246, 314
Winder, Charles S., 51–52
Wirz, Henry, 238
Wood, William N., 160, 175, 184
Women, role in Civil War, 87–89, 90–93, 95–97, 195, 226–27
Women's Christian Temperance Union, 293
Woolsey, Jane, 31, 87, 92, 99, 244
World War I, 17, 18, 98, 154, 210, 271
World War II, 12, 18, 74, 149–50, 268
Wounds
  in combat, 128–30
  desirability of, 31–32
  honorable, 12, 32, 296–97
  "million-dollar," 12

Young, William H., 49–50